EurographicSeminars

Tutorials and Perspectives in Computer Graphics

Edited by W. T. Hewitt, R. Gnatz, and D. A. Duce

L. Kjelldahl (Ed.)

Multimedia

Systems, Interaction and Applications

1st Eurographics Workshop, Stockholm, Sweden
April 18/19, 1991

With 129 Figures

Springer-Verlag
Berlin Heidelberg New York
London Paris Tokyo
Hong Kong Barcelona
Budapest

EurographicSeminars

Edited by W. T. Hewitt, R. Gnatz, and D. A. Duce
for EUROGRAPHICS -
The European Association for Computer Graphics
P. O. Box 16, CH-1288 Aire-la-Ville, Switzerland

Volume Editor

Lars Kjelldahl
Numerical Analysis and Computing - NADA
Royal Institute of Technology - KTH
S-100 44 Stockholm, Sweden

ISBN-13:978-3-642-77333-4 e-ISBN-13:978-3-642-77331-0
DOI: 10.1007/978-3-642-77331-0

Library of Congress Cataloging-in-Publication Data
Multimedia: systems, interaction, and applications/1st Eurographics Workshop, Stockholm, Sweden, April 18/19, 1991; L. Kjelldahl (ed.). p. cm. - (EurographicSeminars) "Record of the first Eurographics Workshop on Multimedia, held at the center for Numerical Analysis and Computing Science ... Royal Institute of Technology" - Pref.
Includes bibliographical references.
ISBN-13:978-3-642-77333-4
1. Hypermedia systems - Congresses. I. Kjelldahl, L. (Lars) II. Series: Eurographic seminars.
QA76.76.H92M85 1992 006-dc20 92-8000 CIP

Softcover reprint of the hardcover 1st edition 1992

Typesetting: Camera ready by author

45/3140-543210 - Printed on acid-free paper

Preface

This volume is a record of the first Eurographics Workshop on Multimedia, held at the department of Numerical Analysis and Computing Science (NADA), Royal Institute of Technology, Stockholm, April 18–19, 1991.

Eurographics is the European Association for Computer Graphics. It is a non-profit organization, one of whose activities is organizing workshops to provide an interface between academic and industrial research in the field of computer graphics.

The idea of holding a Eurographics workshop on multimedia was put forward at the Eurographics conference in 1989. Following the success of this first workshop, a second workshop has been announced, to take place in Darmstadt, May 4–6, 1992.

The Stockholm workshop met with great interest and many good contributions were received by the program committee. There were approximately 40 participants and 23 presentations were given – so many indeed that one might characterize the workshop as a working conference – and there were many discussions focusing on the presentations. The presentations dealt with a range of topics, including the clarification of ideas about the different concepts in multimedia, object-oriented methods for multimedia, multimedia from psychological perspectives, synchronization problems in multimedia, cooperative work using multimedia, and building multimedia interfaces.

The presentations were the focus for numerous discussions. There was also a small exhibition of four different multimedia systems, representing the spectrum from research prototypes to commercial products.

At the end of the book there are two chapters written after the workshop which present its conclusions. The first is a contribution on one of the major applications of multimedia, namely education, and the second is a collection of conclusions assembled from the contributions of some of the participants at the workshop.

The program committee consisted of D. Eckardt, Darmstadt, P. Egloff, Berlin, R. Guedj, Evry, C. Hornung, Darmstadt, L. Kjelldahl, Stockholm (chairman), H. Marmolin, Linköping, P. Stucki, Zürich, P. S. Ward, Leeds, and P. Willis, Bath. I thank them all, especially Peter Egloff and Christoph Hornung, and Matthias Muth (who joined the committee in March 1991).

In addition, I thank Ivan Herman from Eurographics, who gave much good advice as well as support in sending out information on the workshop. Financial support from the Swedish Board for Technical Development (STU) is gratefully acknowledged, with special thanks to Barbro Atlestam from STU.

The local organizer was NADA, where many people worked to prepare the workshop. Among them were Björn Eiderbäck, Konrad Ericsson-Tollmar, JoAnn Gerdin, Lars Kjelldahl, Ingrid Melinder, Ragge Sundblad and Yngve Sundblad.

The success of the workshop was due to the participants. On behalf of all concerned, I give sincere thanks to those who gave their time to prepare papers and attend the workshop.

April 1992 L. Kjelldahl

Table of Contents

Part I

Fundamentals

Chapter 1

Introduction

Lars Kjelldahl

Multimedia is a rather new area in the computer field. Many vendors are trying to put the label multimedia on their systems because it is something that most people understand will be part of future computer systems. When one examines the facilities offered it might be questionable whether the systems really are multimedia systems.

So what is multimedia? The word has been misused and made it harder for people to be precise when they want to speak about the area. Thus there is a need to find a good definition of multimedia that is generally agreed upon among researchers and practitioners in the field. Let us discuss multimedia from a language point of view:

Multi refers to many, i.e. at least two.

Medium can refer to storage, transmission, communication, representation, presentation, input, interaction and perception. This means that medium can refer to different levels of abstraction.

Media is the plural form of medium.

Multimedia is sometimes used as an adjective, sometimes as a noun.

These simple definitions of the words explain to some extent why there are so many different interpretations of the "multimedia". There are however also unclear aspects concerning e.g. how integrated a system should be to be a multimedia system. How many output media should the system provide? How many input media should the system provide? Could you use the term multimedia even if the system has no input facilities at all? What kind of synchronisation and parallelism are needed? One preliminary goal for this workshop was to try to find a definition of multimedia. However it turned out that it would be too ambitious and that there is a need to study the area more before one can come to a consensus on what multimedia really is.

In order to give a background to the question of definition of multimedia we quote a definition that was given at the UIMS workshop, Portugal, June 1990 (User Interface Management and Design, eds Duce, Gomes, Hopgood, Lee, Springer, 1991, page 57):

"1. Multi-media is concerned with both input and output (including their combination called interaction).

2. For output, multi-media is concerned with multiple streams operating in parallel (for example, vector graphics, raster graphics, text, video, sound etc). Streams may not be the best word, channel tracks or modes were alternatives.

3. For input, multi-media is concerned with simultaneous input events generated by one or several different devices (for example key chords, foot pedals, spoken commands, dataglove, datasuite, five-finger-mouse, touch screen, eye tracker, musical instruments etc) all being used in parallel.

4. On input, it is concerned with the composition of higher level input tokens in terms of more primitive input events. For example, gesture input could be derived from a set of dataglove positions."

Hypermedia is often discussed together with multimedia. It seems to be clear that hypermedia should not be considered as a subset or a superset of multimedia. Hypermedia is an area where the main idea is to use links between different parts of a system with information and thereby giving the user the possibility of following these links interactively. Hypermedia and multimedia are very often used together.

Let us discuss some characteristics of multimedia:

Popular area: Multimedia is one of the buzzwords that gives a good flavour to products, conferences, books, etc, i.e. many people will find it interesting.

Few applications: There are not many applications where multimedia has been used. They are e.g. education, museum presentations and computer supported cooperative work. However the systems constructed show the possibilities of the technique.

Interdisciplinary area: People work with multimedia from different points of departure, e.g.:

- Media people working with TV, film, radio and press
- Interaction designers
- Computer graphics designers
- Applications developers

Different people have different wishes and expectations of the use of multimedia. A computer scientist may not produce a good multimedia system from a user´s point of view and the media people may have problems to build the systems they want to have and may not always realise the limits and/or the possibilities of the technique.

Technology driven: The area has evaluated mainly as a result of the development of the technology with faster computers, audio and video technology including CD, better compression techniques, new and better storage devices and more use of computer networks.

Great potential development: It is very clear that the area of multimedia is very immature. We do not yet know how this new technique will be used in the future. Will it be used by everyone as a ubiquitous tool incooperated in all the things we have around us or will it be used solely for production of specialised applications including highly sophisticated presentations. The technical development will of course continue and will influence multimedia, even if we hope and foresee that needs from the users will have more influence. From a technical point of view we can expect better animation techniques, better techniques for the generation of photorealistic pictures as well as a continuation of the development of getting faster computers and better storage devices.

Standards needed: Many different techniques are combined within multimedia and different kinds of equipments are used together. This is very much simplified if one can agree on standards. There is a need for standardization on different levels.

Research topics: Within multimedia there are research problems of great interest. Examples of problems are e.g. synchronization and image synthesis as well as the design, organisation and integration in the multimedia systems. This workshop and this book intend to show that important research work is going on within the area of multimedia.

Chapter 2

A Proposal for a Reference Model for Cooperative HyperMedia Systems

Christoph Hornung and Adelino Santos

Abstract

At the time being, there is a lot of different systems claiming to be either multimedia, hypermedia, or supporting collaborative/cooperative work. In the following paper, a first attempt to clearify the notions of these concepts is tried. Multimedia content, hyperstructure organization and cooperative access will be identified as different features of an intelligent document. These features will be discussed under formal, information technology and implementation aspects.

1 Introduction

There are three key concepts that are likely to be combined and integrated to form the basis of a reference model for Cooperative HyperMedia: cooperative work, hyperstructures and multimedia.

The term *Cooperative Work* refers to a cooperative manner of dealing with entities (which can be resources, servers, users, processing, communications, etc.) at the same time. More specifically, here, cooperative work refers to the nature of the computations that take place between a resource server (or more) and a resource user (or more). The users can be distributed over more than one machine as well as the server and the resources. The distributed properties of the users, servers and resources are independent of each other (Greif 1988).

The term *Hyperstructures* can be used to refer to the set of structures that make possible a non-sequential organization of documents. The prefix *hyper* always refers to a certain scheme where sequential relations are substituted by arbitrary non-sequential relations in order to facilitate some human-oriented task (consulting, presentating, etc.) (Streitz et al. 1989), (Frisse 1988), (Conkline 1987).

The term *Medium* refers to a basic information type like text, graphics, image, video, or sound. The integration of several media in the same information unit is then defined as *Multimedia* (Santos 1990).

Given the informal definitions of these three key concept, we can devise certain relations that can be established between them in order to create a new notion, namely *Cooperative HyperMedia* (*CHM*).

An informal definition of *Cooperative HyperMedia (CHM)* can be given saying that this concept defines documents that integrate several media, have a non-sequential (hyperstructure) organization and enable cooperative/collaborative processing among the users. A CHM document is the basic processing element of a *CHM system*.

Attempting to develop a proposal for a reference model for CHM systems, different aspects haven to be considered: formal conciseness, information technology and implementation strategies. These three aspects will be discussed in this paper.

The paper is organized as follows. In chapter 2, the so called CHM cube as a model to describe Cooperative HyperMedia systems will be presented. This model allows a description and classification of different CHM systems. In chapter 3, the formal aspect of CHM will be shortly discussed. In chapter 4, information technology issues and in chapter 5, implementation strategies follow.

2 The Components of a CHM System

The current state of the art in information technology can best be described as a time of fundamental change. We can denote any processing as the processing of an underlying *document*. Of course, this notion goes far beyond the traditional understanding of document processing. We can distinguish three main topics: the media defining the content of the document, the structures defining the internal organization of the document, and the possible access to the document.

2.1 The Content of a Document

With respect to the media defining the content of a document, we can state that, nowadays, there is a variety of systems for the processing of documents encompassing a single medium only. Text processing systems, graphics systems as well as image processing systems are available on the market. The state of the art is represented by well-understood and stable standards. Corresponding hardware is also available. Especially in graphics a certain point of maturity has been reached. The trend goes no longer towards more and new functionality, but rather towards higher integration and more performance.

However, only little has been done towards the integration of different media into a single document - the so-called multimedia document. Here, we are only at the beginning. The integration of graphics or images into text is possible, but integrated editing environments are not yet available. The integration of video in a window and the support of sound is mostly technology-driven today. Nice and impressive demos can be shown, but there are not yet sufficient really convincing applications of the new technology. Moreover, we are still far away from an integrated multimedia standard.

2.2 The Organization of a Document

Nowadays, there are only few alternatives to define the internal structure of a document. In graphics systems, complex pictures can be structured either linearly in form of segments or hierarchically in form of trees and graphs. However, these structures are static and establish connections between data objects only.

Here, we need new types of connections known as links. A link establishes a connection between two parts of a document. But, rather than a reference, it is executable. This means, that it can be seen as a method of an object. It may be time-variant or change its value, the execution of a procedure may be associated with it, it may be intelligent in the sense that it can learn during the lifetime of the document, and so on. The principal change is from a static document, consisting of data primitives, towards an intelligent document consisting of active objects interacting with each other.

2.3 The Access to a Document

In the past, most research was done based on the so-called *desktop computing paradigm*. This means that the focus was on the support of individual work. While multiple users may have access to the resources of a computing network, they do it in a concurrent fashion. This means that all the users compete for the resources which the system distributes fairly among them. However, the different users still are virtually alone in the system. The possibilities to interact with each other are rather spare and, as the different forms of mail, not interactive.

The need for cooperative access to documents has been recognized and there is reseach in that area. One important form is the so-called joined editing. This approach means that several users have read access to an open document at the same time. Communication channels between the different users can be established and they can, for example, interact by distributing their cursors. This allows conferencing about a document and, in a certain sense, a support in decision finding. However, one of the users has the master's role. He is the only one to be allowed to do modifications in the document, hereby avoiding conflicting or inconsistent accesses. Future work will concentrate on allowing multiple users to access cooperatively to a document, herewith establishing the new *conference computing paradigm*.

2.4 The CHM Cube

In the figure below we schematize the relations that, we think, exist between the three components of CHM. We can say that the three concepts are orthogonal meaning that they do not relate and do not touch each other. A system can have each one of the concepts without incorporating either of the other two. This leads to the representation of CHM in a 3D subspace defined by 3 orthogonal axes representing the three concepts. In the origin of the subspace are represented the systems that use just one medium, with sequential organization and that support just single access. Along the growing sense of each axis are the systems that enable more and more capacities represented by the axis.

It should be noted that the axes are not continuous, but there are features placed at discrete positions. For example, along the content axis, the different media may be grouped. However, this does now mean that one medium is more important than another one. Inside of each medium, classes like primitives and attributes may be identified. Each class may consist out of subclasses (like surfaces as a subclass of the primitives of graphics). All the features, that a certain system covers may be identified as points in the CHM cube, whereby the position of this point represents the corresponding medium, its organization and its access capabilities. The cube surrounding all feature point of a system may serve as a first guess to estimate the capabilites of a system and to compare different systems. However, this cube is not completely filled, and therefore, for a detailed comparison of systems, the concrete features have to be considered.

This way, the systems that integrate cooperative work and hyper structures (Wiil and Osterbye 1990), (Wiil 1991). Systems using just one medium would be in the CH plane. In the same way, the hypermedia systems (Akscyn et al. 1988), (Catlin et al. 1989), (Garg 1988), (Garret et al. 1990), (Phillips 1990), (Richartz and Ruedebusch 1990), (Santos 1990) would be in the HM plane. The localization of the systems in the subspace depends on the relative amount of each of the components that the system incorporates. Following the same reasoning, we can say that the successive and balanced integration of C, H and M would be represented in the line that traverses the subspace origin and makes an angle of 45 degrees with each of the planes. We can measure the power of a system (in terms of CHM) by its distance to the origin.

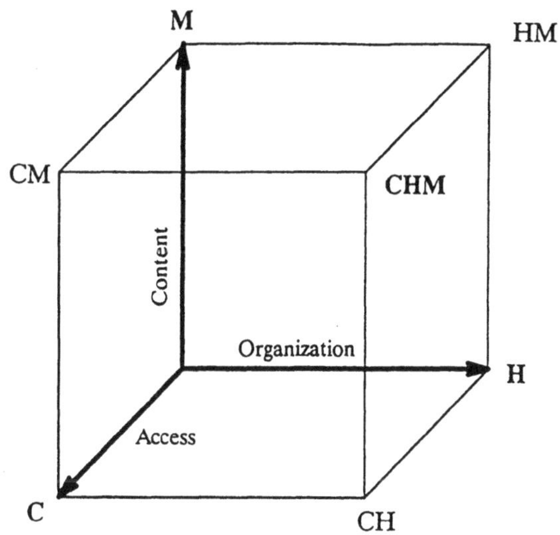

Fig. 1: The CHM cube

We intend, with this work, to touch the problem of integration which is one of the most actual and serious problems of multimedia and cooperative work. Other approaches are included in (Benford 1988), (Kuna and Klehn 1991), (Meiser 1990).

2.5 An Example

As an example of the classification of systems according to the CHM cube, graphics systems will be considered in the following.

First generation graphics systems, like PLOT 10, were passive and rather unstructured. The focus was at that time on the development of the graphics functionality and, therefore, using our terminology, on the content axis. These systems describe by and large, images and are well suited to drive plotter devices. However, they provide only little support for structured graphics and interaction.

Second generation graphics systems, like GKS, addressed then the problem of interactivity. GKS may best be described as an interactive graphics system. Conceptually, both graphical output and graphical input are covered, although not equally mature concepts exist. The concept of picking has been introduced to support access to graphical elements. In the CHM cube, this means that interactive system allow more functionality on the access axis. However, there is only little support in the area of organization. Graphical information can just be stored in the form of segments.

This problem has been overcome in PHIGS. This is a representative of a hierarchical interactive graphics system. It allows organization of graphics information in the form of DAGs (directed acyclic graphs). Therefore, following our terminology, PHIGS provides more functionality on the organization axis compared to GKS.

However, today's graphics system still have drawbacks in all the aspects content, organization and access. Concerning content, a more precise definition of primitives and attributes is necessary; still to much is left open implementation- or device dependent. Concerning organization, the pure data-oriented view of a structure storage is not the appropriate concept for the future. Instead, object-oriented approaches have to be considered. The access of multiple users to resource, while allowed in window systems, has to be more carefully handled by future systems. Tools for the management of cooperative access have to be included.

3 Aspects of a Reference Model for Cooperative HyperMedia Systems

Attempting to define a Reference Model for CHM Systems, we first gathered some ideas about what could be the basic rules for such a model. We think that three different aspects should be considered:

- the formal aspect
- the information technology aspect
- the implementation aspect

The formal aspect primarily covers the theoretical foundations of such a reference model. Such a reference model must be as precise as possible, complete and verifiable.

The aspect of information technology concerns the basic technological components of such a reference model. For example, how to represent such a system, how to present and how to interact with its components.

Finally, the implementation aspect, covers the issues of how to realize a CHM system. For example, how to organize services, users, communications, interfaces, etc..

These three aspects should not be seen as independent, but rather as complementary. So, an implementation should reflect in some modules (defined by the information technology aspect) and these modules should themselves be verified and proved according to the rules defined by the formal aspect. A method to prove the correctness of implementations similar to the one used in (Guttag et al. 1976) can be used. These different aspects will now be outlined.

4 The Formal Aspect

From an abstract point of view, a clear and precise definition of what we mean by CHM systems is necessary. Of course that we are now just at the beginning and, therefore, the development of a concise formal description of the model will take some time.

The goal of this effort is to develop a definition of CHM systems. This definition should be based on the concept of *abstract data types (ADTs)*. An ADT consists of both data and methods. The data can be defined as words over an alphabet and the methods as algorithms using appropriate tools. The definition using ADTs will also support directly the object oriented approach for implementing a CHM system.

4.1 Multimedia Content

We will call text, graphics, full-motion video, pictures, sound etc. as *media*. A medium is defined over an alphabet and, in a certain sense, is a formal language. The symbols of the alphabet form the lexical entities of such an alphabet. Over this alphabet, we can define *words* as the basic syntactic entities and collect words into *single medium documents*, forming semantic entities. By building the union of different media alphabets, we get a *multimedia alphabet*, and accordingly *multimedia words* and *multimedia documents*.

4.2 Hyperstructure Organization

Hyperstructuring defines the organization of the different media. Media have an intrinsic organization already covered in part 3.1. For example, text is intrinsically organized as a sequence of characters. What we intend to define here are manners/ways to compose/organize more complex documents out of simpler/sequentially-organized ones. For example, sets, linear lists, trees and graphs are forms of organization. From the beginning, it should be emphasized, that this organization does not need to be static. In contrast, it may be dynamic, time variant and encompass some actions. Therefore, we will introduce the notion of a *link*. A link is a connection between two documents that can be *executed.* The link has a "leave point" on the origin document and an "entry point" in the destination document. Of course there can exist several links between two documents. The execution of a link may take many forms. It can be a *navigation* execute, a *fetch* execute, *execution* execute, etc. (Abramowicz 1990), (Akscyn et al. 1988), (Catlin et al. 1989), (Collier 1987), (Garg 1988), (Meis 1990), (Nielsen 1990).

More formally, links themselves are objects and consist of data and methods. The data are defined over a so called *link alphabet.* The methods transform words over that link alphabet into other words of the same alphabet. By allowing words over a media alphabet as well as words over a link alphabet in a document, we reach a *hyper (single medium) document* or a *hyper (multi) media document.* Examples for the former would be hyper text documents or hyper picture documents (Kirste and Hübner 1991), the latter are often called hyper media documents for short.

4.3 Cooperative Access

Up to now, documents were just described as entities existing *per se.* Cooperative defines the type of access that is allowed to the different media and to the different links. With the access aspect, the interaction between users and documents comes into consideration. The access rights and the system behavior under cooperative access defines a new dimension not yet covered by the content and the organization. It can be described using so called *access objects,* which are also defined as ADTs. Here, the data describe the access rights over an *access alphabet,* and the methods reflect the operations allowed over the access alphabet. We say that the cooperative aspect is very different from the organization aspect although both can be realized by the link concept. Related literature can be found in (Benford 1991), (Durfee et al. 1989), (Meiser 1990), (Rad and Keith 1989), (Richartz and Ruedebusch 1990).

Three classes of systems can be distinguished with respect to their access capacities: passive systems, interactive systems and cooperative systems. Traditional passive systems can be described using the following schema: only the application program has access to all objects, and the user has no access rights at all. In a certain sense, all objects are private. In interactive systems, both the application program and the user may access the objects. But now, not all objects are accessible at any time. Therefore, access rights are provided. Often a so called *PickId* is used to distinguish accessible objects (having a PickId) from non-accessible ones (having no PickId). Herewith, objects with different scope (private and public) exist in an interactive system. In cooperative systems, the situation becomes even more complex. Both different user groups as well as the according application programs may have access to the objects. Therefore, mechanisms to deal with this situation have to be developed.

In a cooperative environment, user groups may be formed and, consequently, hierarchies of access rights can exist. Different users may have different authorities (access rights) (e.g. a teacher and a student). Therefore, the user groups themselves are heterogeneous and each user still has personal access rights.

Cooperative access may also be classified as follows: single user access, concurrent access, joint access, cooperative access. Using single user access, a document is related to one user only. No other user may ever have access to it. Concurrent access is defined for a document which may belong to a community of users, but only one user has access to it at a time. Joint access defines a slightly higher degree of cooperation. Now, even parts of documents may be exchanged between different users. But, still, the document belongs for a rather long time to one user and the exchange is driven by the users. Cooperative access tries to implement the idea of a document that belong to a community of users at the same time. The entities where only single access is possible may be either a whole document, words or even characters. On the other hand, a wide variety of access rights has to be supported.

5 The Information Technology Aspect

While in the formal aspect, we are more interested in a precise definition of the different components of a Cooperative HyperMedia system, the information technology aspect is more oriented towards a functional description and functional specification of these components. By and large, the mapping of a formal definition to a concrete information processing system is described. Data are mapped to data types, methods to algorithms and interfaces. The functional description gives an overview over the functionality of the components, while the functional specification defines the data types, the interfaces and the behavior of the methods.

Intuitively, a model for describing the information technology aspect may be based on the different types of *abstract device classes* available in an information processing system. Such abstract device classes may be classified as follows:

- processing
- storage
- presentation
- interaction
- transfer

Consequently, a CHM system must provide tools for processing, storage, presentation, interaction and transfer of all the different aspects multimedia content, hyperstructure organization and cooperative acces of a CHM document.

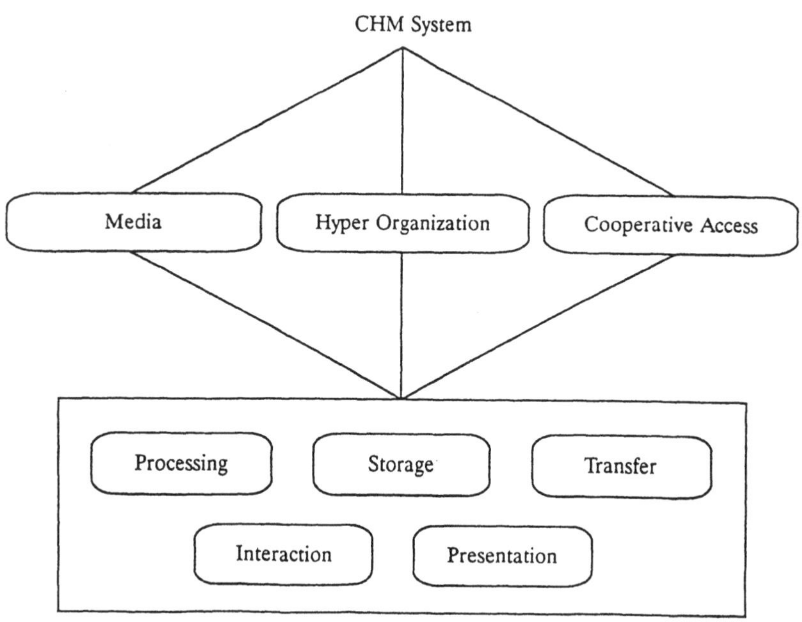

Fig. 2: The Information Technology Aspect

5.1 Processing

First, for each of the components mentioned in chapter 3.1, multimedia content, hyperstructure organization, and cooperative access, representations must be defined. It must be guaranteed that these representations fulfil the requirements of the abstract definition. Especially, the different aspects of time variant media (like video) have to be taken into consideration. It should be noted, that, on the representation level, primarily the information inherent in a document is considered. The internal representation of a document is the basis for the processing.

5.2 Storage

The storage of documents covers the problem of saving a document on a long term storage device. While it must be possible to store all the information of a document, its representation on a storage device and its internal representation may differ. The former one is, in general, optimized for size (for example by using compression techniques), the latter one is, in general, optimized for speed, since it is used for processing purposes. A good reference is (Mariani 1991).

5.3 Presentation and Interaction

Presentation and interaction form the interface between a document and the user. The presentation defines the output side, while the interaction defines the input side. Presentation and interaction should be clearly distinguished from the representation of a document. Also, it should be emphasized, that presentation and interaction covers not only the media aspect, but also organization and access. When presenting a hyper document, the visualization of the organization of such a document is essential to avoid "getting lost in hyper space". When cooperatively accessing a document, the presentation of the actual status of this document is very important. Moreover, tools to negotiate with other users about the access to parts of the document must be provided. A good reference is for example (Foss 1988).

5.4 Transfer

Transfer of documents is another important issue. When transfering a document between CHM systems, consistency is the main issue. Special problems can occur for time variant media. Synchronicity and isochronicity must be provided. Synchronicity means the consistent transfer of the different media of a single document. So, for example, sound and image of a video sequence must be "synchronous". Isochronicity, in contrast, here means, that the single frames of a sequence are transferred in equal time intervals. This is essential to guarantee a continuous transfer of a sequence (Benford 1988).

6 The Implementation Aspect

The implementation aspect is the most concrete one in the outlined hierarchy. Here, the concepts developed in the information technology aspect are realized following general rules for the implementation of information systems. Questions like the following are asked here and have to be answered:

- Software Architecture of a CHM system
- Hardware Architecture of a CHM system (supported devices)
- Hierarchy of services

We believe, that the architecture of a CHM system should be based on the client/server model. This allows a clear definition of modules serving higher level components and being clients of lower level components. While the client server concept is clearly understood today, it does not cover the different access requirements of a CHM system. The client server concept establishes independent client server connections. It does not support the cooperative access of different users to the same document. Therefore, the concept of a cooperative server has to be developed.

At least the following classes of devices may be distinguished: processing devices, storage devices, presentation devices, interaction devices and transfer devices. All these devices form the hardware platform. Related literature is for example: (Catlin et al. 1989), (Collier 1987), (Delisle and Schwartz 1987), (Ruedebusch 1991), (Wiil and Osterbye 1990), (Wiil 1991).

Based on this platform, a hierarchy of services will be implemented. The devices themselves are driven by low-level and very general services. On top of them are higher level and more specific services. In this way, a hierarchy of more and more complex and specialized services is constructed. On the top of this hierarchy, the application kernel is located. It should be as small as possible and make use of (application specific) services as far as possible.

An advantage of this approach is, that already defined services for the different components (for example, transfer services or graphics standards) can be integrated in this architecture. On the other hand, this concept provides a conceptual framework for a critical evaluation of the different single services as components of a complex information system. In such a system, the interfaces between the different services on different levels are essential and crucial.

It is essential for a CHM system that all the services are conceptually distributed. For the reference model, this means, that all services can use the transfer service. On the other hand, the distributed nature of a service should be hidden from the user. For a client, a service should just be available, while the details of a distributed service are handled by the server itself.

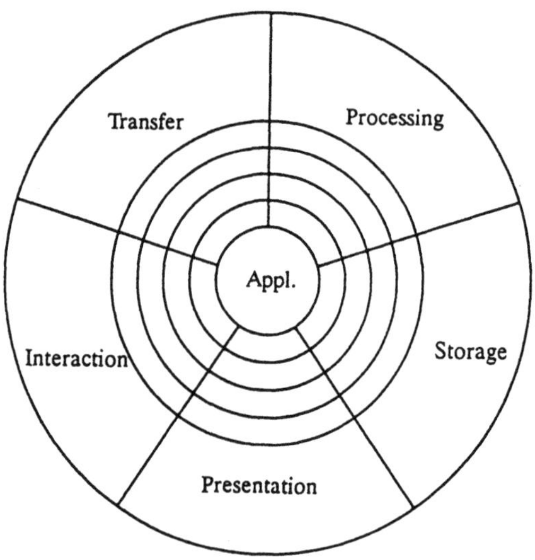

Fig. 3: Hierarchy of Services

7 Conclusions

In this paper, a first proposal towards a reference model for cooperative hyper media systems has been outlined. The purpose of this attempt is more to separate different areas of future work than to provide solutions for these areas. As a first work in this direction, existing systems may be described according to the terminology sketched above. This may improve both the understanding of these systems as well as the different aspects of the reference model.

Bibliography

Abramowicz W. (1990): "Zur Modellierung von Hypertexten" - Proc. of the workshop "Integrierte, intelligente, Informationssysteme", Sep. 1990

Akscyn R., McCracken D., Yoder E. (1988): " KMS: A Distributed Hypermedia System for Managing Knowledge in Organizations" - Communications of the ACM, July 1988.

Benford S. (1988): "" - Research into Networks and Distributed Applications, EUTECO'88, Apr 1988

Benford S., Smith H., Shepherd A., Howidy H. (1991): "INFORMATION Sharing in CSCW: From Models to Architecture" - Proc. International Workshop on CSCW, Apr. 1991

Blum B. (1988): "Documentation for Maintenance: A Hypertext Design" - Proc. conf. on Software Maintenance, 1988

Catlin T., Bush P., Yankelovich N. (1989): "InterNote: Extending a Hypermedia Framework to Support Annotative Collaboration" - Proc. of Hypertext'89, Nov. 1989

Collier G.H. (1987): "Thoth-II: Hypertext with explicit semantics" - Proc. Hypertext'87, Chapel Hill, 1987

Conklin J. (1987): "Hypertext: An Introduction and Survey" - IEEE Computer, Vol.20, N.9, Sep.1987

Conklin J., Begeman M. (1988): "gIBIS: A Hypertext Tool for Explaratory Policy Discussion" - ACM ToOIS, Vol.6,N.4, Oct. 1988

Delisle N.M., Schwartz M.D. (1987): "Neptune: A Hypertext System for Software Development Environment" - Database engineering, Vol.10,N.1,Mar. 1987

Durfee E.H., Lesser V., Corkill D., "Trends in Cooperative Distributed Problem Solving" - IEEE Transations on Knowledge and Data Engineering, March 1989

Ehrich H.D., Gogolla M., Lipeck U. "Algebraische Spezifikation abstrakter Datentypen" - B.G.Teubner Stuttgart, 1989

Foss C.L. (1988): "Efective Browsing in Hypertext Systems" - Proc. RIAO'88, MIT Press, Cambridge, Mar 1988

Frisse M. (1988): "From Text to Hypertext" - Byte, Oct. 1988

Garg P.K. (1988): "Abstraction Mechanisms in Hypertext" - Communications of the ACM, July 1988, Vol.31, N.7

Garret N., Smith K., Meyrowitz N. (1990): "InterMedia Issues, Strategies, and Tactics in the design of a Hypermedia Document System" - Institute for Research in Information and Scholarship, Brown University

Gibbs S.J. (1989): "LIZA: An Extensible Groupware Toolkit" - MCC, Software Technology Program

Greif I. (1988): "CSCW: A Book of Readings" Morgan-Kaufmann Publishers, San Mateo, 1988

Guttag J., Horowitz E., Musser D. (1976): "The Design of Data Type Specifitions" - Information sciences Institute, 1976

Heck N. (1984): "Abstrakte Datentypen mit automatischen Implementierungen" - Fachbereich Informatik der Universität Kaiserlautern, 1984

Jones C.B. (19xx): "Software Development - A Rigorous Approach" - Prentice-Hall

Kuna M., Klehn N. (1991): "A Three Level Approach to Model Systems for CSCW" - Proc. International Workshop on CSCW, Apr. 1991

Mariani J., Rodden T. (1991): "The Impact of CSCW on Database Technology" - Proc. International Workshop on CSCW, Apr. 1991

Meiser D. (1990): "Die abstrakte Hypertextmaschine DAHM als Basis für große verteilte Hypertextsysteme" - Proc. of the workshop "Integrierte, intelligente, Informationssysteme", Sep. 1990
Nielsen J. (1990): "The Art of Navigating through Hypertext" - Communications of the ACM, Mar. 1990, Vol.33, N.3
Phillips D. (1990): "Interactive SIGGRAPH Proceedings: A New Form of Publication" - Computer Graphics, Vol. 24, N. 1, Jan. 1990
Rada R., Keith B. (1989): "Collaborative Writing of Text and Hypertext" - Hypermedia Vol.1,N.2, 1989
Richartz M., Ruedebusch T. (1990): "Collaboration in Hypermedia Environments" - Designing Hypermedia for Learnning, Chapter 18, 1990
Ruedebusch T.D. (1991): "Supporting Interactions within Distributed Teams" - Proc. International Workshop on CSCW, Apr. 1991
Santos A: (1990): "State of the Art Report on Multimedia" - FAGD-90i034, Dez. 1990
Streitz N.A., Hannemann J., Thüring M. (1989): "From Ideas and Arguments to Hyperdocuments: Travelling through Activity Spaces" - Proc. Hypertext'89, November 1989
Thomas P., Robinson H. (19xx): "Abstract Data Types - Their Specification, Representation and Use"
Wiil U., Osterbye K. (1990): "Experiences With HyperBase - a multi-user back-end for Hypertext Applications with Emphasis on Collaboration Support" - Institute for Electronic Systems, Allborg, Denmark, 1990
Wiil U. (1991): "Using Events as Support for Data Sharing in Collaborative Work" - Proc. International Workshop on CSCW, Apr. 1991

Chapter 3

CDAM - Compound Document Access and Management. An Object-Oriented Approach[1]

Wolfgang Herzner and Erwin Hocevar

Abstract

This paper describes an object-oriented database approach for a direct access and memory management system which covers the needs of storing compound resp. multimedia documents in a multi-user and distributed environment. Document components may be distributed over several physical locations, documents may share components, and multi-user access is supported. In addition, the model allows to represent much of the document semantics, giving the opportunity to define and access components favourably through their properties. Rapid access and manipulation (using for example, associative methods) as well as encapsulation of data to minimize side effects are also considered.

1 Introduction

The socalled *desk top publishing*-revolution, which brought the integration of 'traditional' document domains like text, (line) graphics, (raster) images, and spreadsheets at the hand of almost every user, was only a first step towards a completely new view of documents and their processing. Some aspects of this new view are

- integration of *continuous* media into compound documents like sound, movie and video; making compound documents really *multimedia*;
- extensive use of component-sharing among documents;
- support of documents whose components may be distributed over nodes of a (computer) network;
- support of simultaneous access by different users to (different components of) a document;
- support of nonsequential resp. nonhierarchical document structures like the hypertext model (Gloor et al. 1990).

In the light of this new perspective, several projects have been carried out at Seibersdorf. One of them aims towards the integration of music and synchronisation notations

[1]This project has been funded by Digital's European External Research Project 376/AU-014.

into compound document formats in revisable form (Kuhn et al. 1991), while another, CDAM, is aimed towards a system which allows to store and manipulate documents with no restriction about their content in a distributed multi-user environment, where document-specific semantics are widely supported (Herzner et al. 1991), (Zdonik 1989).

To explain the functionality and intended goals of CDAM, the next section discusses the underlying view of documents in general, their structure, their contents, and other related aspects. As a result, requirements for a system for storage, access and management of such documents are formulated. Based on this, the adapted architectural model for (multimedia) documents is described in section 4. Section 5 then deals with a prototype realisation, carried out at Seibersdorf, with emphasis laid on the API (Application Program Interface). The final chapter gives a summary of the achieved results.

2 A View of Multimedia Documents

2.1 What's a Multimedia Document?

The first question which has to be discussed is the term *multimedia*. It is felt, however, that in the context of this journal (resp. these proceedings) that term is well known (although its definition is possibly a major issue to be solved) and shall therefore not be dealt with here in much detail.

One aspect to be kept in mind is the distinction between different *content categories* like text, drawings, images, or spreadsheets on the one side, and sounds or movies on the other. The first could be called *static* because their presentation is usually of that form, while the latter could be called *dynamic* because dynamic changes are a crucial property of their presentation.

Multimedia documents then simply means, that the content of a document is not restricted to one category. (According to some stronger views, all static categories belong to one *medium* and only audio and video are different media, but we keep more flexible in that point.)

It should be noted here that all mentioned document media rely on waves as final *information carriers* from the computer to the human perception. But there exist some more human senses which are based on other information carriers, namely *smell* and *taste*, which react on molecules, and the sense of *touch*, which is mechanically oriented. Although the smell of an object may be a documentable property, it seems that in the near future such types of information will rather not be integrated into document processing environments, mainly because of technical reasons.

Trying to answer the question "What's a Document ?" will lead directly to our understanding of (multimedia) documents.

To begin with, a document is a piece of structured information. Of course, any information has to be structured somehow to carry its 'message', but what we mean is a property which can be described with sentences like "an article consists of a title, an abstract, the content, and the bibliography."

Therefore, a document is a - possibly ordered - collection of parts or components, and we will call this collection an aggregation. Now, the components may further be divided into subcomponents like "**the content consists of a sequence of chapters**" and build aggregations by themselves, too. Because this repeated aggregationing leads to a sort of tree structure, we will call this an aggregation hierarchy, which is a very important property of any document.

Looking at the apostrophed descriptions above more carefully, we recognize that they describe properties of, let's say, *classes* of documents rather than specific ones. A specific document would be described in terms like "**this chapter has the title 'A View for Multimedia Documents'**". So we can differentiate between document classes and real documents constructed according the rules defining their classes, which we call instances of these classes. Because this dualism also applies to document components, we replace the term *document class* by the more general *object class*. So the difference between object classes and their instantiations is another important aspect of documents.

Back to aggregation, it is evident that such a decomposing process will terminate at some level, when parts are encountered which are atomic from the point of our view like *string* or *video-frame*. Nodes in the aggregation hierarchy which correspond to such elementary types are called leaves, because they don't have other parts as components anymore. These elementary data types are considered to be predefined within the document processing environment, although it could sometimes be comfortable to support the addition of further basic data types (e.g. day names or synchronisation events).

Such data types are completely defined through their *carrier set* (the possible values) and the *operations* on them (for example, (Bauer et al. 1982)); that means that elements of that type can be manipulated solely with the operations provided by this data type, which increases security and consistency. That's also an important aspect.

Now, the concept that the elements of a type can be manipulated only by 'its' functions is worth to be applied to the document and its parts as well and leads to the object-oriented approach. Therefore, the concept that the manipulation of document components is only allowed by functions which are explicitely defined (on them), is a further important aspect.

Functions are called methods in the object-oriented approach, and are either predefined or specified by the application environment. This definability of methods is another essential feature.

In addition, certain aspects of component-classes can be identified which should be inherited from components to their parts, that means the way down aggregation hierarchies. For example, if a *font size* is defined for a document, then it shall become 'known' to all its parts and sub...parts to be applied whenever necessary. (Note that this differs from inheritance which happens within the specialisation schemes of classes).

In our model, we will call such properties attributes. Definability and propagation of attributes down the aggregation hierarchy is an important feature of our compound document processing model.

Finally, it is sometimes necessary to define associations between document components outside both aggregation and generalisation. Examples are *cross references, counters, synchronisation markers* or the hypertext *links*. Support of manipulation and interpretation of such relationships is also important in multimedia document environments.

2.2 Document Processing and Revisability of Documents

The following processes deal with document manipulation:

- Editing process: recording and manipulation of document content, structure, and semantics;
- Store and retrieval process: storing, distribution, exchange, and retrieval (like content-specific search) of documents and their components (within a distributed environment);
- Layout process: preparing documents to be output from the processing environment to an environment accessible to human perception (e.g. page layout, rawMIDI);
- Presentation process: presenting documents to the human perception like displaying on screen, printing or sending rawMIDI data to a synthesizer. (As long as only visual media are concerned, the term *imaging process* is used.)

Evidently, the editing process may use the other processes, essentially when working in a WYSIWYG-environment.

It should be emphasized here that this paper essentially deals with the store/retrieval process, because CDAM can be regarded as a realisation of that process. However, the underlying model (as outlined above) shall be powerful enough to support the other processes. For example, layout or presentation (e.g. for synchronisation) information should be storable together with the documents (which can be done by means of attributes, relationships, and methods).

Fig.1 shows the document processing model which has been assumed for our approach. It assumes three forms of documents:

- the revisable form (is administrated by the store/retrieval process and) contains the highest amount of document specific information of all forms;
- the final form contains the layouted document in a format directly processable by the presentation process;
- the revisable/final form contains the layouted document in a still editable format (e.g. PostScript).

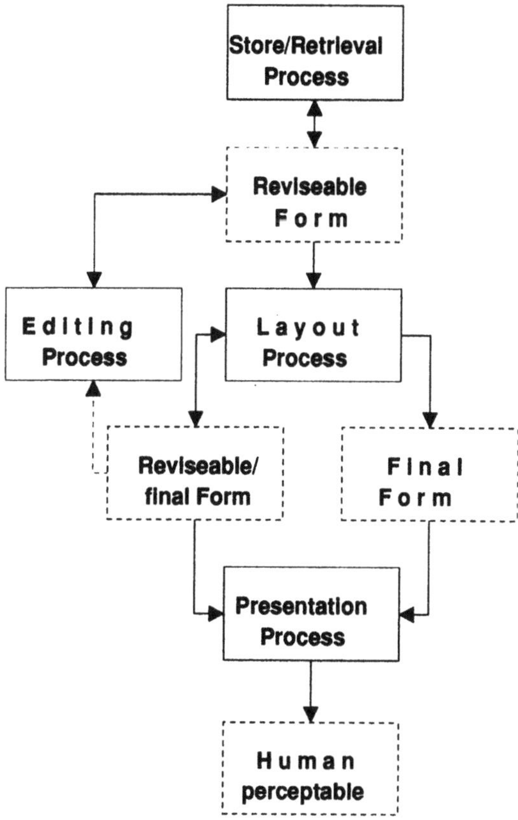

Fig. 1 Document processing model

3 Requirements

For a store/retrieval system of multimedia documents in revisable form (which are structured as outlined before), different sets of requirements exist which are grouped in the three following subsections.

One general requirement is to allow for adaption and update of existing specifications (class descriptions, methods, ...) to the changing user's needs in a consistent way and with as few inconveniences for the users as possible. This applies to all of the following aspects and will therefore not be mentioned anymore.

3.1 Multimedia Document Requirements

These requirements have already been identified in the subsection about the assumed document model and shall only be detailed here.

Aggregation

The most important requirement from documents is the adequate presentation of their structure. Therefore, the aggregation hierarchy of document instances as well as their definition on classes must be supported. Specifically, the following aspects have to be considered:

- it must be possible to mix various document categories within one aggregation,
- complex structures of any depth must be supported,
- sharing of substructures between different components (of different documents) should be possible,
- the valid aggregations - groupings of components of a document part - must be definable (at any depth), e.g. alternatives, repetitions,
- default structures should be definable.

Content

For the presentation of elementary data, some socalled elementary data types have to be provided. For each of them, the following has to be considered:

- the set of possible values and the applicable operations, together with the constraints under which they may be applied, should be defined, at least to such an extent that elementary data can be communicated with application programs,
- it should not be impossible to reference data on external media like CD-ROM,
- generally, the handling of large amounts of elementary data should be optimized, including sharing among documents and the control of their physical representation by some system administrators,
- defaults and constants should be definable.

Attributes

as already described, must be provided. That means that not only their definition and setting has to be supported, but especially their propagation (within aggregations) has to be performed by the system.

Relationships

as already described, must be provided. That means that not only their definition and setting has to be supported, but especially their dereferencing has to be performed by the system.

Access and manipulation

Associative access to (parts of) stored documents must be provided. This access may be based on structure (aggregation), content (elementary data), or specific semantics (realised by means of attributes, relationships, or methods). The same applies for specifications. An example would be the search for a class definition like a 'double arrow' of which the name may be unknown but which has certain inquirable characteristics by which it can be identified.

Furthermore, it should be possible to manipulate (add, replace, move, copy, delete) arbitrary complex document parts as a whole rather than node by node. Of course, these operations have to consider *consistency constraints* automatically.

3.2 Requirements of the Multi-User and Distributed Environments

Concurrent access

Concurrent access to the same data by multiple users must be controlled. For example, we may specify that changes made to a document will not be visible to other documents, until the changes are committed resp. the locks are released. This - the locking of data to be changed - is a straightforward method of concurrency control which is sufficient for many document management applications.

Distributed data

Conceptually, any information like elementary data or class definitions may be distributed over a set of processing nodes. The situation becomes aggravated when relationships among different documents have to be considered, which should be treated dynamically (i.e. changes of one document should be recognized in a related document as soon as possible). The system should be able to keep this distribution transparent to the applications.

Views

A part of a document can be viewed in time as either a snapshot of underlying data at some point or as a window into the underlying data. The selected view will determine if some portion of data is updated when some other data changes. This is the snapshot and view mechanism found in conventional databases. In combination with constraints resp. rule mechanisms, the views can be used for security purposes by allowing only to see the data one is authorized to.

3.3 Requirements of the Object-Oriented Environment

The merits of the object-oriented approach - *data encapsulation, specialisation/inheritance, polymorphism* - are already mentioned and not be further discussed here. Since CDAM shall provide these features, the following requirements have to be considered.

Specialisation / inheritance

One of the fundamental characteristics of the object-oriented model is the property of inheritance. Since this functionality is also a basic issue of the accepted document processing model, the full support of specialization (hierarchy) is important. In particular,

- the definition of subclasses has to be possible,
- instances of subclasses have to be provided with any properties of their superclasses (as long as not overridden),
- collisions raised by multiple superclasses have to be solved.

Methods

A fundamental characteristic of the object-oriented model is that the only way to cause an object to perform some operation is to activate one of its methods (by sending it a *message*). Therefore it is not only essential to support this feature by the proposed model with regard to their usage, but also concerning their definition (and manipulation) by applications. In order to restrict the efforts of the applications to set up a reasonable environment of object classes, methods etc., the provision of a set of predefined methods (like those for elementary aggregation editing) is of great value. This may be realised by defining them on very general object classes from which any other application-specific class may be specialized.

4 The CDAM System

Based on the discussed concepts and requirements, a compound document processing system has been developed by the following steps:

- design of the model,
- mapping the model into a semantic resp. object-oriented database environment,
- realising this environment on a relational database system (Lyngbaek et al. 1987).

These steps shall now be discussed in some detail.

4.1 The Document Architecture

This is described in terms of diagrams which are similar to semantic nets and entity relationship diagrams (Tjoa et al. 1982). The diagrams are directed graphs containing nodes and directed arcs (edges). The nodes represent socalled entities like object classes or data, and the edges represent interrelations between nodes. The model itself is based on works by Woelk et alii (Woelk 1986).

4.1.1 Node types

Five node types (respectively object categories) can be distinguished:

1. (structure/part) class nodes representing document resp. part classes, will be called class nodes for short;
2. instance nodes representing instances of document/part classes;
3. elementary-data-type nodes for value classes;
4. (elementary) data nodes for defaults, constants, and content;
5. method nodes.

It may be surprising that there are no object categories for *attributes* and *relationships*. The reason is that attributes are considered to be of the same type as normal parts (as already mentioned in chapter 2). That means that they can be defined and used in the same way as ordinary part classes and instances. The only difference is that if such an object is to be used as attribute of another, then this is indicated by an own edge-type (see below). Similarily, relationships are regarded as interrelations between nodes rather than nodes themselves.

4.1.2 Edge types

Analogously, twelve edge types can be distinguished. CAN-HAVE.. edges describe possible resp. valid relationships between classes, while HAS-.. and IS-edges represent facts:

1. CAN-HAVE-PARTS: defines an aggregation relation between two (structure or object) classes. An edge of that type from a class node A to another node B means that "instances of A can have instances of B as parts".
2. CAN-HAVE-TYPES: defines a relation between a class and an elementary data type. An edge of that type from a class node A to an elementary-data-type node B means that "instances of A can have data of type B".
3. CAN-HAVE-ATTRIBUTES: defines a relation between two classes. An edge of that type from a class node A to another node B means that "instances of A can have attributes as instances of B".
4. CAN-HAVE-RELATIONSHIP: defines a relation between two classes. An edge of that type from a class node A to another node B means that "instances of A can have relationships to instances of B".
5. HAS-PART: defines an aggregation relation between two instances. An edge of that type from an instance node A to another node B means that "A has B as part".
6. HAS-DATA: defines an aggregation relation between a class or an instance and an elementary datum. An edge of that type from a class or instance node A to an elementary-data node B means that "A has data B".
7. HAS-TYPE: defines an aggregation relation between an elementary datum and an elementary data type. An edge of that type from an elementary-data node A to an elementary-data-type node B means that "A has type B".
8. HAS-ATTRIBUTE: defines a relation between two instances. An edge of that type from an instance node A to another node B means that "A has B as attribute".
9. HAS-RELATIONSHIP: defines a relation between two instances. An edge of that type from an instance node A to another node B means that "A has a relationship to B".
10. HAS-METHOD: defines a relation between a class and a method. An edge of that type from a class node A to a method node B means that "A has method B".
11. IS-INSTANCE-OF: defines a relation between an instance and a class. An edge of that type from an instance node A to a class node B means that "A is instance of class B".
12. IS-SUBCLASS-OF: defines a specialization relation between two classes. An edge of that type from a class node A to a node B means that "A is subclass of B".

Formally, these edges can be regarded as binary relationships or predicates. For example, HAS-ATTRIBUTE (a, b) would mean that a(n instance) node a would have another (instance) node b as attribute. Based on this, functions can be defined which allow to access and manipulate nodes. For example, providing an instance a and a class

B to a function Get_Attribute (a, B), it would return that instance b (if it exists), for which the conditions IS-INSTANCE-OF (b, B) and HAS-ATTRIBUTE (a, b) hold.

Evidently, such functions have to consider constraints to keep the whole document system consistent, but these constraints can be expressed in the indicated way.

Since the network of (part) classes describes the possible document structures, it is also called the *generic (document) structure*, while the aggregation hierarchy of a specific document is called *specific structure*.

Fig.2 defines the graphical representation of the introduced node and edge types, while fig.3 and 4 show simple examples of a generic and a specific structure, respectively.

4.1.3 Aggregation types

A document component together with its parts is called an *aggregation*. Since the ordering of these parts is usually important, five aggregation types are conceptually distinguished:

1. SEQUENCE: an ordered sequence of parts of possibly different classes, denoted by name;
2. SEQUENCE-OF: an ordered sequence of parts of one class with sequence size within a given range, denoted by indices;
3. CHOICE: a choice out of different parts, denoted by name;
4. SET: an unordered set of parts of possibly different classes, denoted by name;
5. SET-OF: an unordered set of parts of one class with set size within a given range, denoted by indices.

(Since SET(-OF) are not used in our example, they are not presented in figure 2.)

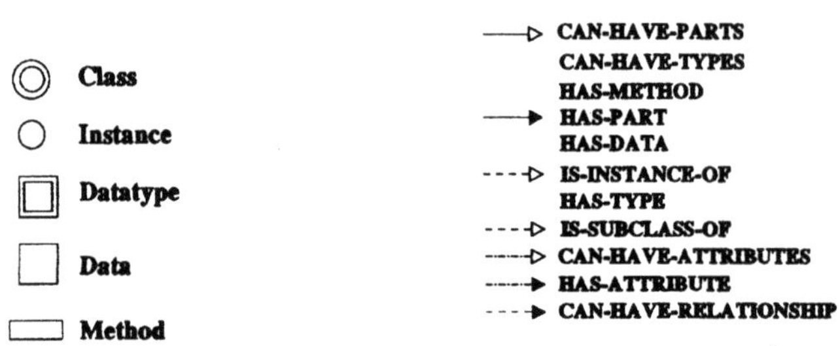

Fig. 2 Graphical presentation of nodes and edges

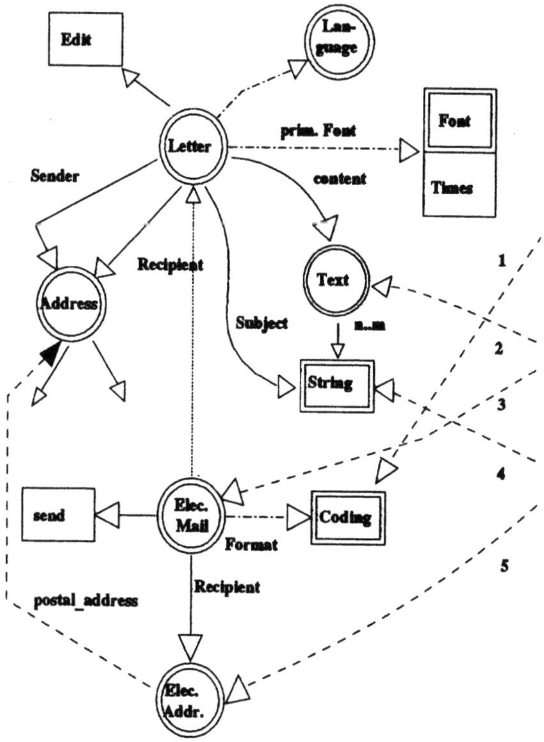

Fig. 3 Example of a simple 'generic' structure

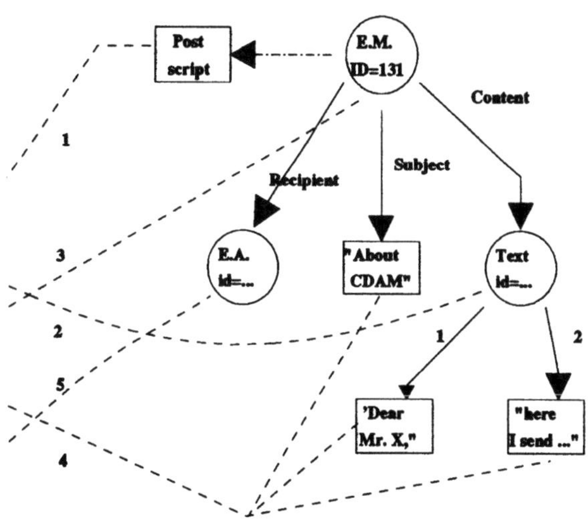

Fig. 4 Example of a simple 'specific' structure

4.1.4 Selectors

As just described, parts can be uniquely selected, either by name or by index. This applies to all edge types within the document architecture where unique selection is not guaranteed otherwise. Hence, relationships and attributes can be named explicitly, while IS-SUBCLASS-OF and HAS-METHOD cannot, because their targets always have unique names.

By this way, each edge can uniquely be identified and therefore serves as *selector*.

4.2 The Semantic or Object-Oriented Database Environment

4.2.1 Operations

The model as described above has to be embedded into an environment which allows to access and manipulate the network of nodes and edges (Herzner et al. 1987), (Woelk et al. 1986). This is achieved by providing functions (resp. predefined methods) for

Creation of classes

When a (part) class is created, the following properties have to be defined:

- its name (has to be unique);
- its superclasses if any, (multiple inheritance (more than one IS-SUBCLASS-OF-edge per class) is possible, which creates a specialisation lattice rather than a hierarchy; this set is ordered to specify precedence if there is a conflict of inherited properties);
- its aggregation type; if it is SEQUENCE, CHOICE, or SET, then for each possible part either a CAN-HAVE-PARTS or CAN-HAVE-TYPES edge associated with its (selector) name and pointing at the part class or elementary data type; otherwise a CAN-HAVE-PARTS/TYPES edge associated with the minimum and maximum number of allowed occurences; for each possible part a *default* if requested and whether it is *mandatory or optional*;
- its attributes; for each possible attribute, an edge CAN-HAVE-ATTRIBUTES associated with its (selector) name and pointing at the corresponding class; a *default* value if necessary;
- its possible relationships; for each possible relationship, an edge CAN-HAVE-RELATIONSHIP associated with its (selector) name and pointing at the referenced part class;
- its methods; for each user-defined method for that class, an edge HAS-METHOD to the referenced method (with unique name within the set of methods of that class).

This is performed by a method CREATE_CLASS with the described properties as arguments.

Modification and deletion of classes

All properties as just described can be modified. Whole classes can be deleted. See 'constraints' below.

This is performed by methods MODIFY_CLASS and DELETE_CLASS.

Retrieval of class descriptions

With a method like INQUIRE_CLASS, all properties of a class as described above, especially any inherited ones, can be inquired.

Creation of (user-defined) methods

Before methods can be referenced by class definitions, they have to be created. Conceptually, this happens by providing their source code to the system, which (compiles and) integrates them into its API.

Creation of instances

When an instance (document part) is created, the following properties have to be defined:

- its *class (name)* resp. *data type*;
- if it is a *class* instance, its mandatory and not defaulted parts; this happens, for example, by providing the appropriate object identifiers with the corresponding selectors;
- if it is an *elementary data element*, its value (if not defaulted);
- values for the attributes, which are defined for its class and not defaulted; these are either elementary values or object identifiers, depending of the attribute type. Remember that attributes are propagated down the aggregation hierarchies and may be redefined at any level.

This function CREATE_INSTANCE returns an identifier of the created instance.

Modification and deletion of instances

With DELETE_INSTANCE, instances can be deleted. (See however 'constraints' below.)

All properties as just described can be modified. In addition, relationships can be set. This happens with methods like SET/REMOVE_ATTRIBUTE, SET/REMOVE_PART, SET/REMOVE_RELATIONSHIP.

Retrieval of instance properties

With methods like GET_PART, GET_ATTRIBUTE, GET_RELATIONSHIP, the corresponding information can be inquired, when the identifier of the instance and the corresponding selector is provided to them. (GET_PART may return elementary data or a reference to them if the inquired part is of appropriate type.) These methods automatically resolve inheritance and propagation (of attributes).

In addition, with methods like GET_CLASS the class of a given instance can be inquired. Finally, a method like GET_OWNER could return the identfier of the predecessor in the aggregation hierarchy. (Special treatment is necessary on shared parts, which have multiple predecessors.)

Execution of user-defined methods

is performed by calling the specific methods with the object identifier as argument (and additional arguments of course, if necessary).

Note that the methods as described do not fully support the access and manipulation of substructures more complex than a single node and its associated edges. Since, however, in the prototype realisation (as described in the next section) this functionality is provided, these methods are considered to be sufficient. The corresponding is valid for 'views'.

4.2.2 Constraints

To keep the database consistent, all the described functions and methods (including user-defined) have to consider a list of constraints:

- A class may only be modified if its modification does not make existing instances of this class (including instances of subclasses) invalid.
- A class may only be deleted if no instances of this class exist (including instances of subclasses).
- Aggregation types cannot be mixed.
- Each CAN-HAVE-PARTS and HAS-PART edge is associated either with a name or an index to uniquely identify it within an aggregation.
- If an aggregation over class nodes is of one of the types SEQUENCE OF or SET OF, then the aggregation contains exactly one edge CAN-HAVE-PARTS. Corresponding aggregations over instances always consist of a number of HAS-PART/TYPE edges whose value lies within the range defined by the CAN-HAVE-PARTS/TYPES edge.
- If an aggregation over class nodes is of the type CHOICE, then the corresponding aggregations over instances consist of exactly one HAS-PART edge representing the chosen alternative.
- An edge HAS-PART(*X*,*Y*,*name*) may only exist from an instance node X to an instance node Y, if there exists an edge CAN-HAVE-PARTS(*A*,*B*,*name*) from a class node A to a class node B and also the edges IS-INSTANCE-OF(*X*,*A*) and IS-INSTANCE-OF(*Y*,*B*).
- If there exists an edge HAS-DATA(*X*,*d*) for an instance X, as well as an edge IS-INSTANCE-OF(*X*,*A*), and d is of type T, then also an edge CAN-HAVE-TYPES(*A*,*T*) has to be present.

This is only a small excerpt of the full list of constraints to be considered, but it exhibits the basic aspects of their importance.

4.3 The Relational Database Environment

Since no object-oriented database has been available, which provided the described features, its functionality has been built on top of a relational database environment. This has been performed in essentially three steps.

The first step was the development of a set of relations (*tables*), which contain all information. Conceptually, the following tables have been used:

1. STRUCTURE_CLASS: the defined object classes for parts;
2. STRUCTURE_INSTANCE: the instances of part classes;
3. TYPE_CLASSES: predefined and additional elementary data types;

4. DATA: the elementary data resp. references to external presentations.

The second step was to map the functions described in the previous subsection to procedures which perform their task on the given relations.

The final step was the formulation of all constraints in the relational database language and their implementation.

Since specific aspects of the the relational database environment will be discussed in the next section, it will not be treated in more detail here.

5 Realisation and Prototype

The system architecture resulting from the mapping of a conceptual model into a relational database environment is shown in figure 5.

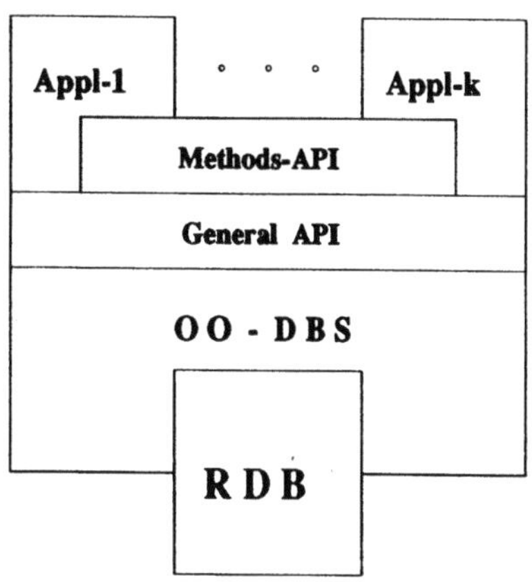

Fig. 5 System architecture

5.1 The Prototype

has been developed on VAXes under VAX/VMS 5.3 or later, is mainly written in VAX/C and uses VAX/Rdb as relational database system.

A demonstration shell, also written in C, uses DECwindows as user interface.

In the following, the individual components of the implemented prototype are described.

5.2 The Relational Database

The conceptual relations as described in 4.3 have been normalized and installed. The consistency constraints have been transformed to work on the normalized relations and implemented.

Methods - as executable pieces of 'data' - cannot usefully be stored in relational databases. Therefore, only references are stored within the 'class' tables, while their code is managed by the object-oriented database system.

Although VAX/Rdb principally supports distributed databases, this feature has not been fully implemented yet.

5.3 The Object-Oriented Database System

is realised as shell around the relational database kernel (see fig.5). Generally, it provides the functions as described in 4.2 and the incorporation of application-defined methods.

Predefined Methods

The methods resp. operations as introduced in 4.2 - for example CREATE_CLASS or GET_ATTRIBUTE - are provided by a set of functions each operating on a single (relational database) table entry. Therefore, four elementary operations exist, namely CREATE, DELETE, MODIFY, INQUIRE (table_entry). Since these can be applied to all tables, a call like MODIFY (CLASS) performs like the execution of the method MODIFY_CLASS. Analogously, the other predefined methods are represented, although not always a 1:1-mapping has been realised.

In addition, by reasons of efficiency, a more powerful inquiry-function is provided, which allows to inquire more table entries (building an aggregation tree) within one call.

The definition of elementary data types by the user is not yet supported.

Definition of Application-defined Methods

To incorporate an application-defined method (or replace an existing one), the following steps have to be performed:

1. An ASCII-file MT_NA_method.SEQ has to be created, (where 'method' is the name of the method,) wich contains defaults for the parameter lists (see the 'methods' API below) and the body of the method.
2. The class for which the method shall be defined (or replaced), has to be created or modified (using the corresponding tree-manipulation function of the general API - see below). If these functions encounter a HAS-METHOD edge, the corresponding .SEQ is read and converted into a complete C-code file MT_NA_methodNNNNNNNN.RC. The extension NNNNNNNN denotes the internal class identifier and is necessary to support polymorphism (different methods with same name for different classes). Simultaneously, its internal name is registered and prepared to be used by EXECUTE_METHOD - see below.
3. This C-code file has to be precompiled (because it contains some VAX/Rdb specific specifications) and compiled. The resulting object is to be put into a corresponding library.
4. Applications linked with CDAM later on can access the new methods.

5.4 The General API

allows applications to access the database on network level (of nodes and edges). The basic concepts of this API (Herzner et al. 1987) are

- Edit pointer: resources which may point at any node of the internal structure; essentially, edit pointer serve as *object identifier*;
- Path: sequence of edges between two nodes;
- Node list/Edge list: together, they describe an arbitrary complex structure like an aggregation.

The functions of this general interface can be divided into the following groups:

Initialisation
Functions to open and initialise CDAM and to provide initial information to the application.

Edit pointer manipulation
Functions to position edit pointer by various methods like

- Define_EP_Relative (IN OldEP, IN Path, OUT NewEP) directs NewEP at a node which can be reached from the node referenced by OldEP via Path;
- Define_EP_By_Tree (IN RootEP, IN CompTree, IN Params, OUT NewEP) points NewEP at a node which is the root of a subtree of 'RootEP' which corresponds to CompTree.

Data retrieval
A set of functions allow to inquire data associated with a node like content (elementary data), associated attributes (considering propagation), parts (considering inheritance), or even an arbitrary subtree of its aggregation tree.

Structure manipulation
Functions allowing to insert, move, copy, and delete trees at nodes selected by edit pointer;

Multiuser Environment control
Functions for locking (and unlocking) arbitrary subtrees of a given node, as well as for *transaction control*. Although structures are locked automatically on modifying access, the specific functions provide more control (e.g. locking document parts in advance).

Sometimes it is impossible to avoid inconsistent database states during its manipulation. A sequence of operations transforming a databes from one consistent state into the next is called a transaction.

These functions also serve for the support of *user-specific views* as mentioned in 3.2.

Auxiliary functions
Trees specified in node/edge-lists can be read from and written to external files in a standard format. Additionally, internal structures like class specifications can be listed in a human-readable format.

5.5 The 'Methods' API

To let applications communicate with CDAM in a 'clean' object-oriented way, the function

EXECUTE_METHOD (node, method, node_list, argument_list)

is provided, with the following meanings of its arguments:

node : the object (instance) for which the method is to be executed, denoted by a edit-pointer/path - pair;

method : the name of the method to be executed;

node_list : list of further nodes possibly needed by the method, denoted by an array of edit-pointer;

argument_list : list of further methods parameter, denoted by an array of (C-)pointer to the argument variables resp. values.

EXECUTE_METHOD maps node/method to the registered internal function name, provides the identified function with the further arguments and executes it. The executed function may call other methods or functions from the general API to perform its task.

Due to the richness of the general interface, no predefined methods are currently provided.

6 Conclusion

The approach presented in this paper allows to store, retrieve and manipulate multimedia documents in an object-oriented way within a multi-user and distributed environment. Thus, integrating the proposed model into a multimedia document architecture (including editors, formatters and other document processing tools).

The benefits of this approach are summarized below:

- By adaption of the object-oriented approach, its advantages like encapsulation of data and behavior, object class refinement through specialisation, and inheritance are available at the application interface.
- By extending the object-oriented model for aggregation, attributes, and relationships, important characteristics of documents are directly supported.
- By the addition of application-definable methods, document specific semantics can be incorporated into the system.
- By using the object-oriented interface to CDAM, application objects may communicate with documents in a way similar to the way they communicate among themselves.
- Document as well as component classes can be defined and manipulated during the lifetime of the system; e.g. for adding a new class no restart or analogous action is necessary.

- The underlying relational database system automatically accomplishes the task of multi-user access, distributed environments, and integrity control (constraint checks, transaction control, roll back, ...).
- Documents may be distributed over different locations and still be accessible as a whole.
- An arbitrary number of users may access a document simultaneously.
- For document editing, two levels of application program interfaces are provided. One pure object-oriented (by calling only methods) and another which allows access to the database at a lower level, but still providing most of the security of an object-oriented interface.
- Only those document parts have to be processed, which are needed at a given point in time.

Semantic (resp. object-oriented) databases are currently in most cases built on top of relational databases. This approach has also been taken in the project described in this paper, mainly for two reasons:

- the underlying database (RDB) was readily available
- no appropriate implementation of a semantic database has been available on the market at a development stage beyond that of prototypes or research tools.

So, any information about object classes and structure as well as content of specific documents is stored in relations within RDB, while methods - realised as C-modules - are treated specially: their source is stored mainly with the 'creator' of the functions, while the objects are either collected in directories or libraries. The remaining semantics - like inheritance, aggregation or attributes - are exclusively treated in the CDAM software shell around the database.

This compromise suffers to some degree from reduced efficiency (but performance was not the major issue of this project).

References

Alagić, S. (1989) Object-Oriented Database Programming. Series of Text and Monographs in Computer Science. Springer, New York-Berlin-Heidelberg

Bauer, F.L., Wössner H. (1982) Algorithmic Language and Program Development. Springer Berlin-Heidelberg-New York

Gloor, P.A., Streitz N.A. (ed.) (1990) Hypertext und Hypermedia. Informatikberichte 249. Springer, Berlin-Heidelberg

Herzner, W., Hocevar, E., Kuhn, W. (1987) Dynamic Access Layer / Dynamic Access Structure to DDIF/DDIS-Documents. DAL/DAS User Guide, V1.0. TR OEFZS-A-1060. Austrian Research Center Seibersdorf

Herzner, W., Hocevar, E., Zoubek, R. (1991) Direct Access and External Memory Management of Multimedia Documents - An object-oriented approach. Austrian Research Centre Seibersdorf (in press)

Kuhn, W., Kummer, M., Vorlaufer, G. (1991) CDA/DDIF Music and Synchronisation Extension. Austrian Research Centre Seibersdorf (in press)

VAX Rdb/VMS Reference Manual (1987) Digital Equipment Corporation. O.N.AA-N039D-TE.

Lockemann, P.C. (1988) Multimedia Databases: Paradigm, Architecture, Survey and Issues. Universitt Karlsruhe.

Lyngbaek, P., Vianu, V. (1987) Mapping a Semantic Database Model to the Relational Model. Proceedings of Association for Computer Machinery Special Interest Group on Managment of Data ACM. SIGMOD San Francisco.

Tjoa, A., Vinek, G., Rennert, P.F. (1982) Datenmodellierung (Theorie und Praxis des Datenbankentwurfs). Vol. 2. Physica Verlag.

Woelk, D., Kim, W., Luther, W. (1986) An Object-oriented Approach to Multimedia Databases. Proc. of ACM SIGMOD '86, Int. Conf. on Managamenet of Data. Washington D.C.

Zdonik, S.B. (1989) Object-Oriented Database Concepts, A Research Perspective. Tutorial of OOPSLA'89 - Object-Oriented Programming Systems, Languages and Applications. New Orleans

Part II

Interaction

Chapter 4

Multimedia from the Perspectives of Psychology

Hans Marmolin

1. Introduction

The present report discusses multimedia technology from the perspective of theories and models in psychology. It describes multimedia as the result of new theories about the capabilities of man and as the result of new visions about the role of computers. It discusses the fundamentals of multimedia and relates it to new trends in perceptual, cognitive and social psychology. In addition some basic interface problems in current implementations are discussed.

Multimedia has become a very popular term today, and almost everyone claims that they are designing multimedia systems. One way of defining multimedia is to list common technical characteristics of systems claimed to be multimedia systems. This could be referred to as a technological definition. Examples of such technical characteristics are multidimensional presentation techniques, multimodal interaction techniques, hypermedia or hypertext techniques enabling the user to explore the information in an active way, and broadband communication techniques supporting cooperation between users. All of these techniques are of course not used in every multimedia system, but most of them use at least two of these techniques.

Multidimensional presentation techniques could be described as the integrated use of text, pictures, video, sound etc for representing different characteristics of the information. Such techniques constitute the bases for a new kind of media industry developed by combining computer media, ether media (TV, movies etc) and graphical media (Brandt 1987). The development in the area has just started, but it is predicted that products like interactive video newspapers will be available within 10 to 20 years.

Multimodal interaction techniques enable the user to use different modalities such as voice, gestures, pointing, commands etc, for controlling the computer[1]. The VPL DataGlove that makes the use of gesture possible is one example of a new input device developed within this approach (Weimar & Ganapathy 1989).

---

1 Computing without keyboards. In Byte, pp 202-251, July 1990

Hypermedia or hypertext are nonlinear data structures composed of nodes and links. Nodes can be any kind of information element as a table, a picture, a word, a document etc. Nodes are related through a network of links that enables the user to jump from one node to another, i.e to explore the information in a non-sequential way (see e.g Halasz 1988, Conklin 1987). Hypermedia and hypertext is the focus of most computer science research in this area.

This technological definition is, however, focused on the medium or technology rather than on the user. From the users point of view, the technology is not as important as the possibilities offered by the technology. A user centred definition would characterize multimedia systems as systems enabling the usage of multiple sensory modalities and multiple channels of the same or different modality (for example both ears, both hands etc), and as systems enabling one user to perform several tasks at the same time and several users to perform the same task at different or same time. That is, multimedia is viewed as a multisensory, multichannel, multitasking and multiuser approach to system design (Buxton 1990). In addition multimedia systems put the user in control, i.e could be described as a user centred approach.

In this context, it is important to emphasize that the multimedia approach is based on new visions about the usage of computers. It all started with the vision of Vannervar Bush reported 1945 in his famous article "As we may think" (Bush 1945), where he described a new kind of computer tool, that should enable the user to link documents, notes, drawings etc according to their needs into an associative network. In this way it would be possible to create and to browse through a personalized hypertext library. This vision was implemented by Doug Engelbart 15 years later (see e.g Engelbart 1968, 1984 and 1988) in order to provide a set of tools for extending the human intellect. His goal was to design tools that augmented the capabilities of the people using them, rather than systems replacing a limited intellect. Other milestones in this development were Ted Nelson's vision about a global hypertext library 1965 (see e.g Nelson 1980) that partly have been realized, and Bill Atkinson's vision about hypertext capabilities for the ordinary user, realized in the form of Hypercard™, Supercard™ and similar products (see e.g Hooper 1989).

Computers are thus viewed as tools for extending and augmenting the capabilities of mind and not as systems compensating for the intellectual limitations of man. The four techniques described above should then only be regarded as current attempts to implement these visions and other and better ways may be realized in the future.

To summarize, multimedia should rather be regarded as a new approach to system design than a new technology and a definition of multimedia should not be based on the current implementations, but on the common theoretical bases behind these implementations, i.e on the visions about computers as tools for the mind. In order to characterize this new approach it could be compared to the traditional approach, although such a comparison will be unfair as twenty year old views are compared with visions that have not yet been realized. Traditionally, computers are regarded as calculation machines, while the multimedia approach views computers as windows to the world that enables the users to get new experiences. The traditional approach is focused on compensating for the limitations of man and tries to develop intellectual prosthesis, while the multimedia approach is focused on the capabilities of man and tries to develop tools that enable the user to utilize all their perceptual, cognitive and social capabilities. The goal of the traditional approach is to replace the user, while the goal for the multimedia approach is to augment the user. Traditionally, users are regarded as controllable, rather mechanical and unreliable components in the man-computer system, while the multimedia approach regards the user as uncontrollable, dynamic and qualitatively different from the computer. The user is not viewed as a component in a system, but the system as a tool for the user.

2. Views on man and man - machine interaction

It is important to realize that this development in system design corresponds to a similar development in both general psychology and human factors. In general psychology, there was a paradigm shift in about 1960's. Earlier, man was viewed as controlled mainly by signals from the environment, as a passive receiver of information. In addition, it was assumed that man could be studied in the same way as any physical linear component. Subjects were exposed for simple stimuli in artificial situations and one measured their reactions, assuming that more complex behaviour could be explained in terms of these simple reactions.

Perceptual psychology regarded our senses as more or less independent channels that could be studied in isolation, and the stimuli used to study e.g visual perception were simple patterns of light that could be fully controlled and mathematically described. In cognitive psychology one attempt to describe man's mind as an information processing system composed of independent memory and processing components, each with their capabilities and limitations. Information processing was regarded as a sequential linear process in which the information was successively refined. In learning the behaviour of man it was assumed to be regulated only by external positive and negative reinforcements and very simple and artificial situations such as labyrinths, wordlists etc were used to study learning. There was a parallel view on man in human factors. Man was viewed as a system component possible to describe by the same terms as other technological components. One tried to build models of the whole man machine system in order to optimize system performance. One tried to allocate functions to man and machine according to their comparable limitations and strengths and one tried to control the behaviour of man through signals from the machine.

This view could best be described as a mechanical view of man. However, there were many problems with this mechanical view. Although, many micromodels explained and predicted man's behaviour in the laboratory situations used in research, the behaviour of man in more natural situations could not be very well understood. In the same way, the system oriented man-machine models developed in human factors were not very successful for optimizing system performance and for preventing human errors and mistakes. Findings such as "50-70 % of all errors were dependent on the human factor, 20-25 % of all errors were caused by human mistakes, 10-15 % of all system errors were directly caused by the operator", were frequently published.

As a result of the limited explaining power of the mechanical model, it became replaced by a more dynamic view during the 70´s. Perceptual psychology did not view man any more as an information receiver equipped with sensory channels of limited capacity. Gibson (1950,1966, 1979) showed that it was not possible to isolate perceptual variables as we seemed to function differently when we are exposed to isolated as compared to integrated stimulation. He argued that our senses have been developed to function in direct contact with our environment and that impoverished and artificial situations elected an unnatural way of perceiving. Although, the flow of information in a natural environment is very complex from a mathematical point of view, our senses are constructed to handle such information and not the simple stimuli earlier used. Simple situations as static patterns of light are on the contrary too complex for our senses and we are then forced to rely on cognitive analyses of earlier experiences, expectations etc. For example Johansson (1958,1974) following the tradition from Gestalt Psychology, showed that our visual system had been developed to handle continuously changing information rather than static pictures. Gibson also argued that we are not passive receivers of information and that there are really no sensory channels with limited capacity. Instead, our perceptual system is characterized by the pick up of information and by the integration of activities in the different senses. As he stated it, we do not hear, we listen, we do not see, we look around. One could also show that the complex flow of information often is redundant in a mathematical sense, but that this redundancy is very important for our ability to pick up and process information.

The information processing view in cognitive psychology was also replaced by more dynamic, non linear and complex models of cognition. For example, Neisser (1976) and Norman (1981) explained cognition in terms of hierarchical structures of inbedded and parallel schemata. Neisser also emphasised the importance of active explorations or with his term, anticipatorical schemata, expectations, that controls the exploration of the environment. He regarded cognition as a constructive active process directed towards preparing and focusing perception. In learning became explanations in terms of simple associations replaced by mental models (Norman 1983) explaining how man achieves understanding by relating new knowledge to old experiences, developing incomplete mental models (Carroll J. & Thomas 1982).

The same kind of paradigm shift occurred later in applied psychology. Man was put into control and work was regarded as a social activity (Rasmussen 1986, Hacker 1985). Man´s behaviour was explained as a "random walk" controlled by both mental goals and social acts. Man was viewed as qualitatively different from and not controllable by machine.

3. Fundamentals of multimedia from a psychological perspective

Using the new theories in psychology as a point of departure, the fundamentals of multimedia could be described as an attempt to adapt the representation of information to all the perceptual and cognitive capabilities of mind, to design systems that are fully user controlled and enable the user to explore the information in an active way and to consider the social context in which computers are used and the need for users to be able to cooperate in a computerized environment.

3.1 Representation of information

The multimedia approach devotes great efforts to the problem of finding good representations of the information. In order to utilize all the capabilities of the mind, the multimedia approach uses multidimensional representation, attempts to design aesthetical representations and is focused on finding natural and direct ways of representing the information. This approach assumes that integrated multidimensional representations are necessary for utilizing all the capabilities of the mind and for extending the usage of computers as tools for the mind to new user groups and new problem areas.

One conclusion that can be drawn from the new theories of perception is that complex, dynamic and integrated representations of information really are necessary for utilizing all the capabilities of mind. The use of integrated multidimensional representations in multimedia systems could be described as an attempt to apply this view when designing tools for the mind. It could be regarded as an attempt to put the users in direct contact with the environment in order to enable them to utilize their perceptual capabilities more effectively.

Multidimensional representations is often redundant, as when both colour and form are used to describe an object. As mentioned above, this redundancy is also very important for our ability to pick up and process information. Colour is often used as a redundant source of information, and there has been an intensive debate about the use of colour displays. One showed rather early that colour presentation was experienced as more stimulating than black and white presentation, but one has now also shown that colour presentation results in better performance, provided that the colouring is made in accordance with how the visual system works. Redundant use of colour has two effects. It facilitates the pick up and processing of information and it results in a more stimulating environment. This may also hold for other kinds of redundant representations, as e.g redundant use of sounds. If sounds were systematically used as a redundant source of information, then the pick up and processing of information should be facilitated and the environment should be experienced as still more stimulating. Studies with sounding interfaces, where each event is characterized both visually and auditory supports such a hypothesis (Gaver 1989). This is not surprising as, according to the modern view of man, our perceptual system is built for a sounding environment and therefore is capable of handling such information, if presented in an integrated and natural way. One might even assume that sounds constitute a necessary source of information for our perceptual systems to function effectively.

The use of multidimensional representations could also be described as an attempt to utilize the whole mind, i.e both our ability to logical reasoning and our ability to creative thinking. According to modern research in cognition, our minds function in two different ways, one logical and one creative, associated with left and right parts of the brain. The logical mode of processing information is characterized by the use of language and an analytical, rule based, sequential and time based processing. The creative mode, on the other hand is characterized by the use of pictures, by synthesizes and by an associative, spatial, parallel and timeless processing. Of importance in this context is that these two modes require different ways of representing the information. Both language oriented representations and visual representations are necessary for utilizing all the cognitive capabilities of mind.

Another characteristic of multimedia is the strong emphasis on aesthetical attractive representations. Much time is spent on picture composition, colouring, interesting effects, dramatical effects and other actions that increases user's motivation and makes the usage of computers more interesting. There are two different reasons for this emphasis on aesthetical aspects. One is related to the assumption that aesthetical layouts are aesthetical because they support the way we pick up and process information. The aesthetical rules are really rules for how one should emphasis relations, improve communication, bring out the message etc. The other is related to the recognition of the importance of interesting and motivating workplaces. Norman (1987) , discussing human computer interaction from a cognitive perspective, points to the importance of motivation when he declares that ".. I have two major goals (1) To understand...(2) To devise systems that are pleasant to use ...neither efficiency, nor ease, nor power, although these are all to be desired, but rather systems that are pleasant even fun .... that produce pleasurable engagement". This emphasis on aesthetical aspects could be explained as an effect of the close relation between multimedia and other media branches, but it could also be described as another manifestation of the dynamic view on man. Man's behaviour is not only determined by perceptual and cognitive capabilities, but also by motivational forces.

3.2 User control

User control and the assumption that users want to be active and exploring constitutes a central point in multimedia. The strong emphasis on user control has put multimedia in opposition to AI, as many argue that intelligent machines undermine the user's sense of control (Schneiderman 1989). Instead of designing intelligent, adaptive AI machines that try to figure out what the user wants, multimedia attempts to design tools that facilitate for the users to do what they want,without any limitations and assumptions imposed by the system. To put the user in control means that systems should be designed as toolboxes as opposed to intelligent machines, as a set of "independent" and powerful tools that the users control and use according to their ideas of how to accomplish the tasks (Boedker et al 1987).

One of the visions behind multimedia is that the user should be able to explore the information in an active way. Neither the author of the information nor the designer of the system should decide how the information should be processed, but the user should be in control. This means both that it should be possible to go from any element of information to any other element and it should be possible to create personalized links between different elements of information. The basic idea is that the users should be able to follow their associations in the same way as one follows the associations of ones mind in creative thinking. One attempts to design systems that imitate the way mind works. Although, one has not accomplished this goal, active exploration facilitates learning. Comprehension increases as the exploration focuses the users on the context, on relations between information elements rather than on isolated facts. In the same way, memory is improved by active processing. Research on learning and education strongly supports these assumptions (Ropa 1990).

This emphasis on user activity and user explorations are other examples of the close relation between the multimedia approach and the modern view of man. The users are no longer controlled by the system, but use the system as a tool to fulfil their goals. In order for a system to be a tool for the mind, it had to support the active pick up of information as described by Gibson, constructive cognitive processes as described by Neisser and explorative activities.

3.3 Cooperation

The social context is one of the most important tools for augmenting human capabilities. Thus, tools that support collaboration and cooperation are central in this new approach to system design. Human factor research has also taught us that the technologies used have a major impact on how the work is performed.

That is, if one does not support cooperation, as in most systems today, this will either change the way people work or the systems will not be used. However an understanding of the collaborative process is lacking.

Perhaps the most important aspect of collaboration is that it is a social process, controlled by social conventions as Kraut et al (198) concluded from their study and emphasized by Harrison et al (1990). Another important aspect of collaboration is that it is a communicative process (Johnson,1989). In any human communication process there are social rules that monitor the communication pattern in terms of social acts like persuasion, negotiation, arguing. In ordinary communication these rules are learned and signaled by a meta-communication language based on gestures, intonation etc. In electronic communication, the development of new rules and tools are necessary for enabling the participants to monitor the communication process and to adapt the rules to special communication needs (Danielson et al, 1986). Winograd's Speech Act model (1988) is one example of how conversational structures can be built into a message system. However careful thought should then be given about the effects of the imposed structure on social control. Collaboration could also be viewed as a process of knowledge integration. Integration of knowledge and experience is obtained by cooperative work execution such as coauthoring, by collaborative idea generation through discussions and brainstorming, by reviewing, annotating and critiquing each other's work etc. However, Kraut et al´s study (1986) points out that the preferred work strategy in collaborative work is to avoid working together, i.e to decrease what could be called *the collaboration load*. Collaborative aspects of work seldom concern work execution. If this is an effect of basic human capabilities or an effect of missing tools for cooperative work could be discussed. However, most groupware, as tools for co-authoring, co-editing, co-drawing (see e.g Beaudoun-Lafon 1990) are built on the assumption that people really want to accomplish tasks together.

Thus, although tools supporting collaboration are central for the multimedia approach, much has to be learned about the socio-psychological aspects of collaboration, before any useful tools can be designed. In this case, maybe the development in computer science will direct psychological research into new problem areas.

4. Interface problems in current implementations

4.1 The usage of different media

One of the main problems in current implementations concerns the usage of different media. Multidimensional representations could be used for representing multidimensional properties, for representing information on different levels of abstraction and for presenting the same information in different redundant ways. However, the different media are often used in a unsystematic way without considering how man's mind is best augmented. The question about when to use what media is not easily solved, but there are some research findings that may give a first answer to this problem (Figure 1).

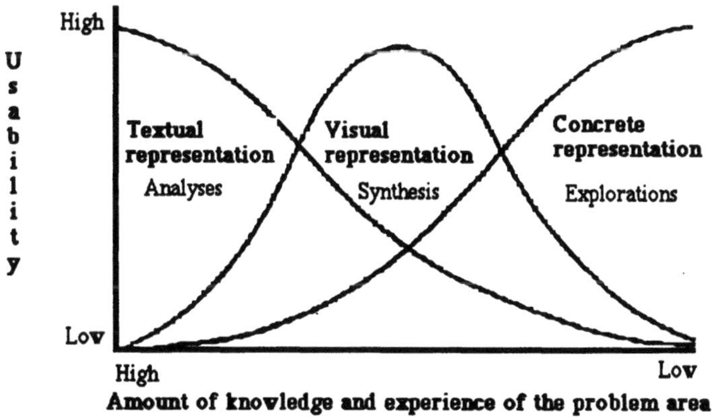

Fig 1: When to use different media

When the problem is new for the user, representations that enable explorations seems to be the best ones. On the other hand, when the user has a lot of experience and knowledge about the problem area, then a textual form of representation seems to be best. Between these two extremes a visual representation seems to be preferred. Many studies have demonstrated the importance of visualizations for problem solving. Such a representation seems to support creative thinking. It facilitates for the user to restructure and transform the problem so that it can be approached from new perspectives. For example many argue that visualization is one of the most important tools in design (Bally, 1987)

A second problem in current implementations of multidimensional representations concerns the need for parallel representations controlled by the user. As each user is unique with respect to their domain knowledge and as each users knowledge changes over time, there is a need for parallel representations and for possibilities for the users to choose the kind of representation that best matches their knowledge and experiences.

Another problem with current implementations concerns the design of multimedia displays and the integration and coordination of different media. Modern perceptual psychology emphasizes the importance of "natural" stimulation for utilizing all the capabilities of our perceptual system and that means that the different medias have to be designed, integrated and coordinated in a natural way. In order to fulfil this goal a lot of effort has to be devoted to the design of multimedia interfaces and this is not always realized. According to the traditional view there is a risk for perceptual overload in multimedia systems.

However, if the information is integrated in a natural way, there is no evidence for such a risk. The main problem is not a question of the amount of information, but of the way information is integrated.

4.2 Aesthetical design

Very few multimedia implementations of "real" applications exist today. Current implementations are mostly toy examples or design examples trying to demonstrate possible uses of multimedia. However, in real applications there will be a problem concerning the trade off between entertainment and work, between having fun and accomplishing the task.

Another problem that procurers of multimedia system will meet concerns the specification of aesthetical and motivational requirements. In principal, one could always improve a multimedia interface from an aesthetical and motivational perspective. There is no way to define any stop condition for such improvements. As aesthetical requirements is not possible to specify, the multimedia approach will require a new design methodology comparable with the ones used in TV, Movies etc.The development of such a methodology and it´s integration with more traditional ones will offer a serious problem, as soon as "real" multimedia applications are designed.

4.3 Direct manipulation and powerfulness

Another characteristic of multimedia is the use of what have been called direct manipulation, a form of man computer dialogue in which the user acts instead of typing commands (Schneiderman 1983). Direct manipulation could be regarded as the point of departure for the multimedia approach and it is still a central part of this new approach.

Direct manipulation is very popular today, but, current implementations have not solved the problem of combining simple direct manipulating interfaces with powerful functionality and the problem of designing interfaces that allows users to increase their craftsmanship (Boedker 1989).

4.4 Hypertext and problems of navigation and orientation

The currently used tool for active exploration is a data structure consisting of nodes, i.e information elements and links that allows the user to go from one node to another. Each node is equipped with links to other nodes and the user explores the information by following the links in a nonsequential way. The main interface problem with this implementation concerns navigation and orientation problems. When the users jump from one node to another, following their associations they will have difficulties in knowing where they are in the document, they will forget where they started, they will be unsure where to go and they will get lost in details loosing their general view. One attempts to solve these problem by implementing browsers in the form of maps or flow diagrams that are intended to give the user such information. However, when there are many nodes and links, these browsers will be very cluttered and of little help.

In order to elucidate some important aspects of this problem, one could compare the exploration of hypermedia documents with our ability to explore scenes. A hypermedia document could be regarded as a scenery of knowledge where the links make it possible to get both a general view of the scene and detailed knowledge about interesting parts of the scene. Using this metaphor as a point of departure it could be interesting to discuss how our perceptual system handles similar navigation and orientation problems. Traditional perceptual theories regarded the eye as a camera and explained the perceptions of scenes in terms of first registering and storing different independent pictures of the scene then adding these pictures to a perception of the scene as a whole. The new theories of perception have a totally different explanation of how we perceives scenes. Gibson (ref) e.g, argues that we perceive the scene directly without any involvement of interpretations or cognitive memory processes. He explains the perception of scenes in terms of our ability to pick up common structures in the flow of information from different parts of a scene. These common structures define the scene that we perceive, and constitute the base for our ability to navigate. Many current hypertext systems have been designed according to the traditional view, and this has in turn resulted in serious navigation and orientation problems. That is, the user is demanded to first store the information in more or less independent nodes and then add the stored information to a more general view in order to be able to navigate. Instead one could argue that it is the common components between the nodes that constitute the bases for navigation. One should therefore put a strong emphasis on designing the linked nodes so that there are dependencies and common structures. For example one should elucidate the relations between nodes and if no relations exist one should design the links so that the user really perceives it as different scenes. In short, current implementations have neglected the problem of authoring nonlinear documents. We have a long tradition and education in the authoring of linear documents, but very little is known about the authoring of nonlinear documents. Writing a nonlinear document is much more difficult than writing a linear one, and as long as little is known about this art, there will always be navigation and orientation problems.

Finally, although the user can explore the information in an active way, there are few possibilities for processing the information actively. There is really much to be desired in this area, e.g possibilities to add comments, to restructure the information, to define own links, to add new material etc. For example, the possibility for the user to create his own links played a central part in Vannevar Bush's vision, but is missing in most current implementations. The reasons are partly implementation problems, partly that one assumes that this will create a too strong cognitive overload for the users. Already the choice and exploration of links and nodes in current implementations results in a cognitive overload and if one demands that the user should create own links the systems may be too complex to handle. However, this problem may be solved by better interfaces and by better support for cognitive processing as memory cues, information about the contents of the nodes that the user intend to go to, different kinds of links etc.

4.5 Cooperative work and earlier failures

Computer supported cooperative work is a very popular area today and much effort is devoted to implement different kinds of collaborating systems as intelligent mail systems, conference systems etc. However, current implementations in this are driven by technology instead of knowledge about user needs and user capabilities. They are still based on a system-oriented view instead of augmenting the collaborative capabilities of man.

Maybe, the design principles put forward in Moran & Andersson (1990) WorkaDayWorld points to another possible approach. They argue that computer supported cooperative work should be designed from an understanding of how people work together. They distinguish three aspects of the WorkaDayWorld, the technology, social and work practice and concluded that the most important aspect of the WorkaDayWorld is how people slide to and fro between formal and informal interaction. A similar approach has been applied by Marmolin et al (1990). They discussed the danger of designing specific tools supporting specific collaborative tasks as brain storming, conferences etc. The danger with this approach is that the tools then assume a certain way of performing the tasks. One creates a system controlled environment instead of a user controlled and this is especially dangerous when one attempts to support collaborative tasks as they are very dependent on the social context. They concluded that another approach, is to be preferred. Instead of designing tools based on some analysis of the task to be fulfilled, one could attempt to design very generic collaborative tools, that the users can use and combine as they want in order to accomplish the collaborative task. Some combination of tools could be used for conferencing, some other for coworking, some for understanding the problem and some other for selection of alternatives etc. In some situations the tools could be used for formal in other for informal collaboration, in some for one-to-one collaboration in other for many-to-many collaboration, in some for explicit and in other for implicit collaboration. This design paradigm is very similar to the paradigm of the Workaday World proposed by Moran and Anderson as it is not task oriented, but focuses on the social process of collaboration and on giving the users tailorable tools that they can control and attend to according to their needs. As discussed by Moran and Anderson these tools should not only support the users, they should enhance and encourage people in their work and allow creative deployment and development of job skills.

Thus any technology supporting collaboration has to be based on research concerning the social behaviour of man, and had to be designed according to the new view on man discussed in this report.

References

Bally J.: *An experimental view of the design process.* In Rouse W. & Boff K (eds) System Design, Elsevier Science Publishing Co, New York, 1987

Beaudouin-Lafon B. *Cooperatiev Development of Software.* In S. Gibbs & A.A Verrijn-Stuart (Eds) Multi-User Interfaces and Applications. Elsevire Science Publisher, North Holland, 1990

Boedker S., Ehn P., Kyng M., Kammensgard S., Sundblad Y.: *An Utopian Experience.* In Bjerkers G., Ehn P., Kyng M. (eds) Computer and Democracy, Avebury, Aldershot, 1987.

Boedker S.: *A Human Activity Approach to User Interfaces.* Human Computer Interaction,4,3,1989.

Brandt S.: *The Media Lab, Inventing the Future at MIT,* Penguin Books Ltd, 27 Wrights Lane, London W8 5TZ, 1987.

Bush V.: *As we may think.* Atlantic Monthly 1945:176:101.108

Buxton B: *Smoke and Mirrors.* In Byte, pp 202-251, July 1990

Carroll J. & Thomas J.: *Methaphor and the Cognitive Representation* . Computing Systems IEEE transactions on Systems, Man and Cybernetics, Vol Smc–12, 2, march/April 1982.

Conklin J.: *Hypertext: An Introduction and Survey.* in IEEE Computer, pp 17-42 September 1987

Danielsen T., Pankoke-Babts U., Prinz W., Patel A., PAys P., Smallan K., Speth R.: *The AMIGO project.* In Proceedings of CSCW'86, p 229-246, Dec 1986

Engelbart D., English W.: *A research center for augmenting human intellect.* In Proceedings of 1968 FJCC. AFIPS press Montvale, N.J. pp 395-410, 1968

Engelbart D.: *A conceptual framework for the augmentation of man's intellect.* In I. Greif (eds). Computer Supported Cooperative Work. A book of readings. Morgan Kaufman Publisher Inc, San Mateo, California, 1988.

Engelbart D.: *Authorship provisions in Augment.* In Proceedings of the IEEE COMPCON. New York, pp 465-472, 1984

Gaver W.: *The SonicFinder. An Interface That Uses Auditory Icons.* Human Computer Interaction, 4,1,1989

Gibson J.: *The Ecological Approach to Visual Perception.* Houghton Mifflin , Boston, 1979

Gibson J.: *The perception of the visual world.* Houghton Mifflin, New York., 1950

Gibson J.: *The Senses Considered as Perceptual Systems.* Houghton Mifflin , Boston, 1966

Hacker W. Activity: *A fruitful concept in industrial psychology.* In M. Frese & J. Sabini (eds). Goal directed behaviour: the concept of action psychology. Hillsdale, New Yersey, Lawrence Erlbaum Associates, 1985.

Halasz F.: *Reflections on notecards: Seven issues for the next generation of hypermedia systems.*

Hooper K.: *Interactive multimedia design 1988.* San Fransisco CA: Apple Computer, 1989.

Johansson G.: *Projective transformations as determining visual space perception.* in R. MacLeod and H. Pick Jr (eds) *Perception: Essays in the honor of James J. Gibson.* Ithaca: Cornell University Press, 1974

Johansson G.: *Rigidity, stability and motion in the perceptual space.* Acta Psychol.,14, 359-370, 1958

Johnson B.: *How is work coordinated? Implications for computer-based support.* In Olson M (ed) Technological support for work group collaboration, Lawrence Erlbaum Ass, New Yersey, 1989.

Kraut R., Galegher J., Egido C.: *Relationships and tasks in scientific research collaborations.* In Proceedings of CSCW'86, p 229-246, Dec 1986

Marmolin H., Sundbladh Y., Pehrson B.: *A Model of Design and Collaboration in a Distributed Environment,* to be published in ECSCW-91, Amsterdam, 1991

Moran T. & Anderson R.: *The Workaday World As a Paradigm for CSCW Design.* In Proceedings of CSCW'90, p 381-393, October 1990

Neisser U.: *Cognition and Reality.* Freeman and Company, 1976

Nelson T.: *Replacing the printed word: A complete literary system.* Proceedings of the IFIP Congress 1980, S.H. Lavington (ed), North-Holland, pp 1013-1023, 1980

Norman D. & Draper S.: *User Centred System Design* , Kap 2. LEA Publisher, London, 1987
Norman D.: *A psychologist Views Human Information Processing; Human Errors and other phenomena suggesting processing mechanisms.* Proceedings of the International Joint Conference on Artificial Intelligence, Vancouver, 1981
Norman D.: *Some observations on mental models.* In Gentner, Dedre & Stevens Albert L (eds). Mental models, Hillsdale, N.J Lawrence Erlbaum Associates, 7- 14, 1983.
Rasmussen J. *Information processing and human-machine interface. An approach to cognitive engineering.* New York Elsivier Science Publisher, North-Holland, 1986
Ropa A.: *Computers as Communicators. Designing a Multimedia, Interactive Interface to facilitate Cultural Understanding in a Fifth Grade Classroom,* EURIT Conference, Denmark, 1990.
Schneiderman B., Kearsley G: *Hypertext Hand.On. Reading,* MA: Addison-Wesley, 1989.
Schneiderman B.: *Direct Manipulation: A step beyond programmin language.* IEEE Computer, 16, 57-69,1983.
Weimar D. & Ganapathy S.: *A synthetical sicual environment with hand gesturing and voice input.* In Proceedings of CHI'89, pp 235-240, May 1989.
Winograd T.: *A language perspective on the design of cooperative work.* In Greif I (ed) Computer-supported cooperative work. Morgan Kaufman Publisher, San Mateo, 1988.

Chapter 5

The Design Space of Interfaces

David M. Frohlich

Abstract

A framework for describing the design space of human computer interfaces is presented which relates interface modes, channels, media and styles for both input and output interfaces. Language and action modes are said to be supported through use of the audio, visual and haptic channels. Interface media are derived from the combination of modality and channel. Use of these channels within the language mode gives rise to interaction within the speech, text and gesture media, while use of the same channels within the action mode gives rise to interaction within the sound, graphics and motion media. A range of interface styles are allocated to one or other of the two basic interface modes, and the possibility of implementing the same style in more than one medium is noted. Application of the framework is illustrated in relation to so called 'direct manipulation' interfaces such as those to and from the Apple Macintosh operating system, and reveals extensive use of linguistic utterances as well as manipulative actions. The implications of the framework for interface design are discussed.

1. Introduction

Rapid developments in interactive system design have led to a situation in which it is now difficult to describe interface variety. Although a technical terminology has grown up within the user interface field (Chignell 1990), it is not always used clearly and consistently by practitioners in the field. In fact the most commonly used terms in this area, such as 'multimedia', 'direct manipulation' and 'mixed mode', often seem to be the least well defined as descriptors of interface characteristics.

What is needed is a common framework for describing the design space of interfaces which uses these terms in a coherent and technical sense. Without such a framework, it will remain difficult to interpret the progress already made in exploring this design space, and to anticipate or constrain future innovations in design.

Some advances have already been made in providing a framework for describing interfaces through a series of papers by Buxton (1983, 1990), Foley et al. (1984), Card et al. (1990) and Mackinlay et al. (1990). These articles present a number of ways of describing the design space of *input devices* in terms of the transduction of human force or motion energy to logical values within a machine (Card et al. 1990). The work of Buxton, and also of Card and his colleagues, focuses on the combination of transducer functions represented in actual physical devices, while that of Foley and his colleagues deals with the use to which individual functions can be put in the performance of basic interaction tasks.

The current paper can be seen as a development of this work to systematize the description of interfaces, but at the level of the *whole interface* rather than that of the input interface alone. It presents a taxonomy of interface modalities, channels, media and styles in a single framework intended to represent important dimensions of the interface design space. These dimensions are not clearly defined at present, although they continue to be used extensively in discussions of systems which attempt to combine different interface technologies to enhance human computer interaction (cf. Blattner & Dannenberg 1990, Taylor 1988, Taylor et al. 1989).

The framework itself is presented in the next section, together with definitions of each dimension. A method of applying the framework in order to describe complex input and output interfaces is then described, using the standard Apple Macintosh operating system as an example. This is followed by discussion of implications of the framework for the design of multifeature interfaces.

2. The framework

2.1 Two interface design spaces

A useful starting point in the characterisation of human computer interfaces is provided by an information processing model of human computer interaction (e.g. Card et al. 1983). This suggests that interaction occurs with a two way exchange of information between a person and a computer across two different interfaces. Information travelling from the human to the computer must travel across an input interface, in which some energy generated by the user is transformed into some internal representation inside the computer. Information travelling from the computer to the human must travel across an output interface, in which some energy generated by the machine is transformed into some internal representation inside the user.

Given this viewpoint we can see that the transformation of information within these exchanges takes place through human and computer processes to generate and interpret energy distributions and through human and computer input and output devices which transform one kind of energy into another kind.

Consider the specific information transformations which can take place across the input interface. The user can generate force and motion energy by performing limb movements, or acoustic energy by vocalising sounds. These can be transformed by various devices into analogue or digital electronic signals representing audio, visual or haptic[1] information. For example, a microphone transforms sound energy into an analogue audio signal, a touch panel transforms motion energy into an (x,y) position signal, while a button transforms transforms motion energy into a digital position signal. Further computational processes inside the computer serve to interpret the audio, visual and haptic information in terms of interactive events of significance to the activity being supported by the computer.

The situation is reversed for information transformations across the output interface. The computer can generate audio, visual or haptic events through the output of analogue or digital electronic signals to output devices. These devices take the signals as their input and produce the events as their output. For example, a loudspeaker transforms an analogue audio signal into perceptible sounds, while a cathode ray tube or a printer transforms x,y position signals into perceptible light or dark. Devices which transform haptic signals into perceptible textures or positions are less common, but nevertheless possible, as can be seen in the generation of braille output for the blind. This time the processes which serve to interpret the transformed information lie inside the user. More specifically, they operate to encode this information in terms of the development of some conceptual activity being carried out, through the senses of hearing, sight and touch[2].

---

[1] The term haptic is used rather loosely to refer to both tactile information specifying surface contact and kinesthetic information specifying effector position.

[2] It is possible in principle for a computer to generate gustatory and olfactory events perceptible as tastes and smells by a human user, although I know of no interfaces which employ them. For simplicity, these features have been omitted from the framework.

It is this 'conceptual activity' which motivates the design of all interactive computer systems and holds the key to an understanding of the interface design space. To take this analysis of input and output interfaces further we must introduce some notion of the kind of activities which these interfaces support.

All interactive computer systems can be said to support only two basic human activities: language and action (cf. Claassen et al. 1990, Hutchins 1989, Hutchins et al. 1986). These correspond to the social and physical dimensions of interfaces which encourage users to view interaction with the machine, metaphorically, as a conversation with some virtual partner, as a series of manipulations of some virtual world or as a combination of both (Frohlich 1991). Some applications of computers lend themselves more to one metaphor than the other, but the versatility of computers is such that the same application can often be supported through either activity. For example, word processing can be supported through line editors which respond to special linguistic commands, or through screen editors which respond to special physical manipulation.

Laurel (1986) describes how the use of language and action at the interface can fundamentally alter the relationship between the user and the machine. Linguistic interaction appears to lead to a *second-person* experience in which users feel themselves to be instructing some hidden intermediary to perform actions on their behalf: as with various line editing commands. Manipulative interaction appears to lead to a *first-person* experience in which users feel themselves to be engaged in performing actions directly: as with certain screen editing operations. In fact screen editors are typical of many so called direct manipulation interfaces in combining manipulative and linguistic forms of interaction (see Section 3). This leads to a kind of 'collaborative manipulation' (Hutchins 1989) in which users feel themselves to be communicating with some hidden intermediary over the manipulation of computational objects: as in selecting and moving a block of text using 'drag-select' and 'pointing' actions with 'Cut' and 'Paste' commands.

Applying the language/action distinction to the exchange of information at the interface, we find that this information can have quite a different meaning for the user and the computer in the two cases. When audio, visual and haptic information is designed to support apparent linguistic activity, speech, text and gestures are produced at the interface, and will be parsed as meaningful utterances in some domain of discourse. In contrast, when audio, visual and haptic information is designed to support apparent physical activity, sound, graphics and motions result, and will be interpreted as meaningful operations on some world of interest. Furthermore, quite different methods of interaction are involved in each kind of activity. For example, programming languages, command languages, natural language, field filling and menu selection are associated with interaction through language, while windows, icons and formalisms such a spreadsheets are associated with interaction through action.

The above analysis gives rise to the two interface design spaces shown in Figures 1 and 2. Figure 1 shows the input interface design space as a left to right mapping of voice and movement energy in the human (effector) interface channel to audio, visual and haptic information in the computer interface channel. This information is interpreted as comprising events in the speech, text or gesture media within a language mode of interaction, or as events in the sound, graphics and motion media within an action mode of interaction. Different sets of interface styles are shown to be utilised in each mode. Figure 2 shows the output interface design space as a right to left mapping of audio, visual and haptic energy in the computer interface channel to hearing, sight and touch information in the human (sensory) interface channel. Again, communication is shown to take place in different media and through different styles of interaction depending on whether the mode of interaction being supported is language or action.

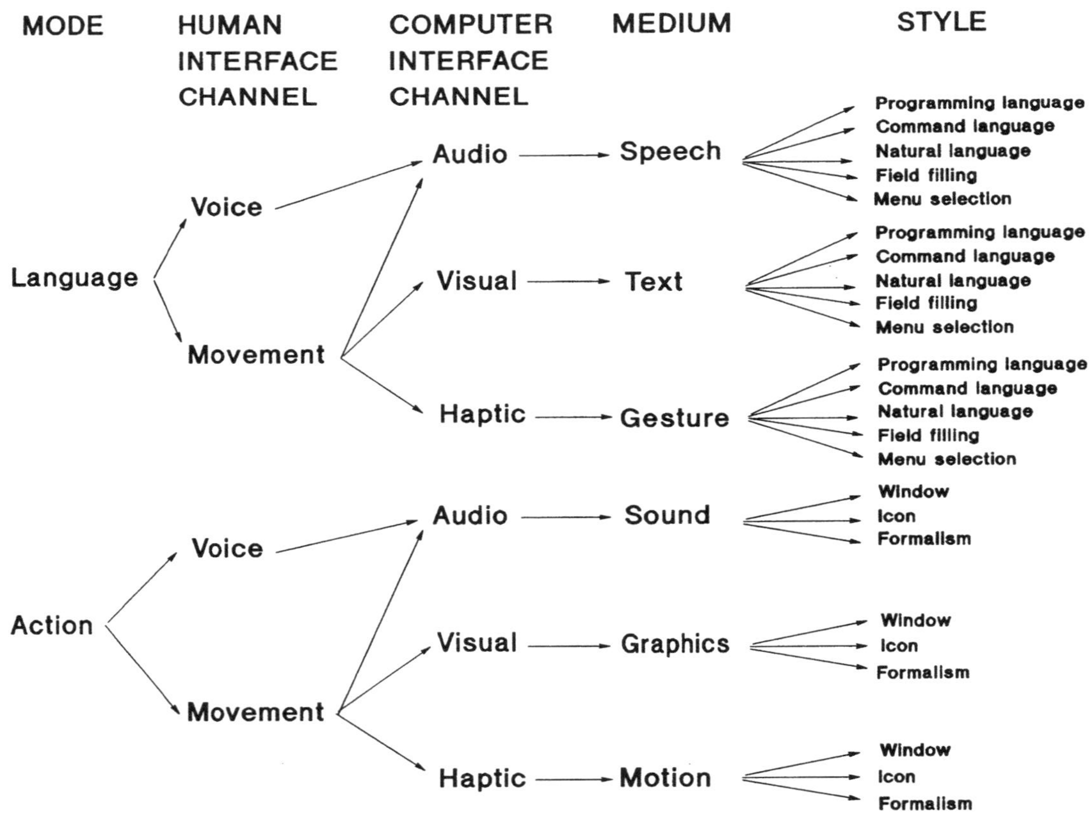

Fig. 1. The input interface design space.

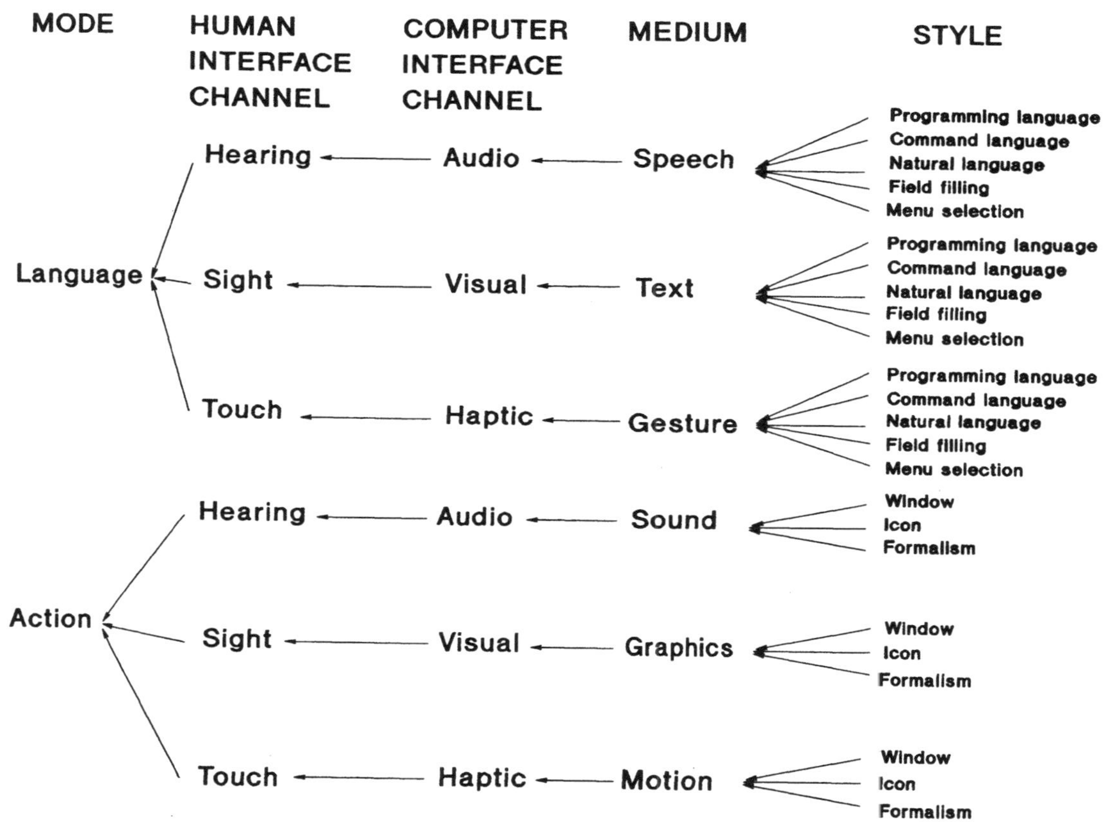

Fig. 2. The output interface design space.

2.2 Definitions of Mode

For the purposes of the framework, interface modes are defined as *states across which different user actions can have the same effects*. Language and action appear to be two fundamental modes in this sense, since they comprise dimensions of difference in human action with important consequences for the methods by which a given effect can be achieved. For example, the effect of deleting a file within an operating system might be achieved by the linguistic activity of typing 'Delete <filename>' or by the physical action of dragging an icon of the file over to a wastebasket icon and 'releasing' it.

This definition allows a contrast with system modes, which usually refer to *states across which the same user actions can have different effects* (cf. Johnson 1990). The ambiguity of this term in the human computer interface literature can be understood through these definitions since they show that mode refers to different sides of the classic problem of motor equivalence (Bernstein 1967, Connolly 1975, Hebb 1949). The problem is that movements of the body have an equivocal relationship to action in the world, such that to perform the same action under varying conditions requires different movements and to perform the same movements under different conditions can result in different actions. A similar relationship exists between user actions and their effects on a computer. Interface modes (or 'modality') describe the *redundancy* of user actions across interface conditions; such that different actions can achieve the same effects. System modes (or 'modedness') describe the *ambiguity* of user actions across system conditions; such that the same action can achieve different effects.

2.3 Definitions of Channel

For the purposes of the framework, a channel is defined as *an interface across which there is a transformation of energy*. A human and a computer interface channel are shown in the framework to acknowledge the various roles of the effector and sensor systems of humans and computers in generating and transforming energy. Over the human interface channel there is a transformation of electrochemical energy within nerve cells into noise and movement energy, and of audio, visual and haptic energy into electrochemical energy. Over the computer interface channel there is a transformation of noise and movement energy into electrical energy, and of electrical energy into audio, visual and haptic energy.

For every channel there is a corresponding device which performs the energy transformation. For example, human interface devices include vocal cords, limbs, ears, eyes and skin, while computer interface devices include microphones, keyboards, joysticks, sliders, mice, loudspeakers, printers, plotters, cathode ray tubes, robot arms and so on.

2.4 Definitions of media

For the purposes of the framework, a medium is defined as *a representational system for the exchange of information*. The framework shows how the particular media employed in human computer interfaces result from the interaction between modes and channels. This is because the language and action interface modes modify the *use* to which the audio, visual and haptic channels are put in human computer interaction.

In interfaces based on the language mode of interaction, audio, visual and haptic energy is interpreted symbolically as part of input or output *utterances* in the language media of speech, text or gesture. Speech is defined here as any communicative vocalization, and includes paralinguistic noises such as filled pauses, grunts and sighs. Text is defined as the visible trace of a communicative movement, whereas gesture refers to any communicative movement which leaves no visible trace.

In interfaces based on the action mode of interaction, audio, visual and haptic information is interpreted more literally as part of input or output *events* in the action media of sound, graphics and motion. Sound is defined as any noise other than speech, graphics as any visible trace other than text, and motion as any literal movement other than gesture.

Thus the function to which some information exchange is put defines the medium (or representational scheme) in which it takes place. This can be seen most clearly in differences between language and action media in the real world. For example, the difference between a human gesture and a human motion lies not in the movements involved but in the functions intended to be performed by the movements; in this case whether it is intended to signify some communicative meaning to an observer or to serve some intrinsic value in interacting with the environment. This is nicely summarised in the following quote by Reed (1982, pp112-3):

> "The fact that the same movements (e.g., a slight nodding of the head) may be a component of balancing in one case or a social gesture in another is of basic importance to our understanding of action. Natural selection operates because the structures and behaviours of organisms have functional significance in the life of a creature. Evolution will therefore result in various action systems in a given organism which are differentiated by their *function*, not by the muscles or movement patterns they involve. Moreover, these functions are not concepts we impose on the phenomena of animal behaviour, but are embodied by any and all animal actions."

In computer systems all this might be more accurately put the other way round. Because the significance of a user action is defined by the computer software, and not by properties of the natural world, functions *are* concepts we impose on the phenomena of human computer-behaviour, largely by the choice of a representational scheme for information exchange. Thus systems which are designed to process speech, text and gestures naturally lead the user to perform linguistic functions through the interface, whereas systems designed to process sounds, graphics and motions naturally lead the user to perform manipulative functions. In a very real sense then, choice of a medium for interaction defines that interaction's modality.

2.5 Definitions of style

For the purposes of the framework, interface style is defined as *a recognised class of methods for supporting interface activity*. There are two sets of interface styles associated with each basic type of interface activity. Language styles support the generation of input or output utterances and include programming languages, command languages, natural language, fields and menus. Action styles support the generation of input or output events and include windows, icons and formalisms.

Conventional definitions of individual interface styles are offered by Baecker & Buxton (1987, pp 427-437). These have been adapted for the framework, by renaming some of them (in brackets) and describing each style in a medium independent way as follows:

Command line *(Command language)* dialogues, in which the user instructs the computer in a formally defined command language.

Programming language dialogues, in which the command language allows its own extension through the definition of procedures.

Natural language interfaces, in which the user's command language is a significant, well-defined subset of some natural language such as English.

Menu *(Menu selection)* systems, in which the user issues commands by selecting in sequence, choices from among a menu of options.

Form filling *(Field filling)* dialogues, in which the user issues commands by responding to prompts given by the computer.

Iconic *(Icon)* interfaces, in which user input and system output is represented metaphorically in terms of some real world activity or event.

Window *(Window)* systems or environments, in which the user and system activity is partitioned by function.

Graphical interaction *(Formalism)* in which user input and system output is represented non-metaphorically in terms of some activity or event whose meaning is particular to the application software.

Baecker & Buxton also define 'Direct manipulation' as an additional interface style, but this can be seen as a composite of other styles as will be shown in Section 3.

Applying each style to each medium within a given modality has been done to suggest that styles are modality rather than medium specific. For example, a natural language interface style can be supported through the speech medium by human or computer 'vocalization' of natural words, through the textual medium by human or computer 'writing' of words, or through the gestural medium by human or computer 'signing' of words.

It is possible, in principle, to step through potential implementations of each style in this way, but we would soon find that many have never been attempted within a particular medium or in a particular input or output direction along its channel. Instances of this kind include the use of field filling for computer output, the use of sound windows to segment the functions of noise input or output within distinct frequency bands, and the use of iconic motions to represent tactile (textural) or dynamic (force, friction, weight, etc) properties of objects in the world.

These examples also show that while styles may be modality specific they are not completely medium independent. Each style was invented within a certain medium and is therefore likely to be best suited to implementation in that medium. This is because, different implementations of a single style across media must use different representational schemes from the elements which make up the style. In the natural language example above, a natural gestural language would not be composed of gestures corresponding to the same 'words' represented by phonemic signatures in the speech medium or by orthographic strings in the textual medium. Gestures natural to any given language will comprise postural and movement phrases taken to signify certain meanings or emotions within that language culture; such as the clenching of fists, pointing of fingers, lifting of eyebrows and so on. These may have no parallel in the other language media, and hence would be difficult to implement faithfully in speech or text.

3. Application of the framework

3.1 Describing the Apple Macintosh

The framework can be used to describe the design of any existing interface by annotating the input and output design space diagrams shown in Figures 1 and 2. Essentially, all combinations of modes, channels, media and styles employed by that interface for the input and output of information should be indicated on the diagrams.

This section illustrates this process by applying the framework to the basic Apple Macintosh operating system. This system has been chosen as an example of a so called 'direct manipulation' interface, and serves to show the value of the framework in highlighting ambiguities in the definition of direct manipulation in the current interface design literature.

Consider first the input interface to the Apple Macintosh. Users are able to manipulate windows and icons representing files and file containers using a mouse input device. Although these windows and icons are displayed visually to users on a computer screen, users influence them primarily through movement of the mouse to specify haptic information in the motion medium. In addition, users are able to perform operations on files and containers by selecting options from menus displayed at the top of the screen, and by typing text into input fields displayed in 'dialogue boxes'. They do this by using the mouse and an alphanumeric keyboard to produce visual information in the textual medium. Finally, a number of special purpose keys and key combinations are available to users as quick methods of performing operations on graphical objects. Since these leave no visible trace on the computer screen they are best described as elements in a gestural command language which is input through the haptic channel. This leads to the characterisation shown in Figure 3.

Note that certain features of the interface, such as the modes employed, 'drop out' of the analysis of other features. Analysis of each dimension can proceed in any order and stop when enough features have been described to connect any single feature with those across all other dimensions. All features should connect to other features in (horizontally) adjacent dimensions.

The output interface of the Apple Macintosh is somewhat different. As mentioned above, the computer displays visual representations of windows and icons together with a trace of any actual or potential textual input from the user (at least for transient periods). In this respect it makes use of both the graphical and the textual media to provide a context in which *possible* user inputs can take place and to give feedback on *actual* user inputs. In addition, it often displays dialogue boxes containing messages in natural language about the state of the machine and the expected behaviour of the user, again through the textual medium. Some of these dialogue boxes occur under 'error' conditions, and are accompanied by a beep from a loudspeaker indicating the occurance of error and an iconic symbol indicating the category of error. A beep constitutes a formalism in the sound medium which signifies 'error' in the semantics of the Macintosh software, and also happens to comply with a longstanding convention in the semantics of other software systems. A graphical icon such as a bomb has the same status as other icons in the system in suggesting some similarity with a real world object. The fact that it is displayed at just this occasion in the system's operation serves to make salient (for that occasion) a class of behaviours normally associated with the object. This leads to the characterisation of the output interface shown in Figure 4.

The combined descriptions of the Apple Macintosh interface are interesting in that they reveal subtleties in design which might escape a more casual analysis. They also allow technical discussion of interface features. For example, if we say that any interface with more than one feature on the same dimension can be described as 'multi-' feature, then the Macintosh input interface can be said to be a multimodal, multimedia and multistyle interface. This also happens to be true of the Macintosh output interface, but it need not have been so. This means that it is not sufficient to refer to an interface *per se* as multi-anything, since the characterisation differs for input and output. Furthermore, the framework leads to a more precise specification of the *respect* in which an input or output interface can be said to be multi-something, by enumerating the combination of features possessed in cases where there are more than two possibilities.

Clearer technical discussion of interface characteristics has numerous benefits, not least in the formulation of rationale or theory to account for design decisions. This is especially true in the case of theoretical ideas advanced to account for the popularity of the Macintosh interface and others like it.

3.2 Description and explanation: Some insights on direct manipulation

The Macintosh is said to be an example of a direct manipulation interface as defined by Shneiderman (1982). It is a direct descendant of the Xerox Star office system (Johnson et al. 1989) which was cited by Shneiderman as one of several systems in the early 1980's to have broken away from a linguistic mode of interaction. Like video games, spreadsheets and graphics packages, the Star (and its relations) were said to support the direct manipulation of computational 'objects' through:

1. Continuous representation of the object of interest,
2. Physical actions or labelled button presses instead of complex syntax, and
3. Rapid incremental reversible operations whose impact on the object of interest is immediately visible.

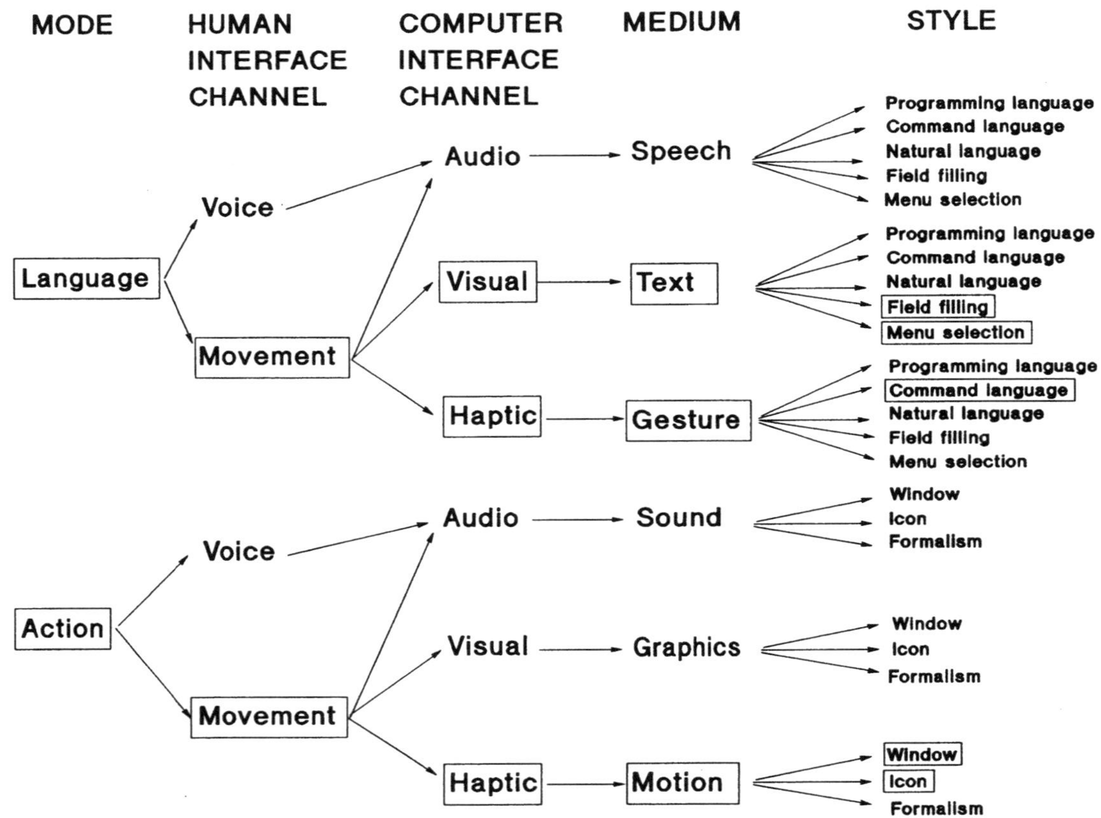

Fig. 3. The Apple Macintosh input interface.

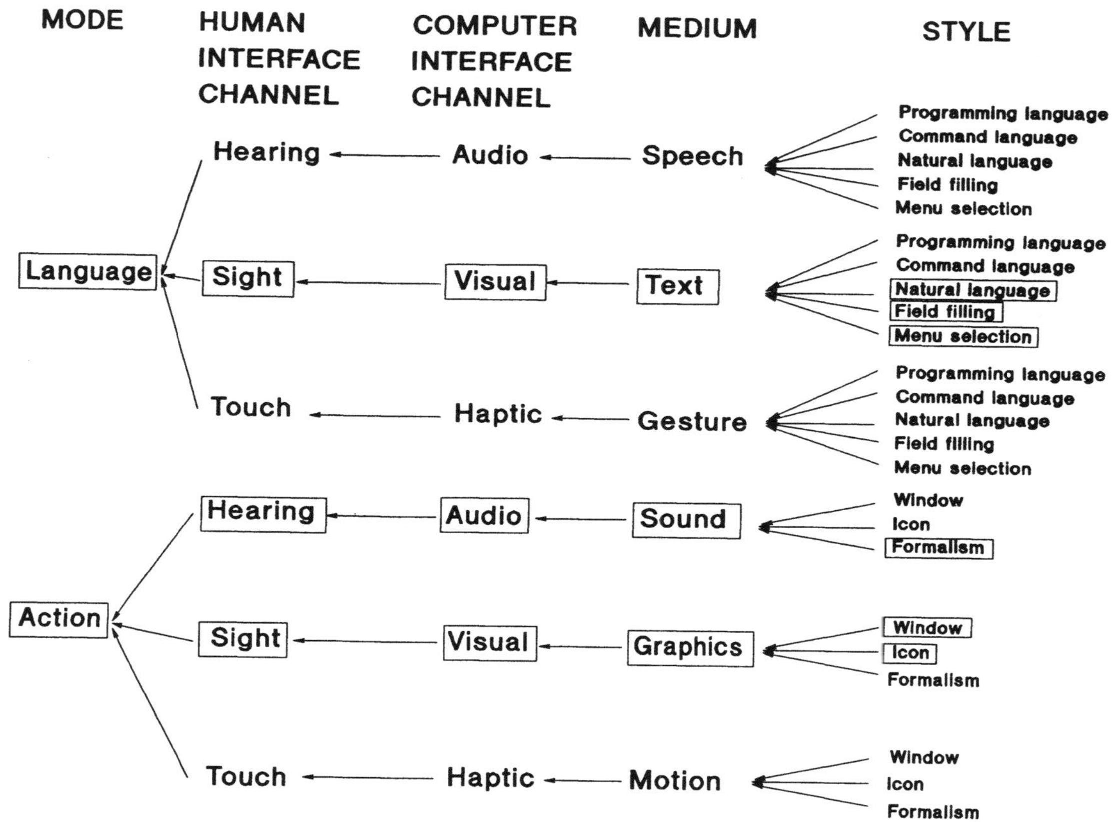

Fig. 4. The Apple Macintosh output interface.

In an analysis of Shneiderman's claims, Hutchins et al. (1986) proposed a theory of direct manipulation in which directness is equated with the psychological 'engagement' of feeling oneself to be controlling the computer directly through manipulation rather than indirectly through instructing some 'hidden intermediary' in language to act on one's behalf (see Section 2.1). The implications of the theory are that the usability of interfaces like the Apple Macintosh derives from the fact that they are action rather than language based, and also that language based interfaces are intrinsically less usable than action based ones.

However, this can't be true as Figures 3 and 4 show. The Macintosh input and output interfaces make extensive use of the language modality, especially through menu selection and field filling in the textual medium. Yet their general attractiveness and popularity cannot be denied. We must ask again what accounts for the improvement in usability over previous interfaces.

Although it may be true that the Macintosh makes *more* use of the action modality than did previous systems, this will not suffice as the only explanation, given the apparently effective use of the language modality tó compliment it. A more likely explanation is that more than the modality of the interface has changed. Compared with interfaces to other operating systems like MS-DOS and Unix, the Macintosh employs quite different combinations of channels, media and styles. For example, command language input from a keyboard has been completely replaced by gestural commands in the form of button pushes and screen menu selections using a mouse. These changes alone could considerably improve usability by speeding up the process of entering an utterance into the computer and by lessening the need to remember the lexicon, syntax and semantics of legitimate utterances.

All this implies that the language modality is not intrinsically less usable than the action modality, but that its usability for particular tasks is affected by the way in which it happens to be implemented in different channels, media and styles. Indeed, there is growing evidence that more rather than less use of the language mode is required to improve the usability of future office systems (Frohlich 1991, Laurel 1990, Stearns 1989, Stenton 1990, Walker 1989, Whittaker 1990).

The simple lesson to be drawn from this critique is that greater precision in the description of interface characteristics can lend greater clarity to theoretical debates about, their usability. The framework for describing interfaces shown in Figures 1 and 2 appears to be of some value in this respect, since its application to describe the Macintosh interfaces has called into question one theory commonly advanced to account for its appeal.

4. Implications for design

We have seen how the interface design spaces explained in Section 2 can be used to clarify interface terminology, to identify the design characteristics of any particular interface, and to improve technical and theoretical discussions of interface properties.

In this section I examine the implications of the framework for interface design. In particular, I consider what the two design spaces tell us about the process of and opportunities for design.

With regard to the process of design, the design spaces point to a variety of levels at which design takes place. At the lowest level, designers must select input or output device technology to support the kinds of energy and information transformations upon which all subsequent human computer interaction will be based. In fact such devices lie between the human and computer interface channels in Figures 1 and 2, and might be selected with reference to the combination of channels thought to be appropriate to any particular system or user population. At the highest level, designers must decide upon the kind of conceptual activity that the interface should support, and in particular upon the social and physical manifestation of this activity. The central design question at this level is whether the activity to be supported is best represented as social interaction carried out primarily through language, as physical interaction carried out primarily through manipulation, or as some combination of the two. In between these two levels, designers must choose a combination of media for the representation of linguistic or manipulational activity and a combination of interface styles through which that activity can be performed.

This multi-levelled nature of interface design seems to reflect three basic levels at which any complex information processing system can be described (see Figure 1-4 in Marr 1982). At the highest level, is the computational theory describing the goal of the computation and the problem it addresses. This corresponds to the choice of mode and mode combination. At the next level is the representation and algorithm by which the theory is implemented. This corresponds respectively to the choice of media and styles. At the lowest level is the hardware implementation through which the representation and algorithm is physically realised. This corresponds to the choice of input and output devices and channels.

Thus at each level of description of any *artificial* information processing system, we see that there are corresponding design decisions which serve to specify that description. Note also that in *interactive* systems, the system's design does not fully specify its description, since part of the information processing is performed by a human user. This is why interface styles can be equated with information processing algorithms and input/output devices can be equated with the physical implementation of algorithms; both enable a certain kind of interactive activity to take place which is itself a solution to some information processing problem. All this suggests that interface design can be seen as part of a larger enterprise to construct a human-computer information processing system, by facilitating certain kinds of interactive activity through which desirable information processing operations are performed.

The question of whether the design enterprise is better served by a top down, bottom up or combined approach to the making of design decisions is not answered by this analysis. However, it does highlight the consequences of making design decisions at one level on choices at other levels (see again Figures 1 and 2). For example, top level choices about modality define the set of media and styles that might be used, while bottom level choices about devices and channels do not. Selection of an interface style implies use of a particular mode, and a set of representational systems or media, but does not specify which medium must be used. Similarly selection of a medium implies a particular mode and a set of possible styles, without specifying a particular style. And so on. In practice, design appears to proceed wholistically as interface designers move freely and repeatedly between multiple levels of abstraction (Guindon 1990). The current framework suggests that, in doing this, designers should attend to at least three different levels of design and to the special relationships which hold between them.

Some of the interdependencies between levels can be seen in various developments and trends in interface design. For example, full exploitation of innovations made at one level in the interface design space may depend on innovations being made at other levels. Thus it is now possible to support interaction over the audio computer interface channel, and future generations of personal computers will probably come with microphone input and loudspeaker output devices built into them. However, full exploitation of the audio channel involving natural speech input to computers awaits further developments in two other technologies positioned at different levels of the interface design space; namely speech recognition and natural language processing. Until these technologies become more reliable, the best use of the audio channel probably lies in the areas of 'non-speech audio' (sound) input and output (Buxton 1989), speech synthesis (Waterworth 1985), non-natural language styles of speech input such as vocal menu selection (Firman 1988), and spoken computer mediated communication in which natural speech input is processed by another user (e.g. Chalfonte, Fish & Kraut 1991).

There is also evidence of interface design at high levels being driven by that at lower levels, as if by default. A good example of this is the work to combine different interface styles and its implications for generating interesting combinations of mode. In fact work on mixed style interaction is sometimes referred to as 'multimodal' research (e.g. Bullinger & Faehnrich 1984). This includes for example, the manipulation of graphical tree formalisms to change the context of a natural language utterance (Cohen et al 1989) and the maintenance of graphical map formalisms by icon manipulation or natural language utterance (Lee & Zeevat 1990). It is difficult to say exactly what these style combinations mean to users in terms of the apparent combination of language and action at the interface, except that linguistic activity can evidently take place with reference to some shared 'physical' reality perceived by both user and computer 'participants'.

This shared reality turns out to be the basis of other more high level attempts to mix interface modes, and leads to a variety of forms of social and physical interaction, *implemented* through the combination of interface channels, media and styles. These include distinct collaborations with some virtual partner to manipulate a virtual world (as with a desktop agent - Stearns 1989), conversations done in the context of some physical framework (as in electronic form-filling - Frohlich 1987, Luff & Frohlich 1991), manipulations of disembodied fragments of conversation (as in reading a hypertext book - e.g. Conklin 1987), and being shown round some virtual space (as in being guided through a hypermedia document - e.g. Oren et al 1990).

The above examples illustrate the subtlety with which high level interface features can be combined. Such subtlety results from the multi-levelled nature of interface design, which means that the same high level feature can be implemented in numerous ways. This leads first of all to multiple forms of the same feature, and consequently to a combinatorial explosion in the possibilities for multi-feature combinations.

Some important kinds of combination can be derived from Figures 1 and 2. Sticking with the example of multimodal interfaces, we see that *cross-mode* combinations are possible in which language and action modes are used to support information transformations in different directions across the input/output interfaces. This leads to Language-in/Action-out or Action-in/Language-out configurations. Furthermore, *separate* (multimode) or *integrated* (mixed mode) combinations are possible in which language and action modes are either presented as alternative input or output methods or as integral components of a single method. Also, it is likely that the *dominance* of any particular mode in a multimodal interface may vary, such that it would be possible to speak of a primary and secondary mode. This aspect of interface design might manifest itself as a default mode presentation in a multimode interface or as the more psychologically salient activity in a mixed mode interface. The same kind of combinational possibilities are also present at other levels of design. For example, cross-media, multimedia, mixed media and media dominance are all terms which could be applied to interfaces which make use of more than one representational medium.

In summary, the proposed design spaces show interface design to be a complex and multi-levelled exercise, in which two fundamental kinds of interactive activity are supported through various representational, software and hardware technologies. The particular relationships which hold between designs at similar and different levels are detailed in the framework, and suggest that design decisions cannot easily be made in isolation from each other. The art of interface design appears to lie in a working knowledge of these relationships and its creative application in the structuring of human activity.

5 Conclusions

Previous attempts to systematise the description of interface characteristics have concentrated on describing properties of the input interface, largely without reference to their function in human computer interaction. This paper has described a framework for describing properties of both input and output interfaces, specifically with reference to the social and physical functions they support. The framework essentially maps the design space of each interface type as a set of possible combinations of modes, channels, media and styles. Definitions have been offered for each interface dimension, and application of the framework has been illustrated by describing the design space of input and output interfaces to the Apple Macintosh operating system. It remains to be seen, what use the framework might be put to, but potential benefits have been indicated in outlining relationships between multiple levels of design, suggesting interface design possibilities, and facilitating clearer technical and theoretical discussions of interface properties.

Acknowledgements

Thanks to Edwin Bos, Phil Stenton, Steve Whittaker, Sean Hayes, Nigel Derrett, Nick Haddock and Steve Loughran for comments and discussion on earlier drafts of the paper, and to participants at the workshop for much helpful feedback.

This work was funded by Hewlett-Packard Research Laboratories Bristol, and a Cognitive Science/HCI Initiative Special Training Fellowship (G106/511) carried out within the Departments of Sociology and Psychology, University of York. The help and support of these respective organisations is gratefully acknowledged.

References

Baecker R.M. & Buxton W.A.S. Eds. (1987) *Readings in human computer interaction.* Los Altos, California: Morgan Kaufmann Inc.

Bernstein N. (1967) *The coordination and regulation of movements.* Oxford: Pergamon Press.

Blattner M.M. & Dannenberg R.B. (1990) CHI '90 Workshop on multimedia and multimodal interface design. *SIGCHI Bulletin 22*:54-58.

Bullinger H.J & Faehnrich K.P. (1984) Symbiotic man-computer interfaces and the user assistant concept. In G. Salvendy (Ed.) *Human computer interaction.* Amsterdam: Elsevier Science.

Buxton W.A.S. (1983) Lexical and pragmatic considerations of input structures. *ACM SIGGRAPH Computer Graphics 17*:31-37.

Buxton W.A.S. (1989) Introduction to this special issue on non-speech audio. *Human Computer Interaction 4*:1-9.

Buxton W.A.S. (1990) A three state model of graphical input. *Proceedings of INTERACT '90* :449-456. Amsterdam: Elsevier Science.

Card S.K., Mackinlay J.D. & Robertson G.G. (1990) The design space of input devices. *Proceedings of CHI '90* :117-124. ACM SIGCHI.

Card S.K., Moran T.P. & Newell (1983) *The psychology of human computer interaction.* Hillsdale, New Jersey: Lawrence Erlbaum.

Chalfonte B.L., Fish R.S & Kraut R.E. (1991) Expressive richness: A comparison of speech and text as media for revision. *Proceedings of CHI '91*:21-26. ACM SIG-CHI.

Chignell M.H. (1990) A taxonomy of user interface terminology. *SIGCHI Bulletin 21* (4):27-34.

Claassen W., Bos E. & Huls C. (1990) *The Pooh way in human computer interaction: Towards multimodal interfaces*. SPIN-MMC Research Report No. 5. Nijmegen: NICI.

Cohen P.R., Dalrymple M., Moran D.B., Pereira F.N.C., Sullivan J.W., Gargan Jr R.A., Schlossberg J.L. & Tyler S.W. (1989) Synergistic use of direct manipulation and natural language. *Proceedings of CHI '89* : 227-233. ACM SIGCHI.

Conklin J. (1987) Hypertext: A survey and introduction. *IEEE Computer 20*:17-41.

Connolly K.J (1975) Movement, action and skill. In K.S. Holt (Ed.) *Movement and child development*. London: Heinman for Spastics International Medical Publications.

Firman T.R. (1988) Empowering the Macintosh interface with speech recognition. *Proceedings of the Voice I/O Systems Applications Conference, AVIOS*. San Fransisco, October 1988.

Foley J.D., Wallace V.L. & Chan P. (1984) The human factors of computer graphics interaction techniques. *IEEE Computer Graphics and Applications, Nov.*:13-47.

Frohlich D.M. (1987) On the re-organisation of form-filling behaviour in an electronic medium. *Information Design Journal 5*:111-128 .

Frohlich D.M (1991) Direct interaction. In preparation.

Guindon R. (1990) Designing the design process: Exploiting opportunistic thoughts. *Human Computer Interaction 5*:305-344.

Hebb D.O. (1949) *The organisation of behaviour*. New York: John Wiley & Sons.

Hutchins E.L. (1989) Metaphors for interface design. In M.M. Taylor, F. Neel & D.G Bouwhuis (Eds.) *The structure of multimodal dialogue*. North Holland: Elsevier Science.

Hutchins E.L., Hollan J.D. & Norman D.A. (1986) Direct manipulation interfaces. In D.A. Norman & S.W. Draper (Eds.) *User centered system design*. Hillsdale, New Jersey: Lawrence Erlbaum Associates.

Johnson J. (1990) Modes in non-computer devices. *International Journal of Man-Machine Studies 32*:423-438.

Johnson J., Roberts T.L., Verplank W., Smith D.C., Irby C.H., Beard M. & Mackey K. (1989) The Xerox Star: A retrospective. *IEEE Computer, Sept.*:11-29.

Laurel B. (1986) Interface as memesis. In D.A. Norman & S.W. Draper (Eds.) *User centered system design*. Hillsdale, New Jersey: Lawrence Erlbaum Associates.

Laurel B. (1990) Interface Agents: metaphors with character. In B. Laurel (Ed.) *The art of human computer interface design*: 355-366. Menlo Park, California : Addison-Wesley.

Lee J. & Zeevat H. (1990) Integrating natural language and graphics in dialogue. *Proceedings of INTERACT '90*:479-484. Amsterdam: Elsevier Science.

Luff P. & Frohlich D.M. (1991) Mixed initiative interaction. In T. Bench-Capon (Ed.) *Knowledge based systems and legal applications*. London: Academic Press.

Mackinlay J.D., Card S.K. & Robertson G.G. (1991) A semantic analysis of the design space of input devices. *Human Computer Interaction. 5*: 145-190.

Marr D. (1982) *Vision*. San Fransisco: W.H. Freeman & Co.

Oren T., Salomon G., Kreitman K. & Don A. (1990) Guides: Characterising the interface. In B. Laurel (Ed.) *The art of human computer interface design*. Menlo Park, California : Addison-Wesley.

Reed E.S. (1982) An outline of a theory of action systems. *Journal of Motor Behavior 14*:98-134.

Shneiderman B. (1982) The future of interactive systems and the emergence of direct manipulation. *Behaviour and Information Technology 1*:237-256.

Stearns G. (1989) Agents and the HP NewWave Application Program Interface. *Hewlett-Packard Journal 40*:32-37.

Stenton P. (1990) Designing cooperative interfaces: Tailoring the channel. In J.R. Galliers (Ed.) Proceedings of the first belief representation and agent architectures workshop, March 1990. *University of Cambridge, Computer Laboratory Technical Report No. 194*:193-197.

Taylor M.M. (1988) Editorial: Special issue on multimodal computer-human interaction. *International Journal of Man-Machine Studies 28*:99-100.

Taylor M.M., Neel F. & Bouwhuis D.G., Eds. (1989) *The structure of multimodal dialogue*. Amsterdam: North-Holland.

Walker M.A. (1989) Natural language in a desk-top environment. *Proceedings of HCI89 3rd International Conference on Human-Computer Interaction* :502-509. Boston, Mass.

Waterworth J. (1985) Speech communication: How to use it. In A. Monk (Ed.) *Fundamentals of human-computer interaction*. London: Academic Press.

Whittaker S. (1990) Next generation interfaces. *Proceedings of the AAAI Spring Symposium on Knowledge Based Human Computer Communication*, Stanford, 27-29th March :127-131.

Chapter 6

Out of the Window: A Multi-Medium

Roger K. Took

Abstract

This paper informally describes a presentation model for multiple media. In contrast to the display platform provided by standard window managers, this model supports richly structured media of high granularity with a wide range of visualisations and with few geometric restrictions. The full formal model (Took 1991c) also integrates graphical and textual media by allowing their arbitrary nesting without imposing a priority between them. In the implemented system *Presenter*, described here, the model is an *objective* structure which can be constructed dynamically and incrementally, and so can act as an interactive communication intermediary between users and applications. Such a presentation module is called a *surface*. A major benefit is that the user can directly manipulate surface objects independently of the application which created them. Such *surface interaction* factors a large proportion of the task of writing highly interactive applications. The *UMA* architecture (Took 1991b) describes how this can be achieved without sacrificing semantic feedback from the application to the surface.

1. Introduction

Most current multimedia systems sit on top of an established operating system and window manager. The operating system therefore ideally needs to provide communication primitives for a range of media such as sound or video. However, traditional operating systems may be unsuited to this. UNIX, for example, is based on communication via files or streams, which lack the bandwidth for effectively channeling sound or video. In the same way, the window managers which are typically used to present multimedia information are based, as the name suggests, on the *window* as the main presentation primitive. While the deficiencies of standard operating systems in providing channels for multimedia information are recognised and are being addressed (Blair et al. 1991), there is currently little exploration of the deficiencies of standard window managers for presenting multimedia information. This paper gives an outline of the rationale, design, and benefits of a new presentation model for multimedia information called a *surface*. This encapsulates a single manifold, or multi-medium, with which, and via which, both users and application interact.

2. Window Manager Deficiencies

The standard window manager is based on a presentation model consisting simply of large-grain display spaces. There are often three major deficiencies in the way in which this is implemented. Firstly, in many widow systems there may be geometric or visualisation constraints on the manipulation and display of windows. Windows in SunWindows, for example, cannot be moved off screen. Other window managers may impose tiling (for example Cedar (Teitelman 1984)), or limit the number of windows available at once. In the Perq window manager, for example, this limitation was due to a strict association between windows and UNIX processes. In hierarchical window managers, like X (Scheifler and Gettys 1986) or NeWS (NeWS 1987), child windows are constrained to be visible only within the area of their parent window, which must itself be visible, or 'mapped' in X terminology. Windows in nearly all systems must be opaque - the 'transparent' windows of X or NeWS are actually input or clipping frames on an underlying opaque window.

Secondly, by reason of the dependence on the window as the major display primitive, in window managers graphical media usually have better support that textual media. Text must typically be written *into* a window by more specialised tools. Often there is an arbitrary division and overlapping of functionality here too between tools that provide simple textual labels, others that provide editable text lines for inclusion in dialogue boxes, and yet others which provide editable blocks of text. These may all be based on a very rudimentary text *drawing* primitive provided by the window manager. While this proliferation of types may be rationalised by an object-oriented type hierarchy, the drawing of text remains bound in to the application, rather than separated into the surface.

Lastly, there is often a poor separation between the underlying presentation capabilities of the window model, and its user interface. Thus the particular desktop metaphor in use, complete with its icons, menus, scroll bars etc., may be difficult to extend or override. While this may lead to a consistent interface over a range of applications, it places limitations on the application designer's expressive freedom and makes user interface experimentation difficult. Such experimentation may be essential for multimedia research.

While rectangular overlapping windows are clearly a powerful organisational aid in multitasking environments their conventional representation can be criticised on a number of points:

- Overlapping windows can lead to a cluttered screen. The clutter is visually confusing and can cause 'thrashing' (Card and Henderson 1987 p.59).

- In window interfaces which indulge in relatively wide window borders filled with functionality like scroll bars and buttons (as on the Mac) the cluttering is exacerbated, since this functionality is duplicated for each window.

- Not all visible objects are rectangular or opaque. In layouts of networked objects, for example, there may be opaque background around and between the objects such that some underlying objects may be obscured unnecessarily. Compare, for example the following (artificial) screen:

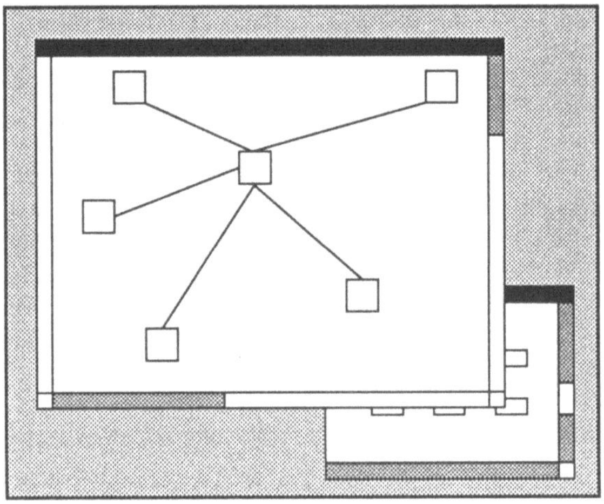

with the following (real) screen from an interactive database (Daly 1989) using *Presenter*:

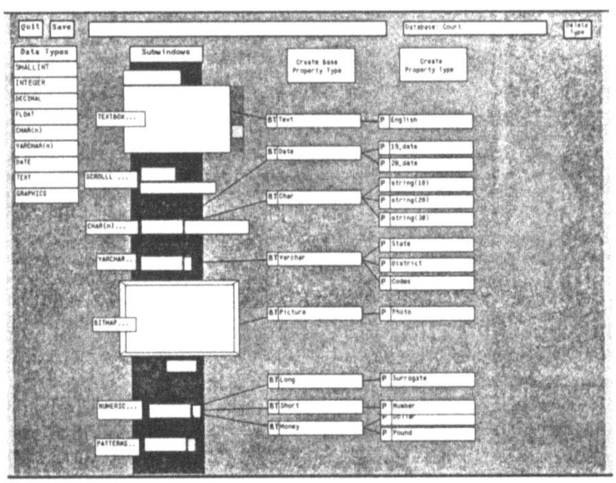

Conventional window interfaces can thus lead to a discontinuity between interaction with the window manger (for example to open, pop, or iconise windows), and interaction *within* a window with the application. This is because user interaction with application objects is managed entirely by the application, which sees all user input events occurring within the window. Thus the interactive tools (menus, scroll bars, etc.) that are created within the window by the application may differ in behaviour from those provided by the window manager in the window borders or on the desktop. To some extent this discontinuity is prevented by toolkits which provide a set of soft interactive devices with a fixed stylistic 'look and feel', such as Open Look or Motif. However, these tools bind a predefined presentation style tightly to the semantics of the application. Thus it may be impossible for the user dynamically to alter the style of the application's presentation, independently of the application.

3. Multimedia Requirements

In contrast, the notion of multimedia ideally suggests highly flexible channels of communication free of such arbitrary constraints. However, multimedia also implies not simply a *collection* of different media types and associated communication channels, but also some *structure* by which these can be integrated. This may be in the form of a *spatial* integration such as the embedding of images in text, or in the form of a *temporal* integration, by which sound, video, text and graphics may be appropriately *synchronised.* It is the design of this integrating structure, rather than that of the media which it supports, which is critical in providing the generality and expressive power needed for the presentation of multimedia. It is especially important that future multimedia presentation platforms do not perpetuate the limitations of window managers by binding in stylistic or domain-dependent constraints which will restrict their range of use.

In particular, it is important that text be given equal status with graphics. Both text and graphics may possess an internal structure. Graphical structure forms a model by which the image can be incrementally recreated and its components picked by direct manipulation. In the same way, text may possess a structure which is presented and formatted in terms of chapters, sections and paragraphs, and allows interactive editing of these. The defining distinction between text and graphics is therefore not their structural richness, nor the details of their respective content (since both text and graphics ultimately consist of *images*), but the different *geometries* which apply to both. Within graphics the manipulative operations are scaling and translating, whereas within text the manipulative operations are insertion and deletion. Thus it is theoretically possible to apply a *textual* geometry to graphics, and a graphical geometry to text. The former is needed for embedding or anchoring graphics (such as diagrams) at fixed textual locations:

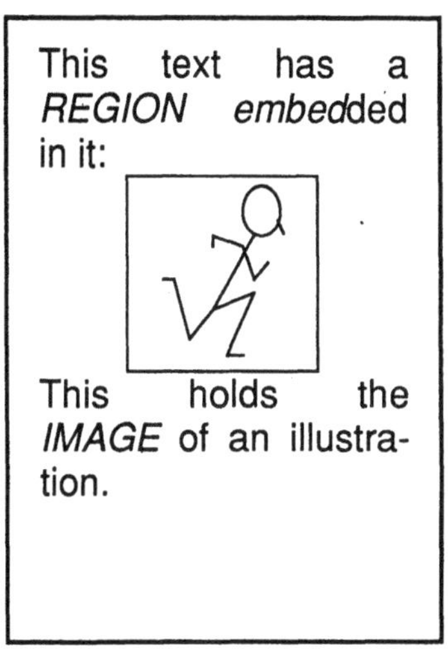

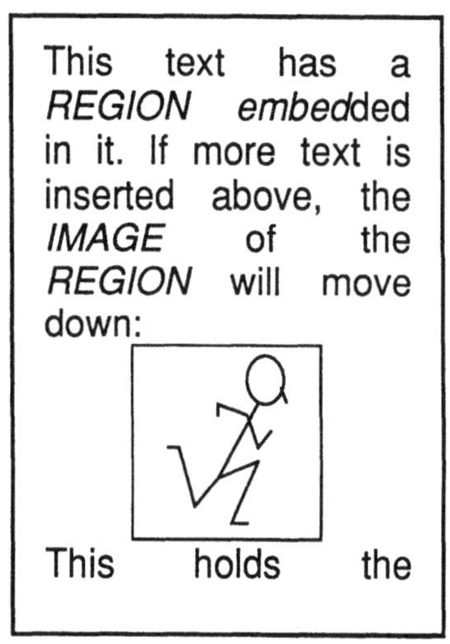

while the latter is needed for laying out blocks of text for labels or document columns, in which text may be framed by a sequence of graphically defined regions such that as text overflows from one, it runs on into the next:

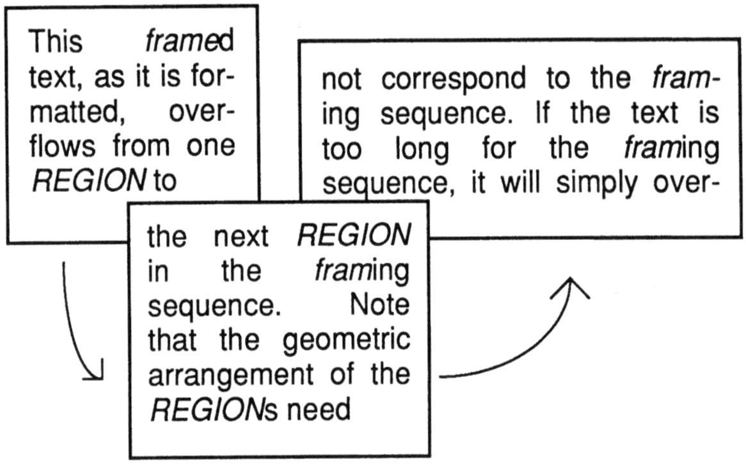

We should also be able to nest textual and graphical geometries to arbitrary depth, without imposing a priority between them, such that the top level space can be either graphical (Cartesian) or textual, depending on the content. Recent work has shown that it is also possible, and intuitively acceptable, to create documents which contain sound, video, or active components. The *document* is thus a powerful integrating paradigm for all forms of multimedia presentation. A formal specification for such a document model is given in (Took 1991c), but has yet to be implemented.

4. The Surface

The paper now describes, within the above context, a particular design and implemented system for such a multi-medium, called here a *surface*. The full design exists only as a formal specification, but the implemented system *Presenter* already instantiates some of the ideals outlined above. *Presenter* has formed the presentation platform for a wide range of applications: an Ada task debugger (Cobbett and Wand 1989), an interactive database management system (Daly 1989), software engineering diagramming applications, and image processing applications. In particular, it has been used in an interactive conferencing system (McCarthy and Miles 1990), and current work is using it as the platform for a (simulated) video manager/editor.

The description of the surface and its implementation in *Presenter* is structured into two main areas: presentation and interaction.

4.1. Presentation

The presentation capabilities of the surface model determine both the range of content that can be displayed, and the structure by which the content can be organised. The structure can also carry attributes which determine the visualisation of the content. We cover the stucture first, and then describe the content.

Structure

Clearly we should wish the structuring capabilities of a surface model to be as rich and generic as possible. That is, we should wish to be able to represent in the surface a wide range of particular configurations and relations of visual objects, and have these structures apply over any of the content types available.

Presenter has a single node type, called a *region* (in the C interface, a pointer to the region structure is the only external type that the application has to import). Regions come into existence dynamically through a *create* operation. Regions represent both simply a coordinate space, and at the same time a logical node in the application domain. It is up to the application to maintain the deep semantics of regions (that is, to associate with them some particular application behaviour), but managing the display and manipulation of regions is performed by *Presenter* in the surface.

Presenter supports both a display-oriented tree structure, and a more general network structure. Both of these are constructed on regions as the nodes, and the same node can be part of either or both structures. The tree structure has a single root, which acts as the display root. The tree structure is constructed simply through *paste* and *cut* operations. It is *ordered*, in the sense that a parent has a *sequence* of children, and so the paste operation specifies, as well as the parent region and the new child region, a *location* in the sequence of existing children in which the new child is to be pasted. This ordering of the tree maps to display layering of the visible content.

The more general *network* structure is constructed by a *link* operation which specifies the two regions to be linked. The direction of the link is preserved in the surface. Both the tree structure and the network structure can be traversed and queried, and so form a surface *database* for the visible objects. Optionally, *Presenter* can give a generic visualisation for this network structure. It does this by maintaining empty regions between the linked regions which change shape as the linked regions are moved or scaled. The application can insert any content into these empty regions. Typically this might be lines with labels, for example. Here is a networked database schema presented using this linking mechanism:

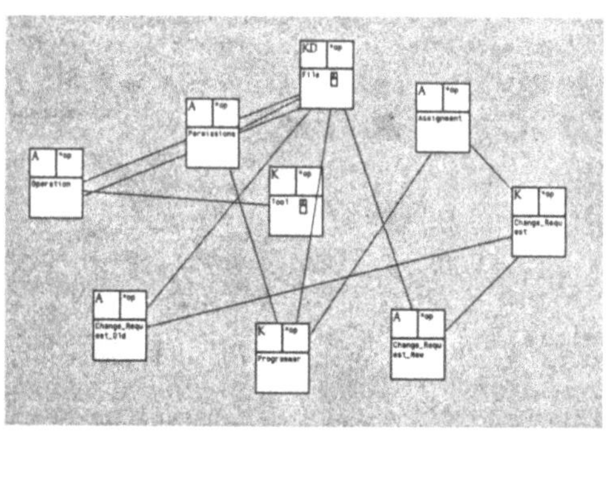

and here is the same schema rearranged interactively by the user:

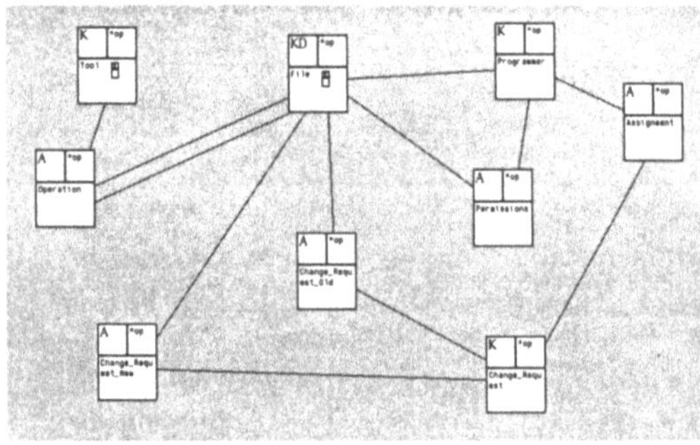

Attributes

Regions have attributes (properties) which determine their surface visualisation and behaviour. These similarly can be set dynamically. An important region attribute is a geometric transformation which is interpreted as applying to the region in the space of its parent on the tree structure (by contrast, transformations in PHIGS (ISO 1987b) do not apply to the structures in which the transformation is set, but to *child* structures of these). The particular geometric tranformation is set by separate operations which change the size, shape and position of a region. In contrast to most window systems, there are no restrictions on these operations: children can be at any size, shape or position with respect to their parent. In particular, they may be widely dispersed from their parent, allowing sparse groups of regions to be constructed. A set of buttons, for example, could be logically grouped in this way while remaining physically dispersed:

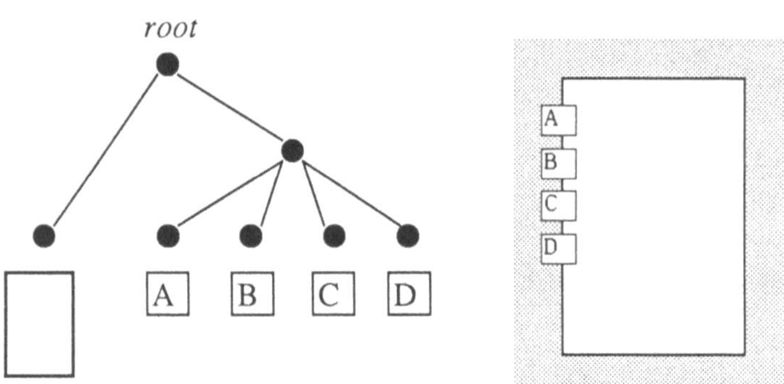

logical view *surface view*

Attributes in addition control the visualisation of content. This may be in any display mode: AND, OR, XOR or opaque in monochrome. Although colour has yet to be introduced, the implementation of *Presenter* is such that any colour combination operation could easily be incorporated. The display mode of a visible content is interpreted as occurring between that content and all underlying content. Thus *transparent* regions can be overlapped to any depth:

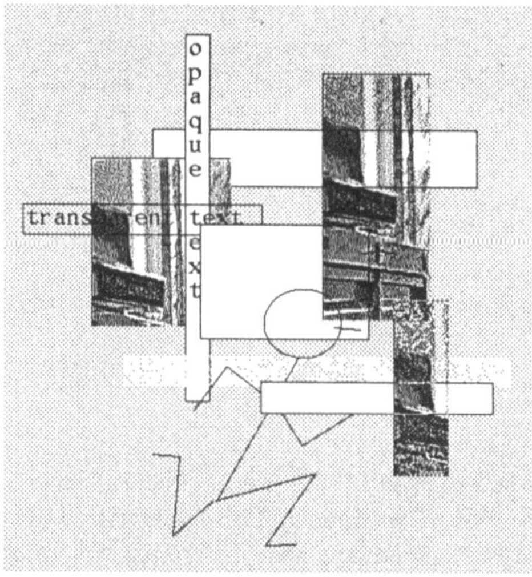

A *clip* attribute also causes a region to clip all its prior siblings. Any region can be set to clip, but clearly only transparent regions usefully clip their underlying regions. This clipping similarly can be nested to any depth:

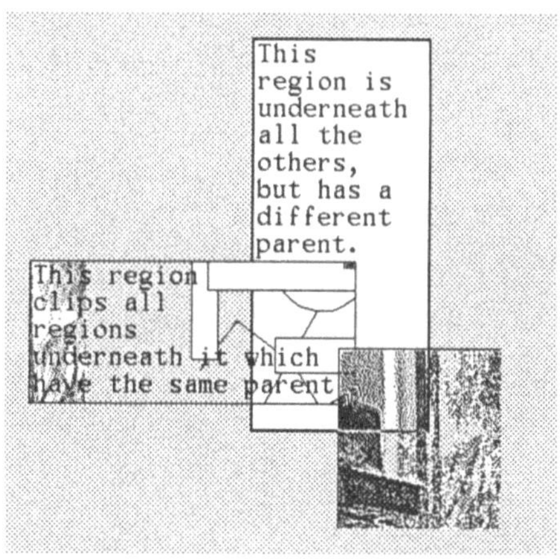

Finally, other attributes determine features of the behaviour of regions during surface interaction. These behavioural features are designed as simple constraints on the default capability of interactively moving or scaling regions. For example regions may be set to move or scale only horizontally or only vertically. Further attributes control the propagation of geometric transformations down the tree structure. The *noscale* attribute (which can be specialised to either dimension) causes a region to maintain its absolute size irrespective of changes to the size of ancestor regions. The *nogroup* attribute has a similar effect with respect to moving. Other attributes allow a region to be moved only inside, or only outside, the area of another region.

The effect of these attributes can be illustrated by the example of a slider, which is constructed out of a group of regions, some representing the background and its scale, and another representing the slider button, which is constrained by its attribute setting to be moved only vertically, and only within the bounds of its background:

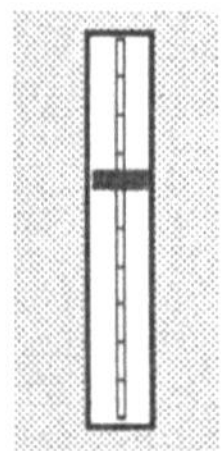

Further effects can be achieved by the use of other attributes. For example, the slider might be attached to the side of a window. The geometric properties of the tree structure immediately give the desirable behaviour that if the common parent region of the window and the slider is moved, then the slider and the window, from the point of view of the user, remain attached. However, if the parent changes size, then the slider changes size proportionally, that is, both its height and width may change. The commonly expected behaviour of such a slider, on the other hand, is for it to change size along its length, so that it stays the same height as its associated window, but to remain the same absolute width regardless of the width of the window. This can easily be achieved in *Presenter* using the *noscale* attribute in one dimension only. In this example, the slider group is set *noscale* horizontally. The slider button itself is in addition *noscale* vertically:

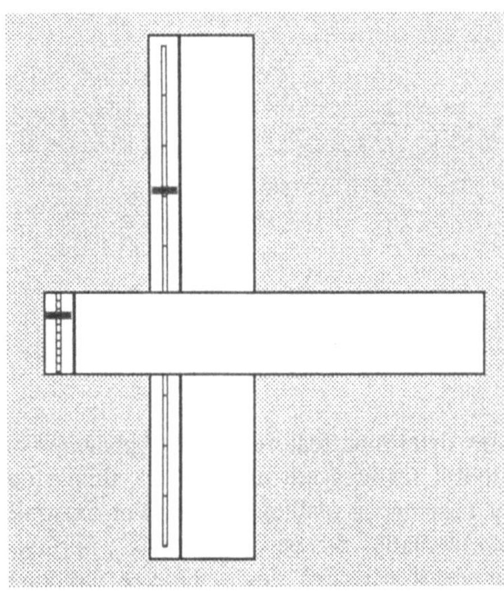

Content

Again in contrast to existing hierarchical window systems like X or NeWS, the visible content which *Presenter* supports can only be loaded at the *leaves* of the tree structure.

This scheme is similar to statically defined, grammatically-driven models such as ODA (ISO 1987a), or to graphics programming systems in which the *call* structure represents the model, such as PHIGS (ISO 1987b) or PostScript (Adobe 1987). The advantage of this scheme is that structure and content remain orthogonal, such that any element of either can be changed in isolation. By contrast, moving or changing the visibility of a window in X unavoidably results in similar changes to all its sub-windows. For example, changing the position of one of the diagonally shaded windows in the following illustration would result in both sub-contents also changing position:

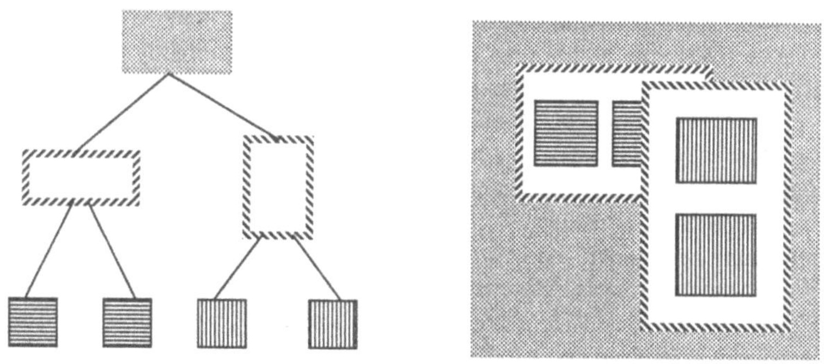

logical view *surface view*

A similar display in *Presenter*, on the other hand, would be modelled by the more verbose but more flexible structure:

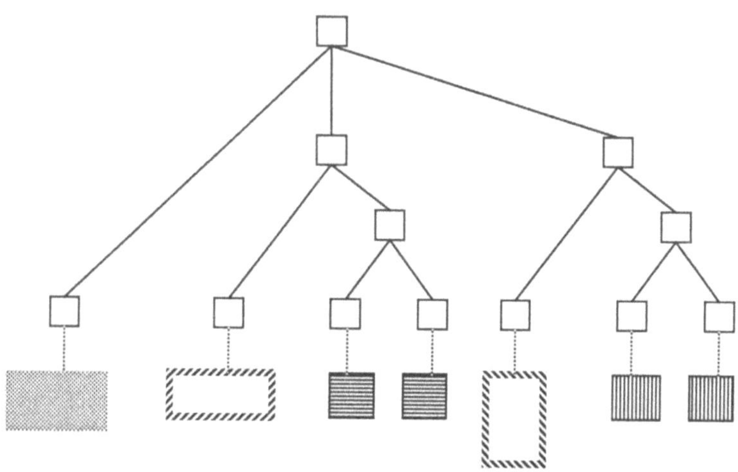

Presenter supports both text and graphics (bitmap and line-oriented). Leaf regions can contain either text or graphics, but not both. Composite objects incorporating both text and graphics are constructed instead by means of the tree structure. This, however, as pointed out above, is not an ideal scheme since it makes text subordinate to graphics.

4.2. Interaction

A feature of the model implemented in *Presenter* and described in (Took 1990b) is its *objective* nature. By this is meant that the model is both *dynamic* and *encapsulated.* The top level of most window systems is objective in this sense: windows can normally be created dynamically and manipulated by the end user independently of the applications using them for display. However, in many window systems this advantage is not carried through to other objects in the environment. For example, sub-constructs of the window (which can go by various names: sub-windows, tiles, panes, panels, frames, boxes etc.) exist in a static *type* hierarchy which can only be instantiated within the application.

A surface model based on an objective structure has the advantage that its objects can cache temporary display details like current pixel extent. This enables such objects to be *picked* interactively by a pointing device like a mouse directly and randomly (in contrast, for example, to objects created in PHIGS or PostScript, whose current extent, for interactive picking, can only be determined by re-executing the display script). An objective structure also facilitates incremental redisplay when only a small number of objects change.

A more important advantage of an objective structure is that its internal representation can be hidden and modification only allowed through well defined operations rather than by direct reference. Thus it can be supported by a separate server process, and can be distributed from the client application. An objective surface can thus be run on hardware optimised for handling the display of its media. An objective surface can also easily be made persistent, in the sense that its lifetime can be decoupled from that of the application which uses it. This only requires some hidden transformation of the objective structure to a format suitable for longer term storage.

Distributable window systems, like X and NeWS, use encapsulation in this way. However, the X server is fixed in functionality and limited in the ways outlined above, and, while the NeWS server is extensible via PostScript and its imaging model is more powerful than X, it too is bound by a restricted top level windowing model inherited from the older SunWindows system. In contrast, in addition to its more general geometric scheme, *Presenter* exploits a further benefit of a surface with an objective structure: all objects on the surface can be manipulated by the user *independently* of the application which creates them. This can factor a large part of the task of maintaining a highly interactive, direct manipulation user interface.

Such *surface interaction* (Took 1990b) only requires a dedicated user agent at the surface which translates the user's actions into operations on the surface objects. The involvement of the application in the events of surface interaction can be determined in advance, and on a per-object basis, by the application. Taking the slider above as an example, the application which creates this may be interested only in the position of the slider button, and may only wish to be informed of this when the user *releases* the mouse button. Thus maintaining the display of the slider button as it is interactively moved up and down the scale can be factored out of the application and into the surface. Other attributes of the slider, such as its position or overall size or aspect ratio, may be irrelevant to the application. However, these attributes may be important to the user (the slider may obscure some relevant information at some point during the interaction). It may therefore be very useful to allow the user to move or scale the slider as a whole. Using surface interaction this can be done without involving the application.

The communication architecture for allowing surface interaction to occur independently of *deep* interaction with the application is described formally (using CSP (Hoare 1985)) in (Took 1990b) and (Took 1991b). More informally, this *UMA* architecture can be illustrated diagrammatically:

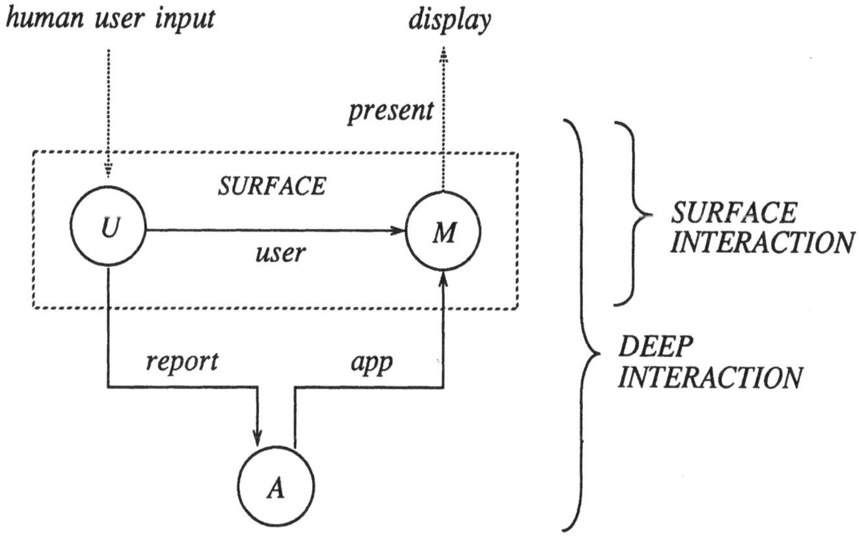

The surface consists of two processes, the medium (*M*), which maintains the objective structure described above and a presentation mapping of this to the display, and the User Agent (*U*), which monitors all input. The range of application processes is represented here by a single token application (*A*). These processes communicate via the channels *user*, *report*, and *app*.

Interaction that is event-driven (i.e. caused by user actions) occurs in the following way. User input (for example, a mouse click) is registered by the User Agent. This then asks the Medium (via the *user* channel) for the identity and attributes of the surface object (if any) currently under the mouse cursor. If the attributes of the picked object require that the current event be reported to the application which owns the object, then the User Agent informs this application via the *report* channel. On the other hand, if the attributes indicate that the application is not interested in the current event, then the User Agent is free to manipulate the object on behalf of the user directly via the *user* channel.

The *UMA* architecture also permits interaction that is driven by the application since, asynchronously, the application may update its surface objects by communicating directly with the Medium along the *app* channel. This style of interaction may be required for process monitoring applications, for example.

5. Conclusions

The objective structure which is used to integrate multiple media types in this model, and the *UMA* architecture which manages user interaction with the objects of the model, stress the importance of the *medium* of interaction in providing a level of independence between different users and different applications, and in factoring interactive tasks from applications. In particular, the medium is an ideal site in which to maintain the structures of multiple media. Thus the medium can ideally form a kind of interactive, perceptual *database* (Ciccarelli 1985, Scofield 1985) (or, in AI terms, *blackboard*) for the application's semantic objects (Took 1990b). This has several advantages.

Firstly, these objects can *persist* in the medium. That is, they can exist there for possibly longer than the lifetime of the application which created or channeled them. This also enables interactive objects to be created in advance by specialised tools (for example, user interface editors) for subsequent use with an application which provides their semantics.

Secondly, because the medium objects thus have some independence from their application, they can be manipulated both by the application, and (possibly concurrently) directly by the user independently of the application. If the medium is *shared*, then these objects can be tokens of communication between different users or different applications, as well as between user and application, and can thus form the basis for computer supported cooperative work (CSCW) or 'groupware' (McCarthy and Miles 1990).

Thirdly, by building the medium to support objects themselves, rather than simply to be a display area for objects maintained within an application domain, we can factor out a large proportion of the interactive operations which applications built within a standard window manager have to support. Thus we can make the *architectural* division between the application and its interface media correspond to the *conceptual* distinction between semantic objects and multiple views of these.

The models presented here and implemented in *Presenter* do not immediately address the technical issues of incorporating content with multiple media types into a single interface, for example issues of image compression and transmission. Nor do these models address the special user-computer interaction issues raised by multimedia interfaces. They seek instead to provide a flexible platform for the integrated display of any visible content, without imposing the restrictions common in window-managed presentation.

However, a distinguishing feature of multimedia presentation over more usual window-managed presentations is the inclusion of sound and video channels. The *UMA* architecture, by allowing surface objects in the Medium to be active through the User Agent, also shows a possible way to model the integration of sound and video in an interactive surface. These media types can be modelled as surface processes, with asynchronous events such as 'new sample' (sound) or 'new frame' (video). Such a scheme could certainly account for the temporal behaviour of sound and video channels. The problems of image and sound synchronisation could also be adequately expressed using a process algebra. This possibility is left for further research. Issues of inheritance in presentation objects are also being examined in related work (Took 1991a).

6. References

Adobe Systems Inc. (1987) PostScript Language Reference Manual, Addison-Wesley.

Blair G., Gallagher J., Hutchinson D., Shepherd D. (eds.) (1991) Object Oriented Languages, Systems and Applications, Pitman, pp. 244-269.

Card S. K., Henderson Jnr. A. (April 1987) A Multiple, Virtual-Workspace Interface to Support User Task Switching, in *Proc CHI + GI 1987*, ed. J. M. Carroll, P. P. Tanner, ACM SIGCHI Bulletin, 18(2), pp. 53-59.

Ciccarelli E. C.(1985) Presentation Based User Interfaces (PhD Thesis), MIT.

Cobbett A. P., Wand I. C. (September 1989) The Debugging of Large Multi-Task Ada Programs, Ada User, Volume 10, pp 122-131.

Daly W. (1989) A Graphical Management System for Semantic, Multimedia Databases (PhD Thesis), University of York, 1989.

Hoare C. A. R. (1985) Communicating Sequential Processes, Prentice-Hall International.

ISO (July 1987a) Information Processing - Text and Office Systems: Office Document Architecture (ODA) and Interchange Format, ISO DIS 8613 part 1-8.

ISO (October 1987b) Information Processing - Computer Graphics - Programmers Hierarchical Interactive Graphics System (PHIGS), ISO DIS 9592-1:1987(E).

McCarthy J. M., Miles V. C. (May 1990) Elaborating Communication Channels In Conferencer, in Proc IFIP WG8.4 Conference on Multi-User Interfaces and Applications, pp 181-193.

NeWS Manual (1987) Sun Microsystems, 1987.

Scheifler R. W., Gettys J. (April 1986) The X Window System, *ACM Trans. Graphics*, **5**(2), pp. 79-109.

Scofield J. A. (August 1985) Editing as a Paradigm for User Interaction (PhD Thesis), Computer Science Dept., Univ. of Washington, Seattle, Tech. Rep. No. 85-08-10.

Teitelman W. (1984) A Tour Through Cedar, *IEEE Software*, **1**(2), pp. 44-73.

Took R. K. (April 1990a) Surface Interaction: A Paradigm and Model for Separating Application and Interface, in Proc CHI '90, pp. 35-42, ACM.

Took R. K. (1990b) Surface Interaction: Separating Direct Manipulation Interfaces from their Applications (PhD Thesis), Computer Science Department, University of York.

Took R. K. (1991a) Integrating Inheritance and Composition in a Persistent Presentation Model for Multiple Media, Proc. Eurographics '91.

Took R. K. (1991b) The Active Medium: a Conceptual and Practical Architecture for Direct Manipulation Proc. HCI '91.

Took R. K. (June 1991c) Integrating Graphics and Text in an Objective Presentation Model, Proc. Eurographics Workshop on Formal Methods in Computer Graphics, Marina di Carrara, Italy.

Part III

Synchronization

Chapter 7

Synchronizing the Presentation of Multimedia Objects - ODA Extensions

Petra Hoepner

The presentation of Multimedia Objects requires simultaneous and/or sequential presentation of several representation types (text, graphics, images, audio and video sequences). Therefore the presentation has to be structured and the temporal relations of different actions have to be described. The temporal relations are realized by applying synchronization mechanisms. In this paper a general synchronization model for the description of presentation sequences of Multimedia Objects is introduced. This model is applied to the Open Document Architecture (ODA) Standard and ODA Extensions are defined to integrate temporal relationships into ODA.

1 Introduction

This paper has been written in the context of the project "Multi-Media-Dokumente im ISDN-B" (BERMMD) forming a part of the BERKOM program. As part of this project an analysis of standards [1], [2] has been made to explore their usability for multimedia applications (see also [3]). Furthermore a framework, called *BERKOM Reference Model - Application-Oriented Layers* [4], has been developed to structure distributed applications into three parts: Communication, Information- and Datastructures and Application Environment, based on the current work of Open Distributed Processing (ODP) [5]. According to this reference model, the paper can be related to *User Access*, one topic in the *Application Environment*, and there concentrating on synchronizing the presentation of multimedia information.

Presenting a Multimedia Object means not only displaying some time-invariant representation types such as text or graphics or images, but involves also time-variant representation types such as audio or video. That means the presentation of a Multimedia Objects consists of a set of actions temporally related to each other, which have to be executed in a special intended sequence defined by the author, user or some other instance. This scheduling is generally called synchronization of actions. A notation based on path expressions for the description of synchronized actions is presented in this paper.

In *Section 2* the paper describes a synchronization model usable for Multimedia Objects. The temporal relations between actions are viewed and classified to extract the requirements. Then a notation is provided to describe the synchronization of actions based on path expressions.

Section 3 introduces the ODA Standard to the unfamiliar reader.

A standardized document architecture is the Open Document Architecture (ODA) [6]. The current version of ODA supports only time-invariant representation types such as text, graphics and images. To extend ODA to support Multimedia Objects, other representation types such as audio and video have to be integrated. As a consequence ODA documents have to be imaged in a synchronized presentation order. To provide such a presentation order new attributes have to be defined. *Section 4* describes possible enhancements to the Open Document Architecture (ODA), that integrate the general synchronization properties modelled.

2 Abstract Synchronization Model for Multimedia Objects

2.1 Concept of Actions

A general definition of the terms *action* and *event* is found in [7]: "An *action* is the representation of something which happens. An *event* is an atomic unit of action."

The concept of action is built, in specifications, out of a composition of events, which are taken as primitives [8]. As described in [9], a partial ordering of these events can be defined. Only some events are of interest in the scope of synchronization, namely the events corresponding in some way to events of other actions. We call those events *synchronization points*. The alignment of actions at synchronization points is done by applying some synchronization mechanisms.

An action in our level of abstraction is delimited by the following events: the action starts in time at some *startpoint* and ends at some *endpoint*. It is appropriate to use the start- and/or endpoints of actions as synchronization points. Start- and endpoints do not have to be defined in absolute units of time constituted by some time reference system, but can also be defined in terms of temporal relations to other actions.

The startpoint of an action can be described as an absolute startpoint defined by some system-clock or as a relative startpoint defined by some precondition, i.e. by the end of another action or by a user interaction.

The endpoint of an action can be described as an absolute endpoint defined by some system-clock or as a relative endpoint either defined by some precondition (i.e. by the end of another action or by a user interaction) or defined by a duration (execution time) of an action relative to the startpoint.

Two different kinds of actions can be distinguished, depending on the (non)existence of synchronization points between the start- and endpoint of an action. *Atomic actions* are actions that are not subdivided into partial actions for the purpose of synchronization. This means, that there are no synchronization points during these actions. *Composed actions* are actions that are composed from atomic actions or composed actions. The participating actions of a composed action have to be synchronized to fulfill a defined order of execution.

For synchronization purposes, actions have to be decomposed into atomic actions, which are synchronized by applying appropriate synchronization mechanisms at the start- and endpoints. The semantics of the composed action will not change by a logical decomposition of the composed action.

2.2 Temporal Relations of Actions

Allen [10] defines thirteen temporal relations between two intervals of time. These temporal relations are: *before, meets, during, overlaps, starts, ends* and *equal* plus the inverse relations (except equal). He claims, that this set of relations is complete regarding *two* intervals of time. The left side of Figure 1 shows these temporal relations, thereby the intervals of time are associated with the actions A and B.

To define general temporal relations for presentation, vacant time intervals of Allen's temporal relations are replaced by a timer action (called T). A shift in time is then modelled by a sequence of a timer action and the shifted action. The right side of Figure 1 shows the complete set of general temporal relations between actions developed from Allen's temporal relations by inserting a timer action T. These relations are *sequential, parallel-first* and *parallel-last*; they are described in Section 2.4.

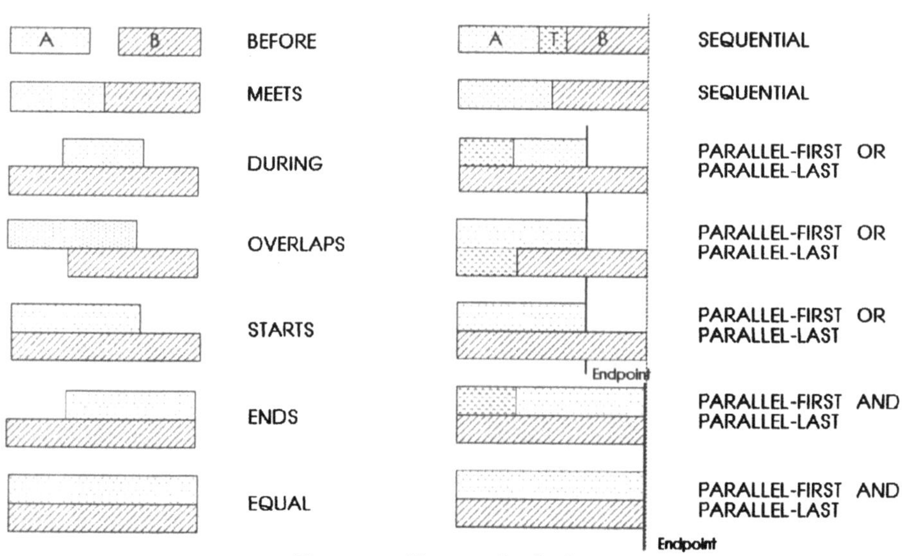

Figure 1 : Temporal relations

2.3 General Model Based on Path Expressions

As defined in the previous sections our goal is the definition of a general notation for specifying the synchronization of the presentation of Multimedia Objects.

General synchronization mechanisms are described in [11], [12] and [13]. Only *path expressions* specify the synchronized order of operations; they were introduced by [14]. A path expression describes which *paths* are allowed for operations respectively which order of operations on an object is executable. In a path expression the *path operators* define the synchronization of operations. They define the flexibility and power of path expressions with regard to their synchronization properties.

By generalizing the term of an operation, our term of an action is easily usable within a path expression. The *path operators* define the semantics of the behaviour of a synchronization mechanism used, without imposing a specific synchronization mechanism. Any mechanism fulfilling the specific semantics will be usable. The set of path operators will be defined in Section 2.4.

The definition of *actions for the presentation* is part of the specification but not part of the synchronization model. Any action that includes synchronization points between the start and the end of an action has to be logically decomposed into atomic actions, that are synchronized only at startpoints and/or endpoints.

2.4 Definition of Path Operators

For the specific purpose of synchronizing the presentation of Multimedia Objects (based on the temporal relations defined in Section 2.2) the following set of path operators was chosen (thereby A and B are actions and N is a positive natural number). The path operators are named and listed in increasing priority ordering:

$A \wedge B$ *Parallel-last*: Actions A and B are started at a common startpoint and are executed concurrently. The composed action terminates, when all participating actions (A and B) terminate.

$A \vee B$ *Parallel-first*: Actions A and B are started at a common startpoint and are executed concurrently. The composed action terminates, when the first (in time) participating action (either A or B) terminates.

$A \,;\, B$ *Sequential*: It is only allowed to execute B if A is executed before. The endpoint of A equals the startpoint of B. The composed action terminates, when the last action in the sequence terminates.

$A \mid B$ *Selective*: It is permissible to execute either A or B. The selection depends on a condition which is not part of the path expression, but has to be evaluated by some other instance. The composed action terminates, when the selected action (either A or B) terminates.

A^{i*} *Repetition*: Action A will be repeated i times. If i is not present, A will be repeated zero or more times; the exact number of repetitions has to be supplied by some other instance (i.e. the user).

N:A *Concurrency*: Action A is allowed to be executed N-times concurrently. If N=1, then the execution of A is mutual exclusive. If N=infinite, then no execution or any concurrent execution of A is allowed. The default value used is N=1.

EXAMPLE of a path expression:

path A ; $((B \wedge C) \vee (D \wedge E))$; F^* end

DESCRIPTION:
Action A is started; exactly at the end of action A the four actions B, C, D and E are started. Action F can be executed as soon as action B and action C or as soon as action D and action E terminate. Action F might be executed zero or more times. The whole path of actions is allowed to be executed only once at a time (mutual exclusive).

2.4.1 Parallelism in Path Expressions

The parallel path operators (parallel-first and parallel-last) support parallel actions. Any of the parallel actions might have to be synchronized solely with other actions, which have no synchronization points in common. In that case at least two path expressions exist for the description of the behaviour of actions. This does not imply a multiple execution of the same action used in different path expressions.

EXAMPLE:
Actions A and B are started at the same time. After A terminated some action C should be started. After A and B terminated D will be started.

path $(A \wedge B)$; D end
path A ; C end

Actions C and D have no common synchronization points. Action A is only executed once.

3 Basic Concepts of the Open Document Architecture (ODA)

An abbreviation of the concepts of the Open Document Architecture (ODA) as described in [15] and [16] is given:

The key concept in the document architecture is that of structure. Document structure is the division and repeated subdivision of the content of a document into increasingly smaller parts. The parts are called objects. The structure has the form of a tree.

The document architecture permits two structures to be applied to a document: a logical structure and a layout structure. In the *logical structure*, the document is divided and subdivided on the basis of the meaning. Examples of logical objects are chapters, sections, figures and paragraphs. In the *layout structure*, the document is divided and subdivided on the basis of the layout. Examples of layout objects are pages and blocks.

An object that is not subdivided into smaller objects is called a *basic object*. All other objects are called *composite objects*.

The basic elements of the content of a document are called content elements (e.g. characters, picture elements, lines...). A set of related content elements that belong to one basic logical object or one basic layout object is called a *content portion*. A content portion may have a more detailed internal structure. The rules governing such an internal structure depend on the type of content and are called a *content architecture*.

An *attribute* is a property of a document or of a document constituent (i.e. a logical object, a layout object...). It expresses a characteristic of the document or document component concerned, or a relationship with one or more documents or document components. The set of attributes associated with a document as a whole is called a *document profile*.

In a document, the logical objects and/or layout objects can often be classified into groups of similar objects. Therefore the concept of *object class* is introduced. An object class or a document class is a specification of the set of properties that are common to its members. Such a specification consists of a set of rules to determine the values of the attributes that specify the common properties. The set of logical object classes and layout object classes associated with a document, and their relationships, are called *generic logical structure* and *generic layout structure*. The structures that are particular to a given document are named *specific logical structure* and *specific layout structure*. The generic logical structure can be used as a set of rules from which specific logical objects and structures are derived during the editing process. The generic layout structure can be used as a set of rules from which specific layout objects and structures are derived during the formatting process.

The processing of a document is performed by three processes:

Editing process: The document editing process is concerned with creating a new document or modifying a previous one. Upon completion of editing, the resulting document can be interchanged. Such a document is said to be interchanged in "processable" form; it is suitable for input to either the editing or layout process.

Layout process: The document layout process is concerned with defining a page-oriented organization (i.e. a layout) for the document content. The layout process can generate a document which is not intended to be modified, the "formatted" form; it is suitable only for input to the imaging process. This process can also generate a "formatted processable" form which can be processed further if desired; it is suitable for input to any of the imaging, layout or editing processes.

Imaging process: The document imaging process is concerned with presenting an image of the document in a form perceptible to a human, for example, on a paper or on a screen. The imaging process is not defined by the standards and is regarded as a locally defined process that depends on the presentation device used.

4 Open Document Architecture (ODA) Extensions for the Synchronization of the Presentation

The presentation of Multimedia Objects requires a time-variant presentation resulting from time-variant representation types as well as temporal relationships between objects. The current version of ODA provides a time-invariant presentation resulting from time-invariant content portions as well as pure spacial relationships between objects.

The spacial relationships of objects in general are expressed by the *location in space* and the temporal relationships of objects are expressed by the *location in time*. The *location in space/time* is defined: "The set of points in space/time at which a given event can occur" [7]. The layout structures in the current version of ODA provide a description of the location in space for the presentation. Thus the layout structures should be extended by attributes describing the location in time to unify the location viewpoints within a single structure.

The logical structures of ODA documents are not directly concerned with timely aspects; this is meant in the sense of the partitioning of content, not for presentation-oriented features such as layout directives or author intended timing for the presentation. The proposed ODA extensions for temporal relationships only will be applied to the layout structures of ODA documents and possibly to the layout directives. Extensions to the logical structures of ODA documents are for further study.

The integration of time-variant content into ODA also requires the definition of new content architectures; these content architectures are not part of this paper.

The following proposed extensions are partially based on the work of [17].

4.1 ODA Extensions in Relation to Path Expressions

The abstract synchronization model is based on path expressions; as outlined in the preceding sections, it is possible to describe the synchronization of the presentation by path expressions. To define the ODA extensions, the semantics of path expressions as defined by actions and path operators should be integrated into the layout structure.

The concept of composed and atomic actions constituting a special presentation effect relates directly to the structuring concept of ODA, namely to composite and basic layout objects. Reorganizing a path expression in a prefix notation leads to a hierarchical tree structure, where path operators are nodes and actions are leaves. This corresponds to the hierarchical structure of ODA and leads to new attributes for the basic and composite layout objects.

Path operators define the synchronization between actions; they impose a presentation ordering for the participating actions. Presentation ordering within the current version of ODA is predefined by the sequential order or specified by the attribute Imaging Order. The sequential order presents objects in the order of tree traversal. The attribute Imaging Order allows the definition of a precedence order in a layout object with respect to the immediately subordinate layout objects. Analogously to the attribute Imaging Order, the semantics of path operators have to be integrated into composite layout objects, by adding attributes which impose processing rules for the imaging process.

Thereby the startpoints and endpoints of the presentation including time constraints and user interactions have to be regulated.

4.2 Attributes

CONTENT TEMPORAL TYPE (basic layout objects)

A basic layout object is associated with a content portion. The content is either time-variant or time-invariant; a basic layout object is thus enhanced by an attribute *Content Temporal Type* with the following specification: The attribute value *static* specifies that the associated content is time-invariant; the attribute value *dynamic* specifies that the associated content is time-variant. The default value is *static*.

DURATION (basic layout objects)

As soon as dynamic basic layout objects are included within an ODA-document, time coordination features have to be considered during the presentation. Dynamic basic layout objects are presented for a specific duration, which is defined by the presentation time of the content of the object, i.e. an audio sequence lasts five minutes. A static basic layout object also can be presented for a specified time, i.e. a picture is presented for one minute.

This leads to the definition of another new attribute called *Duration*. The attribute defines the presentation duration of a basic layout object in Basic Time Units (BTUs). Permissible values are '0' or a positive integer. The default value is '0'.

A static basic layout object with a duration of '0' will be presented until it is terminated by some other instance, this means that the endpoint is undefined. For this reason the endpoint will not be evaluated for continuing the presentation. This guarantees compatibility with the current version of ODA. A static basic layout object with a positive duration value will be presented for the specified duration and is then terminated.

A dynamic basic layout object with a duration of '0' will be presented for its own inherent presentation time. A dynamic basic layout object with a positive duration value will be shortened or stretched for the presentation as needed, to match the duration value.

OBJECT SYNCHRONIZATION TYPE (composite layout objects)

The type of synchronization of actions is semantically defined by the path operators; within ODA this semantic has to be expressed by an attribute. The attribute will be called *Object Synchronization Type*. Assuming a prefix notation for a path expression, a path expression can be mapped onto a hierarchical tree with the path operators as nodes and the actions as leaves; thus only the composite layout objects will be enhanced by the attribute Object Synchronization Type.

The attribute defines the timely ordering of the presentation of the immediately subordinate basic and/or composite layout objects. The default value is *sequential* (for compatibility with the sequential order of the current version of ODA). The attribute values are defined as follows:

parallel-last: All immediately subordinate layout objects are started at the same time, the current layout object is terminated as soon as all of the immediately subordinate layout objects terminate.

parallel-first: All immediately subordinate layout objects are started at the same time, the current layout object is terminated as soon as one of the immediately subordinate layout objects terminates.

sequential: The immediately subordinate layout objects are started one after another (sequential order: from left to right in the tree). The current layout object is terminated as soon as the last immediately subordinate layout object in the sequence terminates.

selective: Only one of the immediately subordinate layout objects will be selected. The determination of the layout object is made by the imaging process, depending e.g. on the user's choice. The current layout object terminates when the selected immediately subordinate layout object terminates.

REPETITION (composite layout objects)

Within a path expression a repetition of actions might be defined. This repetition will be expressed by an attribute *Repetition*. This attribute will be applicable only to composite layout objects; basic layout objects will thus be kept simple and usable as subordinate layout objects for different composite objects. The attribute specifies a factor ('0' or a positive integer) of how often the current layout object will be presented by the imaging process before the immediately following layout object is processed. The default value is '1'. A repetition of '0' means no presentation of the current layout object.

START FIRST (composite layout objects)

An atomic or composed action starts at some startpoint. The startpoints might not only be related to other actions, but also to time constraints or user interactions. This will be expressed by an attribute called *Start First*.

This attribute defines the start of the composite layout object for the presentation in relation to time constraints or user interaction. The attribute consists of two parameters: 'delay-type' and 'delay-value'. The first parameter specifies, if the start of the current object is regulated by time constraints (value 'time') or user interaction (value 'user').

If the first parameter is 'time', then the second parameter specifies the delay in Basic Time Units until the start of the immediately subordinate object(s). If the first parameter is 'user', then the start of the object is user defined. This means, starting of the immediately subordinate object(s) is done on user demand. The second parameter then specifies the location in space of the user interaction (i.e. an icon or button). If '0' is specified, the location of the current object is used.

Start First has different effects depending on the attribute Object Synchronization Type: If the Object Synchronization Type of a composed layout object is *parallel-last* or *parallel-first*, then the start of all immediately subordinate objects will be delayed by the specified time or by user interaction; if it is *sequential*, then the start of the first immediately subordinate object in sequence will be delayed by the specified time or by user interaction or if it is *selective*, then the start of the selected immediately subordinate object will be delayed by the specified time or by user interaction.

The default value of the first parameter is 'time' and of the second parameter '0'. This means, that the immediately subordinate layout object(s) start(s) without any delay.

START FOLLOWING (basic and composite layout objects)

If a sequence of atomic or composed actions is specified, not only the first layout object in the sequence is related to time constraints or user interactions (attribute Start First) but also the immediately following object(s). These relations will be expressed by an attribute called *Start Following*.

This attribute regulates the termination of a current layout object and/or the start of an immediately following layout object in sequence (next layout object immediately subordinate to the current superior layout object) based on time constraints or user interaction. If the current layout object is the last layout object of this sequence this attribute imposes the endpoint of the immediately superior layout object.

This attribute is *only* interpreted, if the immediately superior object contains the value *sequential* for the attribute *Object Synchronization Type*. All other values of the attribute Object Synchronization Type do not impose a sequence, that means no following layout objects have to be regulated.

The attribute consists of three parameters: 'delay-type', 'delay-specification' and 'delay-value'.

The first parameter specifies that the termination of the current object and the start of the immediately following object is regulated by time constraints (value 'time') or user interaction (value 'user').

The second parameter specifies the termination of the current object and/or the start of the immediately following object (value 'stop', 'go' or 'end'). The values 'stop' and 'go' impose offsets from the *start* of the current object to the start of the following object; 'stop' stops the presentation of the object, as soon as the following object starts, 'go' continues the presentation of the object when the following object starts. The value 'end' imposes an offset from the *end* of the current object to the start of the following object.

The third parameter specifies a time interval in Basic Time Units (first parameter 'time') or a location in space (first parameter 'user') of the user interaction (i.e. an icon or button). If '0' is specified, the location of the current object is used.

The default value of the first parameter is 'time', that of the second parameter is 'end' and of the third parameter '0'. This means, that the immediately following object(s) start(s) without any delay after the termination of the current object (corresponds to the sequential order). (Note that the endpoint of a static basic layout object with the duration '0' is not evaluated, and the next layout object is presented immediately even if the preceding object is still presented (it is terminated by some other instance). This guarantees compatibility with the current version of ODA.)

4.3 ODA Processes

EDITING PROCESS

The editing process is concerned with creating a new document or modifying a previous one. Within the proposed ODA extensions the logical structure keeps its original meaning. Content type specific editing has to be integrated.

LAYOUT PROCESS

The layout process is concerned with defining the layout for the document content. Thereby the logical structure is traversed and the layout structure is generated automatically using the layout directives. If the newly proposed attributes are also used for the layout directives, then the rules for the generation of the layout structure have to be expanded.

IMAGING PROCESS

The imaging process is concerned with presenting an image of the document in a form perceptible to a human being. In the current version of ODA the presentation is time-invariant; the layout structure of the ODA document can be processed by the imaging process in a determined sequence. The presentation of time-variant documents imposes new requirements for the imaging process. Before the presentation starts, the layout structure has to be evaluated and the temporal relationships have to be extracted. A presentation order has to be set up, which is controlled during the presentation by the imaging process. The presentation order is defined by the attributes described in Section 4.1; it is a complex system of real-time conditions such as startpoint and endpoint control of actions, user interactions, timer control, and last but not least the presentation of the contents itself.

5 Example of a Path Expression Related to ODA Attributes

Presenting a Multimedia Object involves the following actions: Show a movie, consisting of a moving picture part (M) and a lip-synchronized audio sequence (A) presented simultaneously. Afterwards start a picture sequence of 3 pictures (P1, P2, P3). The pictures turn automatically every 30 seconds (T30). With the first picture a button B is shown. If the button is pushed (B') a voice comment (V) is started. The termination of the voice comment instead of the termination of T30 then starts the next picture P2.

PATH EXPRESSION:

path X1 = (A $\wedge$ M) end
path X2 = (P2 $\wedge$ T30) ; P3 end
path X1 ; P1 $\wedge$ B $\wedge$ (T30 $\vee$ B') ; X2 | (V ; X2) end

EXPLANATION:

The timer actions T30 have to be integrated into the ODA attributes. A timer for static basic layout objects such as B and P2 is defined by setting the *Duration* of these objects to the corresponding value of 30 seconds (for simplification value 30 in the following descriptions). P1 will not be associated with a timer, because its duration is defined by the objects B or V, that means either the termination of B (if the button is not pushed) or the termination of V (if the button is pushed) ends the composite layout object and thus removes also P1.

A tree of composite and basic layout objects is constructed in Figure 2 based on the prefix notation of the path expressions. Timer actions and user interactions are not separately modelled as layout objects, because they are contained within the layout objects (specification within attributes). The basic layout objects (A, M, P1, B, V, P2, P3) are the leaves of the tree; they relate to the actions. The composite layout objects are modelled as the nodes of the tree and are specified by the Object Synchronization Type which relates to the path operators.

The nodes and leaves of the tree, that means the layout objects of the ODA document, are numbered for the association of attributes following in Table 1. The example describes only the proposed temporal attributes for the ODA document. For this reason only basic and composite layout objects are distinguished and no concrete association to blocks, frames and/or pages is made.

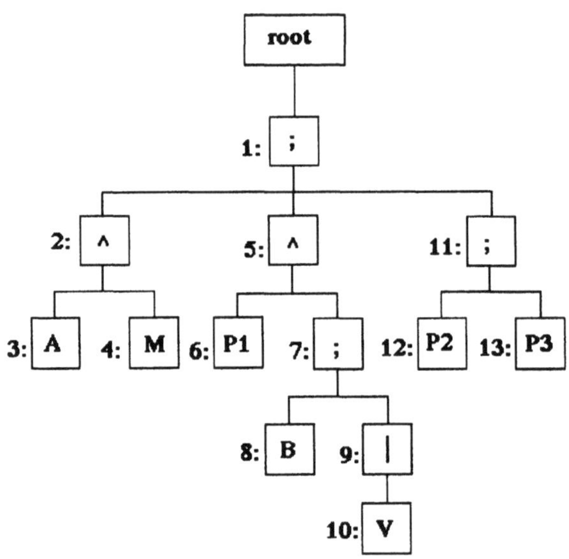

Figure 2 : Example - ODA Tree Structure

	ATTRIBUTES					
Node No.	Content Temporal Type	Duration	Repetitions	Object Synchronization Type	Start First	Start Following
1	-	-	1	sequential	time, 0	not used
2	-	-	1	parallel-last	time, 0	time, end, 0
3	dynamic	0	-	-	-	not used
4	dynamic	0	-	-	-	not used
5	-	-	1	parallel-last	time, 0	time, end, 0
6	static	0	-	-	-	not used
7	-	-	1	sequential	time, 0	not used
8	static	30	-	-	-	user, go, 0
9	-	-	1	selective	time, 0	time, end, 0
10	dynamic	0	-	-	-	not used
11	-	-	1	sequential	time, 0	time, end, 0
12	static	30	-	-	-	time, end, 0
13	static	0	-	-	-	time, stop, 30

Table 1 : Example - ODA Temporal Attributes

6 Conclusion

The abstract synchronization model presented provides a notation to describe the synchronization of actions for the presentation of Multimedia Objects. This model has been applied the Open Document Architecture (ODA) Standard [6] to enhance the current version of ODA with attributes specifying the temporal relationships of ODA objects for the presentation [18].

Also the model can be used as a basis to define a user interface for specifying the synchronization part of the presentation. Thereby the user should not be confronted with the usage of path expressions but with a tool for building them.

Acknowledgements

I would like to thank all colleagues in the BERMMD project "Multimedia Documents in Broadband ISDN" forming part of the BERKOM project for their constant availability for discussion.

References

[1] "Analyse relevanter Normen und Empfehlungen zur verteilten Bearbeitung multimedialer Informationen im ISDN-B", DETECON, Technisches Zentrum Berlin, Voltastr. 5, 1000 Berlin 65, Germany (May 1989), Version 2.0, BERKOM Dokumentation Band V (in German).

[2] RACE Project 1091, "Evaluation of Existing Communication Standards and Mapping on Requirement Analysis (upper layers)" (June 1990).

[3] G. Schürmann and U. Holzmann-Kaiser, "Distributed Multimedia Information Handling and Processing", *IEEE Network*, vol. 4, no. 6 (November 1990).

[4] "BERKOM Reference Model II – Application-Oriented Layers", DETECON, Technisches Zentrum Berlin, Voltastr.5, 1000 Berlin 65, Germany (March 1991), Version 3.2.

[5] ISO/TC97/SC21/WG7 N4883-4888, "Information processing systems – Open Systems Interconnection (OSI) – Open Distributed Processing (ODP)" (June 1990).

[6] ISO 8613, "Information Processing – Text and Office Systems – Office Document Architecture (ODA) and Interchange Format" (1989).

[7] ISO/IEC JTC1/SC21 N4888, "Working Document on Recommendation X.9yy: Basic Reference Model of Open Distributed Processing Part 2: Descriptive Model" (June 1990).

[8] ISO/IEC JTC1/SC21/WG7 N4886, "Working Document – Partial text of the Basic Reference Model of Open Distributed Processing", *Part I : Overview & Part IV : User Requirements* (August 1990).

[9] L. Lamport, "Time, Clocks, and the Ordering of Events in a Distributed System", *Communications of the ACM*, vol. 21, no. 7, pp. 558–565 (July 1978).

[10] J.F. Allen, "Maintaining Knowledge about Temporal Intervals", *Communications of the ACM*, vol. 26, no. 11, pp. 832–843 (November 1983).

[11] R.G. Herrtwich and G. Hommel, *Kooperation und Konkurrenz*, Springer-Verlag, Berlin (1989).

[12] T. Axford, *Concurrent Programming, Fundamental Techniques for Real-Time and Parallel Software Design*, Wiley, Chichester (1989).

[13] M. Ben-Ari, *Principles of Concurrent and Distributed Programming*, Prentice Hall International Ltd., Hemel Hempstead (1990).

[14] R.H. Campbell and A.N. Habermann, "The Specification of Process Synchronization by Path Expressions", *Lecture Notes in Computer Science No. 16, Operating Systems*, ed. G. Goos and J. Hartmanis, pp. 89–102, Springer-Verlag (1974).

[15] ISO 8613-1, "Information Processing – Text and Office Systems – Office Document Architecture (ODA) and Interchange Format", *Part 1: Introduction and General Principles* (1989).

[16] CCITT Draft Recommendation T.411, "Document Transfer, Access and Manipulation (DTAM) – Document Architecture (ODA) and Interchange Format – Introduction and General Principles".

[17] H. Gerloff, "Dokumentenarchitekturmodelle für Multimedia-Dokumente", ETH Zürich, Diplomarbeit (1988).

[18] P.Helbig et al., "Synchronizing the Presentation of Multimedia Objects", GMD-FOKUS, DETECON, Berlin, Germany (October 1990), Version 1.0.

Chapter 8

An Object-Oriented Framework for Multimedia Composition and Synchronisation

Simon Gibbs, Laurent Dami and Dennis Tsichritzis

Composition and synchronisation are discussed within an object-oriented framework for programming multimedia applications. The framework is based on a conceptual model of interconnectable multimedia components and can be used to construct complex multimedia applications involving audio, video and graphics.

1. Introduction

In specifying complex multimedia "objects," such as overlaid graphics and video, or an animation sequence accompanied by an audio track, two basic problems arise: *composition* – or how the object's parts are related to the whole; and *synchronisation* – or the nature of the temporal relationships and constraints which control the *presentation* of the object.

In this paper we discuss the treatment of composition and synchronisation within an object-oriented *framework* [1] for multimedia applications. The framework has been developed both to assist in the implementation of multimedia applications and to provide a conceptual model for their specification. At present there seems to be a tendency to develop such applications in an *ad hoc* one-of-a-kind fashion, and so, we believe, some form of unifying conceptual model is needed.

The object-oriented approach appears suitable for designing the framework for a number of reasons: First, objects can be used to encapsulate hardware devices and so provide a single interface for both software-based and hardware-based components. Second, object-oriented programming techniques, such as specialisation, can be used to extend the framework. Third, organising the components and connections of complex multimedia objects becomes a form of programming within an object-oriented language. Such programs then provide unambiguous, executable, representations of complex multimedia objects. Finally, the components and connections within complex multimedia objects can be specified using high-level description techniques [2][5], in which case their specification by non-programmers becomes feasible.

2. Multimedia Objects

The object-oriented framework has been described elsewhere [3], so here we provide just a summary. The framework is based on *active objects* [6], which, like ordinary or *passive* objects, have state (instance variables) and behavior (methods). In addition, an active object may perform actions even when no messages are sent to the object. A *multimedia object* is an active object with a number of *ports* through which multimedia data flows. We can divide multimedia objects into three categories: *sources*, *sinks*, and *filters*. It is convenient to use a graphical notation for multimedia objects and represent them by circles (see Figure 1) with attached boxes for their ports (extruding for output ports and intruding for input ports).

Figure 1 Multimedia Objects.

The framework includes a hierarchy (or, more correctly, a lattice) of multimedia classes, and a hierarchy of multimedia datatypes (such as video, audio, music and, used for animation, sceneDescription). Instantiating a multimedia class produces a multimedia object and its ports. Ports are typed, i.e., only data of a particular multimedia datatype may flow through the port. The types of an object's ports are specified by the object's class.

Multimedia objects may correspond to hardware devices (for example, a video disc player could be represented by a source object with a video port) or software processes (for example, a graphics renderer could be represented by a filter which obtains scene descriptions from its input port and produces raster images on its output port).

All multimedia objects inherit from the classes MultimediaObject and ActiveObject, and so support the methods of these classes. A partial specification of these classes, written in C++, is:

```
class ActiveObject {
public:
    bool                    Start();
    bool                    Stop();
    bool                    Pause();
    bool                    Resume();
};

class MultimediaObject {
protected:
    objectTime      now;        // current value of object time
public:
    //
    // temporal coordinates
    //
    objectTime                   CurrentObjectTime();
    objectTime                   WorldToObject(worldTime);
    worldTime                    CurrentWorldTime();
    worldTime                    ObjectToWorld(objectTime);
    objectInterval               WorldToObjectI(worldInterval);
    worldInterval                ObjectToWorldI(objectInterval);
    //
    // composition
    //
    void                         Translate(worldTime);
    void                         Scale(float);
    void                         Invert();
    CompositeMultimediaObject*   Parent();
    //
    // synchronisation
    //
    void                         Sync(worldTime);
    worldInterval                SyncInterval();
    worldInterval                SyncTolerance();
    syncMode                     SyncMode();
```

```
        void                    Cue(worldTime);
        void                    Jump(worldTime);
};
```

The methods of ActiveObject provide basic activity control for a multimedia object. For a software-based object, these methods manipulate a process associated with the object. For a hardware-based object, these methods issue commands directly to the hardware.

The methods of MultimediaObject can be divided into three groups, those dealing with temporal coordinates, with composition, and with synchronisation. The last two groups will be dealt with in the sections on composite multimedia and multimedia synchronisation. Here we briefly describe the first group.

In constructing complex multimedia objects, two temporal coordinates are used: *object coordinates*, which vary from object to object and are measured in units convenient to the object, and *world coordinates* which are shared by all objects and measured in conventional time units (in the current implementation, world coordinates are single precision floating point values corresponding to seconds). Each multimedia object maintains its current position in object time (also called *local time*) and can convert between its local coordinates and world coordinates (e.g., ObjectToWorld converts an objectTime value to worldTime).

3. Composite Multimedia

In analogy to how complex graphics objects are composed by specifying geometric transformations applied to their constituents, complex multimedia objects are obtained through the use of temporal transformations; we call this *temporal composition*. The motivation for temporal composition comes from situations where a number of multimedia components are simultaneously presented. Television and films are two obvious examples, each containing both audible and visual components.

As an example, suppose we want to construct a multimedia composite, c_1, which consists of a video background and an overlayed animation sequence. The video, produced by a video object, $video_1$, starts at time t_0. At time t_1, the animation $anim_1$ begins and is completed at time t_2. Finally, at time t_3 $video_1$ is stopped.

Both $video_1$ and $anim_1$ are source objects – $video_1$ produces video on its output port and $anim_1$ produces a sequence of raster images. If we present the composite via a single video value then three additional objects are needed: videoOut, a video sink (e.g., a video monitor); $fbuf_1$, a framebuffer for converting raster values to video; and $ovrl_1$, a device which overlays one video signal with another.

The temporal relationships of a composite object are depicted with a *composite timeline diagram*. Such a diagram contains one timeline for each output port within the composite. The diagram for the composite c_1 is shown in Figure 2.

Components are placed within a composite by applying *temporal transformations*. In general a temporal transformation is a function from one time frame to another. The class MultimediaObject provides three temporal transformations: Translate, Scale and Invert; others can be implemented by the programmer.

In constructing a composite timeline, the Translate transformation is used to adjust the positioning of the components; Scale and Invert may also be applied to alter presentation timing. In general, each component's "placement" within the composite is specified by its translation offset, scale and orientation. For instance, the $anim_1$ component of composite c_1 in Figure 2 has been translated t_1 units of world time.

The timeline representation shows the concurrency within a composite due to the superimposition of a number of multimedia *channels* (each horizontal bar in the timeline diagram), it

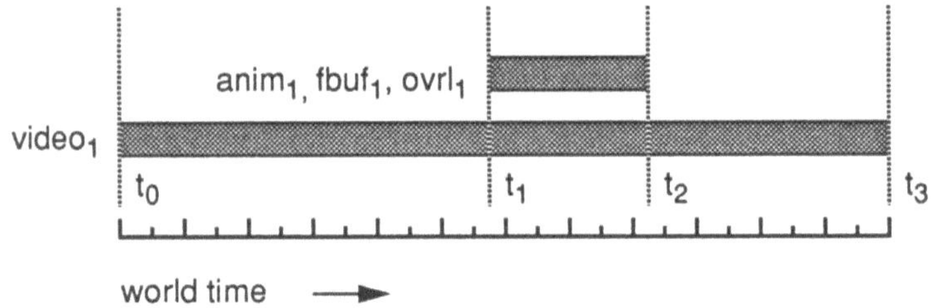

Figure 2 A Composite Timeline.

also identifies *transition points*, i.e., times where sources start or stop. For composite c_1, there are two channels and four transition points: t_0, t_1, t_2 and t_3.

Transition points divide world time into a number of intervals. A composite must specify, for each such interval, the connections between input and output ports of its components. This information can be depicted with a *component network*, where nodes correspond to components of a multimedia composite and edges to port connections. The component network for c_1 during the interval $[t_1, t_2]$ is shown in Figure 3.

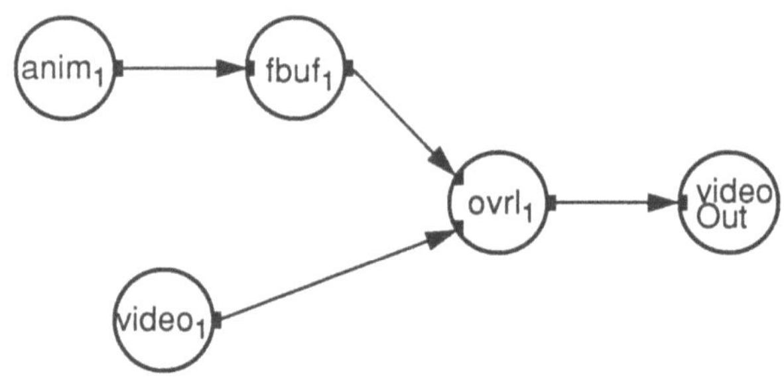

Figure 3 A Component Network (for the interval $[t_1,t_2]$ of Figure 2).

Within the framework, both ports and connections between ports are represented by objects. Partial specifications for the classes Port and Connector are:

```
class Port {
public:
        DataType        DataType();
        bool            IsConnected();
        Port            ConnectedTo();
        int             QueueSize();
        int             NumQueued();
        int             Read(void*, int);
        int             Write(void*, int);
};

class Connector {
public:
        Port            From();
        Port            To();
```

```
        void            Attach();
        void            Detach();
        int             QueueSize(Port);
        int             NumQueued(Port);
        int             Read(Port, void*, int);
        int             Write(Port, void*, int);
};
```

Methods are provided for querying the state of a port or connector and for connecting two ports via a connector. The methods QueueSize, NumQueued, Read and Write are used by multimedia objects to pass data over a pair of connected ports. The Connector class has a number of subclasses which provide different implementations for these methods. Current subclasses are: BufferedConnector, CableConnector, DelegateConnector, and SharedConnector. For example, if two multimedia objects communicate via shared memory then an instance of SharedConnector must be used to link their ports.

All composites are instances of the class CompositeMultimediaObject (or one of its subclasses). A partial specification for this class is:

```
class CompositeMultimediaObject : public MultimediaObject {
public:
        //
        // composition
        //
        errCode         AddComponent(MultimediaObject, TemporalTransform);
        errCode         AddConnection(Port, Port, TransitionPoint, TransitionPoint);
        bool            IsTopLevel();
        //
        // synchronisation
        //
        void            OutOfSync(MultimediaObject, worldInterval);
        void            SlaveTo(MultimediaObject);
};
```

The first two methods allow components to be placed in the composite, the third is used to determine whether a composite is the top-level object in a composite/component hierarchy. The remaining methods will be discussed in the next section.

4. Multimedia Synchronisation

During presentation, composites are involved with a collection of tasks. These include:

- starting or stopping components at appropriate times,
- establishing or removing connections between components at transition points,
- maintaining the information needed to perform temporal transformations,
- ensuring global synchronisation between *activated* components (activated components are those which have been sent a Start message without an ensuing Stop).

The first two tasks are traditional scheduling problems, and therefore will not be studied further here. We shall concentrate on the two latter tasks with particular attention to the interplay between temporal transformations and synchronisation.

Synchronisation is based on a *continuous time model.* In this model, each multimedia component progresses along a local time line ("object time") during presentation. It can tell its current time position using methods CurrentObjectTime and CurrentWorldTime, and it can be asked to move to another location on a time line by using methods Cue and Jump – Cue is intended for initial positioning of an object prior to activation, while Jump is intended for activated objects. The jumps in time can be dynamically determined by the needs of the presentation: for instance, if the top-level composite object realises that synchronisation is being lost, it may decide that the next jump in time will be bigger, so that synchrony will be recovered.

The framework provides a precise definition of synchronisation. In particular, we say that a composite object c is *synchronised*, iff for all activated components, c_i:

$$\text{Abs(c.CurrentWorldTime() - } c_i\text{.CurrentWorldTime())} < \Delta_i$$

where Δ_i is the *synchronisation tolerance* allowed by component c_i.

In general a composite is responsible for maintaining synchronisation of its components. Since composites may themselves become components of higher-level composites, the overall responsibility for synchronisation belongs to the top-level composite. Ultimately, however, each composite must maintain synchronisation of its own components.

Because components are reused within composites, synchronisation cannot be hardwired into the components. Components are built independently; then they are composed and modified via temporal transformations. Consequently, only the composite knows about global synchronisation requirements. However, because of the varying nature of components (i.e., hardware-based and software-based), composites must be flexible and support a variety of synchronisation techniques. In the framework, each component has a *synchronisation mode* attribute. Depending on the value of this attribute, which can be queried by the method SyncMode, the composite adopts different approaches to synchronisation. Presently there are four synchronisation modes: NO_SYNC, DEMAND_SYNC, TEST_SYNC, and INTERRUPT_SYNC. The actions a composite takes for a component of each mode can be summarised as follows:

NO_SYNC: the composite ignores the component as far as synchronisation is concerned.

DEMAND_SYNC: the composite initially queries the component's SyncInterval which returns a world time value. When the component is activated, the composite periodically invokes the component's Sync method passing the component the composite's value of current world time.

TEST_SYNC: the composite initially queries the component's SyncInterval and SyncTolerance methods. When the component is activated, the composite periodically queries the component's CurrentWorldTime method and issues a Jump if the component is out of sync.

INTERRUPT_SYNC: the component takes it upon itself to periodically "interrupt" the composite by querying its CurrentWorldTime method. If the component is out of sync with the composite it must take some action. Typically this involves issuing a Jump and/or calling the composite's OutOfSync method.

Cue and Jump requests are handled differently by different objects. For example a 30 frame/second video disc player would round requests to multiples of 1/30 of a second, and a real-time recorder would ignore requests to go backwards in time. This is relatively straightforward for hardware-based components, but composite and software-based components deserve a more detailed study.

Composite objects handle Jump and Cue requests by forwarding the request to their subcomponents. For a composite c with components $(c_1 \ldots c_n)$, the implementation of Jump(worldTime t) is:

```
foreach ci in (c1... cn)
    if ci is activated
        ci.Jump(t)
```

The implementation of Cue(worldTime t) is simply:

```
foreach ci in (c1... cn)
    ci.Cue(t)
```

For software-based components, i.e., components that are based on processes, the concept of a local time line is problematic. Associating temporal progress to the number of instructions executed would not make much sense, because the execution time depends on external factors like the load of the processor, the number of other processes, or the process scheduling policy. Therefore we choose an approach where the programmer explicitly declares progress along its local time line. Moreover, process instructions can be parameterised by local time, so that the process adapts its progress to the synchronisation requirements of the presentation in which it participates [2].

To illustrate this adaptation, and the interaction of temporal transforms with synchronisation, we will look at a composite object in some detail. Consider an interactive animation where various processes and input devices generate an animated scene on the screen and an accompanying audio track. Our requirements are:

1. to be able to temporally transform the composite during presentation (e.g., run the animation at various speeds, or backwards, or cue and start at various points),
2. for the animation to remain in synchronisation with the accompanying audio,
3. to provide graceful degradation as animation processing requirements increase. (For animation to appear visually continuous, a certain frame update rate, e.g., about 8 frames per second, is needed; however as animation complexity increases, or available processing resources decrease, it may no longer be possible to update frames at this rate. We would like the frame rate to be dynamically reduced, in order to maintain audio synchronisation, when the composite detects the components involved with animation dropping out of sync.)

Using the multimedia framework, real-time animation with audio accompaniment can be performed by an instance of the CompositeAnimator class. Such objects contain an "animation pipeline" (and possibly other objects) as shown in Figure 4. This particular composite, c, consists of objects belonging to seven classes. Brief descriptions of these classes are:

Animator (output port: animEvent)
: Animator objects generate a sequence of animator events.

Model (input port: animEvent, output port: sceneDescription)
: A Model object collects animator events and produces a sequence of scene descriptions.

Render (input port: sceneDescription, output port: image)
: A Render object graphically renders a sequence of scene descriptions producing a sequence of images.

FrameBuffer (input port: image; output port: video)
: A FrameBuffer object converts an image into a video signal.

Monitor (input port: video)
: A Monitor object displays a video signal.

AudioFileRead (output port: Audio)
: Produces an Audio value by reading samples stored in a file.

AudioOut (input port: Audio)
: Writes values from its input port to an audio output device (e.g., a digital to analog converter).

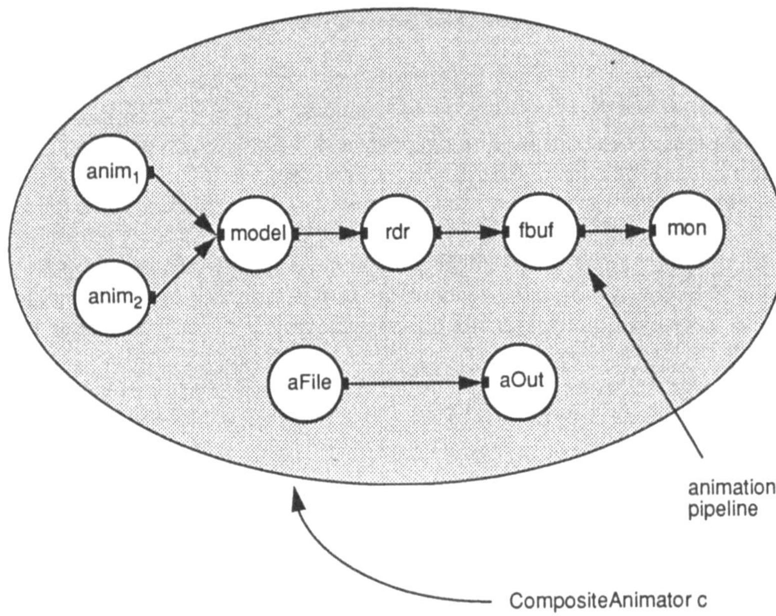

Figure 4 Real-time Animation with a Multimedia Composite Object.

Each Animator object is "attached" to a graphical object (graphical objects consist of geometry and shading information); once activated, an animator generates "animator events," such as movement or change in shape, for its graphical object. Graphical objects are arranged in a hierarchy maintained by a Model object (not every graphical object in a model, however, need be attached to an animator).

The operation of CompositeAnimator relies on the observation that the synchronisation frequency need not be higher than the frame update rate. CompositeAnimator has a method called FramePeriod which returns a world time value indicating the current interval between frames. We now look at how the frame period is used by components in the animation pipeline.

FrameBuffer and Monitor objects are hardware-based and have NO_SYNC as their synchronisation mode. Model basically copies information from its input ports to its output port, because it is a simple component it also uses NO_SYNC. The Animator and Render objects are more interesting. Both are software-based (and so contain an internal process initiated by an invocation of the Process method which belongs to the class of all software-based active objects). Animator uses DEMAND_SYNC, its Sync method operates as follows:

```
void Animator::Sync(worldTime w)
{
    now = this->WorldToObject(w);
    this->Resume();
}
```

The Resume method awakens the animator object which is typically paused in its Process method:

```
void Animator::Process()
{
```

```
        CompositeAnimator*          p = this->Parent();
        objectInterval              fperiod;

        while(TRUE) {
              this->Sample(now);
              fperiod = this->WorldToObjectI(p->FramePeriod());
              now += fperiod;             // update object time
              this->Pause();              // wait for next Sync
        }
}
```

Sample generates a stream of animator events. For instance, the following could be used to move a graphical object along some trajectory:

```
void Animator::Sample(objectTime t)
{
      // calculate new position and tell associated
      // graphic object to move to the position
      // this generates an animator event
}
```

This code shows that the subdivision of the trajectory into a sequence of discrete moves is not hardwired in the animator, but is generated by the Sample method which is, in turn, triggered by the Sync messages received during presentation. Furthermore, since the animator uses object time in calculating positions, the animation will behave correctly under temporal transformations.

Render uses INTERRUPT_SYNC, i.e, a Render object's process must periodically query the composite and synchronise the object. The Process method for Render is of the form:

```
void Render::Process()
{
      CompositeAnimator*          p = this->Parent();
      objectInterval              fperiod;
      worldInterval               delta;

      while(TRUE) {
            this->Sample(now);        // renders scene description on input port
            fperiod = this->WorldToObjectI(p->FramePeriod());
            now += fperiod;
            delta = p->CurrentWorldTime() - this->CurrentWorldTime();
            if(Abs(delta) > this->SyncTolerance()) {
                  p->OutOfSync(this, delta);
                  this->Jump(p->CurentWorldTime());
      }
}
```

By invoking OutOfSync a Render object causes the frame rate to be reduced. Doing so will not change the world time needed to perform the animation, but will affect the number of frames displayed in that interval, thus providing graceful degradation as animation complexity increases.

We have not discussed how CompositeAnimator handles the audio components. Both AudioFileRead and AudioOut use INTERRUPT_SYNC. On receiving a Jump, an AudioFileRead object skips data in the file it is reading while an AudioOut object flushes data from its buffers (both these actions may result in an audible click).

Finally, one problem we have overlooked is how a top-level composite determines its own position in time. By default, CurrentWorldTime for a top-level composite uses a real-time clock.

However, by invoking SlaveTo a composite can be told to obtain its current world time from that of another object. Thus the CompositeAnimator, c, of Figure 4 supports the following alternatives:

1. sync both animation and audio to real-time (the default),
2. sync animation to the audio (by invoking, for example, c.SlaveTo(aOut)),
3. sync audio to the animation (by invoking, for example, c.SlaveTo(rdr)).

The first case will keep both animation and audio in pace with real-time, however the animation may appear jerky and audio may be skipped if processing capacity is insufficient. In the second case the complete audio track is played but insufficient processing capacity will result in pauses. In the third case the animation may not occur in real time and the audio will sound jerky with possible repetition.

5. Test Application

We intend to apply our framework to a specific domain which relies on the integration of interactive 3d graphics with video. Our chosen application is "virtual museums," that is, the audio-visual rendering of artifacts in virtual settings [4]. The active aspect of the objects allows the virtual museum to be dynamic and provides user or group interaction. Our system configuration for a virtual museum prototype is shown in Figure 5, here the rectangles indicate separate pieces of equipment. At present we are using a NeXT as the main development platform (the "envi-

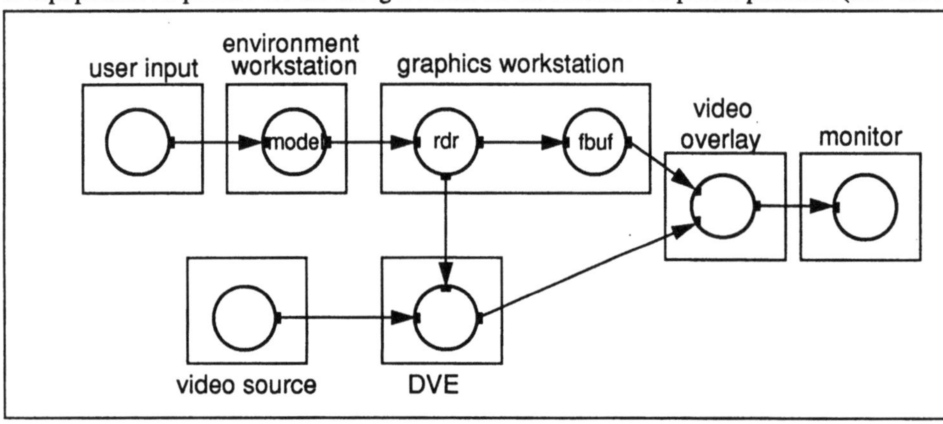

Figure 5 Configuration for Virtual Museum Prototype..

ronment workstation") and a Silicon Graphics GTX for 3d rendering. User input is provided by a 6-degree of freedom trackball, the video source is a Sony LDP-3600D video disc player. The DVE (used here to warp a video signal of a museum artifact prior to placement in the rendered 3d scene) has not yet been obtained but we plan to use a Sony DME-5000, an Abekas A53-D, or possibly Intel's ActionMedia DVI board. Finally, video overlaying is performed by a RGB/View 2000.

6. Conclusion

Two basic problems in constructing complex multimedia objects are composition and synchronisation. We have shown how these may be treated within an object-oriented framework for multimedia programming. It is too early to evaluate the framework, but we believe that object-orientation can be used to design groups of inter-connectable multimedia components.

References

1. Deutsch, L.P.: Design reuse and frameworks in the Smalltalk-80 system. In T.J. Biggerstaff, A.J. Perlis (eds.): Software Reusability, Vol. II, ACM Press, 1989, pp. 57-71
2. Fiume, E., Tsichritzis, D., Dami, L.: A temporal scripting language for object-oriented animation. Proc. Eurographics'87, Amsterdam, Aug. 1987, pp. 283-294
3. Gibbs, S.: Composite multimedia and active objects. Proc. OOPSLA'91, Phoenix, Arizona, Oct. 1991 (in press)
4. Tsichritzis, D., Gibbs, S.: Virtual museums and virtual realities. Proc. of the International Conf. on Hypermedia and Interactivity in Museums, Pittsburgh, PA, Oct. 1991 (in press)
5. Tsichritzis, D., Gibbs, S., Dami, L.: Active media. In D. Tsichritzis (ed.): Object Composition, Centre Universitaire d'Informatique, University of Geneva, 1991, pp. 115-132
6. Wegner, P.: Concepts and paradigms of object-oriented programming. OOPS Messenger *1* (1), 7-87 (1990).

Chapter 9

ASE – Audio and Synchronization Extension of Compound Documents[1]

Matthias Kummer and Walter Kuhn

Abstract

This paper describes extensions of CDA/DDIF by audio and synchronization information. Audio information can be split into analog audio primitives (like LPs or tapes), digital audio primitives (sampled sound, like that on CD or DAT), and music primitives. Music data are described by two different content types: the logical content and the layout (visual and gestural) content. The logical content describes audio/music events by means of basic events like notes, rests, chords, or user-defined events, which allows for describing not only western tonal music but also a wide variety of musical forms like Hindu or African music. To this logical content the layout (score and/or the dynamic interpretation) can be related. For the layout, more hardware-oriented encodings like MIDI (Musical Instrument Digital Interface) and more revisable symbolic notations are provided. The synchronization aspects, imported with the audio extensions into the compound document format, have been generalized to be applicable to the other document domains. Three different forms can be used: trigger-point, continuous, and related synchronization. Trigger-point synchronization aligns events (like the start of a music output or the display of a picture) at certain points in time. Continuous or relative synchronization allows duration times to be adjusted (e.g., display some image as long as some sound is heard), while related synchronization couples the start times of specific events with termination times of other events.

1 Introduction

Based on the international standard IS8613 ODA (Office Document Architecture), DEC (Digital Equipment Corporation) developed its own "Compound Document Architecture" (CDA) environment, where DDIF (Digital's Document Interchange Format) is the exchange format for documents in revisable form (DEC 1989, DEC 1990a,b, Blake 1990). As an extension of ODA (ISO 1987), it supports text, graphics, images, and spreadsheets. Although there exist a lot of computer applications and implementations for music manipulation (notation programs, sequencer programs, bankloaders, librarians, or editor programs for synthesizers) on PCs and home computers, mainly for controlling and synchronizing synthesizers. But there is no general solution for integrating acoustic information into compound documents. Since existing CDA domains are not sufficient for that purpose - a presentation of music as text, graphics, or images do not allow to modify it due to its intrinsic laws, (which also accounts to pure acoustic encoding) they can neither be used in a satisfying way to rep-

[1] This project has been funded by Digital's European External Research Project 377/AU-016.

resent music and sound information, nor in synchronizing them with other information like video or graphics.

Documents that contain dynamic multimedia information have to deal with an additional factor not present in simpler cases: the *time*.

A (CDA) multimedia document can be regarded as a 4-dimensional structure:

$$(x,y,n,t)$$

x,y	... x,y coordinates,
n	... number of pages (or other presentation units), and
t	... the time.

With the introduction of time in (multimedia) documents there is a necessity of specifying the temporal relationships between events - that means the events have to be synchronized with each other.

2 Current State of CDA/DDIF

2.1 The CDA Architecture Model

The CDA architecture model identifies a four-stage applications pipeline which culminates in the display or printing of a document (see Fig. 2-1).

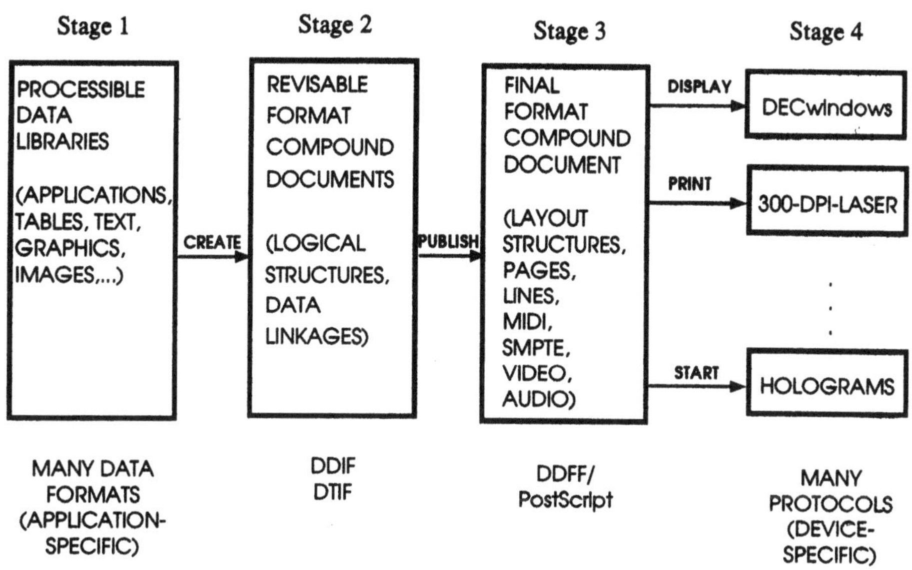

Fig. 2-1 Compound Document Processing Model

The first stage encompasses applications that are the source of information (e.g., tables or sound patches) for inclusion into documents. The second stage is a revisable compound document, where content is added and manipulated. This stage is dominated by logical structure and data cross-linkages. In the third stage, a final compound document results from applying formatting rules and layout characteristics to a revisable compound document. The fourth stage is the transformation of a final document into device-specific language for display or printing.

The processing steps and data formats of the first stage are diverse and very domain specific, since they are determined by the needs of many different processing environments. The first stage is important to the CDA model because it is the foundation for the LiveLink between the stage one and stage two functions. (LiveLink is a DEC product to support live links. A live link is a powerful mechanism which allows an user to access and manage external information from within one application. It ensures that the link-to information is up-to-date and allows the sharing of information in an automatic and orderly fashion.)

Data interchange can take place in all four stages, but the CDA architecture primarily focuses on the second one. Revisable compound documents, their processing and interchange, are at the heart of the CDA architecture.

The revisable form of a document contains abstract relationships between components of the document. Because these relationships are abstract (logical) rather than concrete (representational), any aspect of the document that the user has stated or implied to the creating application(s) can be changed, updated, or recalculated more easily than in final form documents. Applications that involve processing and data interchange are more easily developed and operate more efficiently by dealing with revisable rather than final form document data.

The revisable form for spreadsheet and data tables is specified by the DTIF table interchange format. The revisable form for structured text, graphics, and image is specified by the DDIF. Both DTIF and DDIF provide for the inclusion of related or underlying data in other formats. The CDA Toolkit implements a data interchange hub using these two interchange formats. The toolkit also provides general processing access to in-memory representations of the data.

The final form of a document represents the abstract document component relationships as resolved display attributes. These attributes include for example text fonts, character positions, positioned and sized graphics frames, and final page layout. Final form is produced from revisable form by a formatting process. A final form document is specifically formatted for a particular class of display. The final form for compound documents in the CDA architecture is the DDFF format; the current version of this is based on PostScript.

2.2 DDIF Architecture

Each DDIF encoded document consists of three variable-length elements: the document descriptor, the document header, and the document content (see Fig. 2-2).

The descriptor contains information about the revision level of the data syntax and the name of the application that created the document.

The document header contains global document specific information such as time and date of creation and a list of authors.

The document content generally contains the largest quantity of data, and describes the part of the document that is displayed, printed, and edited. The content of a document is organized in DDIF as a hierarchy of bounded document content portions, called segments. Each DDIF segment may be text, graphics, image, and/or nested segments. (Segment nesting is the main structuring feature of DDIF.) Additionally, a segment's content may be computed by a standard or application-defined function. Each segment represents document content that is distinguished from its surrounding content by a difference in its presentation and processing. Attributes not declared for a given segment are generally inherited from the segment that encompasses that segment. The values of attributes bound to a segment override the value of the same attribute bound to an outer-level segment. The physical occurrence of a segment within a document is significant for its appearance. That means, if segment A is occurring before segment B in a document then segment A also appears before segment B for example on a certain display. Thus a CDA document (using current DDIF) uses a sequential synchronization by default. No parallel synchronization is possible.

Descriptor: Data syntax version, application identification **Header:** Authors, revision dates, ... language references, external references, ... **Content:** Content primitives arranged to form segments containing text, graphics, images, nested segments. Segment attributes control appearance and processing. Segments can refer to external applications and data.

Fig. 2-2 Top-level Structure of a DDIF Document

3 Proposed Extensions

To be a multimedia document interchange and storage format some extensions have to be made. First of all there is a need of audio extensions. But with the extension of audio content there is an implicit need to synchronize events with each other.

3.1 Music Extension

As already mentioned the current DDIF supports text, graphics, images, and spreadsheets but no audio information. There are activities within DEC to support audio information but that proposal (Morris 1990) supports only to store digitized audio (sampled and quantisized audio signals). Our approach (Kuhn et al. 1991) provides three types of audio information (see Fig. 3-1):

3.1.1 Digital Audio Primitive

Specifies a time sampled and amplitude quantisized representation of an analog signal. A primitive is represented by its duration (relative offset to start of recording), a set of attributes (sample rate, channel indicator, compression type, bit and byte order) and the quantisized data itself (CD, DAT).

3.1.2 Analog Audio Primitive

Specifies any (analog) recordings (LPs, tapes) which can be related to a particular duration. Attributes specify the medium, the recording speed, and other still to be defined attributes.

Note that these kinds of audio primitives are of final resp. formatted form rather than revisable.

3.1.3 Music Primitives

To describe music content in revisable form five primitives can be used: notes, rests, chords, graced events, and user-defined events.

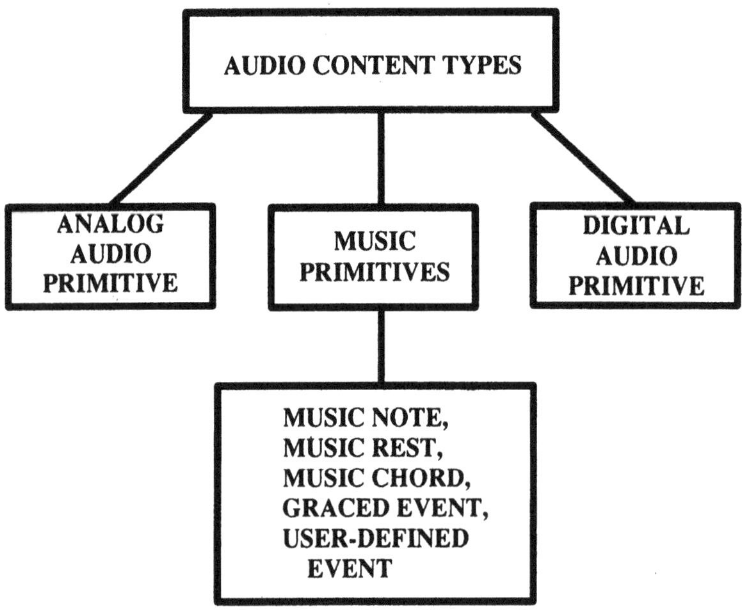

Fig. 3-1 Audio Content Types and Music Primitives

Music note specifies a single sounding musical event by its virtual duration (in music time) and its pitch.

Music rest specifies a single non-sounding musical event by its virtual duration.

Music chord specifies a single chord (some notes with same start and end time) by its virtual duration and its representation (either in terms of the harmonic spelling or explicitly specifying each note forming that chord). A chord in harmonic spelling can be specified using figured bass (or thoroughbass) notation - a reference pitch (the bass) and a set of intervals is used - or chord change notation - a reference pitch, a set of intervals, and an optional bass note is used, e.g. Cmin7.

Graced event specifies a compound event consisting of a main event and graced by a modifier which can either precede or follow the main event. The main event can be either a single music primitive or even a sequence of events. The virtual duration given for a graced event is only related to the main event that means the modifier will not consume time. An example of a graced event would be a mordent.

User-defined event specifies user defined information about timed events other than conventional musical occurrences. Its content will be application specific (a formula describes its content).

These five primitives specify the content of audio information, the pure logical information. But there is no specification of the layout that means for example, how a note has to be displayed or how a note has to be performed using MIDI (Anderton 1986, IMA 1983), or another performance language. To have a more efficient way to manage most audio information lookup tables are used. Thus in most specifications only references to such lookup table entries are used.

Lookup tables can be specified for

- *pitch gamuts* - relating a pitch name to a frequency,
- *tempo lists* - relating a tempo name to a tempo value (e.g., presto can be associated with a metronome marking of 180 beats per minute),
- *rate lists* - relating names of changes to an expression (e.g., linear change),
- *articulation lists* - relating articulation names to a value indicating how long the event is active in relation to its virtual duration (e.g., legato can be associated with a value of 100 percent, indicating that the event is active all the specified duration),
- *controller lists* - relating a controller number to a controller value (for MIDI data),
- *chord tables* - relating a chord name to its concrete representation,
- *added real time lists* - relating a name (like fermata) to a value specifying how long an event has to be extended,
- *stress pattern template lists* - specifying the rhythm,
- *stress pattern use lists* - relating a stress pattern to a tempo in a tempo map,
- *click track lists* - marking each beat in a musical piece; it provides a means for relating beats in the logical content to real time,
- *tempo map lists* - serves as a conductor track by specifying a list of time stamped tempo modifications which govern the tempo of any part of a musical piece which use it,
- *microtuning unit definitions* - specifying the smallest unit of pitch used to specify a detuning. In most cases cents are used, that means the interval between two adjacent pitches is divided into 100 subparts,
- *sound descriptor lists* - relating a sound name to sound patches,
- *sound intensity lists* - relating sound intensity names (like forte or piano) to corresponding values (e.g., decibel, or for MIDI, values in the range from 1 to 127),
- *pitch variation lists* - relating pitch variation names (like vibrato or portamento) to corresponding expressions,
- *instrument lists* - relating sound patches or sound numbers (for MIDI) to particular instrument names,
- *clef lists* - specifying the staff line position of a clef (e.g., treble clef or bass clef).

4 Synchronization Extension

The integration of audio/music information in CDA strongly enforces synchronization within the content as well as with other contents or domains, that means a temporal relationship between events or sequences of events has to be specified. To achieve this, three different kinds of synchronization can be identified.

Trigger-point synchronization: is the alignment of time-variable events at certain points on the time axis that means for example, an event or a sequence of events is starting at a predefined time stamp. Note that trigger-points may also be related to user actions (e.g. inputs like mouse clicks), which allows the human operator to interact with the presentation process and control synchronization by herself.

Continuous or relative-time synchronization: is the ability to adjust the length of an event to the duration of another one, that means, based on the start time and the end time for an event or a sequence of events, the actual duration is stretched or compressed to fit the range given by the start time and the end time.

Related synchronization: is the ability to relate the synchronization start of a segment to the end time of the previous segment(s) without explicitly specifying the start time. That means, the current segment starts when the previous one ends without knowing how long the previous one is active.

4.1 Synchronization Aspects

In current CDA processing model, the formatting and presentation stages are handled implicitly as one functional block. To support multimedia related functionality it is necessary to split them.

The used model applied the concept of *cue based synchronization*. In opposition to an event path definition based synchronization model, which presents an external view of time dependent and inter-related entities, the cue based synchronization model faces the problem from inside of a multimedia document. A cue based synchronization model uses terms and takes references to the virtual world of an application. Such a virtual world provides for the specification of document content, and for the specification of mutual relationships of content elements, within application specific (i.e. virtual) definition of space and time.

In such a model the role of a multimedia document formatter is to relate the virtual world of each multimedia document segment, considering specific constraints, to space and time of real world rather than to produce a code performing rendition of segment content on particular output device. Extending basic CDA idea of a common hub, an appropriate designed logical environment will connect all the plurality of client applications with available heterogeneity of physical rendering environments.

The key issue for a formatter is to detect existing logical, spatial, and temporal relations, and to construct inter-related strands of sequentially processed segments of content.

The role of the multimedia document presenter is to render formatted documents according to a socalled *'script'* produced by the formatter. Key issue for a presenter during the rendition process is to implement synchronization of formatted document content along specific strands.

In DDIF, segment attributes are inherited by nested segments. When dynamic documents are rendered, it may be helpful to override this form of inheritance by inheritance along the processing path.

4.2 Synchronization Model

Segments are the basic elements to be synchronized. To force the content of a segment to participate in the representation, it has to be associated with a socalled *'time stamp'*, a new kind of segment attributes. A time stamp specifies all synchronization information needed to present a segment: the conditions which cause begin or the termination, of the presentation, *'time frames'* to be considered, or specific presentation aspects (e.g. repetition or stretching). Another important concept of the model is the usage of individual time units. Consider, for example a document consisting of a video, an audio segment, and a set of subtitle segments. Dealing with the video, a time unit *'frames (per second)'* may be preferred, while the audio content may be handled in *'RTUs'* (real time units) and the subtitles possibly in seconds. Two aspects are to be distinguished there: the mapping of such *'logical'* time units to other, already defined (e.g. *'1 frame = 1/30 seconds'*) and relative to some other, which may not be known until the presentation takes place (e.g.: *'twice as fast as the current one'*). The latter shall be called *'virtual'* time. Since a segment may have a set of each of these characteristics associated with, segments attributes are extended as shown in Fig 4-1.

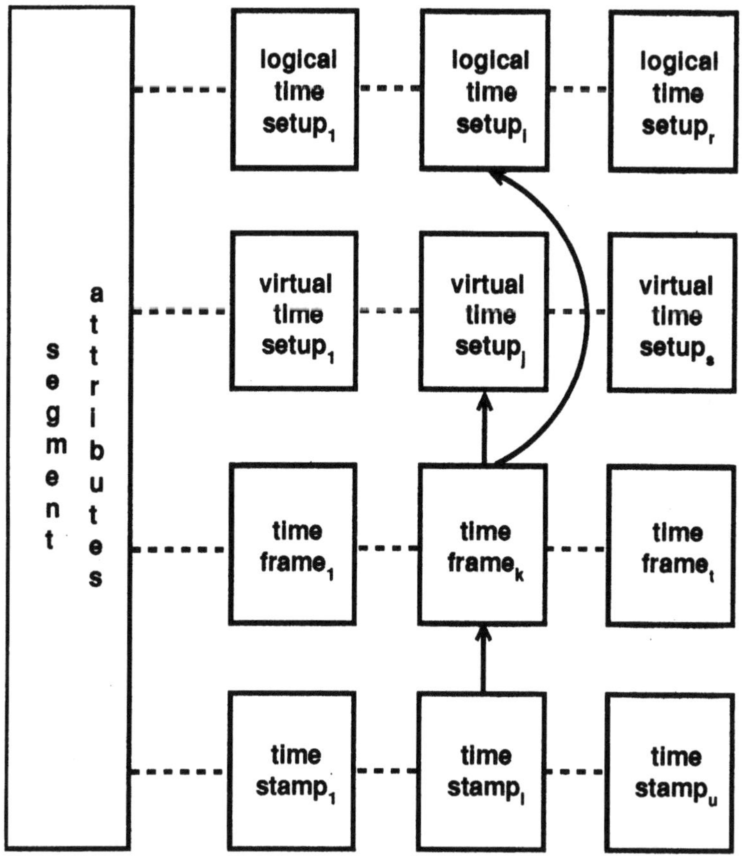

Fig. 4-1 Relation of Synchronization Attributes

Note that these attributes are propagated along segment hierarchies, so global definitions are possible. In the following, these attributes are described in some detail.

Logical time setup:

Provides a set of definitions which specify the logical time units which may be applied within the segment and nested segments.

In a time coding definition the *time base* specifies a value which is used to describe relation between logical and physical time, and the *time code* specifies the nature of physical time measurement (Dahlin 1970) used as a basis for the definition of logical time (e.g., SMPTE time code).

Virtual time setup:

Provides a set of virtual time coding definitions (the time defined in terms of application specific events rather than in units of physical time). The definition of virtual time is application dependent and should be specified in the semantics of an application. An example of such virtual time are the relationships between the scores used to define the melody and a rhythm of a music piece. This concept is similar to HyTime's concept of *baton (*ISO 1990d, Goldfarb et al. 1990, Newcomb 1990*).*

Time frames:

Especially, a time frame defines when the rendering of a presented segment is not suppressed. In analogy to spacial layout, only those parts of a presented segment are actually rendered, which fall into the time frame referenced by the time stamp specifying the segment's presentation, while parts *'outside'* (before or after) the time frame are *'clipped away'* resp. suppressed. In addition, time shields may be defined for a time frame which serve for additional suppression.

Time stamps:

Each occurrence of the segment content during the presentation process is the result of an explicit time stamp specification. An optional *frame reference* points to the definition of a time frame which shall be used to render the current segment. If omitted the segment content will be rendered within the time frame of the parent segment.

What has to be defined for a time stamp, is the condition under which the presentation of the corresponding segment shall commence. This is achieved by the definition of a *start-cue*. In addition, the conditions under which the presentation shall stop, may be defined by another cue, namely a *stop-cue*. (If no such stop-cue is given, the segment will be rendered until its natural end; for time dependent content, this means to render all its content, for time independent content - e.g. some still image - this means *'immediately'*.

The optional *content behaviour* specifies generic temporal features of the segment content rendition process: translation in time, repetition within specific time frame, and the relative direction of the time axis. Flags control if for particular semantic reasons segment content can be transformed in time, shall be repeated, or if it can be rendered in reverse order.

And finally, the (virtual) *time unit* may be selected to be used within the time stamp.

Cues:

The basic idea behind cues can be described as follows. A cue is a flag or a signal, associated with a condition which specifies the point in time when it shall be set. When it becomes set, it triggers all associated actions. Note that cues are always defined locally within time stamps or time frames, where they just trigger the action they are defined for. To reference them from somewhere else, cues may be named. A cue condition is essentially an expression over time. Examples are *'immediately'*, *'100 frames after cue X'*, *'jan 1, 1991, 0h GMT'*, *'cue Y or mouse click, whatever happens earlier'*.

Conceptually, a cue is represented as boolean variable, bound to a segment, initialized to FALSE and switching to TRUE at the moment defined by its condition. The switch is called cue event and triggers associated actions.

4.3 Synchronization Flow

As in current DDIF, where a document is built up of segments, this approach is a synchronization of segments. Each segment which has to be synchronized must be related to a time stamp or a sequence of time stamps, specifying the time(s) when that segment has to be 'active'. Here, active can be interpreted for example, as the start of an acoustic recording, or the start of a MIDI event, or the display of a particular video sequence. If no time stamps are given the segments are executed sequentially according to the current DDIF content streams philosophy where the ordering of the segments within a document is governing the processing. Sometimes it is necessary to adjust the length of a segment to the duration of another event. Thus a time slice has to be defined to fit that requirement. Within this paper we have to distinguish between two different types of time: the document time and the clock time or absolute time. The document time is related to the processing/rendering of a document, that means it is a relative time in opposition to the clock time. To synchronize primitives with each other, in worst case there is only one primitive in a segment.

The control flow is completely governed by the synchronization information specified within the segment attributes. Specifically, the interrelationships and dependencies among segments to be presented are described by the set of time stamps and cue expressions. These have to be resolved prior to presentation (by the formatting process), where inconsistencies (e.g. referenced, but undefined cues, time frames or time units or circular definitions) have to be identified. This formatting may result in some sort of script, which then controls the synchronization flow during presentation. Note that only those segments of a document are considered during presentation, which are either time stamped or nested in time stamped segments. Segments without dependent content have exactly the duration as defined in the time stamp by means of start and stop cues.

5 Sound Extension

Within a DDIF segment a font is related to a particular text by a font number which is associated with a font name (following the X-11 font naming convention). A similar approach is to describe sound patches which can be referenced within a document. Sound patches can be either sampled patches (sampled from anywhere), or patches produced by electronic instruments using different synthesis techniques (that directly generate sounds, or possibly process existing sounds). The most often used synthesis techniques are (Alles 1980, Gordon 1985, Moog 1986, Moorer 1977, Snell 1987):

Additive synthesis
This technique often serves as a standard against which other synthesis techniques are measured, because the highest quality sounds have traditionally been generated by this technique. The spectral components of sound look like the sine or cosine curves (sinusoids) of trigonometry. Ordinarily we don't hear the separate spectral components of a sound. However, it is possible to replicate a given sound to a high degree of accuracy by adding together the proper audio spectral components; hence the name additive synthesis. Sinusoids, also called partials, are the basis functions used in Fourier-based additive synthesis methods. Depending on the tone, up to 30 sinusoids are required to minimize perceptual differences between the natural and synthesized sound. The particular over-tones of a given sound are produced separately, each with its own frequency and envelope, before they are accumulated to a synthetical version of a whole sound.

The generation of a sound patch using additive synthesis implies the specification of a number of overtones (amplitude envelope, frequency envelope, wave form type).

Subtractive synthesis
Another large class of synthesis techniques is subsumed under the term subtractive synthesis. Rather than adding together a selected number of spectral components, as in additive synthesis, the subtractive approach starts with an easily generated signal rich in spectral components (such as noise or a pulse train) and attempts to produce the desired result through a series of filtering operations (time-varying). This technique has been used extensively to produce synthetic speech waveforms.

To produce a sound using subtractive synthesis implies the specification of oscillators and filters.

Frequency Modulation
Like additive synthesis, Frequency Modulation (FM) permits control of the audio spectrum with enough precision so that the composer has adequate control of the resulting sounds. In many cases FM turns out to be more economical in terms of the hardware required to produce a given sound and the amount of data needed to specify a sound.

FM is the variation of the frequency of one repeating waveform, the *carrier*, by an amount proportional to the instantaneous amplitude of a second waveform, the *modulating wave*. The ratio of the carrier to the modulator determines what overtones are possible, and the amount of modulation determines what overtones are present. So very good timbres can be generated by using only oscillators.

FM simulates a dynamic spectrum rather than reproducing it faithfully. This simulation has proved to be sufficient, especially if care is taken to represent other characteristics of the instrument tone. This technique is very good at synthesizing certain classes of sounds such as brass sounds and percussive sounds.

The parameters of a frequency-modulated signal are: carrier frequency or average frequency, modulation frequency, time dependent envelope functions (modulation index), and a sample interval.

6 Layout Extension

Depending on conditions specified in the document header appropriate layout specifications are used. In our layout extension two different layout types are specified: layout for music notation and layout for performance (MIDI).

The layout for music notation is based on the Calliope V2.0 editor (written by William Clocksin), a notation program developed under ULTRIX on a VAXstation 2000 and now running under VMS 5.4.

A typical music notation layout example would be: where to place which note on a staff, regarding if there are beams, slurs, ties, dots, and a lot of other attributes.

The layout for music performance is entirely based on the MIDI standard. That means, MIDI messages (MIDI channel and MIDI mode messages), system exclusive messages, and meta event messages are specified according to the standardized MIDI standard file format.

7 Implementation

7.1 Hardware Configuration

- VAXstation 3100,
- Apple Macintosh IIx,
- MIDI interfaces (JamBox 4+ for the Macintosh and/or MIDIC for the VAX),
- master-keyboard (ELKA MK55),
- sound-module (ROLAND U-110),
- amplifier and loud-speakers.

7.2 Software

- the VAX is running VMS 5.4,
- DECwindows,
- Calliope V2.0 (a music notation program written by W. Clocksin for the VAX),
- Performer 3.3 (MOTU's MIDI sequencer program for the Macintosh),
- Composer 2.3M (MOTU's music notation program for the Macintosh),
- CommUnity-Mac (networking software).

7.3 The Demonstration

The input is based on three data streams

- the *MIDI Standard File Format* (MSF - a standard for the interchange and storage of MIDI data),
- the *Calliope data* (specifying music notation information), and
- the *DDIS based data* stream (including our proposed extensions).

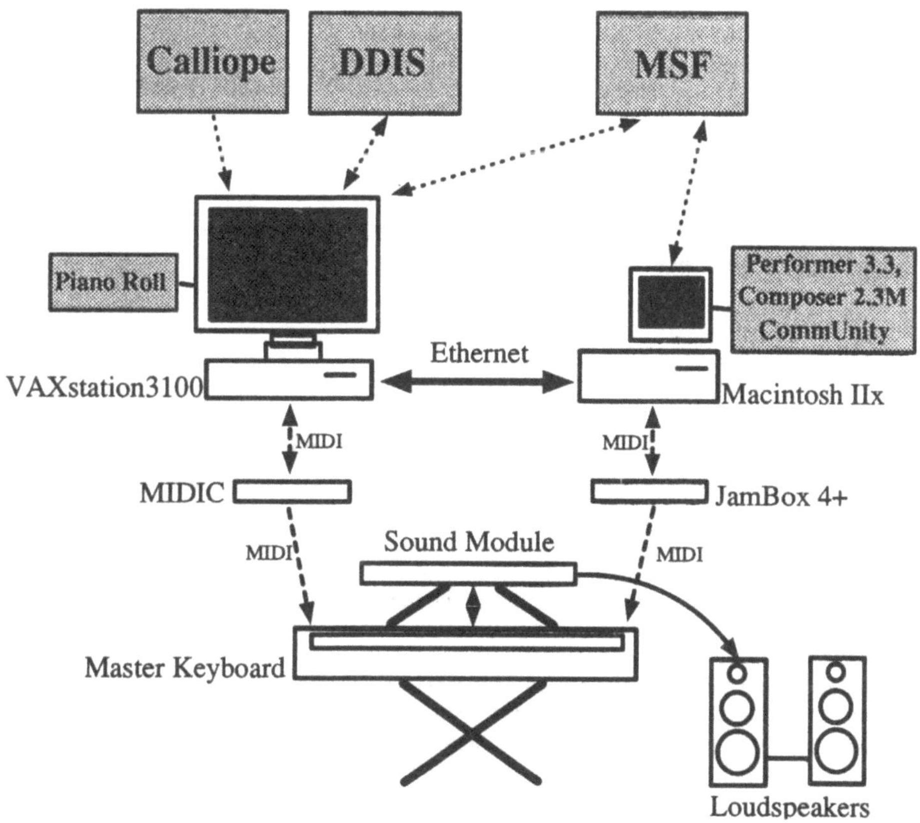

Fig. 7-1 The Demo Equipment

A MSF can be generated in our configuration in two kinds:

- by MOTU's Performer (MOTU is the abbreviation for Mark Of The Unicorn) by sequencing the MIDI data played on the master-keyboard or by converting MOTU's Composer data; or
- by our written MIDI editing software (supporting the conversion of the internal data representation to MSF).

Calliope data and DDIS based data can be imported by first converting them to MSF.

From a MSF, data are converted to internal representation. In this internal representation editing of MIDI messages and synchronization messages is supported. At the moment only *note on* and *note off* specific messages - editing of the key number, used channel(s), velocity on, and velocity off data - and their placement within a track - which track, start measure, start beat, start offset, duration - is supported. The editing of synchronization messages is restricted to determine the start measure, the stop measure, and the sync measure units. The latter is used to specify the number of measures to which text or graphics has to be rendered.

Besides music information the synchronization data can only be imported by the DDIS data stream because a toolkit supports conversion from DDIS to ASCII and vice versa.

All applications running on the VAX are written in VAX C 3.0 and all applications running on the Macintosh are written in THINK's Lightspeed C 3.0.

Starting playback forces to look through all tracks for the next *note on* or *note off* message and sending the corresponding message to the MIDI equipment. The sending can be executed in two different ways: using the MIDIC device or using the Macintosh. Using the Macintosh, the data (status byte and data byte(s)) are sent via Ethernet from the VAX to the Mac. There, a bypass program generates from the data and additional timing information raw MIDI data which are then sent to the MIDI equipment!

Using the MIDIC will be much simpler because this device is directly connected to the VAX using RS232 and so the data have not to be bypassed to the Mac.

8 Conclusion

The approach presented in this project shows two things:

- audio data can be specified in revisable form within compound documents, and
- a tool is specified to synchronize any existing (multimedia) domains with each other.

But this tool implies that the current CDA processing model, which handles the formatting and presentation stages implicitly as one functional block, has to be changed. In the changed model the role of a multimedia document formatter is to relate the virtual world of each multimedia document segment, considering specific constraints, to space and time of real world rather than to produce a code performing rendition of segment content on particular output device.

The key issue for a formatter is to detect existing logical, spatial, and temporal relations, and to construct inter-related strands of sequentially processed segments of content.

The role of the multimedia document presenter is to render formatted documents according to a socalled script produced by the formatter.

Key issue for a presenter during the rendition process is to implement synchronization of formatted document content along specific strands.

9 References

Alles, H.G. (1980) Music Synthesis Using Real Time Digital Techniques, Proceedings of the IEEE, Vol. 68, No.4, 436-449.

Anderton, C. (1986) MIDI for Musicians, Amsco Publications, New York/London/Sydney.

Blake, J.C. (Ed.) (1990) Compound Document Architecture, Digital Technical Journal, Vol. 2, No. 1.

Dahlin, E.K. (1970) Standardization for Time and Control Code for Video Tape and Audio Recorders, SMPTE Journal 79(12), 1086-1088.

DEC (1989) DEC STD 081 - Digital Data Interchange Syntax (DDIS), AX03.

DEC (1990) DEC STD 078 - Digital Data Interchange Format (DDIF), AX05.

DEC (1990) DEC STD 083-1 - Canonical Form Expressions (CFE), Section II, AX03.

Goldfarb, C.F., Newcomb, S. R. (1990) X3V1.8M Journal of Development ANSI Project X3.749-D Hypermedia/Time-based Structuring Language (HyTime), X3V1.8M/SD-7 (HyTime) Sixth Draft - ISO/IEC JTC 1/SC 18/WG 8 N1077.

Gordon, J.W. (1985) System Architecture for Computer Music, Computing Surveys, Vol.17, No. 2, 191-233.

Helbig, P. (1990) ODA Extensions for Synchronizing the Presentation of Multimedia Objects - ISO/IEC JTC1/SC18/WG3/N1797.

IMA (1983) MIDI 1.0 Detailed Specification, The International MIDI Association.

ISO 8879 (1986) Information processing - Text and office systems - Standard Generalized Markup Language (SGML).

ISO 8613 (1987) Information processing - Text and office systems - Office Document Architecture (ODA) and interchange format.

ISO/IEC JTC1/SC 18 N1975; ISO/IEC JTC1/SC 18/WG 5 N711 (1989) Liaison Statement to ISO/IEC JTC 1/SC 18/WG 1, WG 3, WG 8 and CCITT SG VIII SWP 4 From SC 18/WG 5 on New Work Item or Audio Content Architecture.

ISO/IEC JTC1/SC18/WG3/N1817 (1990) Technical Requirements for ODA/Hypermedia.

ISO/IEC JTC1/SC 18 N2190; ISO/IEC JTC1/SC 18/WG 3 N 1444, 1442, 1443 (1990) Liaison Statement From ISO/IEC JTC1/SC 18 to ISO/IEC JTC1/SC 21/WG 5 on Temporal Relationships in ODA Documents.

ISO/IEC JTC1/SC 18 N2197; ISO/IEC JTC1/SC 18/WG 8 N1071; ISO/IEC JTC1/SC 18/WG 5 N829 (1990) Information Processing - Text and Office Systems - Office Document Architecture (ODA) and Interchange Format - Part 9: Audio Content Architecture.

ISO/IEC JTC 1/SC 18 N2330; ISO/IEC JTC 1/SC 18/WG 8 N1009 (1990) NWI Proposal on Standard Music Description Language (SMDL) Hypermedia and Time-based Subset of SMDL (HyTime).

ISO/IEC JTC1/SC 18 N2458 (1990) Recommendation to SC 18 From Ad hoc Committee on Hypermedia.

ISO/IEC JTC1/SC 18 N2469 (1990) SC 18 Recommendation to JTC 1 on Hypermedia.

Kuhn, W., Kummer, M.,Vorlaufer, G. (1991) CDA/DDIF Audio and Synchronization Extension, Austrian Research Centre Seibersdorf.

Moog, R.A. (1986) Digital Music Synthesis, BYTE, June, 155-168.

Moorer, J.A. (1977) Signal Processing Aspects of Computer Music: A Survey, Proceedings of the IEEE, Vol. 65, No.8, 1108-1137.

Morris, T. (1990) CDA Audio Extensions Version 0.6.

Newcomb, S. R. (1990) Tutorials on HyTime - ISO/IEC JTC 1/SC 18/WG 8 N1057.

Pedersen, P. (1990) An Extended Interpretation of The ODA Processing Model for Formatted-processable Documents - ISO/IEC JTC1/SC18/WG8 N1053; ISO/IEC JTC1/SC18/WG3/N1558.

Pedersen, P. (1990) An 'Extensions' approach to document WG3 N1408 - ISO/IEC JTC1/SC18/WG3/N1559.

Snell, J.M. (1987) Professional Real-time Signal Processor for Synthesis, Sampling, Mixing & Recording, 83rd AES Convetion 1987, October 16-19, New York, preprint 2508.

Part IV

Demonstration Presentations

Chapter 10

SAL, A Hypermedia Prototype System

Anita Lundeberg, Tomoyuki Yamamoto and Takashi Usuki

SAL, a hypermedia prototype system developed at Sony Corporation, was designed to support the presentation of multi media information so that it can be easily retrieved and manipulated by the user. It is a navigation system based on the node and link model, and provides a general hypermedia environment on top of which individual applications can be built. This article describes the design and implementation of SAL, along with system characteristics including navigation and authoring support. One application is furthermore presented, and comments from authors and end-users of the application are discussed. We conclude by an evaluation of the current prototype and a discussion of important issues for designing future hypermedia systems.

1 Introduction

SAL (Super Active Literature) is a hypermedia prototype system developed in the Information Systems Research Department at Sony Corporation, Japan. The SAL project is aimed at finding a way of presenting multi-media information gathered from a variety of sources, so that it can be easily retrieved and manipulated by the user. The hypermedia system demonstrates, using Sony's audio and video technologies how multi-media information can be integrated and controlled by the computer.

Hypermedia is an information handling model in which separate units of information are linked together in a structured network. One way of representing such a structure is as a directed graph, in which each unit of information is associated with a *node* that may include various kinds of media. The relations between nodes are represented by directed arcs, *links*, and a user/system navigates through the network of information in a non-linear fashion by traversing links connecting the nodes. While browsing the hypermedia network, depending on the media, the user views/hears/experiences the information in the nodes [3]. Hypermedia systems aid in the organisation and manipulation of irregularly structured information, and in this respect complement the use of traditional database management systems (DBMS) in managing highly structured information [15]. Furthermore, since hypermedia systems support unstructured writing, it is possible to effectively and efficiently organise ideas, *idea-processing*, and to support collaborative work, *groupware.* The information management method employed in hypermedia systems is thought to be closely related to the way in which we human beings handle information, perhaps more so than the traditional database retrieval methods.

Hypermedia systems have been loosely classified as either general purpose systems (such as NoteCards, Intermedia, Guide, HyperCard) or as application specific (EUCLID,

KMS, Xanadu) [5]. General purpose systems, like SAL, are often created as experimental platforms rather than to address a specific application requirement.

SAL is a navigation system based on the node and link data model, and provides a general hypermedia environment on top of which individual applications can be built. It supports four types of media: *text*, *colour image*, *sound* and *video* media. A node is displayed in a window on the screen, presenting the media data, such as a paragraph of text, an image or sound data, as well as some additional node information. In the current prototype version, each individual node is restricted to a single media type. Logical connections between two pieces of information are made by the use of directed links. The user can easily explore information in a database by following existing links, or can create nodes and links to build new information structures for special purposes.

The user searches for information by traversing links from node to node. In addition, SAL provides two navigation support functions. The first, built on top of a relational database management system, is a conditional search facility which retrieves nodes by matching node attributes such as name, date and keywords. The second is a browser which graphically shows the network of nodes that are currently displayed and the links that connect them.

In this article we describe the SAL system: the system design, main characteristics, implementation and an example application. We conclude by an evaluation of the current prototype and a discussion of important areas for future research and development.

2 System Design

When designing SAL, we put a high priority on building a system which would provide an intuitive environment for the user to interact with an information base. This resulted in designing a user interface with an emphasis on simplicity and consistency, introducing as few new concepts to the user as possible. In the following section we discuss the system uniformity and the user interface.

2.1 Uniformity

SAL's model is based on the node and link model. We believe the model is not only useful for information retrieval and organisation, but also very powerful as a framework for unifying various kinds of media. This has been found to be useful for a broad range of applications, and the model has been adopted by many hypermedia systems designers [3], [4], [11], [12], [15].

A node in SAL is an abstract unit of media information and functions as a means of abstracting away media-specific differences. To the extent that is possible, media information is handled uniformly regardless of the media type. Information handling methods which are common to all media and can be treated in a uniform manner are, among others, functions for creation, deletion, retrieval, spatial movement, and attribute addition. Attributes are additional node information specified by the user and include node name, owner, date, authors and keywords. The attributes can be used as keys for a database query search.

A single link type is supported in SAL — a directional, referential link. The usefulness of additional organisational link types (hierarchical or inclusional relations), has been pointed out in [4], [6]. Despite such usefulness, these link types have not been provided for in SAL for two reasons. Firstly, we considered an additional link type to be a potential "threat" to the clear and easily understandable user environment enforced in

SAL. Secondly, SAL is a navigation-based system which supports both non-hierarchical and hierarchical networks of information. Moreover, if an author intends to create organisational relationships among nodes, it is possible to realise them with the referential link type.

We separate the media-specific parts of a node from those that are common across all media types. A node appears as a window, divided into a media-specific part, in which the media data is displayed together with link sources, and a surrounding frame, which holds buttons that provide access to functions common to all media.

2.2 User Interface

SAL's user interface is based on an object-oriented concept. In SAL, a node as an object has all of its procedures attached to it; therefore, a node can be manipulated by simply selecting a procedure, requiring only a single action. This is unlike the traditional user interface, like that of the Macintosh computer, which consists of two operations; First an object is selected, second a procedure is invoked through a gesture or mouse click. The main advantages of the approach taken in SAL are that 1) fewer actions are needed, 2) the number of user mistakes is reduced, and 3) the user's choice of actions is clearer. A disadvantage, on the other hand, is that several objects cannot be manipulated as a group at one and the same time. Furthermore, the available display space gets crowded by user interface gadgets, although this problem can be alleviated by placing buttons and other objects in a hidden panel (see Section 3.1.2).

Additionally, simplicity is emphasised in SAL's user interface design. Modifying the network of information, by adding or deleting nodes or by creating or removing links, is easily done one with button action. For example, in order to create a new link, the user simply marks a rectangular area on the node which is to become the source of the link, and selects the destination by a button click on another node.

3 System Characteristics

Each node in SAL is displayed in its own window, a large number of which can be displayed simultaneously. The nodes are independent from one another in that, for example, scrolling information in one node does not affect the information in any other node. A link is easily established between two nodes by specifying its source, normally a smaller part of a node, and its destination, an entire node. When the user follows a link the destination node is displayed in a separate window. If the destination node was already displayed but hidden from the user, it is brought to the front, otherwise it will be retrieved from the database. At the same time, the source node remains accessible. Figure 1 shows a display of six nodes from a SAL database. The rectangles outlined around words, expressions and images represent the source of a link. A user follows the link by clicking the mouse in the marked area.

All nodes, regardless of media, have the same basic appearance to the user. That is, basic functions such as creating or following a link, editing attributes, deleting information and closing a node, are the same for all types of media. The nodes are resized, lowered, moved, et cetera, by using the user's favourite window manager running on X Window System.

In this section we focus on some important characteristics of hypermedia systems and how these have been implemented in SAL. Section 3.1 discusses the importance of

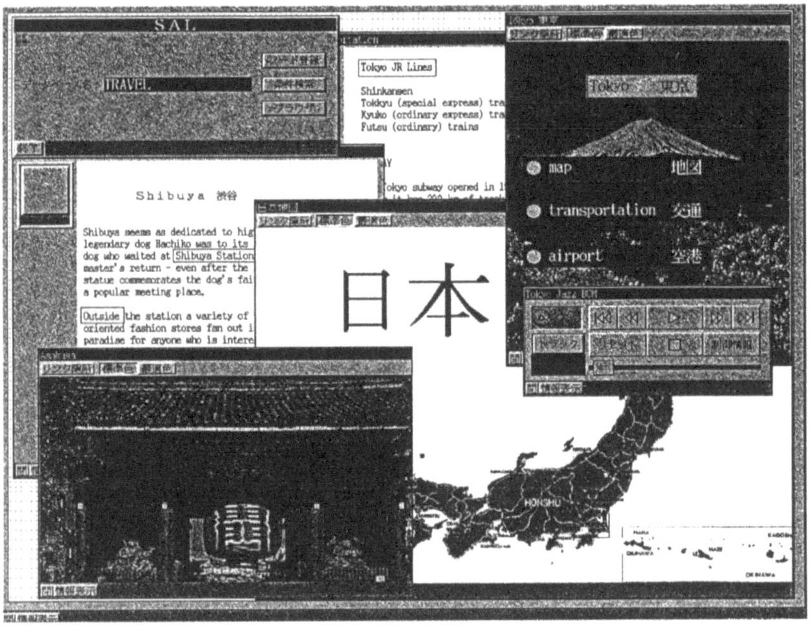

Figure 1: Nodes in SAL

including system support to aid the user in finding the appropriate information in the database. Two major solutions for navigation support and coping with disorientation are graphical browsers and query/search mechanisms. The implementation of these functions in SAL are described in the same section. Section 3.2 describes a simple authoring facility, the storyline, followed in Section 3.3 by an explanation of how real-time media, especially Laser Disk and CD media, are abstracted as nodes.

3.1 Navigation Support

Browsing is the typical means for accessing information in hypermedia documents for both readers and authors. The user searches for, and retrieves, the information required by following links. It has been pointed out that browsing through nonlinear networks often leaves the user with a general feeling of disorientation. This is a spatial disorientation problem, which has been described by Conklin [6] as not knowing where you are in the information network, or not knowing how to access some information that you believe exists there. Hypermedia systems offer a greater freedom to move around in a database; however, along with this freedom comes a greater potential for the user to get lost. It is therefore of great importance to simplify the orientation in, and navigation through, a database in different ways. Many suggestions to overcome this problem have been made, such as enforcing more hierarchical structures, coarse grained networks (a few, large nodes as opposed to many, small nodes), and special navigation and backtrack commands [11], as well as graphical history lists, and summary boxes for note taking while browsing [9].

3.1.1 Browser

The *browser* in SAL is a graphical map which shows the relations between nodes, allowing the user to orient himself in the information space. It displays a network of miniature icons of all the nodes which are either:

- current nodes, that is, nodes which are currently displayed;
- nodes which can be reached from a current node by traversing one link; or
- nodes whose links lead to a current node.

The appearance of an individual node icon depends on its media type. (See Figure 2.) The icon for an image node is simply a miniature version of that image, and is proportional to the size of its parent image. A fixed bitmap is used for all sound icons, and another for video icons, whereas a text icon consists of a rectangle with a number of lines proportional to the size of the text data it represents. By using the browser, the user can quickly get an overview of the current situation and easily display a node by clicking on its corresponding browser icon. This is especially useful in situations when a node has become "buried" behind other nodes and cannot easily be found, or when an explicit view of the relations (links) between nodes is desired.

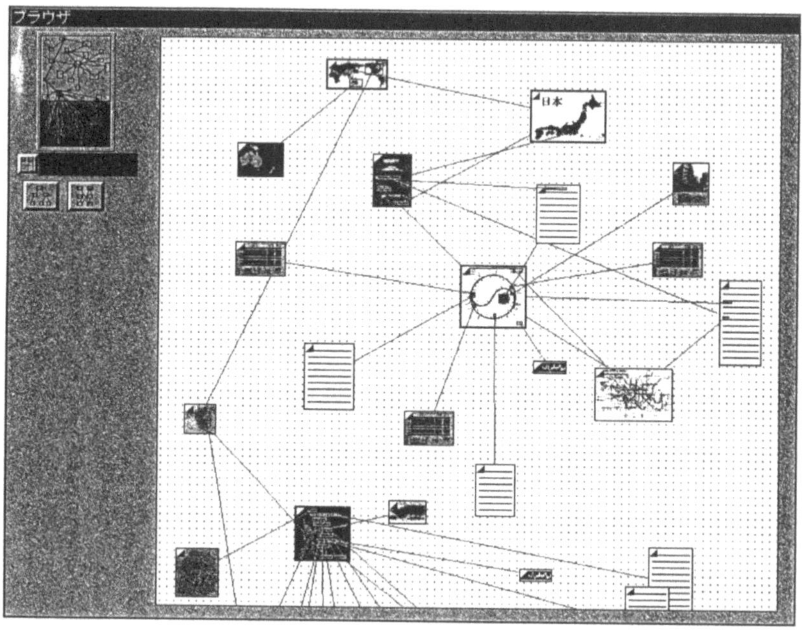

Figure 2: The Browser

The main functions to be performed on a browser icon include showing the name of the corresponding node by moving the cursor over the icon, displaying the corresponding node by clicking the mouse on the icon, and repositioning the icon in the browser.

While a graph representation is a good way to display a complex information structure and can be a great aid to the user, a poor drawing can be equally confusing or misleading. It is thus important to consider the aesthetic layout of graphs, to make them eye-pleasing and easy to understand and remember. The browser in SAL offers two different layouts, one in which the icons simply are placed evenly on vertical lines. The second layout employs an algorithm based on a general method for drawing directed graphs according to four aesthetic criteria [13]:

- all arcs should follow the same general direction,
- vertices should be distributed evenly over the page,
- there should be as few arc crossings as possible, and
- the arcs should be as straight as possible.

If the browser window is not large enough to hold all of the icons, the viewing area can be scrolled, both horizontally and vertically. Both the scrolling button and its movable bitmap are sized proportionally to the entire icon field and view area respectively, indicating to the user the exact position in and size of the icon field. To further simplify orientation, the entire network of icons can be viewed in miniature on the scrolling button. (See Figure 2.)

3.1.2 Conditional Retrieval

The ability to browse a network of information by following the links makes hypermedia a powerful tool for managing loosely structured information [12]. However, navigational access by itself is not sufficient for many applications, and needs to be complemented by a *query/search*-based access mechanism. In a large hypermedia database, a search facility considerably lowers the time required for the user to find an appropriate starting point for further browsing. It also helps to prevent user confusion and potential loss of context from viewing irrelevant information along the way [10]. Moreover, in the case of SAL, the initial node is often retrieved from the database using the conditional search facility.

The search mechanism functions in SAL as a complement to the graphical search provided by the browser. Each node has a number of fields designated, to which a search may be restricted, as mentioned in Section 2.1. This information is normally hidden from the user, but is easily retrieved; a button click opens an information panel giving access to this additional node information. Figure 3 shows two nodes, an image node with with its attributes displayed, and a storyline node (see Section 3.2) with its additional information hidden. Two conditions were specified for the search resulting in the display in Figure 3: node-type (image, written "イメージ" in Japanese) and the date of creation (90/11). The only node in the database matching these conditions was the image node called "Sydney".

3.2 Storyline

Authoring capabilities provide a means for the users to design their own environments, to establish new relationships among information, and to specify functions to be automatically invoked when information is accessed. Authoring tools provided in existing hypermedia systems vary from support for establishing relationships among collections of information (creating links), and customising environments (buttons, fields etc) to extensive scripts, directing what operations are to take place at each navigational step — a well-known script programming languages being Hypertalk, used in Apple's HyperCard [2].

In addition to the necessary basic hypermedia facilities for creating and deleting node and link information, SAL provides a simple form of authoring, the *storyline*, which enables the user to specify a sequence of nodes in order to "tell a story". The nodes included in a storyline are automatically displayed when a storyline is invoked, without any further interaction needed. The order of the display of the nodes, along with the display interval are specified by the user, as is shown in Figure 3. For example, the storyline node "Yamanote tour" contains a node called "Tokyo Tower" which will be displayed 19 seconds after the storyline is invoked, and disappear 16 seconds later.

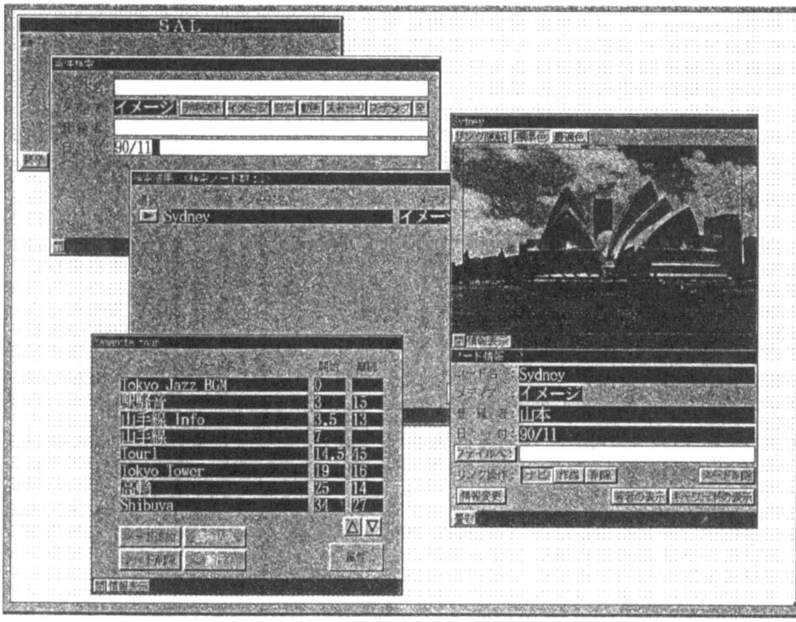

Figure 3: The Storyline Node

An executing storyline can be halted and then continued at any time during the display, which makes it especially suitable for presentations and demonstrations. The scheduling process is very easy, requiring no programming experience. A new node is added to a storyline in a similar way to the creation of a referential link. In this way, the relationship between a storyline and a contained node may appear to the user as a kind of link. The execution of a storyline puts no restrictions on the system—links may be followed, and nodes can be opened and closed as normal (even those included in the storyline).

By using many media, one piece of information can be presented to the user in different ways, for example, information about a dog can be presented to the user in terms of a picture of a dog, text describing a dog, the sound of a dog's bark and so on. Hence, each media represents a different *view* of the same information. The storyline, displaying a collection of nodes, can be seen as a representing a particular view of the information stored in a SAL database. Conforming to the concepts underlying SAL's design— unification, consistency and simplicity—all views, the storyline included, are implemented using a single type of node. Thus, a storyline is created and manipulated like that of any kind of media.

3.3 Real-time Media

Real-time media, such as video and sound media, are defined in SAL to be sequences of video frames or digitised sound. The visual representation of real-time media as nodes include control panels which have basic functions and form already familiar to the user. Some real-time media information is stored separately from the database, and hence requires an external device. Currently, SAL supports CD-ROM and LaserDisk players as external devices. Figure 1 shows an example of a CD-ROM sound node and its control panel with which the user can further control the media data by playing, stopping, rewinding, and so forth. The only media data contained in a node that controls an external device is the the beginning and end of a track, or part of a track, on a sound CD or a LaserDisk. Digitised sound and video nodes, on the other hand, contain the actual media data stored in the database.

Several real-time media can be synchronised by using the storyline function. Although a particular external device can only present data of one real-time node at a time, one digitised media node may be played concurrently with the real-time media node stored externally.

4 Implementation

As mentioned in Section 1, SAL supports four types of media: text, image, sound and video media, each of which is treated equally as a node in the system. The entire system is implemented in an object-oriented fashion using the C++ programming language, an extended version of C supporting an object-oriented programming environment.

In the following section we describe the general architecture of SAL, followed by the details of the node and link model and the relational database. The user interface implementation is discussed, and finally, the hardware configuration is described.

4.1 Architecture of SAL

SAL consists of three parts, as shown in Figure 4: the main SAL body, a database management system (DBMS) "DrTalk", and a user interface management system (UIMS) "DrSheet". The system runs on top of the X Window System Version 11 and the UNIX operating system. Both DrSheet and DrTalk were developed for in-house use at Sony Corporation.

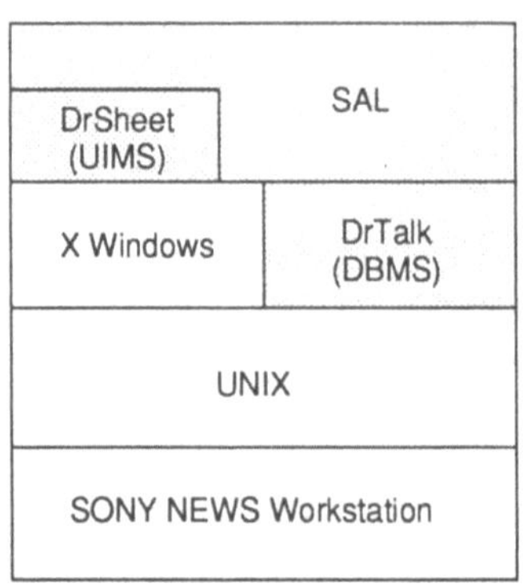

Figure 4: Architecture of SAL

As discussed above, the SAL body provides browser and storyline operations as well as basic functions for user interface operations, such as node and link operations. DrSheet

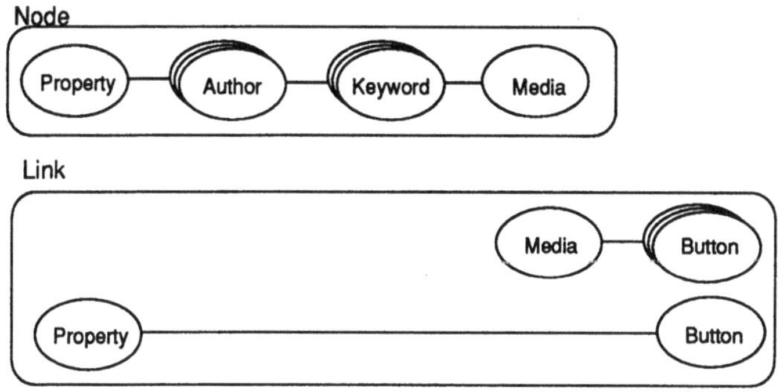

Figure 5: Relational Models for Nodes and Links

supports window primitives such as button, field, and window operations. DrTalk provides storage for media data, as well as node and link information and functions for the search mechanism. The different parts of the system communicate with each other by message passing.

4.2 The Node and Link Model

As shown in Figure 5, nodes and links contain the following five attributes:

- node property; node id, node name, window information to display media data, owner name and creation date,
- author; author's name and affiliation of the media data,
- keyword; can be used for conditional retrieval,
- media; actual media data, media type, control information, and browser icon data,
- branchbutton atom; link source coordinates.

The database management system has the follow features that make it especially suited for a hypermedia system:

- DrTalk has an object-oriented programming interface so that it can behave as if it were an object-oriented system.
- An object (*e.g.*, a node) can have multiple instances of an attribute (*e.g.*, keywords, authors) each instance of which is treated individually. In SAL this allows for a flexible definition of a node and link.
- An object has no logical limit on its data length. This features makes it possible to deal with a very large amount of data such as that required by colour images and digitised sound and video.

More detailed information about the database can be found in [14].

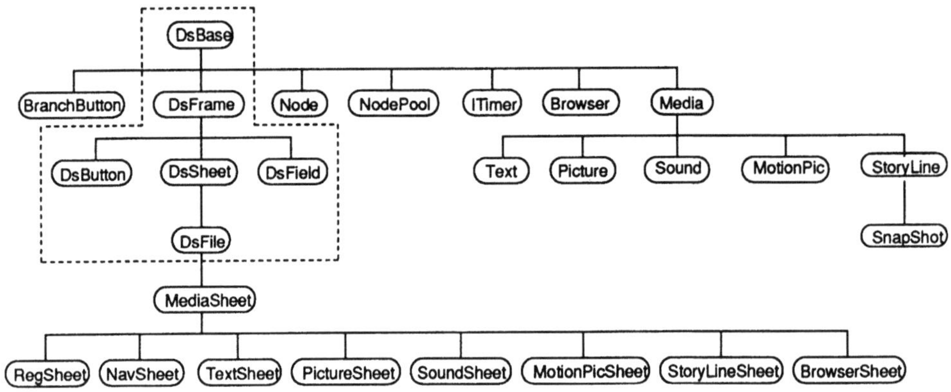

Figure 6: Class Hierarchy of SAL

4.3 User Interface Management System

SAL's user interface is implemented using our object-oriented UIMS, DrSheet. DrSheet allows the the installation of event handlers for all X events (like button and key press events) and supports basic window functions for user application programs. DrSheet is depicted as the dashed outline in Figure 6.

In SAL, the user interface and the model are implemented separately, similar to Smalltalk-80's Model-View-Controller (MVC) model [7]. The classes underneath *DsFile* in Figure 6 function as the user interface (View and Controller in the MVC model). Each media has a corresponding *sheet* class which provides a media-specific interface. Functions common to all media are included in the *MediaSheet* class. The Model part of the MVC model is realised by the *Node* class which also provides the interface to the database.

4.4 Hardware Configuration

SAL currently supports the following equipment:

- a colour scanner for images
- a CD-ROM drive for digital sound including CD
- a Laser Disk player and a write-once drive as an analogue video source
- a microphone for voice input

Each of these is connected to and controlled by a Sony NEWS workstation which embeds digital audio and video capabilities as well as conventional capabilities found in a UNIX-based workstation. The embedded hardware includes a 1024 by 768 dots colour monitor which can display a video frame rate signal on a bitmapped screen with 32768 colours out of 16,700 thousand colours at the same time and a sound board which is able to record and play back straight PCM data (both 8-bit and 16-bit formats), ADPCM format audio data conforming to CD-I and CD-ROM XA specifications, as well as three types of logarithmically compressed PCM format audio data (8-bit) corresponding to the μ-law and A-law data formats.

5 Applications

Applications which have been built using SAL include an on-line manual for an expert system, as well as several demonstration applications. The following section discusses the implementation of the on-line manual application in further detail, along with author and end-user comments on experiences from using the application.

5.1 Expert System On-line Manual

The on-line manual was written for an expert system used as a support tool in LSI (Large Scale Integrated) circuit design. The main reason for choosing an on-line manual in favour of a hard-copy manual was that the hard-copy manual for an earlier version of the expert system was found hard to use. The expert system has a complicated menu structure with many layers of menus, and the users found it difficult to find the right entry in the manual. This problem is alleviated in the on-line version built using SAL, in that the user can "jump" straight to the information desired by following links.

The on-line manual has a strong hierarchical orientation like that of a book (with chapters, sections etc.), and supports linear browsing (i.e. viewing the next or previous page) as well as the non-linear browsing offered by the typical hypermedia link-references.

The user is given several options to start reading the manual. They are:

- A *table of contents*, which outlines the chapters and sections of the manual in a traditional manner. By clicking on a title, a link will be traversed and the corresponding text will be displayed.
- A *graphical map* which displays the expert system's menu hierarchy. The user can get more information about a particular menu by clicking on one of the menu boxes in the graph.
- A *special purpose menu* containing objects of special interest to the LSI designer, objects which he is likely to frequently request detailed information about.

In all three cases, having chosen a starting point the user will search his way through the manual by following existing links. A node in SAL corresponds to one manual page and provides links to the previous/next page (node), referenced topics and drawings, the three starting points, as well as to internal details about the expert system and its reasoning mechanism.

As a result of specifying fixed starting points, one of the search facilities, the conditional retrieval, is abandoned. The reason behind this choice is that the manual is intended for non-computer users and for users with little experience in LSI design, who need directions as to where to "open" the manual and who may find it difficult to make use of a search facility. The manual application uses only two types of media — text and image media. It could benefit from using sound and video media in simulating user actions, but due to lack of time the authors chose not to make any such real-time simulations for the initial version.

5.1.1 Using the On-line Manual

The expert system on-line manual application is currently being used by seven persons, all of whom have had previous computer experience, although none had used any hypermedia-type software before using the on-line manual. The mouse-driven interface was found very easy to use, and most functions were intuitive to the users. Without further instructions, they were able to start the application, and soon became familiar with mouse operations, scrollbars et cetera, and how to click on links to retrieve more information. Thus, most users learned how to operate the manual by "trial-and-error". When facing a new application, most computer users expect to have to set aside time for learning the system and reading user-manuals. This was not found necessary for this SAL application, which surprised and pleased the users.

General comments on the differences between using a hard copy and an on-line copy of the expert system manual made by the end-users include:

- Diagrams are a very straightforward and readable form in which to display information.

- Browsing based on a graphical map is much easier than one based on a table of contents, and the special purpose menu which allows for searching for the three different objects of special interest was also found very useful.

- The main advantage of an on-line manual over a hard-copy one is the alternative search facilities (map and purpose-oriented search) that are provided. It is more convenient, however, to read the actual text from a hard copy.

In the following sections we list and discuss some of the more important comments made by the authors and the end-users of the on-line manual application.

5.1.2 Author and End-user Comments

The current version of the on-line user manual is a static hypermedia application; that is, the user is not supposed to make any alterations to the database, but to merely use it as a reference. Hence, comments made by the users differ somewhat from the ones made by the authors. Many points, however, were stressed by both categories of users, which is the case in the list below if nothing else is stated.

- *Edit text or drawings.* Once the media information has been registered as a node in SAL, it cannot be edited. Changes can be made to the original file outside SAL, and a new node registered. This caused some difficulties for the authors, since all related links are removed along with the old node, however, and as a result have to be re-created.

- *Combining media information into one node.* In the current version of SAL, each node holds information from a single medium. A composite node containing, for example, text and image information, would have made explanations clearer in some cases. This problem can be partially alleviated by using the storyline to simultaneously display one text and one image node.

- *Faster retrieval.* In some cases, especially for large image nodes, the retrieval and display of a node is unacceptably slow.

- *Sorted list of nodes.* A facility for sorting the list of nodes which results from a search would be useful. Preferably, the user should be allowed to specify which key to sort the list on.

- *Fixed geometry and position of nodes.* If a node is moved to a new location and then closed, it will appear in this new location the next time it is opened. From the authors' point of view there may be an "ideal" node layout for reading the on-line manual, which will disappear if the user is allowed to change the location of nodes. On the other hand, as was pointed out by the end-users, users tend to have personal preferences on layout and colours, and would like to be able to customise the environment accordingly. One possible solution to this problem would be to specify a fixed location for start-up or for new users, but to allow users to customise the layout according to their preferences.

- *History list/Back command.* Following a chain of cross-references while browsing through a manual may lead to problems such as losing the main path, losing orientation in the network, and forgetting to return from digressions. This problem has been called *The Embedded Digression Problem* [9] and is an undesirable consequence of browsing observed in most hypermedia systems. A common approach to alleviate this problem is to provide various types of browser such as, for example, history lists. The users of the on-line manual experienced the same problem, and suggested an additional back-tracking facility which would take the user back to the original "main" path, that is, to the point where he left the sequential browsing and started to digress.

- *Automatically closed nodes.* Both authors and end-users commented on the fact that normally a great number of nodes are opened during a browsing session, which may disturb and confuse the user. The authors suggested that, in an application such as the on-line manual where nodes have a parent-child relation, closing the node could additionally cause its child, the destination node, being closed. However, this is not a desired function in a non-structured hypermedia database. In such a network, where the notion of a parent-child relationship does not exist, automatically closing the destination node of a link could cause a "snowball effect", that is, it may result in all nodes in the entire structure eventually to be closed. The on-line manual is, in many cases, read sequentially page by page. The end-users suggested that "previous" pages may be closed, so as to avoid too many nodes to be displayed at the same time.

  An alternative solution, possibly more appropriate for the general application, may be to give each node a time stamp when visited. This way, all "old" nodes, older than a specified threshold, could be automatically closed.

- *Print-outs.* It is possible, however a little cumbersome, to print out a paper copy of node information, by first writing the node data into a UNIX-file which then, in turn, can be printed. A more easily accessed function is highly desired.

6 Evaluation and Future Work

6.1 System Performance

One of the more important aspects to consider when evaluating the user interface of a hypermedia system is the system response time [11]. As part of the performance evaluation of SAL, the access time of a node was measured. The results, based on an average of three trials, are shown in Figure 7. It should be noted that the test results varied considerably

Table 1: Browser Creation and Refresh Time

Number of Nodes	Time (sec)	
	Create	Refresh
0	1.16	
6	16.37	1.10
15	33.66	3.15
28	44.11	6.38
47	53.72	9.65
59	58.13	11.55
80	65.42	13.88

6.2.1 Navigation

Navigation, or following links, is recognised by most users as an easy and intuitive way of retrieving information. In SAL, each node is assigned to a window. As the user browses through a database by following links, a large number of nodes will be opened, covering most or all of the screen, as mentioned in Section 5.1.2. The user soon becomes unable to keep track of where he started, how the nodes are related, and how to return to a particular node in the network. The browser was found to be useful for these situations, considerably alleviating the disorientation problem. A node which has been retrieved from the database but whose window may be hidden behind a number of other windows can be easily found in the browser's iconic display.

6.2.2 Browser

As mentioned in Section 3.1.1, the browser in SAL displays icons corresponding to open nodes and those that neighbour by a single link. Thus, the browser presents only a local map, not a global one. A global map of the entire database would present too much information, leading to a spaghetti-like tangle of crisscrossing links [6]. We discovered, however, that such a tangle can be often observed even in a local map. Since nodes remain displayed in SAL unless explicitly closed by the user, the screen tends to fill up quickly. The situation is even worse in the browser, since nodes which are linked to opened nodes, but not yet retrieved from the database, are displayed as well. Users often want to create a node that functions as an index to other nodes. These kinds of index nodes, in general, have a large number of links and thus especially aggravate the problem of tangled links and increase the number of node icons. The browser proved to show a much more tangled web of links than we had originally expected.

One of our solutions to the "spaghetti" phenomenon was to implement a more intelligent icon layout algorithm, as described in Section 3.1.1. One drawback of the algorithm, however, is that it increases the area needed to display all of the icons. It is often the case that the icons cannot all fit in the browser window, requiring the user to use a scrollbar to survey the area in which he is interested. By displaying a miniature version of the icon network on the browser's two-dimensional slider, the user can more easily orient himself when navigating using the browser.

over the trials and thus give only a rough estimate of the time it takes to retrieve and display a node. For all test results, SAL was run on a Sony NWS-3860 workstation (20 MHz R3000 CPU).

There are four stages of processing in order to read a node from the database and display it: (1) preprocessing, (2) database access, (3) node construction, and (4) the X server's display processing. The time spent on preprocessing is negligible and hence not shown in Figure 7.

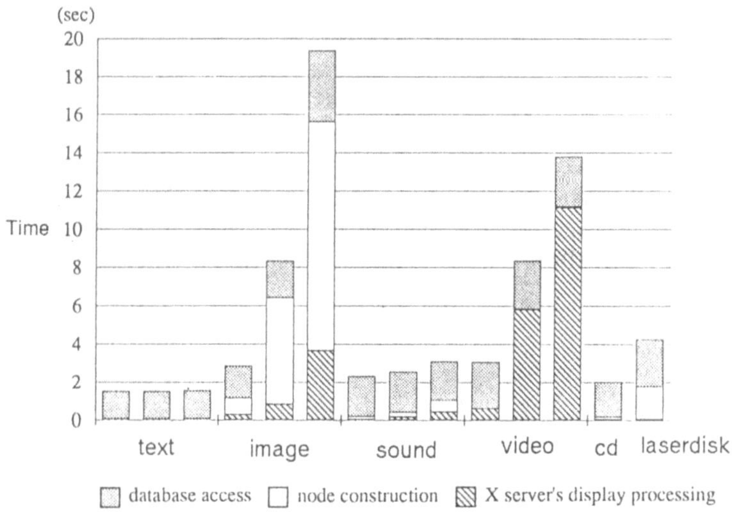

Figure 7: Node Access Times

As shown in Figure 7, image nodes take a relatively long time to construct (3). This is due to the fact that, in general, each image in the database possesses its own colourmap that contains colours optimised for that image. After database retrieval, the image data requires extra processing to convert it to a standard colourmap that can be shared by all images. A relatively large part of the access/display time of any node type is taken up by the X server's processing of display requests. This is especially true for nodes that contain a large number of buttons (subwindows) as is the case with sound and laserdisk nodes.

The access time of a node increases considerably when the browser is open during retrieval, as the browser must update any time a node is opened or closed. Table 1 shows the time it takes to create and re-display the browser. Although the browser is useful in giving an overview of the database in general, it is clear from Table 1 that the current version is unsatisfactorily slow. According to [1], users become frustrated when response time becomes longer than two seconds. In order to make SAL a more usable system, response time should be significantly reduced, especially for the retrieval of image nodes and video nodes, and for the browser update.

6.2 Usability

In this section we present a few considerations about the usability of SAL, such as the ease of navigation, browsing and conditional retrieval.

6.2.3 Conditional Retrieval

Each node in the database can possess a number of attributes. A user can query the database, giving any number of attribute values as a condition, and continue navigation from the retrieved nodes. This retrieval method provides a filtering mechanism for nodes and is an easy way to find the starting point for navigation. Furthermore, it allows the user to switch to nodes unrelated to the nodes currently being displayed.

In order to use the conditional retrieval effectively, it is of course necessary for nodes to have appropriate attribute values to begin with; however, authors often find it troublesome to input attributes, such as keywords, by hand and tend to omit them. Even if the user does add attribute information, there is no guarantee that the information will be useful for succeeding retrievals, as the user might use a different keyword at a later time. Instead of relying on keywords, allowing a full textual search of text nodes[1] would be ideal for textual information, but useless for other media types. Problems such as synonymy (many keywords may have the same meaning) and polysemy (a single keyword may have many meanings), make conditional retrieval difficult [8]. As long as these problems are not solved, conditional retrieval will be only marginally helpful.

6.3 Future Work

Using our experiences from developing the SAL prototype system, we are now beginning development on a new hypermedia platform system on top of which various applications can be built.

One of the most important requirements of a hypermedia system from a user's point of view is uniformity. A system that looks and behaves in the same way across applications is both easy to learn and easy to use. Many current hypermedia systems provide a *local uniformity*—that is, they provide a uniform environment only within a single application. Since the user wants to perform a number of different tasks, he must switch between several applications, each of which might have its own user interface, browsing mechanism, and method of dealing with user history. The Apple Macintosh is a good example of a system that presents the user with a consistent interface. In the same way, a hypermedia platform should provide resources like database interface and networking capabilities that can be utilised by applications in a uniform manner. Our next hypermedia platform will hopefully play such a role. Once realised, such a system will allow uniformity to be expressed not only within single applications, but also among applications.

Our next system will support a unified information representation paradigm based on the node and link model, media manipulation tools, like editors and pre-viewers, network interfaces, the database management system, a script language and so forth. Furthermore, it will provide basic hypermedia facilities likely to be commonly used in many applications, such as dictionaries, authoring facilities, and various navigation support facilities including browsers, history trees, contexts, and search capabilities. The DBMS will be extended to support a distributed database, and the user interface tool will incorporate a basic set of Motif widgets.

The practical use of the hypermedia platform will greatly benefit from conforming to audio and video standards. SAL already uses an audio data format conforming to CD-I and CD-ROM XA specifications, and the next step will be to include video standard specifications and compression technology, conforming to the MPEG specifications.

[1]not currently supported in SAL

7 Acknowledgements

We wish to acknowledge the contributions made by all members of the hypermedia project in the Information Systems Research Department to the system presented in this report. Special thanks to Curtis Eubanks for reading and commenting on earlier drafts of the report, to the authors of the on-line manual applications for valuable user comments, and to Hidetoshi Ichioka for collecting performance data.

References

[1] Shneiderman B. Designing the user interface. *Addison-Wesley Publishing Co. Inc.*, 1987.

[2] Goodman D. *The Complete HyperCard Handbook*. Bantam Books, Inc., 1987.

[3] Stotts P. D. and Furuta R. Petri-net-based hypertext: Document structure with browsing semantics. *ACM Transactions on Information Systems*, 7(1), January 1989.

[4] Halasz F. G. Reflections on notecards: Seven issues for the next generation of hypermedia systems. *Communications of the ACM*, 31(7), July 1988.

[5] Begoray J. An introduction to hypermedia issues, systems and application areas. *International Journal of Man-Machine Studies*, 1990.

[6] Conklin J. Hypertext: An introduction and survey. *IEEE*, September 1987.

[7] Pinson L. J. and Weiner R. S. *An introduction to object-oriented programming and Smalltalk*. Addison-Wesley Publishing Company, Inc., 1988.

[8] Landauer T. K., Dumais S. T., Gomez L. M., and Furnas G. W. Human factors in data access. *The Bell System Technical Journal*, 61(9), November 1982.

[9] Foss C. L. Tools for reading and browsing hypertext. *Information Processing & Management*, 25(4), 1989.

[10] Gallagher L., Furuta R., and Stotts P. D. Increasing the power of hypertext search with relational queries. *Hypermedia*, 2 No. 1, 1990.

[11] Akscyn R. M., McCracken D. L., and Yoder E. A. KMS: A distributed hypermedia system for managing knowledge in organizations. *Communications of the ACM*, 31(7), 1988.

[12] Yankelovich N., Haan B., Meyrowitz N., and Drucker S. Intermedia: The concept and the construction of a seamless information environment. *IEEE*, January 1988.

[13] Eades P. Complexity issues in drawing directed graphs. *Algorithm*, 1989.

[14] Komori S. An object-oriented environment for database management. *The 15th Unix Symposium Proceeding. Japan Unix Society*, July 1990.

[15] Xanadu Operating Company, Inc. Xanadu/server system overview, June 1990. Draft Revision 1.0 B4.

Chapter 11

A Design Proposal for a Hypermedia Abstract Machine

Jerker Andersson

Keywords: Hypermedia, link and node models, HAM, annotation.

1. Abstract

This paper presents some consideration applicable to hypermedia. We suggest a generalized model, HAM, for handling media and navigation without having to integrate the two. By manipulating links and presenting them using different tools we can aid the user in forming a mental model. By separating media and links we remove complexity and allow for a better overview and a more flexible media structure. We can also support the continued evolution of the content into a personalized book.

2. Related Work

In the field of hypertext and hypermedia there is an on-going discussion concerning link and node-models [1, 2, 7]. There have been some systems that have explicitly separated structure and content, e.g. Intermedias concept of "webs" being superimposed on "documents" [3, 9].

Another issue that we address is the granularity of media. In order to construct a seamless media integration different types of media must be parsed into "chunks" that can be handled and referred to consistently [4, 9]. This parsing can be topical and may rely on loose or strict typing of links and nodes [5, 8].

There is also a need for supporting the user in forming a mental model of the hyperspace. This can be done by providing different tools and access points suitable for different information retrieval situations. Providing the right mechanisms for selection and feedback has been identified as a very important factor for hypermedia usability [6].

3. Background

This project is a part of a research programme towards a Personal education environment. The overall goal is to provide the student with a "course" based on a "book" with interactive "classes". The student will be able to add annotations in text, voice or graphic and make his or her own "trails" or "webs" in the "book". One should also consider the possibility of sharing "trails" or "webs" with other students. This scenario envisions an Interactive Book that changes over time to become the owners personal map of the subject, to be used as a reference work as well as for studies and presentations.

The first stage in the programme consists of an extensive body of theoretical text and graphics to be put into a computer system to aid users in retrieval and browsing of its content. The system should allow for continuous development by adding annotations, new paths and specialized navigational tools. It should also have the aspect of being extendible what concerns which and how many media it supports.

In the first phase our work centres on hyperspace topology and information management. It is very much a question of structure vs user freedom.

4. Problem

We would like to design a framework that supports general hypermedia applications. It should allow arbitrary linking between nodes of different media. A very high level of navigational freedom on the part of the user will put severe restrictions on the author of hypermedia documents. We do not know what the user knows or which parts he has visited earlier, thus each node will have to be more or less self-contained.

Even more so than texts, multimedia presentations are context dependent. This is due to the fragmenting aspects of some forms of media. If you want to describe the recent changes in the stock exchange in words you might run in to some difficulty. I might have been better to use a graph or an animated sequence of graphics. Still your recorded voice explanations might make the picture even clearer, supporting the graphical presentation.

Using all of the above will provide a very good explanation indeed. However together they form a context that breeds interdependence between the different media and it has some temporal aspects as well. If someone were to remove a media, say the speakers, the presentation might become incomprehensible. The solution to this problem would be to never allow mixing media on "the lowest level" and require that all media be self-contained in some meaning. With this precondition we can handle all media as separate channels and browse them independently.

4.1. Coordinating Media and Context

So we have the problem of coordinating several media to make a complete presentation. Many authoring systems for multimedia applications have this at their core. By collecting and integrating several different formats and types of media the designer can make his point and build his application to respond to the user. But this requires that he has full control of what is presented and how it is presented. That means that the author decides when and how some particular part of his presentation is displayed.

In a true hypermedia system this might not be feasible. The user may come from one of several different contexts and might be interested in only a tiny part of the information offered on the subject. If we cannot cover all possible scenarios there will be no gradual, well designed build-up of context. Rather the user would experience something like "dropping from the sky" into a "jungle of media".

In the area of hypertext there is an on-going discussion of the disorientation of the user [1, 2, 6, 7]. This problem might well be even worse in a hypermedia environment.

So what we are looking for is one or more mechanisms to provide the user with the ability to move about freely and still give the author a chance to make a consistent and logical presentation. We also need to support the user in forming a mental model of the hyperspace content and how it can be manipulated.

4.2. Extensibility

To further add to the problem, we stated in the background discussion that we would like the users and others to add to the body of material in order to evolve and adapt it over time. To accomplish this we would like the linkage structure to be dynamic or at least additive, so that new links and nodes might be created when needed.

Within the scenario proposal laid down above there also lies the demand for adding and removing media such as video or sound for any particular use of the database i.e. there might be a system that lacks facilities for showing a video or generating sound. This should be possible to accomplish without having to edit the content or change the actual link structure.

5. Proposed Solution

To satisfy the needs in the problem discussion above we designed an abstract model called HAM, Hypermedia Abstract Machine. The idea has originated in the hypertext world where the intermediate level between the actual database and the user interface has been called HAM. It is a strong candidate for standardisation due to its lack of machine dependence [8]. This thought has lead to the idea of generalizing the way one handles different media, so as to make the navigational mechanism separate from the content among which it is set to navigate.

5.1. The Content of a Node

To explain the idea further we must consider the format of our hyperspace. We call each information package a node. We give each node a heading to describe its content, i.e "Impedance and frequency interdependence". The node may consist of different media able to communicate the whole or a part of the information content. We call each such media part a granule. A granule is equivalent to "the smallest meaningful part of any medium", i.e. a page of text, a scene from a film or a chart. Often two media can be combined to provide a better explanation of a concept, but we suggest this is not made at the lowest level. This leaves us with a node containing a handful of media granules, each to be handled separately.

Now the user may browse through the nodes viewing only one specified media or he may select different media in a single node to catch different aspect of a subject. From the HAM's side the different granules and nodes are all handled in the same way. The various modes of navigation and jumps in the hyperspace are translated into absolute addresses in specified media using the HAM's information and an index mapping node names onto granules. From the media's point of view it's just a matter of displaying the requested granule using available channels and settings.

5.2. A Model of the HAM

To further understand this abstraction we should look at the organisation of our HAM, refer to figure 1. There are three levels; the user's navigational tools, the HAM and the media presentation managers.

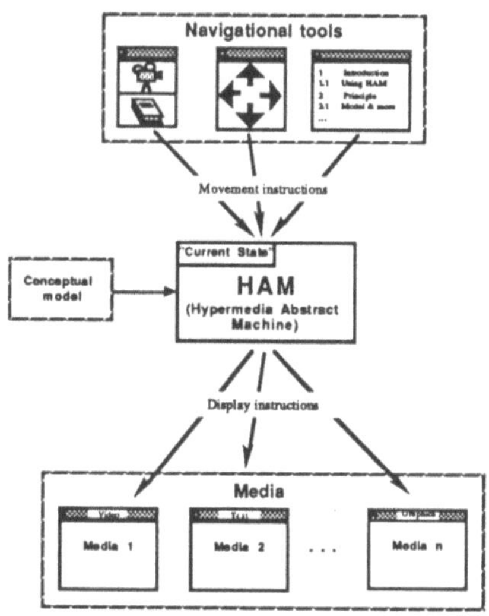

fig 1. Functional view of the HAM

The central part is the actual HAM engine that coordinates and evaluate the users action in order to decide where the user moves and what granules to show. It stores the current state, can evaluate relative movement and absolute addresses and acts as an information server for the other parts. In order to map node-names onto granules it has got an index. It lists nodes by names and show what granules they contain. The index also contains domain topological information such as arrangement of the nodes into chapters and subchapters.

Next there is the top layer in the graph. The user interacts with several different navigational tools, some of which might be custom built for a particular user group or presentation. We have designed a minimal set of generic tools such as the browsing arrows moving forward or backward, topic selections lists and a media selection palette. These, and any other tool we might design, employ a simple language to tell the HAM what actions the user has taken. The HAM in it's turn evaluates what effect that action will have on the current state and issues commands accordingly. We have conducted some experiments using custom built tools to annotate and save "trails" which we will discuss further later on.

Lastly we have the media manager that takes care of retrieval from the various media databases as well as displaying and searching in the different media. Each media manager has display methods and search methods to obey the commands of the HAM engine. A video manager, for instance, knows where to find a particular sequence demanded by the HAM and how to display it in a designated window. The window might be freely movable by the user or under the control of some navigational tool.

5.3. Navigation

The user see two things: the navigation tools and the media managers different presentations. Lets say the user clicked at the "next" arrow. The tool will send a message to the HAM simply saying "next" which is a part of the navigation command set. The HAM in it's turn evaluate the message using the "current state" and the index provided by the conceptual model to see what the "next" node would be. It then issues the appropriate command to relevant media managers, i.e. "show page 35" or "play frames 2345 to 3456". This is an example of a relative link. It links from the current node to whatever the system defines as the "next" node.

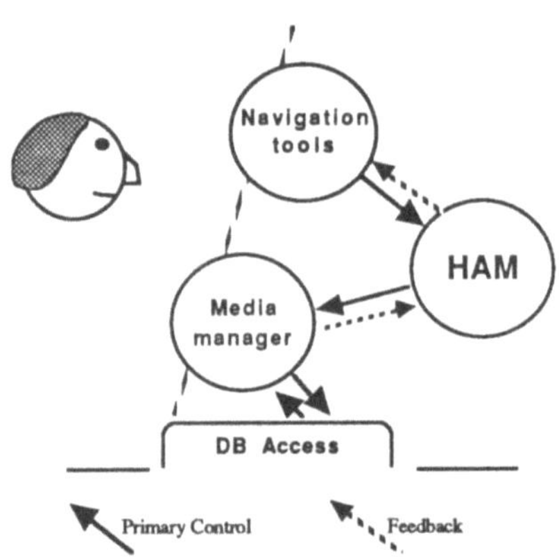

fig 2 Flow of control. Note that Navigation tools and Media managers do not interact directly.

Lets try another example using a search tool. Somehow the user enters a search criterion and a query is formed using a formal language, say SQL. The query is passed to HAM and it passes it on to the relevant media managers. Now the media manager must have some method of querying its particular medium using SQL or translating it into some media dependent search criterion. The result should be a list of nodes fitting the query. The list is passed back to the HAM.

The HAM compiles the different answers it receives and passes a list of node-names to the search tool that issued the query. The tool might do any number of things with the list such as displaying it to the user for selection, randomly selecting a node or using some other function such as picking the first node on the list. If a node is selected it's name is passed back to the HAM and translated into a command for relevant media managers using the index. The node selected is displayed. We call this an absolute link, the action taken by the user specifically naming a particular node to be viewed.

The absolute link may be provided in many different ways: as a reference in a text, as part of an overview or a map, it might be a part of a guided tour or simply a name entered from the keyboard by the user.

6. Findings

In one experiment we provided the ability of making trails and store them. Since the main thread in the presentation follows the authors line of thought another trail may well be rather "jerky". The motivation behind connecting two nodes might not be obvious and the line of thought of the trail blazer can be hard to follow. We might stumble across backwards references put in by the original author that the trail blazer deemed irrelevant. But how can we know whether or not to follow the reference?

If a person provides a trail for someone else to follow it is therefore very important that there is an annotation facility that he might use. The annotations can support the explorer by explaining background facts concerning what we see, pointing out relevant parts of the information presented or simply by telling us why we were guided to this particular node. Otherwise we would once again experience "dropping from the sky" and losing the context.

In our case we used voice and text annotation. We found that the person following a track gets cues as to *why* he has been moved to a particular node. But maybe even more important is that he can be told *what* to look for and *where* he's going next.

7. Conclusion

Firstly we are convinced that the modular aspect of our HAM provides the flexibility that we defined in the problem discussion. Different media might be included or excluded without influencing the overall structure or content. Different user or usage situations might have their special navigational tools or interfaces tailored to suit their needs.

Secondly there is the ability to add to the basic hypermedia link network by designing special tools such as the "trail" tool described in the previous section. A trail tool might be a computer based training "courseware" presentation asking question and showing different nodes depending on the answer. It might also be a special presentation or map overlay that hides the regular interface and reduce the user's freedom in order to make the point clearer.

Using and developing this dynamic information space and with the help of trail tools and the annotational capabilities we believe the user will have an adaptive and changing Personal Book to suit his taste.

References:

1. Conklin, J.:Hypertext: An Introduction and Survey. IEEE Computer September, 1987
2. Halasz, F., Conklin, J.:Issues in the Design and Application of Hypermedia Systems. Tutorial CHI 90, ACM New York, 1990
3. Hodges, M., Sasnett, R., Harward, J., Musings on Multimedia. Unix Review V01 8 No 2, 1990
4. Laurel, B., Oren, T., Don, A.: Issues in Multimedia Interface Design: Media Integration and Interface Agents. Proc of CHI 90, ACM New York, 1990
5. Lundh, J.: Data Models in Hypertext. SISU, Box 1250, S-164 28 Kista, Sweden, 1989
6. Marchionini, G., Shneiderman, B.: Finding Facts vs. Browsing Knowledge in Hypertext Systems. IEEE Computer January, 1988
7. Meyrowitz, N.:The Link to Tomorrow. Unix Review vol 8 no 2, 1990
8. Nielsen, J.: Hypertext and Hypermedia. Academic Press 1990
9. Yankelovich N., et al: Intermedia: The Concept and the Construction of a Seamless Information Environment. IEEE Computer January, 1988

Chapter 12

How to Build a Multimedial Communication/ Creation System for Music and Human Motion

Gunilla Carlsson, Peter Lundén, Magnus Lundin, Gustaf Nyman, Peter Rajka and Tamas Ungvary

A multimedial communication/creation system, called NUNTIUS, will be presented. The ultimate goal of the multimedial communication is to allow both transmission of data between the medial modalities and autonomous evaluation and utilization of that data. This goal presuppose the existence of two creation stations, one for music and one for choreography.

One of the first essential questions is how should we design the interaction between the user and the system of the creation stations ? Both hardware based gestural input devices (sentograph) and software based interactive input dialog methods will be presented. E.g. for choreography a new symbolic notation, symbolic editor, function notation and a computer animation program will be introduced.

In its present form NUNTIUS is concerned primarily with direct communication at either the parametric or structural level. The problems of higher level communication both within each medium and between the medias will also be addressed.

Introduction

The growing complexity of different applications within multimedia and their possible integration into inter- and multi-medial computer systems requires very advanced computer graphic environments. The purpose of this paper is to sketch the diversity and the complexity of the tasks for designing both specific applications and their integration within a Macintosh type of workstation environment.

Definition of Terms

It is suggested by the manufactures of computers, that multimedia means " the integration in a computer the different input- and output- media channel/modes ". The term multimedia, sometimes mixed-media, has however already been used within the artistic community for the long established *concept* (Gesamtkunstwerk) of combining more than one form or area of communication, usually for dramatic effect. (Opera, Son et Lumiere, light show.) In this sense multimedia deals with higher level integration of two (or more) usually independent media specific application systems.

The role of integration in both cases might be different. In the first case the integration serves a better man-machine dialog, in the second case it helps even the communication/collaboration between humans which might result in a "Gestalt" when the separate components of the collaborative elements are amalgamated.

We will use the terms Integrated Media and *Intermedial* Communication to denote the second case, the higher level system.

Background

It is common knowledge that human motion is related to sound as dance is related to music. Both the execution of dance and of music are highly complex motor activities and they both are rooted in utterance and gesture as a function of time.

Over the centuries, music has developed a whole vocabulary that deals with its time dependent aspect, as well as complex notational and extensive theoretical systems. The musical notation system, which emerged between 1400 and 1500 provided the foundation for an increased complexity of structure and cross reference, which contributed crucially to western music's movement towards the harmonic and rhythmic complexity of the early twentieth century.

Oral and physical transmission of information has self-evidently been more important for dance, as a medium with less developed notational traditions, than for western music. Indeed, it is arguable that without kinetic memory or the body's storage of motor functions, the medium of dance could not have developed at all. In current practice, choreography is still dependent to a large extent on the dancer's internalized storage of kinetic and motor functions, and the practicalities of structuring and crossreferencing within a complex dance composition grow organically out of the dancer's abilities to store such instructions accurately, and to provide feedback to the choreographer, not just of the movements, but of the ideas and situations out of which they arose.

Multimedia System for Human Motion

Simulation of sequences of human body motion has long been a subject of computer graphics. Different concepts have been successfully implemented, but computer scientists have always encountered difficulties in describing animation and its dynamic control in an easy and efficient way.

Our approach is based on a symbolic notation system developed by Peter Rajka and used interactively on a workstation. Since a movement notation system may be applied by different users for different purposes, multi-purpose representation of the human movement is also an essential requirement.

Symbolic Movement Notation = Motion Definition

The Symbolic Notation, which formalizes the motor knowledge and expresses it in symbols, provides the tools for structure building and manipulation of movement materials, while remaining efficient at storing and transmitting information.

Graphically, the choreographic score is vertically divided into six sub-areas, called columns. A column contains the motion definition of a group of body parts (e.g. the right arm). Except for one column, each column contains a strongly marked three line system called the angular scale system and lightly drawn parallel, complementary lines outside the angular scale system [Fig.1].

The angular scale systems represent a scaling of the angle axis in 22.5 degree steps between 0 and 180 degrees by the three strongly marked lines (0°, 90°,180°) and six intervening radial lines [Fig. 2]. The placement of a symbol on the scale

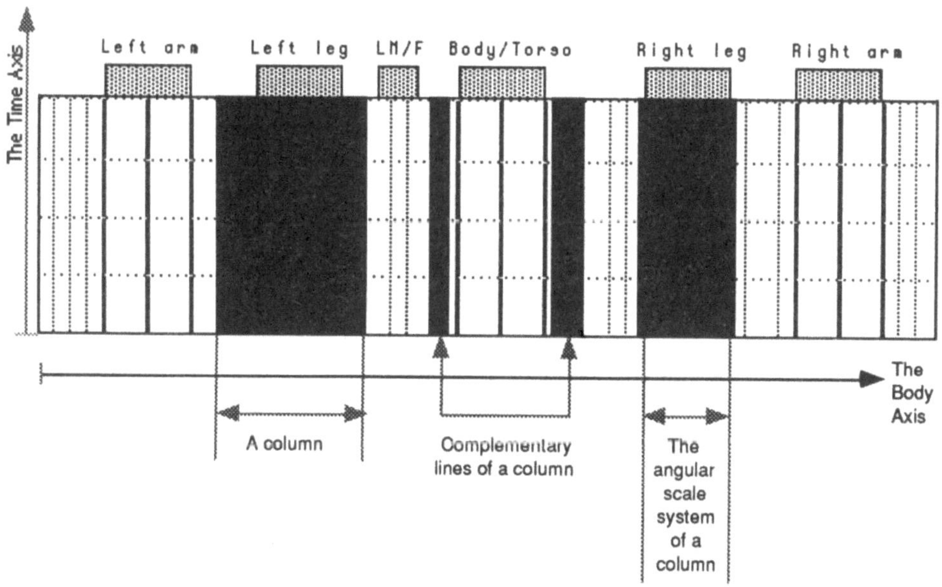

Fig. 1

system indicates the angular relationships between body parts [Fig. 3]. Modifiers allow refined evaluation of these angles.

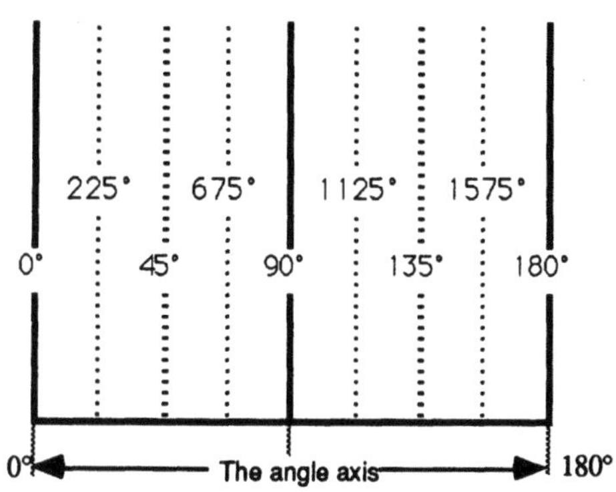

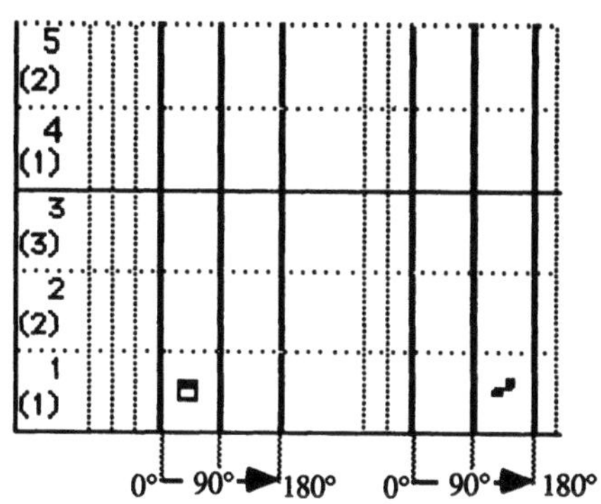

Fig. 2 and 3

Outside of the angular scale systems, the complementary lines serve for supplementary information, indicating, for example, the "state of weight".

The time flow is defined on the vertical axis and scaled in arbitrary time units. The interval represented by a time unit may be evaluated in seconds or metronome units in the comment area. These time units are indicated by dotted horizontal lines, called the time lines. Time lines are grouped by bar lines similar to the bars of a musical score [Fig. 4]. A dialogue window for definition of the counts (2 to 68 counts) is available from the menu.

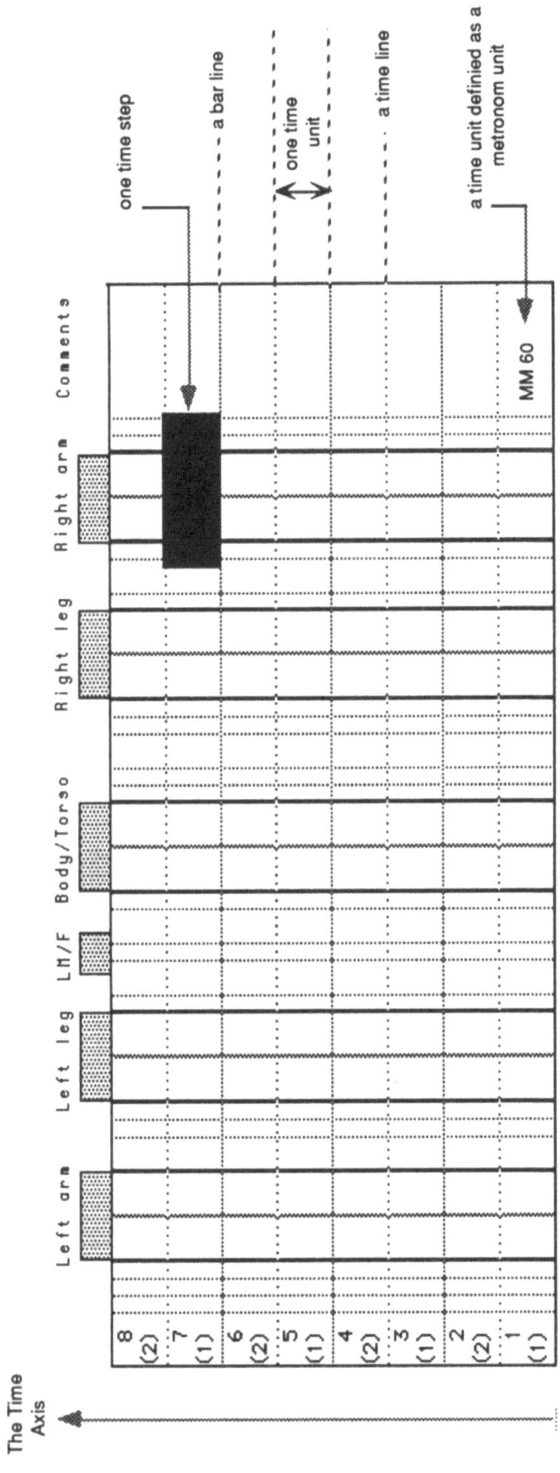
one time step
a bar line
one time unit
a time line
a time unit defined as a metronom unit
Left arm
Left leg
LM/F
Body/Torso
Right leg
Right arm
Comments
MM 60
8
(2)
7
(1)
6
(2)
5
(1)
4
(2)
3
(1)
2
(2)
1
(1)
The Time Axis

Fig. 4

The area between two time lines is called a time step. A time step may contain one or more symbols indicating various positions of the body parts in the column at a given point of time.

In order to give the starting position of the body, the angles between the main body parts (e.g. between upper arm and torso) and subordinate ones (e.g. between upper arm and lower arm) and the position of the centre of the whole body (i.e. the hip) must be defined. This is achieved by placing rectangular symbols with inherent horizontal movement direction indications [Fig.5] on the angular scale system of a column. These rectangular symbols are the "main movement notes" which describe the positions of the main body parts [Fig. 6].

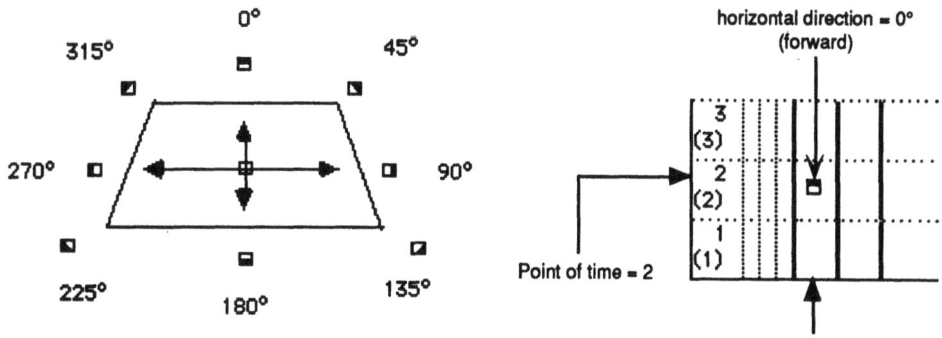

Figs. 5 and 6

The angular relationship between main and subordinate and between subordinate body parts is notated by the placement of signs for secondary, tertiary (etc.) body parts on the angular scale [Fig. 7a].

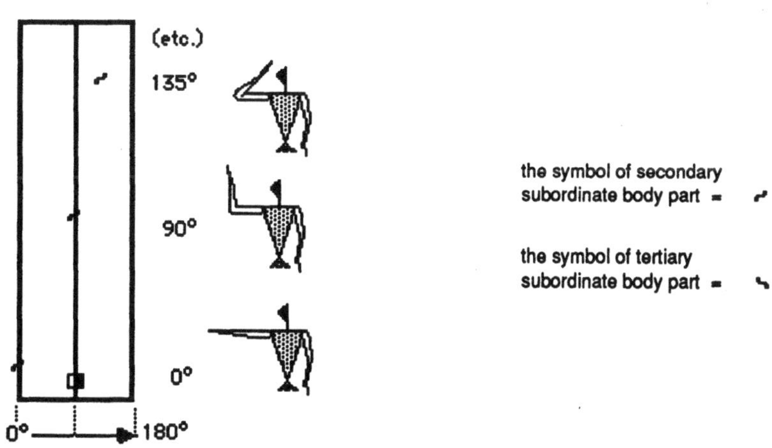

Fig. 7a

If a subordinate body part has its own independent horizontal direction, it is allocated a modifier [Fig. 7b].

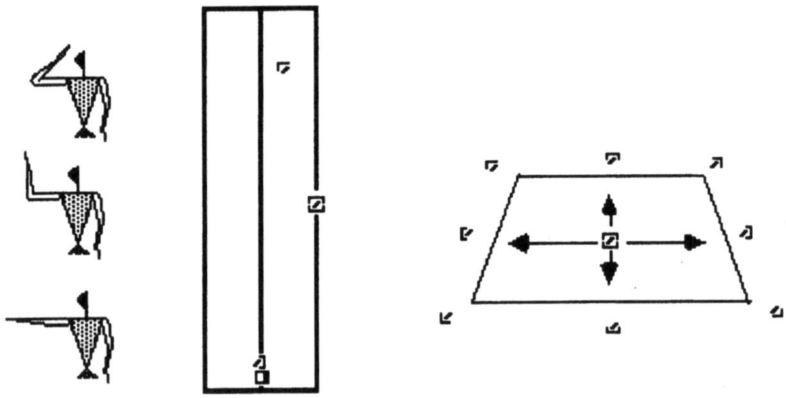

Fig. 7b

New movement notes for the same body part, defining a new position, may be placed anywhere on the vertical time axis. The time span between two positions is either the transition interval (i.e. duration) of the actual movement or a pause between two movements. The duration of a movement is indicated by the length of the duration sign attached to a main movement note or by the distance between the symbols for the subordinate body parts, measured by the time lines [Fig. 8a,b].

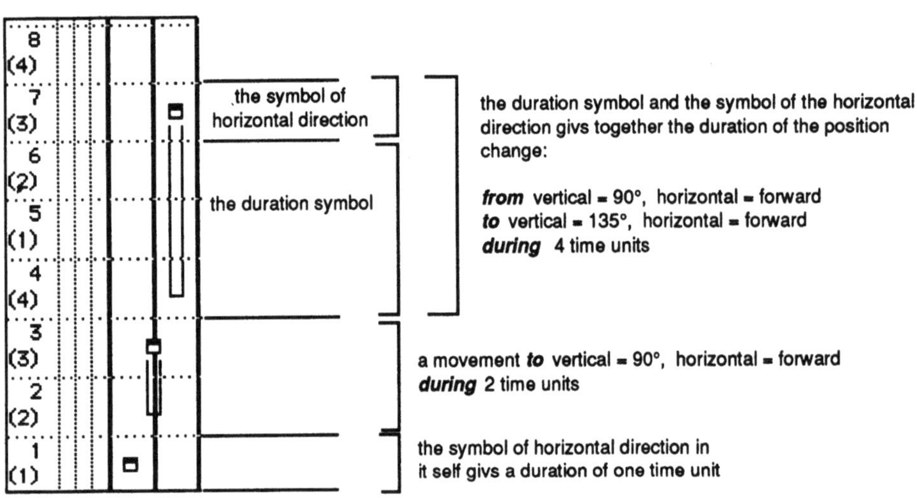

Fig. 8a

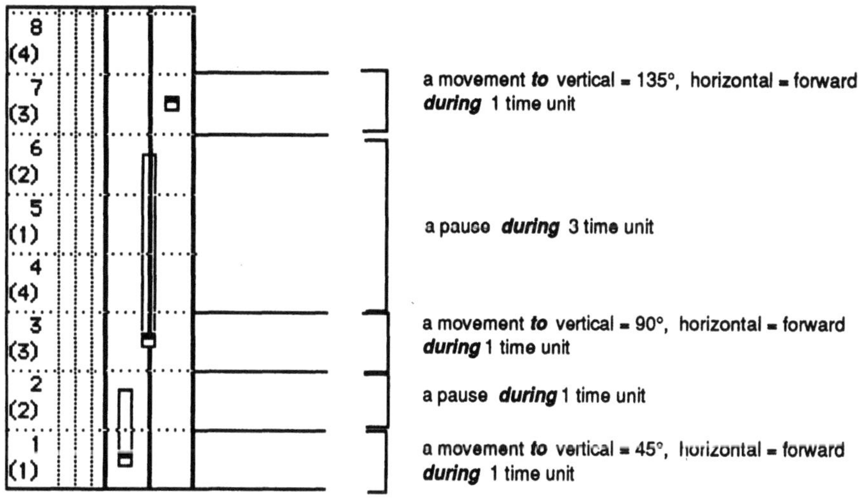

Fig. 8b

The Symbolic Movement Notation Editor = Motion Editor

A few investigations in symbolic motion description editing resulted in some significant results, e.g. the Benesh Notation Editor by Ryman and Beatty. A basic function of all notation editors is that they can be used both to enter new motion sequences and to edit old ones.

In many cases the editor facilities and the internal data representations are highly dependent on the concept and the graphics of the implemented notation system. Motographicon is an attempt to separate the movement data and its graphic representation as far it is possible. This concept facilitates a more autonomous treatment of the motion in itself within the program and data structures, which permits the development of more complex manipulative features.

The Editor of Motographicon involves three integrated parts [Fig. 9] :

1) The Symbol Window, which contains a set of the movement symbols. A copy of a symbol, selected from the Symbol Window may be placed into the Score Window by a mouse click.

2) The Combined Symbol Window, which allows selection of two or three symbols by one mouse click, where upon more than one symbol will be placed at the same position in the Score Window.

3) The Score Window, which contains three main areas:
   - the time reference area
   - the score area
   - the comment area

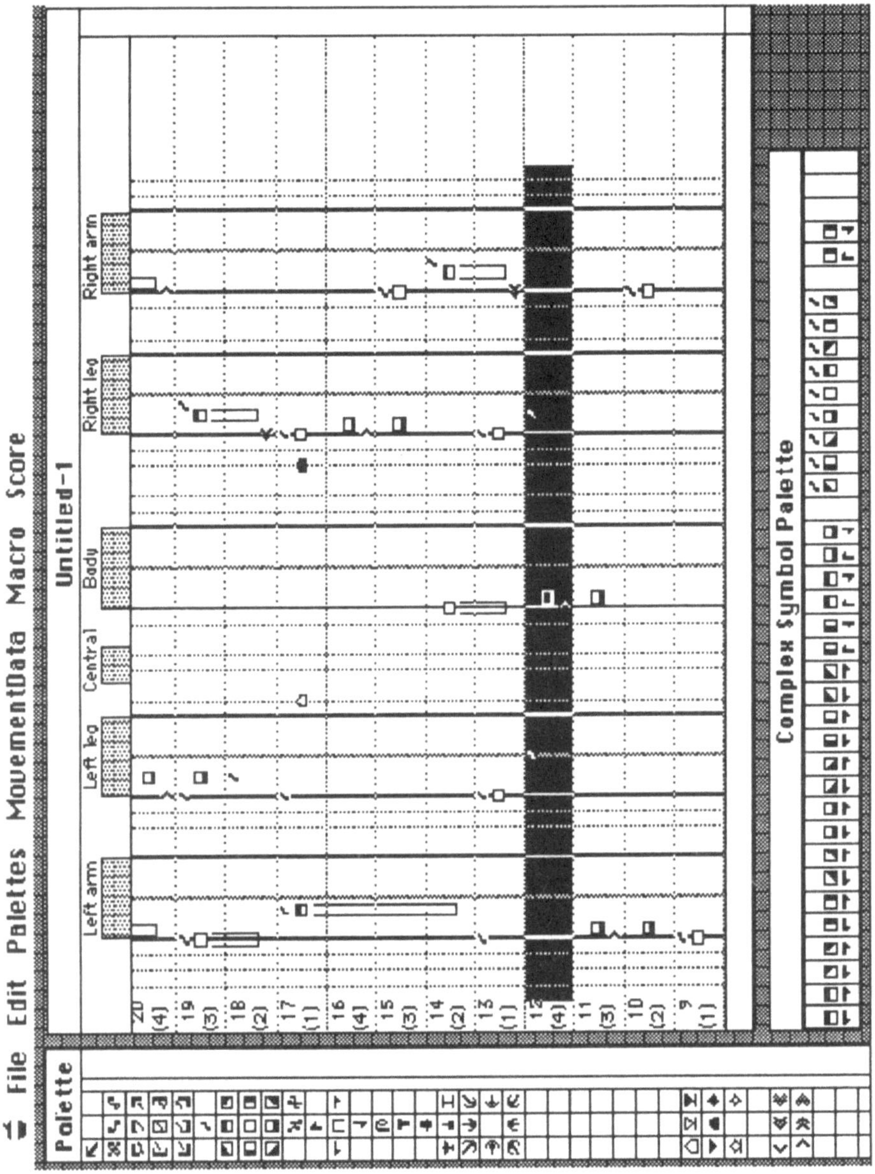

File
Edit
Palettes
MovementData
Macro
Score
Untitled-1
Palette
Left arm
Left leg
Central
Body
Right leg
Right arm
Complex Symbol Palette

Fig. 9

Each of the main areas or elements in these structures may be selected by mouse clicks:

- a row, at a time point in the comment area
- a row of time steps, at a time point in the time reference area
- a column, at a column header
- a time step, at a time step area
- a symbol, on a symbol

Multiple selections (by holding the shift key down) are allowed on each level, except the single symbol level.

Ways of treating selected score elements:

Comments:
- opening a row to enter text information

Symbols:
- move to other columns, time steps or scale positions in a column
- resizing of duration

Time steps:
- move to other columns or time steps
- copy, paste, delete, insert
- saved as movement data

Columns:
- copy, paste
- saved as movement data

Time rows:
- delete, insert
- saved as movement data

Every selected structure element may be cleared.
At any selected time step movement data, stored on a file, may be loaded. Several commands for treatment can be selected from the menu before loading, as augmentation, mirroring, shifting body parts, etc. A loaded movement data file can be assigned to a macro menu for repeated use in the score.

Data Formats. A symbolic score document contains the graphical structure of the symbolic score, while a movement data file contains the position and time definitions in numerical form. The latter format is more suitable for manipulations and interchanges between other programs than the graphical structure which on the other hand facilitates the graphical treatment of the score. Conversion between these two data types is available.

Meta Symbol Editor

With the Meta Symbol Editor the system developer may create his own graphical symbols for the Symbol Notation Editor. The Meta Symbol Editor includes facilities for designing the shapes of the symbols and for the definition of the syntax and semantics of the notation, i.e. rules for allowed placement of each symbol and rules for the generation of the movement data. All this information is saved on a file which has to be read into the data structures of the Symbol Notation Editor.

Function Notation of Movement = High Level Abstraction

As described above, the trajectories of a movement occur between consecutive body positions placed in time, defined by and notated with the Symbolic Notation. Since the positions may be evaluated from angles, a sequence of motion may be represented by a sequence of consecutive trajectories, i.e. by a set of functions. This concept allows the transformation of Symbolic Notation into Function Notation and vice versa. They are interrelated and compatible.

Function Notation Editor

The Function Notation Editor offers visual compatibility between the two kinds of movement representation. This is achieved by using the same time representation and angular scale system in both of them. The Function Notation Editor provides an effective visual record both of the time-space structures and of the evolution shapes of the parameters. Fig.10 displays a movement with three parameters in both symbolic and function notation.

During a transformation of a movement parameter function from the Symbolic Notation to the Function Notation, a rescaling of the movement data also takes place. All of the functions within the Function Notation Editor are normalized to be between 0. and 1.

The rescaling feature of the editor allows the movement characteristics to be displayed in enhanced detail. Additional features allow both the display of any number of overlapping graphs or several graphs in parallel. An option allows generation of new graphs as the difference, sum or average of existing ones. Fig.11 shows the average (b) and difference (c) graphs obtained by comparing two of the parameters (a) of the movement in Fig.10. This facility provides movement pattern detection, even in the case of a delay between two functions.

Animation

The animation programs in our system are based on a parametric keyframe animation concept. It is characterized by objects defined by different sets of parameters at consecutive time steps. The animation program creates keyframes (images) based on the assigned rotation and translation values. In-between frames will be generated by interpolation between the parameters, depending on the assigned duration value and the number of frames per time unit, which is optional.

The User Interface of Anima. Anima is an application for visualization of human movements. It is not intended for rendering purposes, but as a tool for choreographers. Users work with scenes consisting of dancers and a simple floor and a background. Today, it is only possible to view one dancer in each scene, but this limitation will be removed in future versions of the application. A scene is displayed in a window, so it is possible to view several scenes simultaneously. Each scene may be viewed from an arbitrary position in space.

The execution of a choreography is controlled by the user through a window similar to the controls on a tape recorder. There are controls for forward, backward and stop of execution. Full control over tempo and position in the score is maintained with the use of scroll bars.

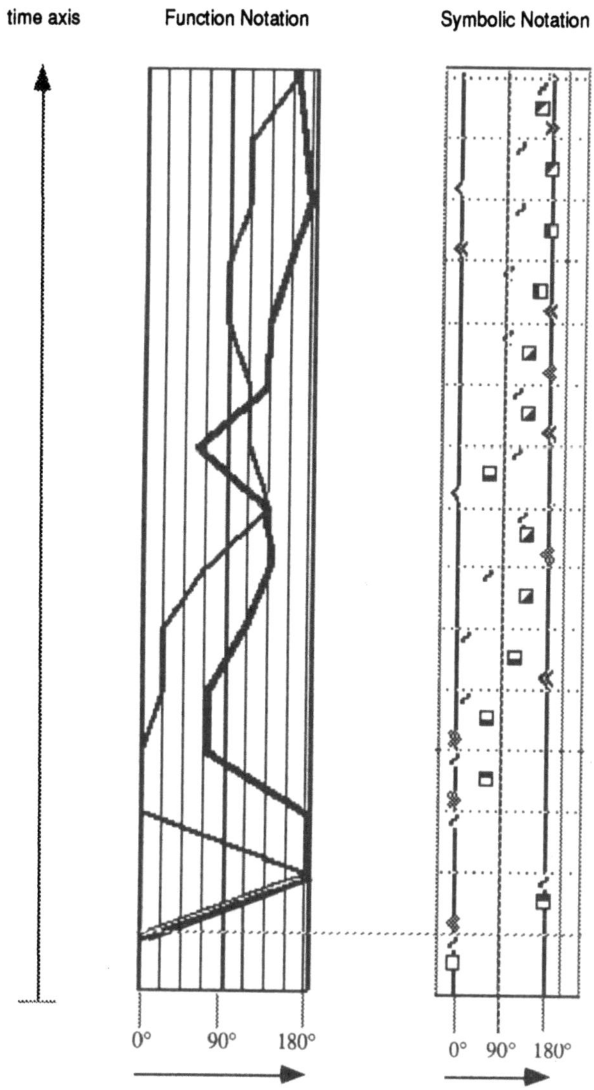

In function notation:

vertical parameters of the main body part (upper arm)

the relationship of angles between main and subordinate body part (lower arm)

Fig. 10

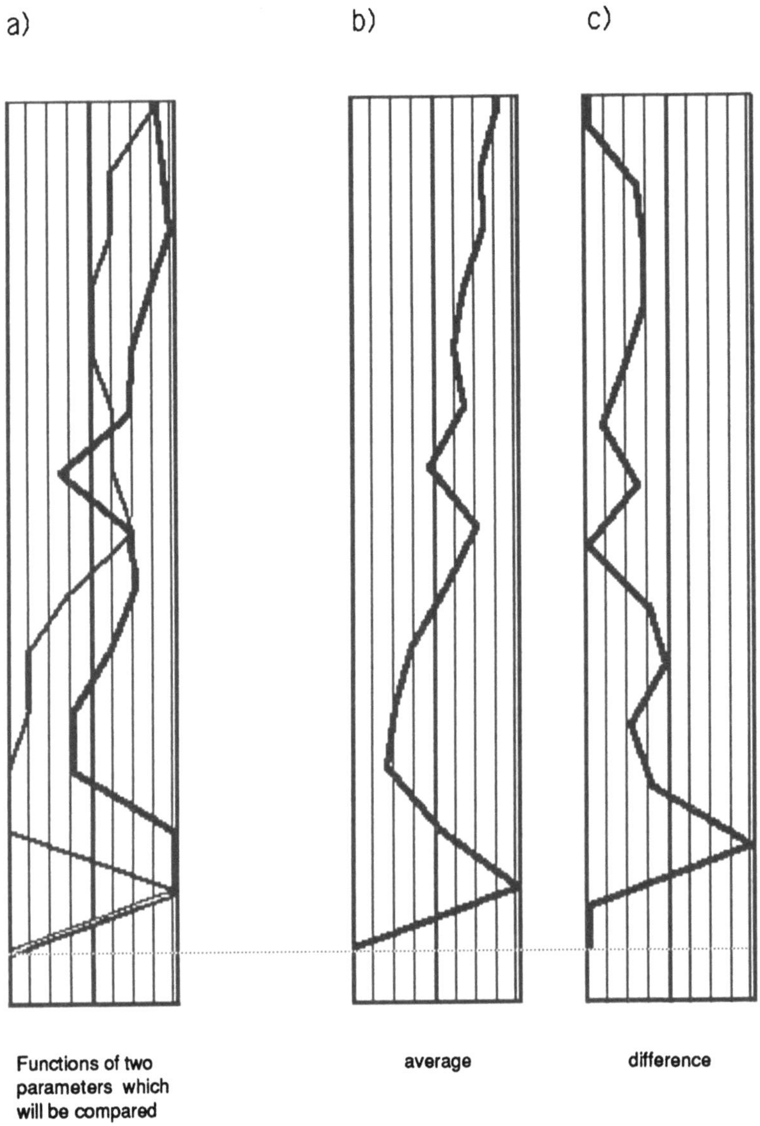

Fig. 11

Animation with 2D Figure. Converts movement data files to a format suitable for generating animated pictures. The animation is performed by a two dimensional cartoon figure, showing movements in 3D space in real-time. The proportions of the figure may be predefined. The animation window contains one moving figure, floor and background references. The movement control panel provides speed, stop, backward and forward functions to steer the motion display. The speed control is scaled in metronome units [Fig. 12].

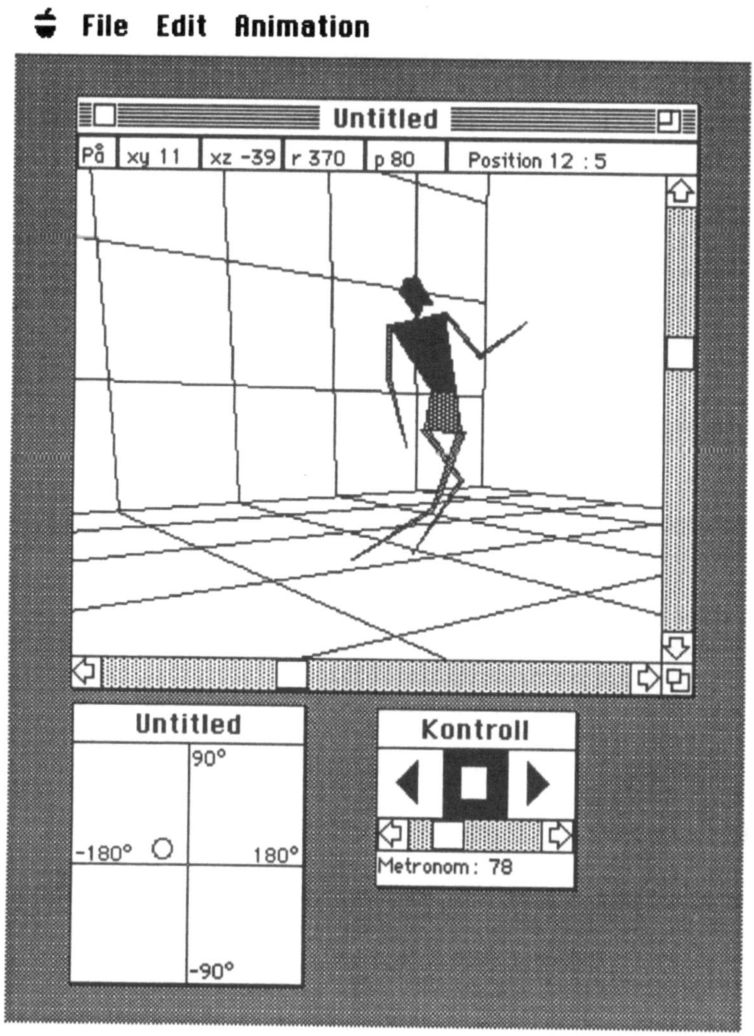

Fig. 12

The camera control panel allows one to change the view-point in 3D, continuously, without stopping the movements. Multiple windows for simultaneous animations are available.

Animation with 3D Figure. It allows interactive editing of the performer figure. It generates a series of bitmap images with a 3D figure for frame-by-frame animation which may be preview with a stick-figure animation.

Movelib. ANIMA is based on a support package for human movement animation, called MOVELIB developed by Magnus Lundin. It is a library if C-language routines developed for the Motographicon programs used in the NUNTIUS project. The

package gives standard support for :
- Reading and parsing MOVE text movement data files
- Computations on moving linked structures representing a human body
- Generating display structures, polygons, for drawing the resulting body shape.

The code is written in ANSI C to be useful on different systems. The main application then has to be linked to system-dependent parts such as a user interface, file handling and interface to the display drivers. The different parts of the library are called using a small number of interface routines and standard data structures, making it easy to change the algorithms used internally without having to rewrite the main application.

MIDI and Anima

MIDI is a wide spread standard for communication between electronic musical instruments, lately including computers. The Macintosh MIDI Manager enables communications between applications as sequencers and composing systems on the Apple Macintosh computer. As one of our objectives is to integrate and enhance the creative process of composing dance and music, we have implemented parts of MIDI, with the MIDI Manager, in Anima. The implementation is limited to timer facilities. It is hence possible to synchronize Anima with various electronic musical devices and applications, either as a slave or master unit.

A user working on a choreography is able to hear music synchronized with Anima as he changes the position in and tempo of his composition.

Multimedia System for Music

A complete Computer Music Workstation is a multimedia system in itself. It's features must include programmability and interactive real-time processing. The audio characteristics together with the control facilities and the available software determines the usability of the workstation.

The Audio Subsystem

The audio subsystem of our Computer Music Workstation consists of: two high quality studio monitors, one DAT tape recorder, one analogue audio mixer used for monitoring, one digital sound processing unit used mainly for reverberation, a synthesizer card and two signal processing cards in the Macintosh [Fig. 13]. The audio signals can be kept in the digital domain throughout the working process, and can be stored on DAT-tape. Audio signals can also be retrieved from the CD-ROM player in the system.

The system can handle 2 audio channels at 48 kHz sample rate which gives a bandwidth of 10-22k Hz and a dynamic range of more than 90 dB. There is disk-space to store 112 track-minutes of sound. External digital audio formats are EBU, SPDIF and optical.

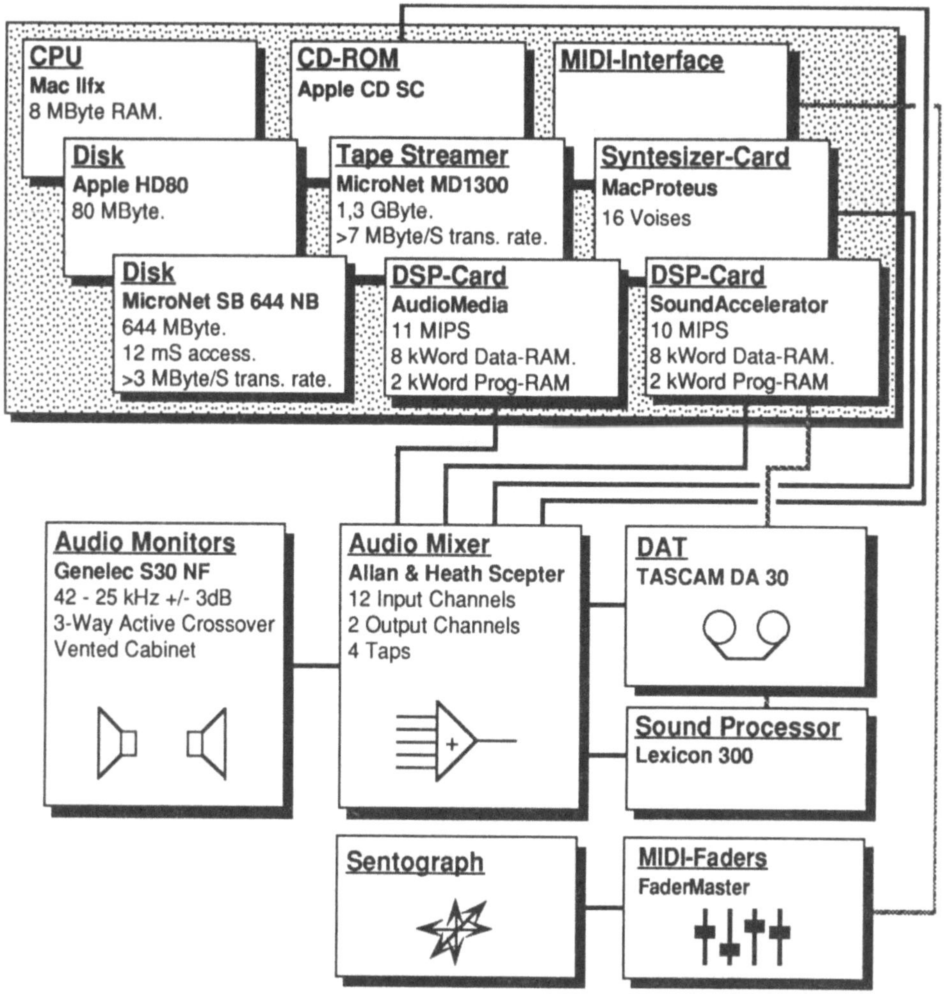

Fig. 13

The Control Facilities

The control facilities determine the real-time usability of the system. Very little research has been done on real-time interactive controlling of a computer music system, especially research on gestural input devices. This leads to a strong traditionalistic influence on the music produced on the system. Therefore the need for new more stylistically neutral input devices is considerable. The Sentograph is such a device which is new to the musical field. More traditional input devices like alphanumeric-keyboard, mouse and MIDI-keyboard are also used in the environment.

Sentograph

The sentograph is a pressure sensitive input organ [1], [2]. The original design which measured the horizontal and vertical components of finger pressure (2D) has been improved by the Dept. of Psychology, Uppsala University, Sweden. The new design allows independent encoding of finger pressure in all three dimensions (3D). This is accomplished by using a linkarm system with ball-bearings to divide possible sideways movement (in finger pressure) into distinctly separated left-right and away-toward directions with separate strain gauges for each direction. A new amplifier with negligible noise is used in the current version. The overall sensitivity of the system is estimated to be 1-2 grams.

Alphanumeric Keyboard

The alphanumeric keyboard is not of central importance in a real-time situation, although it can be used as a triggering and switching device.

Mouse

The mouse is a very flexible tool in this kind of application. It can be used both as a traditional pointing device and as a 2D gestural input device.

MIDI-Faders

The Fadermaster [3] is a MIDI [4] control device with eight sliders. The device transmits MIDI data when the sliders are moved. One can assign both MIDI channels and the type of data (volume, pitch, modulation etc.) to be sent. It has been modified to handle three different voltage inputs from the Sentograph.

MIDI-Keyboard

The MIDI-keyboard is like a traditional instrument keyboard with some additional knobs and thumbweels. It is sensitive to both the hitting force and pressure on the keys. One great problem with this device, especially in a teaching situation, is the stylistic implications that it entails [5].

Musse Dig

An analog singing synthesizer, MUSSE, an important tool for the research on singing, was built in our department in 1976. Recently we have completed the construction of a new digital version, MUSSE DIG. It consists of a PC complemented with a TMS 320C30 floating point signal processor performing real-time computation of sounds. The synthesizer can be controlled either by on-line controllers or from a note-file complemented with text, chords, and phrase markers. The external control system is based on Windows and programed by Sten Ternström.

The note-file is processed by a system of context-dependent pronunciation rules producing reasonably natural sounding consonants and vowels. In addition, the system contains a set of rules providing expressive deviations from the score depending on the musical context, developed under the leadership of prof. Johan

Sundberg. MUSSE DIG can also be controlled from the PC screen by a panel or a keyboard. Other control possibilities are external MIDI devices. The Sentograph has proven particularly useful for attaining expressive sounds.

Problems, Future

Although we are convinced that intermedial communication has a great potential, there are more than a lot of question to be answered before we will even be able to design a system which can be considered as complete.

On the other hand even the realization of our current visions is difficult. The new technologies which could properly serve intermedial and multimedial information systems are just emerging. To be able to store, relate, evaluate, interpret, resynthesize and process both sounds and movements with their respective notations and with a diversity of their classifications we need a very powerful database system. An Object Oriented Database (OODB) might be the answer [6].

To be able to handle the huge quantity of control parameters of the polyphonic processes of the human motion or of the music we need more adequate man-machine interfaces in parallel. Both speech, gesture and eye tracking and even the subcarriers of communication, as shrugging, smiles, body language, winks, gestures might provide additional ways to interact with the computer [7].

Acknowledgement

The development of the multimedial communication/creation system NUNTIUS by the Kineto-Auditory Communication Research Group (KACOR, at the Institute of Speech Communication and Music Acoustics, Royal Institute of Technology, Stockholm), is supported by the Bank of Sweden Tercentenary Foundation.

References and Notes

1. Clynes, M.: "The Communication of Emotion; Theory of Sentics" in: Emotion, Theory, Research and Experience. Volume 1: Theories of Emotion, R.Plutchik and H. Kellerman, eds. ; New York, Academic Press, 1980.
2. Clynes, M., Jurisevic, S. and Ryan, M.:"Inherent cognitive subtracts of specific emotions : Love is blocked by lying but not anger" in Perceptual and Motor Skills, 1990, 70,195-206
3. Lennard, V.: Fadermaster. Music Technology, October 1989.
4. Anderton, Craig : The MIDI Protocol in Music and Digital Technology. The Proceedings of the AES 5th International Conference, 1987.
5. Wishart, T: On Sonic Art. Imagineering Press, York, 1985.
6. Josep, J.V., Thatte, S. M., Thompson, C. W., Wells , D. L.: Object-Oriented Databases : Design and Implementation. Proceedings of IEEE, Vol 79, No 1, January 1991, pp. 42-64
7. Bolt, R. A., Barron, J. J.: The wizards of the Media Lab. Byte, December 1989, pp. 353-360

Part V

Cooperative Work

Chapter 13

Multimedia Conferencing as a Universal Paradigm for Collaboration

P. Venkat Rangan and Harrick M. Vin

Multimedia interaction between users usually takes the form of conferences. We propose a taxonomy of multimedia conferencing, and develop a model that can support most types of collaborative interactions. The model provides sophisticated features such as access control with respect to different media streams, flexibility to use multiple media channels to participate in multiple conferences simultaneously, and nested conferences. Conferences are treated as first class objects, and we define operations to manipulate such objects. We are carrying out a software implementation of the conferencing paradigm at the Multimedia Laboratory of the University of California, San Diego.

1 Introduction

1.1 Motivation

Recent advances in computer and communication technology has led to the development of high performance workstations with digital audio and video capabilities [5]. The advent of such multimedia workstations has given rise to many computer supported collaborative applications. Audio and video interations differ fundamentally from textual interactions [7], and usually take the form of conferences. The task of supporting multimedia conferences consists of two parts: the integration of control of audio and video services with distributed computing, and the real-time transmission of digital multimedia data. The software paradigms to integrate conferencing services with distributed computing constitute the subject matter of this paper.

1.2 Related Work

Mechanisms for person-to-person conferences and shared text-oriented workspaces has been the focus of research in many ongoing multimedia projects. Sarin and Greif [11] have studied conferencing architectures for text and graphics, but they are not flexible enough for audio and video. Angebranndt et al [3] provide a client-server architecture for integrating audio into a graphics workstation environment, but the emphasis is on lower-level audio resource management rather than rich conferencing capabilities. Forsdick et al

This work was supported by the NSF Research Initiation Award No. NCR-9009757, IBM Corporation, Xerox Corporation, UVC Corporation, and the University of California MICRO program.

at BBN [6], Ludwig et al at Bellcore [9], Ahuja et al at Bell Laboratories [2] and Aguilar et al at SRI [1], Casner et al at ISI [4], and the PX system [8] have proposed architectures for multimedia conferencing. Sophisticated connection management facilities, which can lead to the use of conferencing as a general paradigm for interaction and collaboration among any set of participants, are not fully explored. The Etherphone system [10,12] provides basic connection management features such as conference forwarding and visiting, and background/foreground conferencing; our experience with this system has been the initial motivation for the work reported in this paper.

1.3 Our Contributions

We present a conferencing paradigm that can form the basis for supporting most types of multimedia collaborative interactions in distributed computing systems. We propose a taxonomy of multimedia conferencing (*Section 3*), and develop a model that can support sophisticated features such as access control with respect to different media streams, flexibility to use multiple media channels to participate in multiple conferences simultaneously, and nested conferences (*Section 4*). In our model, conferences are treated as first class objects, and we define operations for manipulating such objects (*Section 5*). We are carrying out an implementation of the conferencing system at the Multimedia Laboratory of the University of California, San Diego.

2 Preliminary Definitions

Participants in a conference can be either individual users, or other conferences, or both, thereby leading to two types:

- A *simple participant* represents an individual user.
- A *super participant* represents an entire conference.

Conference Attributes are properties of a conference as a whole, such as its duration of existence, its initiator, etc.

Participant Attributes are properties specific to a participant in a conference, mainly the participant's modes of access to the conference. A mode of access consists of a medium (e.g., video or audio), and the direction (e.g., in or out) of access to the conference. Each participant in a conference has two types of attributes:

- *Permitted attributes* are those specified by the initiator of the conference.
- *Desired attributes* are those preferred by the participant.

Clearly, the desired attributes must be a subset of the permitted attributes.

3 Taxonomy of Multimedia Conferencing

We define a conference as a basic paradigm by which interactions such as (1) communication among multiple participants, and (2) one or more participants accessing one or more servers, are carried out. There are several types of conferences which can be classified as follows:

3.1 Static vs. Dynamic Conferences

Static Conferences do not permit changes in conference or participant attributes after initiation.

Dynamic Conferences permit conference and participant attributes to be changed at any time.

In reality, most conferences are partly dynamic and partly static, with varying degrees of dynamicity. For instance: in an *examination*, participants cannot be changed after initiation; in a *judicial court hearing*, witnesses cannot change their desired mode of participation after initiation; in a *research group meeting*, almost any of the attributes can be changed at any time.

3.2 Simple vs. Super Conferences

Simple Conferences contain only simple participants.

Super Conferences contain at least one super participant representing some other conference, as their participant. If a conference C_1 is a participant in a conference C_2, C_1 is termed as a *sub-conference* of the super conference C_2. Note that a sub-conference can itself be recursively a super conference.

It should be observed that, even though super conferences can always be flattened into simple conferences, the super conference paradigm serves as a better (more natural and efficient) abstraction to satisfy certain collaborative requirements.

Consider a meeting (C_1) among a group of agents in a brokerage firm. The goal of the meeting is to make decisions regarding investments in stocks. An important factor in such a decision making process is the continuously changing information from the stock market. To receive this information, the group joins a conference C_2, which is broadcasting information from the stock market. Thus, C_1 is a simple conference and C_2 is a super conference. Capturing this scenario using only simple conferences introduces special requirements. For instance, a new participant joining C_1 has to determine all the conferences that C_1 is participating in (i.e., C_2 in this case), and then join each of them. Supporting super conference abstraction has the following advantages: (1) Participation in C_1 automatically implies participation in C_2, (2) the mode of participation in C_1 automatically determines the mode of participation in C_2, (3) the duration of participation in C_2 is limited by the length of participation in C_1, and (4) it introduces a concept of group participation in conferences.

3.3 Unrelated vs. Hierarchically Related Conferences

Unrelated Conferences do not share any conference attributes among them.

Hierarchically Related Conferences share semantic context, allowing for (1) *inheritance* of conference and participant attributes (such as, duration of existence and permitted access modes of participants) from a *parent conference* to a *child conference*, and (2) *aggregation* of *sibling conferences* under a parent conference.

Participation in hierarchically related and super conferences are forms of nested conferencing.

A typical example of a conference that uses inheritance and aggregation facilities is an undergraduate course at a university. Such a course usually consists of four different aggregates of conferences: *lectures*, *tutorials*, *laboratory sessions*, and *exams*. Each of these aggregates inherits the duration and the student enrollment from its parent conference, which is the course itself.

3.4 Transient vs. Persistent Conferences

Transient Conferences exist only as long as there are at least two active participants in them, and hence, are usually short-lived. Most work to date in multimedia conferencing falls under this category. Telephone conversations are good examples of transient conferences.

Persistent Conferences have a much longer duration of existence, and can continue to exist irrespective of participants becoming active or inactive. Such conferences usually consist of a sequence of active collaboration sessions among participants separated by periods of inactivity.

Note that since persistent conferences consist of a sequence of active and inactive sessions among participants, it naturally models periodic events (such as, weekly scheduled meetings, lectures for a course, etc.). In addition, there are many reasons for supporting persistent conferences in a connection model:

1. Persistence of a conference (and the knowledge of its activations) provides a mechanism for reserving resources for each activation of the conference.

2. Persistent conferences capture the notion of a meeting room, which exists independent of the participants of the conference and is available during the active periods of the conference.

3. Persistent conferences also capture the notion of semantic continuity between conferences. Maintenance of semantic continuity may involve saving and restoring the context of conference activations (the notion of saving and restoring context is similar to the one used in simple procedure invocations).

3.5 Symmetric vs. Asymmetric Conferences

Symmetric Conferences require all their participants to use the same set of media for communication.

Asymmetric Conferences allow each participant to use media of its choice for communication.

3.6 Homogeneous vs. Heterogeneous Conferences

Homogeneous Conferences do not allow conversion between different media during communication between participants.

Heterogeneous Conferences allow media conversions such as speech-to-text recognition and text-to-speech synthesis.

3.7 Sequential vs. Concurrent Conferencing

Sequential Conferencing allows a user to participate in exactly one conference at any given time. However, users can put a conference on hold (that is, become inactive in), participate in another conference, and later resume the first conference.

Concurrent Conferencing allows users to participate in multiple conferences simultaneously. In real-life interactions, people usually actively interact in one logical context, but can passively monitor information from several different contexts. For instance, while conversing on a telephone, a user may continue to monitor the TV for any interesting news. Thus, concurrent conferencing provides a pragmatic environment for collaboration.

4 Connection Model for Multimedia Conferencing

Connection management refers to the intelligence required to establish and control the progress of conferences. A conference is a progression of the participants through a sequence of states. The *connection manager* handles naming and addressing of participants, mediates negotiations necessary for setting up conferences, performs resource allocation, enforces access permissions, maintains states of all participants, and controls state transitions of participants. Participants may initiate state transitions in response to input from their users. All state transitions of each participant in a conference are reported to the connection manager. The connection manager redistributes the state transition reports to all the other participants, which may then respond with their own state transitions. The *initiator* of a conference becomes its *controller*, and specifies the users who are to be invited (referred to as *invitees*) to join the conference and their permitted modes of access.

Figure 14.1 shows the state diagram of a participant in a conference. Each participant has six possible states, of which the states IDLE, INITIATING, RINGBACK, and ACTIVE are those of an initiator, and the states IDLE, NOTIFIED, RINGING, and ACTIVE are those of an invitee of the conference. The names of the states are derived from the world of telephony, and are self explanatory. Briefly, an initiator enters (1) the INITIATING state just before sending a new conference establishment request, (2) the RINGBACK state when it learns that at least one invitee is currently being prompted to join the conference, and (3) the ACTIVE state when it learns that at least one invitee has accepted the invitation. An invitee enters (1) the NOTIFIED state when it receives a request to join a new conference, (2) the RINGING state if the user is to be prompted to join the conference, and (3) the ACTIVE state when the invitee accepts the invitation.

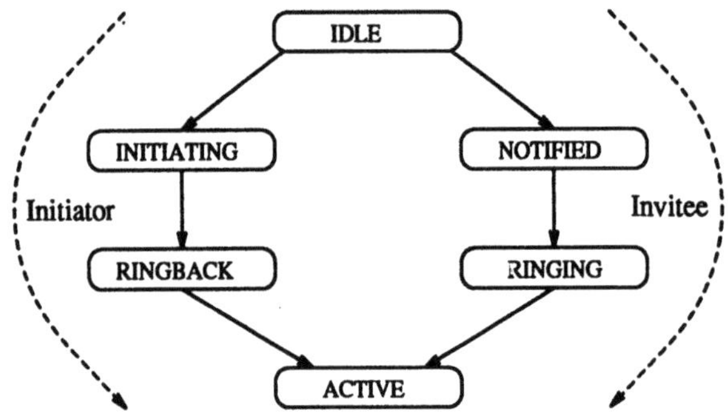

Figure 14.1: State diagram for connection management

Table 14.1: 5-tuple representation of each participant in a conference

participant	— *Unique name*
location	— *Location of the participant (workstation address)*
state	— *State of the participant*
Set of [	— *Permitted access modes*
medium,	— *Medium of transmission*
direction	— *Direction of transmission*
]	
Set of [	— *Desired access modes*
medium,	— *Medium of transmission*
direction	— *Direction of transmission*
]	

The complete information about each participant in a conference can be represented by a *5-tuple* as shown in Table 14.1. The state of a conference is the *set of 5-tuple representations of all its participants.* If each participant can be in one of k states and if there are n participants in the conferences, then there are at least k^n possible states of the conference. That is, the number of states of a conference grows exponentially with the number of participants, and hence a context free grammar (as opposed to a finite state machine) is used to represent the state of a conference (see Table 14.2).

Table 14.2: Context free grammar formulation of a conference state

$S \rightarrow RS \mid \epsilon$
$R \rightarrow (P, L, S_a, A_p, A_d)$
$P \rightarrow p$
$L \rightarrow l$
$S_a \rightarrow R \mid$ IDLE $\mid$ INITIATING $\mid$ NOTIFIED $\mid$ RINGING $\mid$ RINGBACK $\mid$ ACTIVE
$A_p \rightarrow (M, D)A_p \mid \epsilon$
$A_d \rightarrow (M, D)A_d \mid \epsilon$
$M \rightarrow audio \mid video \mid audioVisual$
$D \rightarrow in \mid out \mid inOut$

The state of a conference is maintained in a *Conference Object* created for the conference by the connection manager.

An interesting scenario arises when a conference C_1 participates as a sub-conference in another super conference C_2. C_1's conference object takes on the role of a participant representing C_1 (i.e., becomes a super participant) in C_2, and it obeys the same state transition diagram as that of a simple participant. However, C_1's conference object (recursively) propagates all the requests it receives (e.g., invitation to join C_2) to C_1's conference controller, so as to give him full control over C_1's participation in C_2.

5 Operations on Conferences

We now describe the exact operations that can be performed on conferences.

5.1 Establishing Conferences

A new conference can be initiated using the following operation:

Create[confName, listOf [participant, permittedAccessModes]] $\rightarrow$ confObject

If *confName* is $/C_1/C_2/C_3$, the above operation creates a new conference C_3 nested within $/C_1/C_2$. The initiator (i.e., the creator) of a conference specifies a list of participants, and for each participant in the list, a set of permitted access modes. Since a child conference also inherits access modes from its parent, the permitted access modes of participants are determined by taking the intersection of the given access modes and the inherited access modes.

A participant can accept a conference invitation using the following interface, specifying his own *desired modes of access* to the conference:

Join[confName, desiredAccessModes]

Participants can leave a conference at any time. A transient conference terminates when there is no more than one participant. Both transient and persistent conferences can be terminated by their controllers at any time. The exact interfaces for these operations are:

Leave[confName, agentID]
Terminate[confName]

5.2 Merging Conferences

Multiple conferences can be coalesced into a single conference using the **Merge** operation. The key issue in merging conferences is to determine the state of the resulting conference from those of component conferences, particularly when the same participant appears in more than one component conference, that too with different access rights. Consider the following operation:

$$\textsf{Merge}[C_1, C_2, ...C_n] \rightarrow C_{merged}$$

Execution of this operation terminates all the component conferences (namely, C_1, C_2, ..., C_n). The state of C_{merged} contains the 5-tuple:

$$(participant_i, location_i, state_i, [(m_1, d_1), (m_2, d_2), .., (m_m, d_m)], [(m_1, p_1), (m_2, p_2), .., (m_m, p_m)])$$

if and only if

1. *participant*$_i$ was a participant in exactly one conference, and its state, desired access modes, and permitted access modes in that conference were $state_i$, $[(m_1, d_1), (m_2, d_2), ..]$, and $[(m_1, p_1), (m_2, p_2), ..]$ respectively.

2. *participant*$_i$ was participating in more than one conference (say k conferences), and $state_i$ was the state furthest from IDLE that *participant*$_i$ was in among all the k conferences. Furthermore, let $d_{11}, d_{12}, .., d_{1k}$ be the desired access directions with respect to medium m_1; $d_{21}, d_{22}, ..., d_{2k}$ be the desired access directions with respect to medium m_2; and so on. Similarly, let $p_{11}, p_{12}, ..., p_{1k}$ be the permitted access directions with respect to m_1; $p_{21}, p_{22}, ..., p_{2k}$ be the permitted access directions with respect to m_2; and so on. The access modes of the resulting conference can be generated using either of the following two semantics:

- And-Merge:

$$d_i = d_{i1} \wedge d_{i2} \cdots \wedge d_{ik}, \forall i \in [1, m]$$

$$p_i = p_{i1} \wedge p_{i2} \cdots \wedge p_{ik}, \forall i \in [1, m]$$

- Or-Merge:

$$d_i = d_{i1} \vee d_{i2} \cdots \vee d_{ik}, \forall i \in [1, m]$$

$$p_i = p_{i1} \vee p_{i2} \cdots \vee p_{ik}, \forall i \in [1, m]$$

5.3 Splitting Conferences

A conference can be split into two conferences, each with a subset of the participants of the original conference:

Split[confName, list1Of [participant, permittedAccessModes],
list2Of [participant, permittedAccessModes]] → [conf1, conf2]

The participants of the resulting two conferences need not be disjoint.

5.4 Copying and Moving Conferences

Just like files, conferences can be copied or moved using the following operations:

Copy[sourceConf, destConf]
Move[sourceConf, destConf]

Whereas **Move** terminates the source conference, **Copy** does not. Since the naming convention determines hierarchical relationships, such **Copy** or **Move** operations can be used to create and destroy conference hierarchies. Note that the **Create** operation also provides an interface to create a conference hierarchy. **Copy** and **Move** are the only operations that provide an interface for destroying conference hierarchies (and hence, inheritance relationship). Consider the following operation:

Move[$/C_1/C_2$, C]

The execution of this operation creates a conferences C with the same participants and access rights as $/C_1/C_2$, and destroys the conference $/C_1/C_2$. However, the newly generated conference C does not share any semantic context with C_1 (thus, destroying the inheritance).

5.5 Activating and Inactivating Conferences

A persistent conference becomes *inactive* when either (1) all the participants of the conference leave the conference, or (2) it is explicitly inactivated by its controller. Similarly, a conference becomes *active* when either (1) one or more participants join the conference, or (2) it is explicitly activated by its controller.

5.6 Miscellaneous Operations

The controller of a dynamic conference can (1) change the access rights of any of the participants, and (2) designate some other participant as the controller, using the following operation:

ChangeAccesssAttributes[confName, participantID, newAccessRights]
ChangeController[confName, newControllerID]

If the participantID specified in ChangeAccessAttributes is already a participant of confName, then it is notified about the change in its access attributes. Otherwise, the above operation is equivalent to inviting a new participant to the conference.

6 Modelling Collaborative Scenarios

In Section 3, we have defined a taxonomy of multimedia conferencing. In this section, we will classify and model some of the standard collaborative environments within our taxonomy. The examples that we will consider are (1) examination and (2) shared workspace.

6.1 Examination

An examination is a transient conference, since it exists only as long as there is at least one student taking the examination. When all the students complete their exams, the conference is terminated. Consider a scenario with n students taking an exam. Let the examination be supervised by a proctor. The examination C_E contains two nested conferences C_Q and C_A:

1. C_Q is a n-to-1 conference from all the students to the proctor, and is used by the students to direct questions to the proctor. Whereas the students have permission to transmit, the proctor has only receive permission with respect to the conference. Note that conference C_Q can also be used by the students to send answers to the examination questions.

2. C_A is a 1-to-n conference from the proctor to the students, and is used by the proctor to respond to student's questions. Hence, only the proctor has the permission to transmit media information, whereas the students can only receive information from it.

Note that both conferences C_Q and C_A inherit their duration or existence as well as the list of participants from C_E. Each student in an examination participates in two conferences, and the proctor is the controller for both the conferences. If the proctor decides to transmit some information to a sub-set of participants, then it can do so by changing the access rights of the other participants. A pictorial representation of C_E is shown in Figure 14.2.

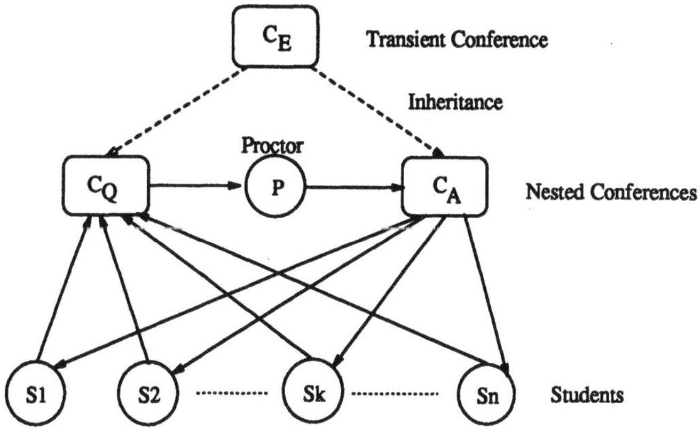

Figure 14.2: Modeling an examination within the taxonomy

6.2 Shared Workspace

In a typical shared workspace environment, only one participant is permitted to modify the shared document at any given time. A floor control mechanism is necessary to support such a collaborative environment. A request for floor control is a special case of a request for modifying the permitted access modes with respect to a conference. In this section, we illustrate that our conferencing paradigm and the operations defined on conferences are sufficient to model this scenario.

Consider a shared workspace environment modelled by a conference C. Let P_1, P_2, ..., P_n be the participants of C. Let P_i be the participant requesting a change in its permitted mode of access. To do this, P_i creates a new conference C_{new}, and invites conference C as its participant. The mode of participation of P_i with respect to C_{new} is the same as the one that P_i desires to have with respect to C. If the controller of conference C accepts the invitation, then P_i can *effectively* participate in C with the new participation rights. Otherwise, the request for change of permitted mode is rejected. Figure 14.3 illustrates this process.

The decision of accepting or rejecting the invitation to join C_{new} can be automatic. For instance, a floor control policy can automatically determine whether a request can be granted or not.

7 Concluding Remarks

We have presented a conferencing paradigm that can form the basis for supporting multimedia interactions in distributed computing systems. The taxonomy of conferences exhaustively captures most types of collaborative environments. The connection model can support sophisticated features such as access control with respect to different media streams, flexibility to use multiple media channels to participate in multiple conferences simultaneously, and nested conferences. We treat conferences as first class objects and define operations to manipulate them. We are carrying out the software implementation

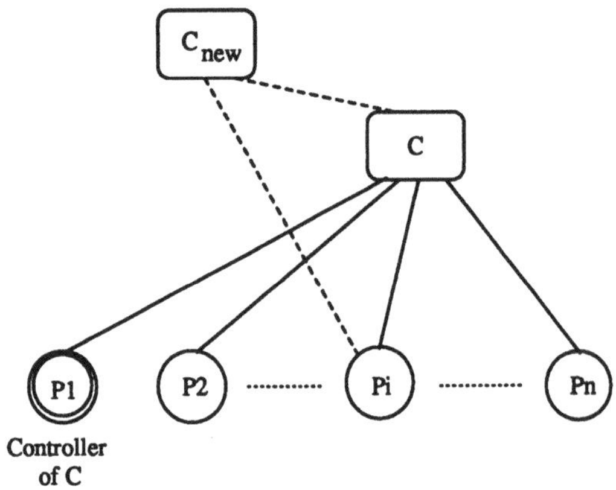

Figure 14.3: Modelling a request for change in permitted access mode

in an environment of workstations and personal computers at our Multimedia Laboratory. The next step is to utilize digital transmission and storage of video, yielding a completely integrated multimedia computing system.

Bibliography

[1] L. Aguilar, J.J. Garcia-Luna-Aceves, D. Moran, E.J. Craighill, and R. Brungardt. Architecture for A Multi-Media Tele-Conferencing System. *Proceedings of the SIGCOMM'86 Symposium on Communications Architectures and Protocols, Stowe, VT*, pages 126–136, August 5-7, 1986.

[2] S. R. Ahuja, J. Ensor, and D. Horn. The Rapport Multimedia Conferencing System. In *Proceedings of COIS'88 Conference on Office Information Systems, Palo Alto, CA*, pages 1–8, March 23-25, 1988.

[3] S. Angebranndt, R. L. Hyde, D. H. Luong, N. Siravara, and C. Schmandt. Integrating Audio and Telephony in a Distributed Workstation Environment. In *Proceedings of Summer 1991 USENIX Conference, Nashville, TN*, pages 419–436, June 10-14, 1991.

[4] S. Casner, K. Seo, W. Edmond, and C. Topolcic. N-Way Conferencing with Packet Video. *Proceedings of the Third International Workshop on Packet Video, Morristown, NJ*, March 22-23, 1990.

[5] P. Cochrane and M. Brain. Future Optical Fiber Transmission Tech. and Networks. *IEEE Communications Magazine*, pages 45–60, November 1988.

[6] H.C. Forsdick. Explorations in Real-Time Multi-Media Conferencing. *Proceedings of the 2nd International Symposium on Computer Message Systems, IFIP*, pages 331–347, September 1985.

[7] J.H. Irven, M.E. Nilson, T.H. Judd, J.F. Patterson, and Y.Shibata. Multi-Media Information Services: A Laboratory Study. *IEEE Communications Magazine*, 26(6):27–44, June 1988.

[8] R. Kamel, K. Emami, and R. Echert. PX: Supporting Voice in Workstations. *IEEE Computer*, 23(8):73–80, August 1990.

[9] L.F. Ludwig and D.F. Dunn. Laboratory for Emulation and Study of Integrated and Coordinated Media Communication. *Proceedings of SIGCOMM'88 Symposium on Communications Architectures and Protocols, Austin, TX*, pages 283–291, August 3-5, 1988.

[10] P. Venkat Rangan and D. C. Swinehart. Software Architecture for Integration of Video Services in the Etherphone Environment. *To appear in IEEE Journal on Selected Areas in Communication*, 1992.

[11] S. Sarin and I. Greif. Computer-Based Real-Time Conferences. *IEEE Computer*, 18(10):33–45, October 1985.

[12] H. M. Vin, P. T. Zellweger, D. C. Swinehart, and P. Venkat Rangan. Multimedia Conferencing in the Etherphone Environment. *To appear in IEEE Computer - Special Issue on Multimedia Information Systems*, October 1991.

Chapter 14

Uniform Integration of Voice in Groupware

Risto Mäntylä and Heikki Hämmäinen

Abstract. In many groupware systems, the three basic voice services – telephone, voice mail and voice database – are implemented as separate subsystems. Such lack of uniformity limits the use of voice services and makes the integration of separate multimedia applications difficult.

This paper describes a uniform approach to voice integration based on multimedia form objects, formbases, and autonomous programmable user agents. A single network architecture (TCP/IP and Ethernet) is adopted for both real-time and non-real-time links for data and voice, which provides several benefits. Distributed multimedia groupware becomes modifiable, or even "user-programmable", because of the uniform treatment of voice as data. Voice can be easily embedded as part of applications, whether the mode is user-to-user (real-time or non-real-time) or user-to-function (local or remote).

1. Introduction

The PAGES system (Programmable Agents for Group Interaction Systems) (HUT 1990; Hämmäinen 1991) was designed and implemented as part of the DIMUN project (Leevers 1990) within the RACE programme. This paper describes the voice extension of PAGES being developed at the Helsinki University of Technology in cooperation with the Nokia Research Center.

In our approach, networked group tasks are viewed as explicit interaction between semi-automated agents representing individual users. This approach emphasises the ownership of information in group tasks. The desired flexibility is achieved through semi-structuredness; inter-agent messages are required to be simultaneously understandable, at least to some extent, by users and their agents. To make the group interaction explicit and understandable, a familiar metaphor for structured cooperation is necessary. Ours is called form, since it derives several properties – such as visibility, persistence, transferrability, replicability, appendices, pasted notes, and the ability to coordinate multilateral cooperation – from its manual counterpart. Users deal with strictly-typed form objects which may contain any structured or unstructured information.

The form abstraction is exploited in providing a collection of asynchronous inter-agent form interchange protocols for semistructured group tasks. In some applications, the underlying protocol is hidden from users by creating the impression of a shared workspace, but more often a user feels that he is sending and receiving messages. PAGES supports inter-agent navigation; if authorized, a user may interactively access the object-oriented formbase of another user's agent. Users accessing the same form have a shared window which facilitates interactive information sharing. It should be noted that a form always belongs to the owner of the agent whereas other users may access his form if authorized. In this paper, we investigate the consequences of encapsulating voice in forms.

2. System architecture

We have implemented the bilateral process architecture of two interacting users (resp. user agents) in the Unix** and TCP/IP environment as described below (Fig. 1). Regarding voice, this architecture provides three different services: telephone, voice mail, and voice databases. The telephone service (link 5) is used in real-time synchronous communication between two users A and B, sitting at computers A' and B' respectively. The voice mail service (link 1) allows the asynchronous exchange of forms containing voice. The voice database feature (links 4 and 2) facilitates the user's access to his formbase containing voice.

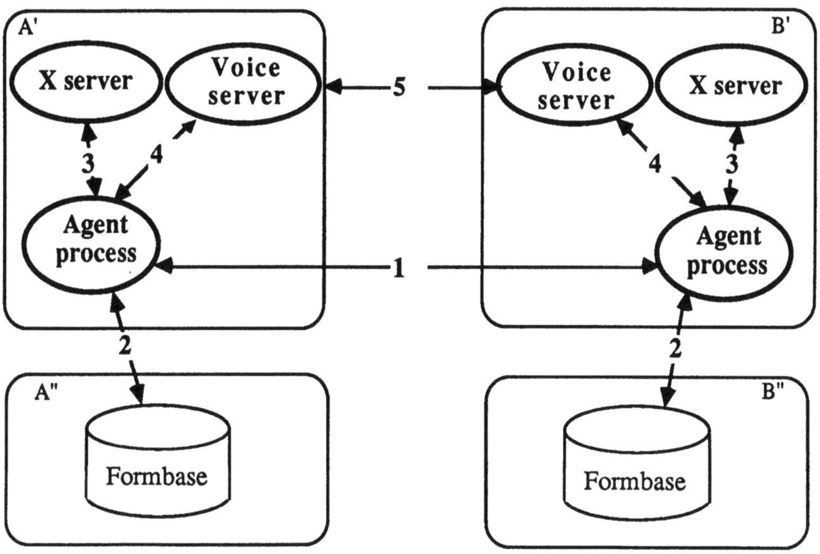

Figure 1. Overall process architecture between two interacting user agents.

The system is implemented on Sun SPARCstations, the sound chip of which supports telephone quality voice (Sun 1989); typically 8 KHz sampling rate with 12-bit precision companded to 8-bit samples (u-law standard). Form fields containing digitized voice are treated like any other data fields. They involve three scopes: class, instance, and paste-on. Voice data in class fields is shared by all form instances of the class, whereas voice data in form fields is private to a form instance. Paste-on fields allow the free attachement of voice notes, i.e. "post-

** Unix is a trademark of Bell Laboratories

it" messages, on any form without affecting its class definition. To manipulate voice within fields, PAGES has a simple voice editor with record and play control. Visually, voice fields appear as icons on forms. The voice editor is opened by clicking voice icons. In addition, the associated forms programming language (FPL) contains functions for accessing voice fields, which allows voice output to be associated as side-effects to other events such as, for instance, opening a form window. The underlying goal of voice integration is to coordinate the X and voice servers so that the complexity of the architecture is hidden from the user and the forms programmer. The visual and audio behaviour of forms need to be coordinated.

The implemented architecture has turned out to be functional. Voice (voice server process, links 4 and 5) and data (X server process, link 3) channels can be synchronized properly on the user interface level. However, this architecture cannot fully exploit the flexibility of distributed windowing.

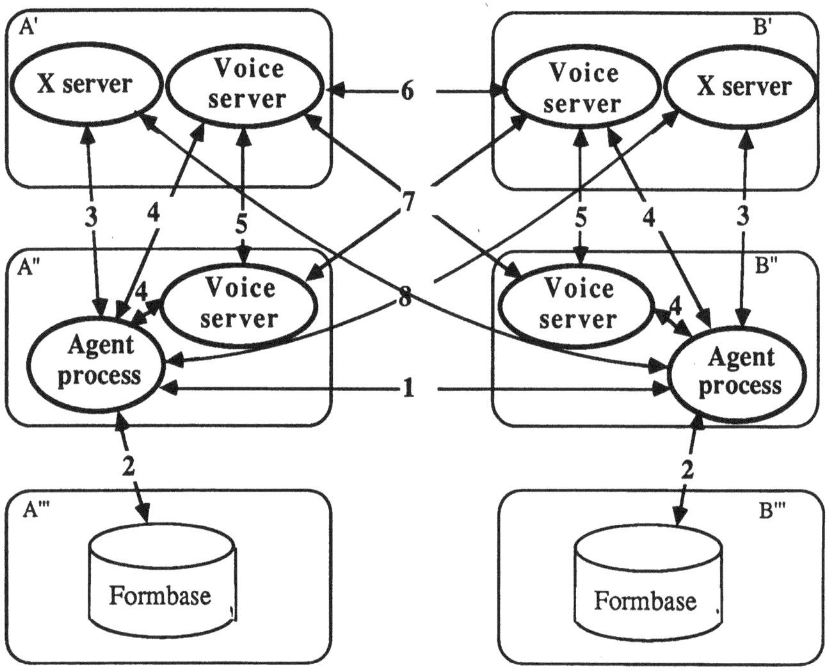

Figure 2. Overall extended process architecture between two interacting user agents.

The prototype architecture (Fig. 1) is being extended to better comply with distributed windowing (Fig. 2). The *X server* and *voice server* processes provide the separation of the user interface from the agent computer. For instance, user A may use a remote workstation (computer A') to access his private agent (computer A") and formbase (computer A''') remotely without losing the voice component. Correspondingly, two users may establish phone connections (link 6) via agents even though they were accessing their agents remotely. Finally, users may have simultaneous real-time voice and data links; the local user A (link 3) and a remote user B (link 8) may view the same local form of A over X and have a parallel voice connection (link 6) between workstations.

3. Telephone service

The telephone service provides synchronous bilateral voice links between the users of separate agents (A and B). Let us imagine that the agent of A runs in computer A" and his X server and voice server in computer A', and that B has a similar configuration (Fig. 3). The connection procedure starts when A (caller) sends B (receiver) an instance of the PhoneForm class. This form asks agent B the name of the computer at which the user interface of agent B is running (links 3 and 4). This address is passed to agent A and forwarded to the voice server process of the computer where the user interface of agent A is running (link 4). The agent B makes the same preparations (link 4) and the connection is established between users (link 6).

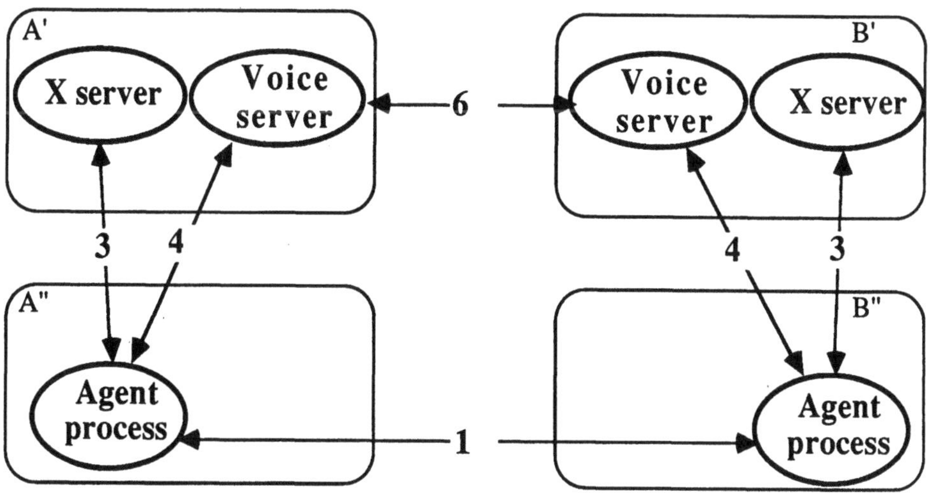

Figure 3. Processes involved in a bilateral phone connection.

This mechanism is limited to bilateral connections. A multilateral setting would require mixing several parallel sound sources which is not supported by the I/O devices and drivers of our hardware. On the other hand, there are results which indicate that voice-only is proper for bilateral interaction, whereas multilateral interaction is difficult without video providing support for non-verbal coordination (Condon 1990).

4. Voice mail service

The asynchronous interchange of forms between user agents supports voice mail through encapsulation of digitized voice (Fig 4.). The sender (A) records his voice message into a form field using the voice editor (voice path 5-4-2), whereafter the form exists in the sender's formbase. The user controls the recording through the X interface (control path 3-4). When A sends the form object to the receiver (voice path 2-1), the receiving agent B saves the new form in its formbase (voice path 1-2). Later on, the receiver B can play the voice encapsulated in the form using the voice editor (voice path 2-4-5).

Each voice server process is controlled by an agent process through socket connections. Thus, each voice server interacts with two other processes: another voice server and an agent. The initialization of connections is based on using standard predefined port numbers for voice servers.

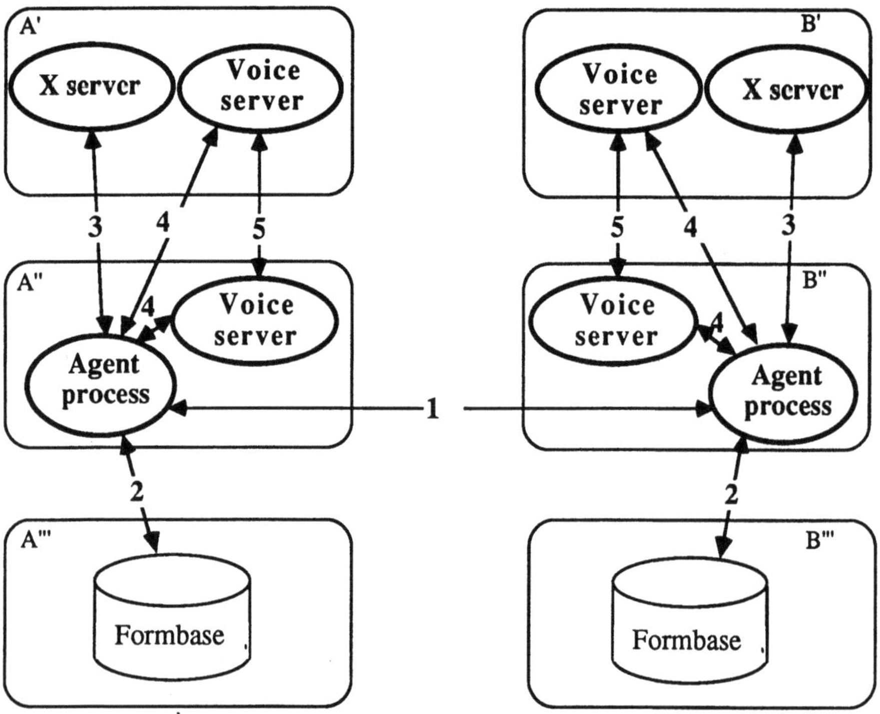

Figure 4. Process interaction in voice mail.

5. Voice database service

The multiuser access to a formbase supports voice through cooperation between voice servers. In addition to the local formbase access (voice path 5-4-2) described above, links for remote access (path 7-4-2) are required.

The procedure for the remote voice access is following. When user B wants to access the formbase of A, he sends a request form to agent A. If a permission is granted the, A creates the necessary X (link 8) and voice (link 7) server connections. These connections are controlled by agent A that may prevent the unwanted actions from the remote user.

Users may access the same form simultaneously using window sharing, that is, the same form is simultaneously used by several users. Also in this situation the agent of the owner of the form controls the form and its shared views. The window sharing and the possibility of using voice raises several questions. What kind of policy should be used in shared forms? Should voice data be played to all users of the shared form or only to the user that requested it? Both these policies have their pros and cons. If the voice is played to all users other users can find it disturbing or it may cause problems (when two voice sources are played at the same time). Should there be the possibility to use shared and private voice workspaces?

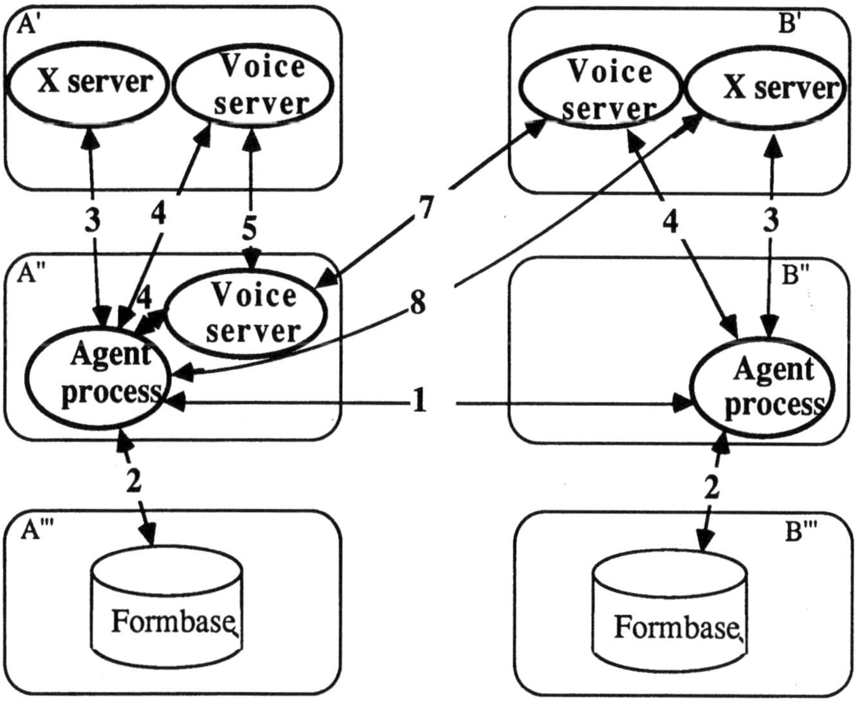

Figure 5. Processes involved in local and remote formbase access.

6. Conclusions

We have developed a distributed architecture that allows flexible combination of voice with shared windowing in the case of bilateral user interaction. Extending this mechanism to support multilateral voice connections (or multiple simultaneous sound sources) is not straightforward, though. Mixing of digitized sound is not supported sufficiently by hardware and device drivers. Instead of point-to-point messaging, efficient multicasting of voice packets would be necessary to spare bandwidth. The control of interprocess communication requires skillful compromises, since managing multiple voice servers becomes complex, if kept decentralized, and inefficient, if made centralized.

We have treated voice uniformly as data, but this clearly is a simplification. For instance, voice is time critical; varying delays can be acceptable when viewing data, but not when "viewing" synchronous voice. Cooperating listeners have to hear same sounds simultaneously with a high level of quality. This sets timing requirements which are difficult to fulfil in a packet network.

We took the original model for voice LAN from the vtalk program (Vtalk 1989) which implements a simple Ethernet phone mechanism on SparcStation. PhoneTalk (Nises et al.

1990) has improved the sound quality by dividing a bilateral voice link into two unidirectional links, by adding a sequencing mechanism, and by developing load balancing algorithms.

As opposed to using separate networks for data and voice, see e.g. MILAN (Condon 1990), we have employed a single network, TCP/IP and Ethernet, for both media. The integrated networking provides uniform addressing for data and audio connections, but suffers from poor audio quality due to the congestion problems in workstations and network. In practice, the functionality is limited to the LAN environment.

As opposed to systems which aim at interpreting voice information, e.g. (Muller et al. 1990), PAGES manipulates voice by encapsulating it in form fields of the user-specific formbases without an attempt to "understand" voice.

References

Condon, C. (1990) Networked Cooperative Work: Usability Issues of MILAN – Multimedia Industrial Local Area Network, proc. of Telematics '90, Bremen University.

Hämmäinen, H. (1991) Form-Based Approach to Distributed Cooperative Work, PhD thesis, Department of Computer Science, Helsinki University of Technology.

HUT (1990) PAGES User's Manual, Department of Computer Science, Helsinki University of Technology, Finland, March 1990.

Leevers, D. (1990) Multimedia communications in DIMUN, proc. of Telematics '90, Bremen University.

Muller, M., Daniel, J. (1990) Toward a Definition of Voice Documents, proc. of Office Information Systems, SIGOIS Bulletin, Vol.11, Issues 2 and 3, pp.174-183.

Nises, P., Wettby, J. (1990) PhoneTalk, MSc thesis, Department of Telecommunication and Computer Systems, Royal Institute of Technology, Stockholm, Sweden (draft).

Soares, L., Martins, S., Bastos, T., Ribeiro, N., Cordeiro, R. (1990) LAN Based Real Time Audio-Data Systems, proc. of Office Information Systems, SIGOIS Bulletin, Vol.11, Issues 2 and 3, pp.152-157.

Sun (1989) SPARCstation 1, SunOS 4.0.3, Release Notes, Sun Microsystems.

Vtalk (1989) User's Manual and source code, public domain Ethernet phone package, Oki Electric Industry Co., Ltd.

Chapter 15

A Distributed Multimedia Interface Builder

Yngve Sundblad

Abstract

Current and coming workstation and high-speed networking technology coupled with processing of different media in digitized form make feasible distributed applications where users can communicate with a computer and with each others using several human senses and presentation forms (media) in parallel. The Swedish research programme MultiG concerns all levels, from applications to fiber technology, in exploration of these possibilities in building distributed multimedia applications in a gigabit per second network. Here we describe DMIB, a distributed multimedia interface builder, a tool under development in Smalltalk-80 for building prototypes of multimedia interfaces. DMIB is based on object-orientation, direct manipulation, constraint and event handling techniques. It is intended for distributed use, i.e. for cooperation between two or more designers and/or end users at different workstations, which raises some functional requirements also discussed.

1. The MultiG Research Programme

MultiG is a cooperative research program concerning distributed multimedia applications in a gigabit per second network. The scope of MultiG is the design of such a network, together with multimedia workstations, which could be used as hosts that utilize the full power of the available bandwidth, and visionary multimedia applications running on these workstations.

MultiG is described in (MultiG 1990) and (MultiG 1991) and consists of a series of projects from advanced user oriented applications to data communication protocols and communication hardware. The different projects are rather loosely coupled, but they are focused on the same application domain and are centred around a shared communication environment. The application domain is a distributed environment for system design and programming and the communication environment consists of a broadband, high-speed network between the partners in MultiG that is intended to operate in the magnitude of Gbps in 1993. The MultiG goals are similar to the goals of the NREN gigabit network testbeds (IEEE 1990).

One of the application oriented projects in MultiG, referred to as the DMIB project, concerns the construction of a distributed multimedia interface builder using and developing programming and user interface techniques such as direct manipulation, constraint handling and event handling. The DMIB is developed in Smalltalk on and for graphic workstations.

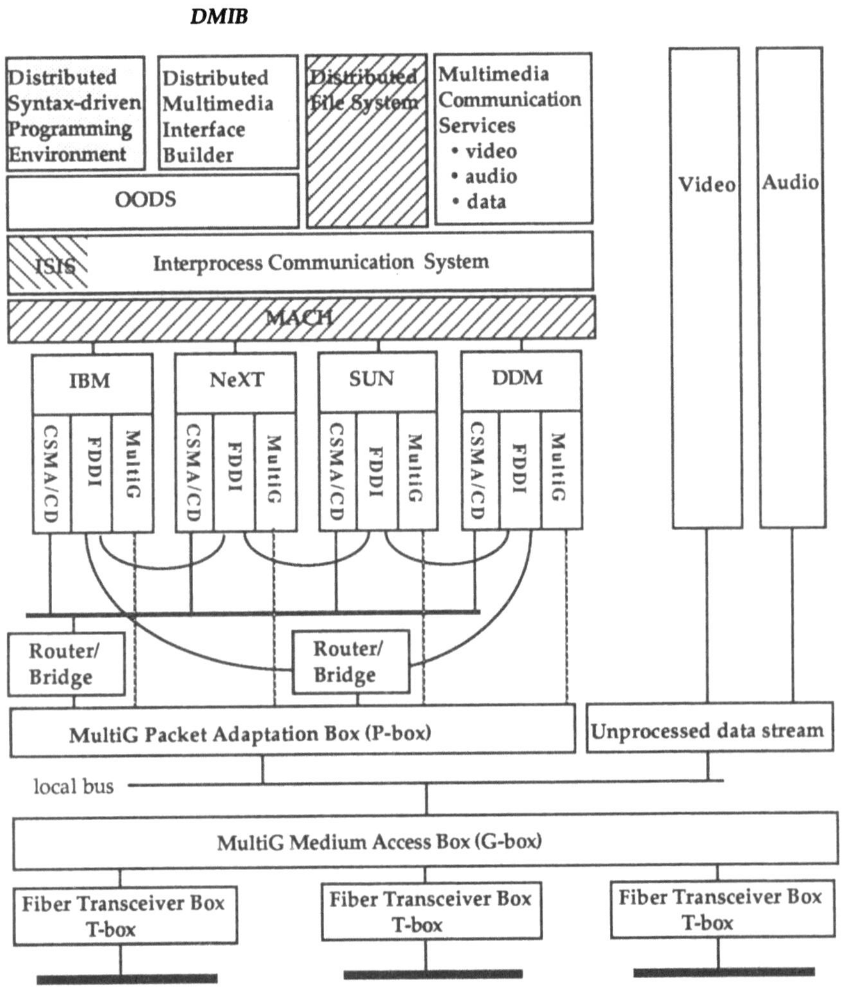

Fig.1 MultiG System Architecture

Another application oriented activity is the CSCW project, concerned with modelling computer supported cooperative design work and specification of a distributed design environment, which has direct bearing on the DMIB.

The MMWS project concerns the functionality of a multimedia workstation, for which both DMIB and CSCW provide requirement specifications.

Projects on "lower levels" concern the runtime environment for the distributed multimedia applications, including interprocess communication mechanisms, the transport and network protocols, the host-network interfaces and the transfer mode protocols and hardware interface to the fibre.

Examples of applications that need flows of bits in the Giga order of magnitude are animated visualisation of data from scientific calculations with supercomputers (2Mb screen x 24 bits pixels x 25 picts/sec ≈1Gbps), comparisons of simulation results, interaction between supercomputers and (on the very visionary side) animated (25/sec) holograms (of 100 Mb each). Such applications require high performance workstations, new algorithms, software and display techniques beyond the state of the art, which create and consume Gbps bit streams, and network interfaces which can process such bitstreams from and to a network. Lots of other applications will certainly evolve when the multimedia and Gbps possibilities become available.

The envisaged MultiG computer system architecture is depicted in figure 1.

2. Distributed Use for Cooperative Work

In this chapter we discuss computer support for cooperative work (CSCW) with direct bearing on the "Distributed" aspect of the DMIB.

The CSCW project within MultiG is concerned with collaborative early design capture, specification and rapid prototyping of interactive and/or embedded real time systems in a distributed MultiG design environment. With early design capture we mean all phases of design from requirement specification to prototyping, but not activities concerned with final implementation, service and maintenance.

The scope of the project is to specify tools for collaboration that enable designers to cooperate as good or better than in a traditional environment. There are then two kinds of tools to be considered, tools for communication between designers at different workstations (e.g picture phones) and tools for cooperative design (e.g tools for collaborative editing). The former kind of tools enable designers to exchange information, while the latter enables designers to process the same information at the same time.

2.1. Multimedial Communication Channels

Interactive multimedia communication, "talk", (and also asynchronous communication, "mail") between workstation users is basic in CSCW. We envisage environments where a user can communicate and cooperate with other users at the same site or other sites through simultaneously seeing each other in screen windows (direct video), hearing and talking to each other (direct audio), seeing the same or different views/aspects of the same information (text, pictures, videos, sound, etc. without and with hyperlinks), using pointing or other control devices (voice commands, gloves with sensors, costumes with sensors, etc) for navigation through, and selection of different aspects of the information.

Basic such functionalites are developed in other parts of the MultiG programme, e.g. the MMWS project.

2.2. Functional Requirements

In the CSCW project we have formulated the following general functional requirements on a distributed environment for collaboration in design, (Marmolin 1990).

• Support informal collaboration
- Communication of social behaviour pattern
- Establishment /development of personal relations
- Drop-in meetings

• Support sharing and record keeping of
- Requirement-, design- and implementation changes
- Design results, design ideas, design concepts
- Commitments, work-plans etc

• Support sharing and integration of background knowledge
- Common frame of reference
- Application domain knowledge
- Knowledge about similar systems, other solutions

• Support presentation/representation of ideas
- Visualizations
- Story board facilities
- Drop-in meetings

• Support task accomplishment
- Review of work results
- Collaborative editing/debugging

• Support strategies reducing the need for information sharing, i.e. the "collaboration load"

2.3. Generic Collaboration Tools

Instead of designing tools based on some analysis of the design task or collaboration task to be fulfilled, one could attempt to design very generic collaborative tools, that the users can use and combine as they want in order to accomplish the collaborative design task. These tools have then to be designed so that they can be used for many different tasks in a distributed design environment. Some combination of tools could be used for conferencing, some other for coworking, some for understanding the problem and some other for selection of alternatives etc. In some situations the tools can be used for formal in others for informal collaboration, in some for one-to-one collaboration in other for many-to many collaboration, in some for explicit and in other for implicit collaboration. This design idea is very similar to the Workaday World proposed by Moran and Anderson (1990) as it is not task oriented, but focuses on the social process of collaboration and on giving the users tailorable tools that they can control and attend to according to their needs. As discussed by Moran and Anderson these tools should not only support the users, they should enhance and encourage people in their work and allow creative deployment and development of job skills.

There is of course no optimal generic tool, but a question about trade-offs between a lot of factors such as system control – user control, specific – general support, automated tools – manual tools, easy to use – hard to use but powerful etc. Based on reviews of collaborative tools reported by Grudin and Poltrock (1990) and on our discussion of the collaborative design task in (Marmolin et al 1991) we suggest the following set of generic collaborative tools, further elaborated in (Marmolin 1991).

The Shared window is shared by one or more users. The user should be able to define any number of windows as shared with a set of other users and to paste any multimedia document and/or to run any application in these windows. It could have both read and write permission attributes, i.e one could either have permission to just read the information in the window or one could have permission to update the information. Such windows could then be used for many different purposes. For example, they could be used for collaborative work execution as coediting, for conferences, for lectures etc.

In *the PicturePhone window* a video of a user's face and/or the whole user is shown and the users voice is heard. There could be many such picturephone windows on a work station, active ones with videos or inactive ones in the form of icons representing e.g the user. One should perhaps also be able to chose between voice communication, picture communication or both and one should perhaps be able to record the information. These windows could then be used for questioning, conferences or for more informal chatter.

In *the MultimediaMail window* the user can paste any multimedia document and/or run any application and that can be mailed to one or more users. There could be many such mail windows and some could be used for sending mail some for received mail. This tool should be designed so that one could put any information in the mail window, e.g sharable interface objects such as buttons, information from the picturephone etc. In principle, it should be possible to transform any synchronous collaborative task to an asynchronous one using this mail window.

In *the Desk window* a video of the real desk of another user is shown. This tool could mainly be used for showing documents and other objects that are not stored in the work station, e.g hard copies of reports. There should be one such window for each user.

The SharedFolder window is a folder that can be used to put documents that should be available for some defined group of users. This folder could act as a kind of group memory. It should have hypertext linking capabilities and inform the user about when new documents are distributed. There could also be SharedFolders tailored to the specific needs of the design situation. For example for distribution and record keeping of design notes.

In *the BulletinBoard window* information available for some defined group of users could be recorded and presented using multimedia techniques. There could be many such windows for different groups of users and for different kinds of information. For example there could be one bulletin for record keeping of changes, commitments etc in a project, one informing about users that can be reached and what other users are doing, scheduling and calendar information, another informing about different kinds of news etc.

The Hallway is a window in the user can browse through a collaborative network map looking for users that one can disturb with questions, brief chatter or with more engaged forms of collaboration. It might be restricted to such information that allows one to determine the presence and availability of others using a video glance and/or sound. The social problems of controlling this process have of course to be considered. In addition this kind of tool should support informal communication. A similar tool has been implemented by Xerox EuroParc.

In *the MeetingProcess* is a process where the user can meet other users using the same process. Any common process could be defined as a meeting process, but processes that involve waiting might be most suitable. In a meeting process there will be picturephone communication and/or audio coummunication between the users involved. For example if a printing process is defined as a meeting process, then when the user is printing and perhaps waiting for the results, videos of other users using the picture process at the same time will be shown, if they have declared printing as a meeting process. In this way an attempt is made to support the kind of informal interaction, that often occurs in a working place when people are waiting for something.

We develop prototypes of some of these windows as collaboration tools and intend to integrate them in DMIB. Use of DMIB will thus be an evaluation of the collaboration tools in cooperation between interface designers and between designers and end users.

3. DMIB Functionalities

The applications envisaged in the MultiG programme are based on multimedial human-computer interfaces. In the activity described here we focus on extension of tools for building graphic interfaces into tools for building distributed multimedial interfaces. Of special interest is the Interface Builder (IB) idea, i.e. construction of user interfaces and whole applications through direct manipulation of objects in the interface. The IB technique is well established for building graphic interfaces and is possible to extend into useful development tools also for handling other interaction media. The intention is to develop, test and evaluate the basic idea of a DMIB, a Distributed Multimedia IB, in parallel with development of theory and metodology, e.g. for using constraints and event handling. We use multiple media both in the interface to the DMIB itself and in the interfaces built.

For functionalities such as "professional" editing of media such as sound and video we rely on software tools developed by others. We restrain the DMIB functionality to tools for connecting sound and video sequences to graphic objects controlling e.g. input, time cutting and playing.

One type of functionality where we go deeper, though, is in animation of graphic images, using techniques such as inbetweening and more general temporal constraints, connecting them to sound and video effects. We explore both the use of animation in interfaces themselves and as a result of using the interface.

Prototypes of the DMIB are implemented in Smalltalk environments on graphic workstations.

3.1. Interface Building Techniques

The *Interface Builder* idea, i.e. construction of user interfaces and whole applications through direct manipulation of objects in the interface, is quite new but well established for graphic interfaces, e.g. through systems by Jean-Marie Hullot, e.g. the NextStep Interface Builder (NeXT 1990), by Luca Cardelli (1987) and by Roger Took (1991) and in a less advanced smaller scale, but widely spread, HyperCard (for the Macintosh). Another example of state-of-the-art in graphic interface builders is GAD (Backlund and Lundh 1991).

The objects' activities can be described through direct manipulation using a pointing device (in cases such as establishing links to and invocating actions in other objects) or through scripts of program text connected to the object. Using text in advanced programming languages for expressing complex actions of the objects and for the core of the model of the application is superior to all ideas of graphic and visual ways of expression presented so far. The IB technique thus has its limitations but is certainly very good for making and experimenting with the interface the user sees on the screen. One important use is in prototyping, which is of decisive importance for achieving powerful systems for the user.

With distributed multimedia the IB technique can be extended in three ways:

1. For distributed cooperative work with the IB using multimedia for human to human communication
2. IB tools för prototyping and building distributed multimedia interfaces
3. Use of multimedia in the user interface with the IB tool

3.2. Multimedia Extensions of the IB Techniques

It is a natural and promising idea to extend IB techniques to building multimedial environments by supporting the following functionalities.

It is of course a formidable task to implement all these functionalities. Within the DMIB project we concentrate on development of techniques, methods and prototypes including the aspects marked with *italics.*

- techniques for description and *integration* of sound, video, still images, graphics (incl animations) in 2D and 3D, text, ...
- parallel use of several media
- description of *dynamic and time dependent processes*, e.g. animations
- construction of *event sequences*, e.g. for a button push, by showing (via the input channels) the IB what should happen (programming by demonstration), including the event operations discussed in section 16.4.2 below.
- describing relations between parts of an interface, objects and/or media, as *constraints*
- visual tools for integrated editing in media (video, sound, pictures, animations, graphics, ...)
- possibility of using human experience of other design tasks, e.g. *sketching* with pencil and paper, through sketchy input techniques, e.g. by pen and tablet, for definitions of objects involved in the interaction.

3.3. Distributed Use of the Multimedia Interface Builder

For distributed use of the DMIB in collaboration between interface developers and/or with end users the following functionalities are of interest.

- support for multiple users in a distributed environment to construct or manipulate the behaviour of a common application
- support for parallel use of several media
- support for common "whiteboard" where objects look alike for all users

- support for common view where objects created by different users look different
- support for different views of the same model, selectable by the users
- support for several views simultaneously
- support for direct ("talk") and asynchrous ("mail") communication with text, graphics, audio, video, executable code, ...

The possibilities to have different views or looks of the same object or model is important for the users' keeping track of the origin and history of ideas in and for discussing different aspects of the interface.

Prototypes of these functionalities will be implemented using some of the generic collaboration tools (windows) described in section 2.3 and will be tested with users of DMIB.

4. Interface Specification and Programming Techniques in DMIB

The most basic functionality of an IB, and thus of DMIB, is the possibility to specify the look and behaviour of the user interface through direct manipulation of objects and their "scripts".

Other important functionalities of the DMIB is handling of events from the different input media and via communication channels, e.g. with other users, and the possibility to specify dependencies, both spatial and temporal, between "objects" presented and manipulated in different media.

In the DMIB project we explore and develop direct manipulation, event handling and constraint specification /satisfaction mechanisms.

4.1 Direct manipulation of interfaces

DMIB will support the construction of user interfaces both for applications that have their own graphical representation and those that do not.

DMIB will contain a comprehensive set of tools that make it easy to design and implement highly-interactive, graphical, direct manipulative and multimedia user interfaces, i.e. it supports development of interfaces that use different media such as text, graphics, buttons, windows, scrollbars, animation, sound, video, etc. DMIB also supports development of dynamic interfaces, i.e. interfaces that change or use motion during the user session.

DMIB will also support distributed and cooperative development of user interfaces. When two or more constructors cooperate with the creation of a user interface they could communicate via a various set of tools that are especially designed for this purpose. Example of tools that are used are common whitebord where both text, graphics, sounds, program text, DMIB objects, buttons, animations, sound and video sequences could be used and exchanged with support of voice connection, picture phone talk, multimedia mail, scrapbooks etc., via some of the generic tools described in by Marmolin (1991).

The interface construction is primarily based on direct manipulative and graphical techniques. It is not only possible to describe graphical interfaces as such but also parts that change dynamically, by direct manipulation of successive states, enhanced with the event and constraint handling mechanisms described below.

We design DMIB for separation of

- the application
- the graphical representation
- the behaviour or interaction

in cases where that is possible.

With such a construction it is easy to, for example, change the look of the interface without changing the behaviour. An interface with windows and buttons in Sun's OpenLook style could then easily be changed into Macintosh style. Conversely one can change the behaviour without changing the representation, e.g. change the meaning of a "resizebox" of an object so it is only possible to change the extension of an object in one direction instead of two.

A user interacting with a direct manipulative program uses some basic operations: select, open and drag an object, extend a selection with a new object, choose an operation etc. The idea is to separate the way the user chooses the operation from how the operation is carried out. It is also possible to separate the basic operations described above from the feedback they should have. There are several reasons to do this separation, for instance to allow different feedback depending on the user-interface standard, and to make an easy switch of feedback-level depending on the host's resourses. It is also easy to change the representation of a graphical object, for example to see a directory of files as a set of icons or as a list of file names. In this example it is only the view of the abstract graphical object, the file, we change, not the way we interact with it or the functionality it represents.

We will thus separate the DMIB into three different parts:

1 A tool-box with buttons, windows, scrollbars, menues, animations etc., but also with different kinds of basic interaction methods, and different kinds of feedback.
2 A language that combines tool-box objects into a user interface.
3 A graphical interface builder that uses direct manipulative methods for constructions of both 1 and 2.

4.2. Event Handling

One important functionality of the DMIB is handling of events from different input media and via communication channels, e.g. with other users. We discuss event handling mechanisms needed for distributed multimedial interaction and communication in (Eiderbäck and Sundblad 1991). We implement the mechanisms by handling the events as instances of objects in a hierarchy, scheduling the events into queues controlled by programmer defined rules and processed by receivers, e.g. controllers (in the MVC sense, (Krasner and Pope 1988)) in Smalltalk.

Here we present some examples of situations in multimedia interaction and communication to motivate the need for event handling mechanisms such as conversion, combination, sequencing and priority. The event handler is expected to send events to some receiver(s) connected to an application.

Normally an event from the keyboard is a "character event". In some cases, e.g. with arrow function keys pressed the event may be easier or "cleaner" to handle by a receiver if *converted* into a "position event".

A spectacular form for humans to express a firm need for a change is to hit the table with the fist. This combination of closed fist, detected by a data glove, and sound when hitting the table might be interesting to use as input to a program as "enough-of-this" command. The glove event and sound event, if occuring within a suitable time frame, should then produce a new event, a *combination*, to send to a receiver in the application.

Another similar example is the use of a flat hand for "stop" only if it is amplified by a "STOP" voice command.

These combination examples are also examples of the need for *sequencing*, i.e. rules stating different handling of events depending on the time frame between them. Temporal order may also be important as when giving the voice command "DROP IT" before or after having picked up a new object with the data glove. In that case a time frame taking human reaction capability into account might also be prescribed, making the drop command concern the new object only if it has been picked for at least 0.2 seconds.

There is also obvious need for *priority rules* for situtions where an event from one input medium, e.g. a video camera, should be given less priority than an event from another, e.g. a pointing device controlling movements of the video camera, or when speech commands should have immediate effect.

Similar situations occur when two users collaborate using the media directly and for interaction with common windows.

An event, e.g. a mouse click in a box with one of the users might be better understood in the framework of the other user as, say, a character event and should thus be *converted*.

An example of *combination* is the event that the two users point at the same object and confirms that it should be treated in a certain way.

Sequencing rules such as suppression of a sound event from the other user if it does not arrive in time for amplifying but rather for confusing another, e.g.pointing, event, are also needed.

Priority is needed e.g. when the two users point in the same window and try to drag an object.

The following inheritance tree shows kinds of multimedia event objects that should be built in. The event handler should be able to treat object from these classes and programmer defined subclasses.

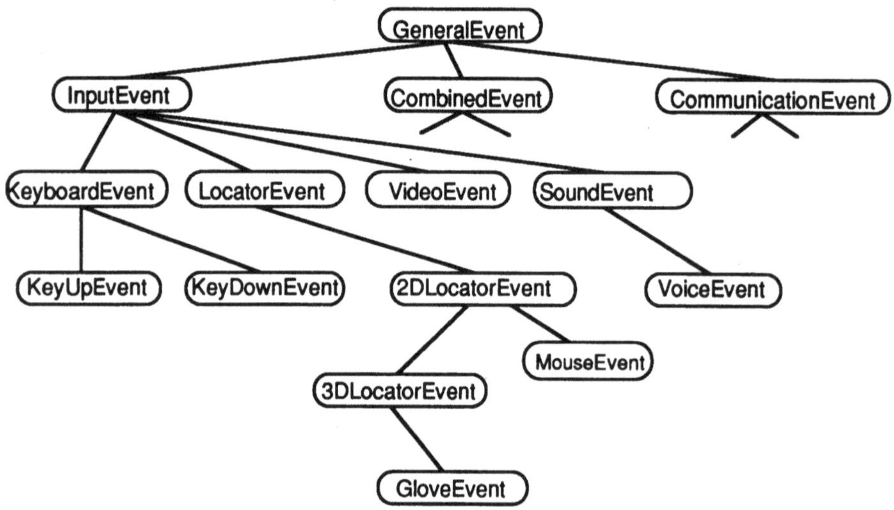

Fig.2 Sketch of event hierarchy

4.3. Constraints

The technique of expressing dependencies between objects as constraints in mathematical (e.g. algebraic) form, evaluated by constraint solving algorithms, has proven useful for user interface design and implementation, (Borning 1981), (Borning and Duisberg 1986). Graphical, direct manipulative methods for defining constraints are demonstrated in (Borning 1986).

Geometric constraints have been studied, developed and used in IPLab for object-oriented graphic editing, (Li 1988). We extend them with mechanisms for keeping consistency when the same object is handled in different media. An example extended to sound and video is

$$soundamplitude = k \cdot videowindowwidth$$

In *temporal constraints*, time is a basic variable.

For *simulated* time it is clear how to use constraints, even in both time directions for deriving history and future. Typical such situations are animations, see below.

In *real* time many of the event dependencies described above can be expressed as temporal constraints, where the time goes in one direction and implementation heavily depends on connection to operating system mechanisms and with temporal constraints. An example from the previous section is

$$| t_{clutch} - t_{sound} | \leq 0.5$$

How to handle this with "classical" constraint mechanisms is not quite clear and might be investigated at latter stages of the DMIB work.

The following examples describing the visual effect of "closing barn door" and a (non-linear) rising sound pitch are meaningful both with *t* as simulated time and as real time.

$$videowindowwidth = screenwidth \cdot (1 - t / duration)$$

$$soundpitch = 440 \cdot 2^{(t / duration)}$$

We put special efforts into giving a DMIB user (interface designer and/or implementor) possibility to specify, test and execute *animations* in the form of temporal constraints. These constraints can be in the form of formulæ including time as a parameter for describing a continuous process (e,g. inbetweening) and/or in the form of dependencies between "film" sequences and snapshots with video and sound events.

Inbetweening from *pict1* to *pict2* is simply described by

$$picture = pict1 + (t / duration) \cdot (pict2 - pict1)$$

These and other relevant expressions in constraint specification for multimedial interfaces are input to other work with constraint satisfaction algorithms, e.g. (Li 1991).

5. Specifying and Evaluating by Building Applications

As a basis for our specification of DMIB and cooperation with other MultiG projects we consider some applications for which we want to be able to build interfaces using DMIB. The applications are needed by other MultiG (ongoing or intented) projects or by DMIB itself.

The first three concern building our interface design tools and strongly depend on and presuppose each other.

The fourth (visualisation) is a "real" very demanding application of our tools.

5.1. Programming Environment

We enhance our programming environment, i.e. Smalltalk under Unix, using it and later on DMIB for making it more directmanipulative, support collaboration and add abilities to use different media like

- dragging and pasting of all kinds of objects, presenting themselves in appropriate form, e.g. to a "printer" for output, to a text window in one form, to a "sound window" in another form, etc.
- voice comments in code
- other sounds in code, e.g. for indication of the depth level of a selected class in a class hierarchy.
- animations, eg. to exemplify how to use a certain editor
- colorised icons that indicates some aspect of a special file

5.2. DMIB Itself

The interface to the DMIB tool is developed in a "boot-strapping", iterative process where the first implementation makes other functions feasible to implement and include in the second implementation etc.

5.3. Generic CSCW Tools

Interfaces to some of the generic tools (windows) for collaboration described in section 2.3 will be implemented with DMIB, at the same time giving DMIB enhanced collaboration facilities.

5.4. Interactive Visualisation Tools

One important and spectacular use of multimedia and high-speed networking is interactive visualisation of massive date, e.g. scientific calculations by supercomputers. In our vicinity at the department are numerical analysts making flow calculations on a Connection Machine. We intend to cooperate with them in using DMIB for building tools for interactive manipulation of and navigation through 3D visualisations of their computations.

6. References

Backlund, B., Lundh, J. (1991) GAD – Graphic Application Developer, demonstrated on NeXT computer at the 2nd MultiG workshop, Stockholm, June 1991

Borning, A. (1981) The Programming Language Aspects of Thinglab, A Constraint Oriented Simulation Laboratory, ACM TOPLAS 3: 353-387, Oct 1981

Borning, A. (1986) Graphically Defining New Building Blocks in ThingLab, HCI 2: 269-295, 1986.

Borning, A., Duisberg, R. (1986) Constraint-Based Tools for Building User Interfaces, ACM TOGS 5: 345-374, Oct 1986.

Cardelli, L. (1987) Building User Interfaces by Direct Manipulation, Digital SRC Research Report no.22, Oct 1987

Eiderbäck, B., Sundblad, Y. (1991) Object-oriented Event Handling in a Distributed Multimedia Environment, accepted for EurOOPe'91, Bratislava, Sept 1991

Goldberg, A., Robson, D. (1983)*Smalltalk-80 – The Language and its Implementation*, Addison-Wesley 1983

Grudin, J., Poltrock, S. (1990) Computer supported cooperative work and groupware. Tutorial at CHI'90, Seattle, April 1990

IEEE (1990) Gigabit Network Testbeds, IEEE Computer, Sept 1990, pp. 77-80

Krasner, G.E., Pope (1988) Cookbook for using the Model-View-Controller User Interface paradigm, JOOP Aug 1988, pp.26-49

Leler, W. (1987) *Constraint Programming Languages*, Addison-Wesley 1987

Li, J. (1988) Using Algebraic Constraints in Interactive Text and Graphics Editing, Proc EUROGRAPHICS'88, Sept 1988

Li, J. (1991) Hierarchical Constraint Solvers for Numerical Equalities, working paper, IPLab, NADA, KTH, Jan 1991

Marmolin, H. (1990) The MultiG CSCW Project, Proc 1st MultiG workshop, Stockholm, Nov 1990

Marmolin, H. (1991) TheKnowledgeNet – An Environment for Distributed Design, Proc 2nd MultiG Workshop, pp. 1-18, Stockholm, Jun 1991

Marmolin, H., Sundblad, Y., Pehrson, B. (1991) An Analysis of Design and Collaboration in a Distributed Environment, accepted for ECSCW'91, Amsterdam, Sept 1991

Moran, T., Anderson, R. (1990) The Workaday World As a Paradigm for CSCW Design. Proceedings of CSCW'90, p 381-393, Oct 1990

MultiG (1990) Proceedings of the 1st MultiG Workshop, Stockholm, Nov 1990, 136 p

MultiG (1991) Proceedings of the 2nd MultiG Workshop, Stockholm, Jun 1991, 118 p

NeXT (1990) The NextStep Interface Builder, NeXT Reference Manual, 1990, ch.8

Took, R.K. (1991) Out of the Window: A Multi-Medium, these proceedings, ch.6

Chapter 16

CoMEdiA
a Cooperative hyperMedia Editing Architecture. The Problem of the Cooperative Access

Christoph Hornung and Adelino Santos

Abstract

We describe CoMEdiA, a Cooperative hyperMedia Editing Architecture. CoMEdiA is a software tool that has been conceived having as main guidelines: cooperative work, multimedia data, hyper features, distributed processing and information edition. Using CoMEdiA users compete for the access of an information server in order to manage the cooperative edition of multimedia data. A first prototype with some of the above features is already implemented and the implementation is described.

We have partitioned this paper in the following manner. In the first section we will describe the problem that we are trying to solve. In the second we give an overview of CoMEdiA. In the third we describe the architecture and in the fourth we will present the algorithm that is used to solve the problems posed by the access. Finally we mention our intentions concerning future work and draw some conclusions.

Keywords: cooperative work, multimedia, hyper features, cooperative server, distributed processing, information edition

1 Statement of the Problem and Goals of CoMEdiA

Creation and usage of information and knowledge are two cornerstones of our modern society. All human work can be subdivided into individual and cooperative work. There is no clear preference for one of these work styles. Indeed, only the synergy achieved by combining both individual and cooperative work will bring out the best results.

The cooperative way of working is becoming a high interest area to researchers, system builders and end users. A change from the connection "single person/single resource" or "single person/multiple resources" to the connection "multiple persons/single resource" or "multiple persons/multiple resources" is required by many actual trends and is being attempted in many fields.

Multimedia applications are also a rising trend in information systems and technologies nowadays. Efforts towards media integration in different application areas are needed. One of these areas is multimedia information editing.

Organization problems are becoming bigger as information becomes denser and more complex. New organization methods are necessary. In this direction hyper features are being studied and applied as a way to solve organization, navigation and information transmission problems.

To summarize we can enumerate/synthesize some of the advantages we see in cooperative work:

- quicker distribution of current knowledge and work;
- more flexible and efficient team work through decentralization;
- easy to transmit on-line and off-line information (help, cooperation) to other users;
- face-to-face audio/video support of partner's communication, conferencing and knowledge transfer;

2 Overview of CoMEdiA

CoMEdiA has been conceived following the above guidelines and a first prototype with some of these features and characteristics has already been implemented. This paper describes some of the main features, problems and solutions. With this system we did not aim at having a powerful text/graphic editor, high multimedia processing power or powerful/state of the art hypermedia system. We put the strongest emphasis in the cooperative and integration features and techniques.

The CoMEdiA system runs on a transputer network of 16 transputers connected to a PC as input/output server. There is a server process for each file and a group of user processes (domain) that simultaneously edit this file. The users login into the server to make themselves known and to potentially request the file. The server manages the editing by making non-intercepting partitions on the file belonging to each user. The intercepting zones are where conflicts appear. To manage and solve these conflicts the server uses an ordering algorithm. Each user sees the changes made by the other users in his domain in their partitions. The partitions are completely user-defined, the user processes negotiate (through the ordering algorithm) their acquisition as well as release*. This way, we can say that the server is completely distributed, the resources are centralized and the access management is distributed. The server just does a fetching cycle fulfilling requests from the users, and the consistency of these requests is ensured by the ordering algorithm. A user can still change the working file, enter another domain or logout from the server. There is no connection between the users. All communications that a user can send to another user are made through the server. This is made this way because the all idea of cooperative work supposes the existence of a resource, several users and the actions of the users are made towards the resource. In this case the resource is represented in processing terms by the server. Having inter-user connections would imply duplication of information because the users would have more decision power (and to decide they would have to have information to base themselves on). Also the resource would no more have the central role of the cooperative philosophy. Also the existence of a care taker of the resource supposes that all the actions that can eventually concern this resource should be known to the care taker.

2.1 Multimedia Features

For the reasons described above and developed in some of the references, we consider multimedia a main issue in COMEDIA. The only media that are treated right now are text and graphics. We are considering the future inclusion of video as a means of realization of a human-human interface. Following the modelization of some multimedia entities we try to treat these objects in a cooperative view (see (Hornung et al. 1991)). The editable unity component entities of these have been formalized and are identified in the editor as the basic editing entities. For example, for the text medium, these entities are the lines (so we can say that the text part of CoMEdiA is a cooperative line editor). For the graphics medium these entities are line segments, circles and closed polygons.

---

* Rather than the human user, the processes that compose each user do these negotiations implicitly in the ordering algorithm.

As was said before the use of just these two media is due to the inclusion of other components (cooperation, hyper features, information editing) that diminished the relative importance of the pure multimedia aspect. Nevertheless, this multimedia treatment will enable us to a latter integration of more media in an already existing cooperative/hyper platform.

Video integration as a way to produce a human-human interface is the next step towards multimedia.

2.2 Hyper Features

In this section we will discuss the problems related with the inclusion of hyper features (structures, storage mechanisms, browsing mechanisms, display mechanisms, etc.) in CoMEdiA. Some extensions to the already traditional view of hyper features are being tried. As was noted in some of the references the navigation through hyper links can have several semantic meanings. The simpler and traditional semantic meaning is what we call *go_see*.

In CoMEdiA we tried to make some extensions of the notion of link. Hyper links can be thought of as mathematical relations that connect two sets (origin and image). The extensions that we make are semantic and syntactic variations over these two sets.

The first and most obvious extension is to allow multimedia links. The other extensions that follow are incremental and apply also to multimedia hyper links.

In order to give other meanings to hyper links, namely *go_execute*, *go_copy*, *go_process* or *go_bring*, we semantically change the image set. This way, the image set can be composed of commands (instead of other information units). This can be another navigate order (through another link), a call to a piece of executable code that does something external to the editor or can be an editing command. This enables something to be constructed closer to a command file or a script file. Providing a beginning hyper node a user could start an interpreter mechanism (the hyper links provide the flow control). This will enable the user to create hyper executable code (the embryo of a programming language) with several interesting properties (various executable entry points, incorporated interpretation, self-modifiable code, etc.). We note that KMS also has some of these features. With the examples above it is simple to imagine a text that (once a hyper link is navigated) can modify parts of the document, connect itself with the document or do any editing command.

One more semantic change is to allow hyper links between users. This enables one user to know what another user is doing (more than editing) or to access the other users' data structures. One step further is to admit hyper links between domains. This way a user can also access other files. These extensions imply some actions related with protection and identification.

Another extension is to syntactically enlarge the origin and image space. This enables a paragraph (instead of a line) to be connected to a picture or a complex polygonal wire frame (instead of a line) to another.

Another syntactic variation is to refine the granularity instead of enlarging it. The user can mark any area of information to be the origin or the end of a link. This allows to connect any two information items independently of how they are understood by the editor.

An extension that can hardly be classified as syntactic or semantic is the realization of volatile and non-volatile links. Volatile links are those that are created within a user edition section and exist just as long as this section exists. These are links that the user uses in the same way as he uses edition features. Non-volatile hyper links are the ones that exist beyond an edition section. They are stored along with the information file. Volatile links can become non-volatile by means of an explicit storing. There is a parallelism between these two types of links and the edition tools.

An integration of the cooperative concept with the hyper idea is to make the access to the hyper features also cooperative. This is a logical extension because the hyper information must be seen just as one more component of all the information. This way a user also has to ask permission to access a hyper feature (when it is shared) and all the concepts involved in the cooperative way of doing things are extended to incorporate this.

2.3 Identification and Authorization

Identification and authorization is also a research field that is touched by this system. A user has an identification code and can have different kinds of access rights based on levels.

A special problem in the cooperative access of multimedia objects is the heterogeneity of the user community. Different resources in the information set can have different access/security statuses. For example, teachers as well as students will have access to a learning document in a teaching environment. But a teacher may have access to more information (for example the results of all students) than a single student. Therefore, on the one hand, tools for identification and authorization must be developed. In some cases, some of the techniques developed for distributed systems will be studied and adapted. In other cases new mechanisms will be developed. But, moreover, even a single document may consist of different parts each having different access rights. The access rights themselves may consist of different levels.

2.4 Information Editing

Information editing is limited to text in the present system. Future extensions will follow from the strategy taken for the media expansion. CoMEdiA is a line editor with a very simple interface that supports basic experimental editing functionalities.

Other aspects related indirectly with information edition concern the user interface and various display information.

Cooperative work implies the existence of a special interface that informs each of the users of a certain domain of the current access status of the resource. In CoMEdiA the possible access status are: REQUESTED_ME, REQUESTED_OTHER, EDIT_ME, EDIT_OTHER, EDIT_ME_REQUESTED_OTHER. The way to reflect this status information in the user interface is done by means of using colors, respectively: light blue, dark blue, green, red, violet. Other hypothesis would be blinking or highlighting.

The supported policy of writing concerning transparency is *Non-Transparent* mode. This way, while a user owns a resource (e.g. text line) and proceeds with changes, the other users of the domain do not see them immediately. Future work will deal with *Transparent* mode which we think is more realistic, natural and user friendly.

Links can have explicit or implicit interfaces. The first one is a kind of button that connects a point of the information to another (not specifically a line, mathematical formula or drawing). This button does not really belongs to the text or graphics. The second one happens when the origin of a link is a sensitive area of information that really belongs to the information. The latter requires no additional interface (more than some blinking or colouring feature). Also concerning a special user interface to deal with the hyper features of CoMEdiA we think that tools must be provided that give information about the structure and contents (summary) of the hyper network. This is very important to avoid the so called problem of being "lost in hyper-space".

3 Requirements in the Cooperative Access

3.1 Cooperative Access

In systems providing cooperative access, there are particular requirements like:

- serialization
- mutual exclusion
- global consistency
- communication

Therefore, we divide this problem into smaller but still related problems, which we will treat: serialization, mutual exclusion and communication.

These problems somehow have a different nature from the ones found in traditional distributed systems. One of the more problematic differences is that they deal with resources that we call "non-stable resources". In a normal distributed system the resources are there and they are requested, used, freed, etc. without being destroyed. Another particularity is that the resource can be far from the users. (Usually in distributed systems the mutually exclusive resources are shared by variables or services that are physically located in each of the users. The users negotiate the access but then the access is local). Also, the requests have to be memorized when they cannot be satisfied immediately. In the user and in the server there must be a memory mechanism associated with the ordering algorithm.

3.2 The Serialization Problem

By the serialization problem we mean the problem of deciding which is the correct issueing order of the messages knowing that the transmission delay is random and unknown. The serialization problem is common to any distributed system. CoMEdiA is intended to be distributed to allow geographically distinct processing, human cooperation and conferencing. Using CoMEdiA, users compete for the access of a resource through a server that manages the cooperation.

3.3 The Mutual Exclusion Problem

The other problem is the mutual exclusion problem. Cooperative processing assumes the existence of just one resource available to several users. Most of the time the resource (or parts of the resource) has to be locked as critical. This means that accesses to these have to be made in a mutually exclusive manner. No two users may edit the same picture or paragraph at the same time.

In fact, the ordering algorithm (below) solves also the mutual exclusion problem providing consistency to documents.

3.4 The Communication Problem

The communication problem is strongly related with the access resulting from the degree of distribution that is used as well as well as from the kind of distribution (network technology - local, national, international - or transputer technology). The communication options, concepts and algorithms influence the system performance and the implementation complexity. All communication done in CoMEdiA can be considered within the ordering algorithm. Therefore during the explanation of this, the type, complexity and other communication aspects will become clear.

In the case of just one user using CoMEdiA the communications are very simple and the algorithm (as a decision mechanism) becomes trivial. Another simplification for one user is that no information, related to one user actions, has to be sent to other users (e.g. when one edits a set of lines, the others must know that these lines are being edited by the first user). This lack of echo information takes away some of the communications complexity.

4 Approaches to an Ordering Algorithm

4.1 First-In-First-Served-Passive

For short, FIFSP is an algorithm without process notification. Here each client sends a request, waits for a reply and, if the reply is positive, executes the action relative to the reply. The server just waits for requests, executes one at a time by the order of arriving. Some advantages are: very simple to implement, has a complexity of *2*. Disadvantages are the imposed syncronocity, there is no notification to other users, a policy for occupied resources is still necessary, resource status changes are not visible and in general terms the changes in the other users are not visible.

4.2 First-In-First-Served-Active

For short, FIFSA is also an algorithm without process notification. The server is divided in $N_u\text{-}1$ parts as shown in the figure below. Each of the users has a part of the server (peripheral part) closer to him. The functionalities that can be treated locally or are not allowed at all are processed here. Just the other cases are sent to the central part of the server. The central part of the server communicates with the peripherical parts. To the peripherical part concerning a certain request he sends the convenient reply and to the others he sends the informations that reflect this reply. Some advantages are that the complexity is still $2+(N_u\text{-}1)$, it is asynchronous, consistency can always be preserved, status changes are visible as well as general changes, there is an event mechanism (instead of a pooling mechanism). The main disadvantage is that there is no memory mechanism to avoid an exception situation when a request can not be satisfied. It can be solved if each of the peripheric servers repeats the request when a negative comes from the central server. Otherwise the inconsistent requests are lost and only one is satisfied.

4.3 First-In-First-Served-Active Multiple

For short, First-In-First-Served-Active Multiple is an algorithm with processes notification. The previous algorithm is augmented with a memory mechanism and a strategy to solve semantic inconsistencies. This way, a user (or more accurately, a peripherical server) just sends a request and always receives a positive answer despite the number of attempts, delay time or accessing conflicts. An example of semantic inconsistency is the simple case where a user asks to delete line *i* and another inserts a line after line *i-5* (before he has been notified of the deletion). If the fulfilling order is insert+delete then the line *i-1* will be deleted.

5 Approaches for Managing Cooperative Access

5.1 Strategies

In the following, different strategies for the management of cooperative access will be discussed. This will serve as motivation for our final approach.

5.1.1 Server Organization

If we realize a central server, then this also implies one central (server) time. Consequently, consistency can only be checked by the server. All requests are handled independently and have a complexity of 2 (request and reply).

On the other hand, a distributed server consists of one central server and several local servers distributed over the network. Each one has its own local time. All requests now go to the central server first. This server negotiates with the (n - 1) other local servers, gets (n - 1), acknowledges, and sends them the reply. This sums up to 2 + 2 (n - 1).

5.1.2 User Update

Another point is the update of $user_j$ after $user_i$ has made a request. Here, we distinguish between passive and active servers. A passive server has the actual version of the document, but the user has to ask for it. This sums up to a complexity of 2 (request and reply). An active server sends an update of each request to all other users. This increases the complexity of the request by (n - 1), but makes the actual status of the document locally available. It should be noted that the implementation of a distributed server implies an active update.

5.2 Comparison and Evaluation

5.2.1 Central Server; No Update

This solution has the lowest request complexity (2). However, this approach does not fit the special needs of cooperative work. Since update is essential, all users have to ask for the actual status, and this on the basis of polling. This leads to an overhead in communication.

More severely, consistency cannot be guaranteed with a central server.

5.2.2 Local Server; Update Only

The concept of a distributed server in combination with update works as follows: The request goes from $user_i$ to the central server. It is handled there, a reply is sent and all other local servers are updated. The resulting request complexity is 2 x (n - 1) now. This approach allows local processing, since the actual status of the document is locally available. On the other hand, the consistency problem is not yet solved. It may happen that a request is locally valid, reaches the server, is still syntactically valid but semantically refers to the wrong object.

As an example, suppose $user_j$ wants to delete line 7, which is actually free. While this request is transferred to the central server $user_i$ deletes line 7 and completes the deletion. Thus, line 8 becomes line 7. Now, the request of $user_j$ reaching the server, line 7 (the former line 8) is free and gets deleted. This, of course, is semantically wrong. The only way to avoid this is the usage of a truly distributed server.

5.2.3 Truly Distributed Server

In this approach, the server is truly distributed. The central server serves only as a central switch. This approach has a request complexity of 2 + 2 (n - 1). But it solves all the problems stated above. Moreover, global consistency is achieved. Remember the example above. If now $user_i$ wants to delete line 7, the central server passes this request to all other users. If it reaches $user_j$ before it starts deletion, $user_j$ accepts the delete. It sends a notify back to the central server. The central server waits for an n - 1 notifies, and then sends an acknowledge to $user_i$. When $user_j$ now tries to delete line 7 the local $server_j$ will not let this request pass.

If $user_j$ starts deletion earlier we have a true conflict. Now $user_i$ gets $request_j$ and $user_j$ gets $request_i$. Because of the total ordering (e.g. the user id), this problem can be solved. Let us suppose that $user_i$ has higher priority than $user_j$. Then $user_i$ blocks $request_j$ while $user_j$ passes $request_i$ and invalidates his own $request_j$. $Request_i$ is passed back to $user_i$, and the request is handled. After completion $request_j$ is passed by $user_i$ and reaches, after a while, $user_j$. $User_j$ now checks the $request_j$ and notices that it is invalid. So, a total ordering and a processing of all requests is reached.

6 Communications Architecture and Access Management in CoMEdiA

Obviously there are a lot of ways we could have organized our communications architecture. As we have in mind cooperative processing we had to allow the distribution of the using entities from the resources. Therefore, CoMEdiA is based on the server/client paradigm having the following general architecture.

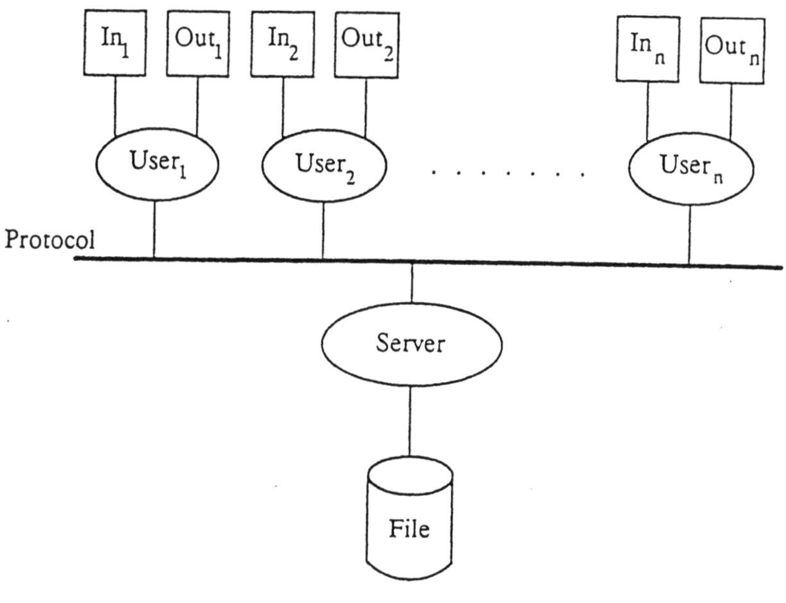

Fig. 1: A general view of CoMEdiA's communications

In the above general communications scheme of CoMEdiA, there is the server process that takes care of the resource (file), there is one user process for each user that makes the local operations (e.g. editing), and there are the communication links.

6.1 Architecture of the Server Process

The server architecture is very simple and consists only of one process. This process communicates with the several user processes through the UserReader and UserWriter (see above - two communication processes that take care of the asynchronous bidirectional message flow between the user and the server) and controls the physical resource.

The server implements the concept of a distributed server and therefore, each user has a local server, $server_i$, in it.

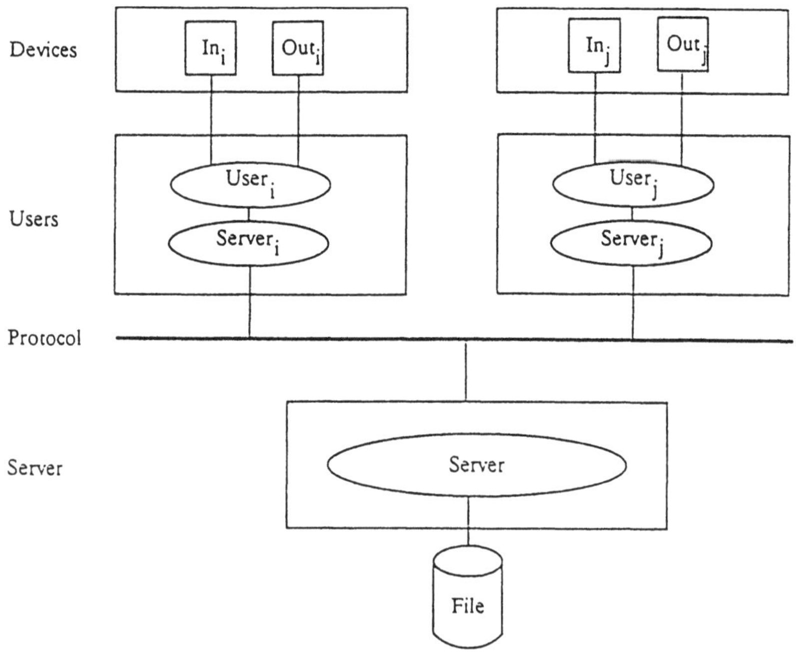

Fig. 2: Architecture of the server process

6.2 Architecture of the User Process

All users have the same architecture which we describe below.

Each user is built up of four processes: the user itself that takes care of the local editing functionalities and makes the main management functions (User), two communication processes that take care of the asynchronous bidirectional message flow between the user and the server (ServerWriter, ServerReader), one process to control the flow of asynchronous information from the input device to the user (Keyboard). Why are so many process needed? As the user can not make a sequential synchronous pool of the input device and server communications (he would loose information) we introduce the buffer mechanisms supported by the Keyboard and ServerReader processes. On the other hand the ordering algorithm enforces the existence of an asynchronous process to act as a care taker of the requests (InvokeReq - this will be explained altogether with the algorithm). Finally, for the same reason there are two buffer mechanisms on the entrance of the server (for each user) and the respective two care takers that connect these buffers with the streams.

The user process is seen as a process that is asynchronously running but interacting simultaneously with the server process, with other users' processes and with the input device. Moreover for each edition that is sent to the server a new process is created that takes care of this request during its server access competition and fulfilment. From here we deduce that CoMEdiA's process complexity (for each domain) is $4N_u+M$ where N_u is the number of users using CoMEdiA and M is a constant that represents the average number of requests that are waiting for the ordering algorithm (referred to below) to let them go into the server. This results in a high degree of process distribution and communication.

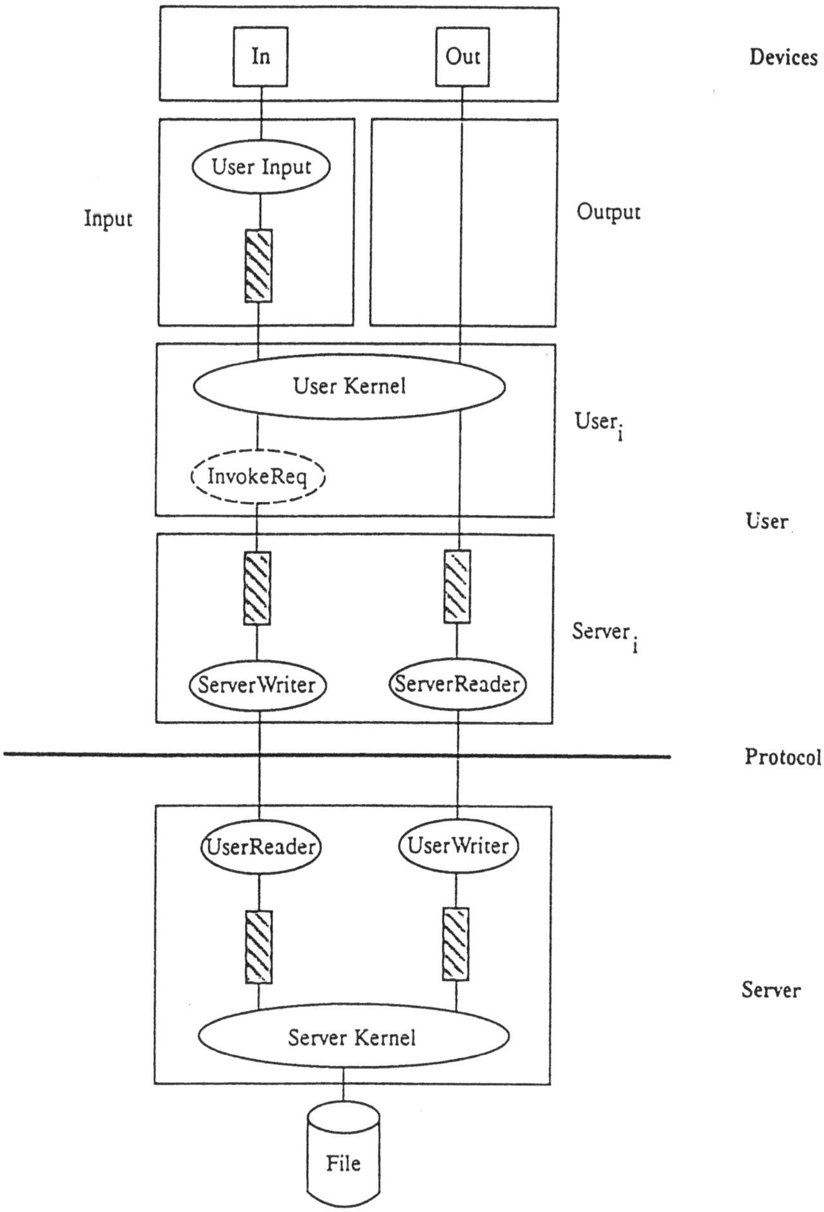

Fig. 3: A detailed view of the CoMEdiA's communications

7 The Ordering Algorithm

In the pevious sections we presented some approaches to ordering algorithms. This one tries to solve the problems presented.

7.1 The Algorithm

The ordering algorithm that was implemented is used to establish an order in the requests that come from a domain of users to the server and to provide mutual exclusive access.

The only possible communication between the users and the server is using messages. There is no common memory. Nevertheless, the several processes of the user have common memory. The only way to communicate among the users is through the server and just users within the same domain can communicate.

The concept of the algorithm is as simple as each user asking the others if he can have the turn to make a request. A user has the turn to send a request, after all other users from the same domain have been notified of the existence of the request and have sent a reply granting their agreement. The algorithm is based on the fact that a user receiving a request notification can immediately determine whether the requesting user or himself should have the turn to issue a request towards the server. The user originating the request notification never knows the result of the comparison (at least directly). A reply message is sent if the originator of the request notification should have the turn, otherwise the reply is delayed. The priority order decision is made by each user based on a time stamp that each request notification brings. Therefore, each user has to have a local time stamp reflecting what he thinks about the global state of the system. This mechanism acts as a sequence (a total order) of slots (of requests) that is being fulfiled. Every user begins from the same slot. When a user sends a reply message he is implicitly admitting that he does not want to use that slot of the requests' total order (therefore, he increments his image of the total order).

More specifically we can say that the algorithm runs as follows: each user runs the same algorithm consisting of one asynchronous process (*InvokeUserSend*) and of routines callable from the main event dispatcher of a user (*TreatAnswer* and *TreatReply*). The first process is created whenever a request is to be sent. It sends request notifications to all other users (in fact just to the server, and this one broadcasts the notifications), then it waits until all the other users have answered. One of the routines is responsible for receiving the request notifications of the other users and process them. The second routine is responsible for waking up the asynchronous process that is stopped waiting for the answers of all the other users.

The process *InvokeReq*:

- poses himself in requesting mode state
- sends a request notification to the user
- waits for every other users' answer (through the server).

When it is awakened

- sends the real request to the server with a number reflecting the total order that was calculated within the algorithm (slot number)
- poses himself in no requesting mode state
- sends replies to all the users who were waiting for him to get out of the requesting mode state

The routine *TreatAnswer*:

- makes the necessary comparisons between its time stamp and the one just arrived in the incoming request notification. This will enable this user to conclude if he is ahead of the one issuing the request notification
- if this happens it will not answer the other user preventing him from having the requesting turn. It will, instead, save the request notification in order that this can be answered later.
- if this does not happen it answers the other user

The routine *TreatReply*:

- when it receives a message saying that all the other users have authorized this user to make a request, it awakes the process InvokeUserSend

When we say that a user sends a request notification to all the other users we mean that he sends a request notification to the server and the server broadcasts it to the other users of the same domain. Also one user does not receive replies from all the other users. The server acts as a filter counting himself the replies. Then, when the total is reached he sends a unique reply to the issueing user. This allows a saving of N_u-2 messages for each request (see complexity analysis below).

A very important point of this algorithm is that it makes the decisions where the needed information is located. This avoids the problems (common in distributed systems) that come from making decisions based on copies of the information. The problems, resulting from message delay, are also avoided this way. Especially in large networks, there may be a substantial and variable time delay between the instant when a user issues a request and its arrival to the server. One problem that this fact poses it as follows: in a system with concurrent access, a request valid at the time when it was sent may be no longer valid when it arrives to the resource server. This problem here is somehow different from the ones that usually appear in distributed systems. In the latter, the resources are considered, by default, stable. This means that a resource is to be requested, used and released. Resources do not *disappear* with the use. A cooperative (and in particular an editing) system is more dynamic. Resources can be legally requested (legally based on user information), but when the request is about to be fulfiled, it can no longer be valid. This happens when, for example, a piece of information is requested for editing and a prior request (the effects of which are not yet known to the issueing user) has, between the issueing and the arrival, deleted this piece of information.

7.2 Complexity Analysis

We can divide the complexity analysis into two parts. One that deals with the general access, made for each and every action of the user towards the server. The other part deals with the editor specific functionality.

The message complexity analysis of the algorithm part that concerns pure access functionality, leads to the number $2N_u$ messages per request. One message to send the request notification to the server. The server broadcasts it to N_u-1 other users. The N_u-1 users, sooner or later, reply to each one with one message more. One more message from the server to the user saying that we can really issue the request taking one slot. This all sums up to $2N_u$. In (Ricard et al. 1981) it is said that for a parallel, distributed, symmetric control algorithm the optimal number of messages per request is $2N_u$-2. The fact that we do not want to have a symmetric system (it would imply direct inter-user communication) and the resource is not in each of the users (therefore we have a resource server) translates into the use of more 2 messages per request. If the system is composed by 2 users the overhead is 50% but as the number of users goes up this overhead becomes more and more insignificant.

The message complexity analysis of the algorithm part that concerns the editing functionalities, leads to the number N_u+1 messages per edition request. The request itself was, this time, authorized by the other users. One message to transmit to the requesting user an acknowledgement about the success of its operation. The server information to all other users (N_u-1) that a certain part of the resource, concerned with this request, is under a certain editing operation (edit, delete, free, etc.).

A slight modification in the presented algorithm can introduce some optimizations concerning the simplicity of the server scheduler. Each of the broadcasts made by the server take information relative to the type of the request notification. This way any user can decide if we still wants to make a certain request knowing that another user made other requests. For example a user that wants to edit a line and has already sent his request notification to the server, can receive a request notification from the server saying that the other user wants to delete this line. If the tests determine that the first user loses the slot to the second one then the first user does not have to send the edit request to the server because it is directed to a line that will, for sure, not exist when the edit request arrives at the server.

This kind of reasoning can be applied in other cases to avoid conflicts, inconsistencies and other situations that would be difficult to deal with in the server.

Instead of using mechanisms like shared windows, system broadcast message techniques, timing channels or receiving-order fulfilment of requests we choose to use a more general approach: a pure software algorithm. This has the advantage of being more easily portable and modifiable. It is cooperative and distributed right from the basic concept. Also, it is reusable for other media independently of the media and of the channels used for the transfers. On the other hand it has the disadvantage of being slower and having more software development costs.

7.3 Evaluation

How does this algorithm solve the serialization problem?

Serialization is achieved because of the slot mechanism. If each user increments the slot counter when he gives a positive reply then he is not taking the opportunity to use this slot. For each request notification issued, all users, except the issueing user, will increment the slot counter. Therefore, only one user takes a slot number to make the request. This implements a total order in the requests. After this, the only thing that the server has to do is to fulfil the requests in the order of the slot numbers.

How does this algorithm solve the mutual exclusion problem?

The mutual exclusion problem is solved by the reply mechanism. Each user just answers to a request notification if he has not issued a conflicting request (it does not matter if the message with the request is still traveling because the decision is taken based on local information, without delay). This way, the entrance in a critical region (e.g. simultaneous editing) is prevented.

In relation with the algorithms presented above, this algorithm is completly asynchronous, there is notification of one user's action to the other users (as well as changings in the resource status), a clear policy for managing occupied resources is defined, there is an event mechanism (instead of a poling mechanism), there is a memory mechanism to avoid an exception situation when a request can not be immediately satisfied.

Some important characteristics that differentiate this algorithm from other known distributed algorithms are: the resources can disappear, non-symmetric decision control and low density of physical communication (geographic distances make it impratical).

8 Future Work

A future goal is the global integration of CoMEdiA in a bigger work that includes other cooperative tools as well as several multimedia tools.

More than flexibility, cooperative work techniques need speed. Cooperative work applications are very communication demanding. Usually they use a high rate of small messages. Therefore another goal is to accelerate the communications between the server and the users. This acceleration would come from the use of different communication techniques, instead of the pure message mechanism. The advantages would be the speed up of the ordering algorithm (main consumer of communication time) and enable the *Transparent write* mode. The disadvantages would be, for example, the loss of portability (to workstations or networks in general).

As referred to above the *Transparent write* mode will be implemented in the near future.

The user should be given the chance to optionally visualize the hyper-links structures. This will imply the devising of mechanisms for visualization (for example, windows are non-existent) and navigation as well as an integrated user interface. We refer to section 2.2 where a lot of future work to be done is described.

Human-human interaction is something that is needed in CoMEdiA. A direct/no-store transfer of data must be accomplished to provide a connection between a camera and a display as well as between a microphone and a speaker. This communication will be the kernel of the interface aiming at the creation of a more communicative and better cooperative environment.

A feature that is desirable to have in CoMEdiA in the near future is the so-called private annotations. These are pieces of information that are attached to some paragraphs of a text, or figure of a graphic picture. There is a certain resemblance of annotations and hyper links. The annotations can be other parts of the document (of the same media or not) or can be external data. The external data can be information specially edited to be an annotation or can be an entire file. This is another way of having inter-file references.

In fact, almost all the work relating identification and authorization has yet to be done. Also, most of the work referred to in section 2.2 is still being implemented.

We do not make any processing related to node (users) failures. We have, until now, avoided this problem.

9 Conclusions

Although we are just at the beginning of our work, we think that we have taken a step forward for solving some of the problems of cooperative work, in particular cooperative information editing.

Moreover, we have put our best efforts in the cooperative access problem. We achieved a cooperative access algorithm that is flexible, powerful and robust enough for this problem and is suitable also for other cooperative work fields.

Acknowledgements

We would like to thank Prof. J. Encarnação for the opportunities given and Rui Guerreiro for useful suggestions and implementation help.

Bibliography

Akscyn R., McCracken D., Yoder E. (1988): " KMS: A Distributed Hypermedia System for Managing Knowledge in Organizations" - Communications of the ACM, July 1988.

Barret E. (1988): "Text, Context and Hypertext: Writing with and for the Computer" - MIT Press, Cambridge

Ben-Ari M. (1982): "Principles of Concurrent Programming" - Prentice Hall, Englewood Cliffs, N.J.

Blum B. (1988): "Documentation for Maintenance: A Hypertext Design" - Proc. conf. on Software Maintenance, 1988

Brown P.J. (1988): "Hypertext: the way forward" - Proc. Int. Conf. on Electronic Publishing, Document Manipulation, and Typography, Nizza, April

Collier G.H. (1987): "Thoth-II: Hypertext with explicit semantics" - Proc. Hypertext'87, Chapel Hill, 1987

Conklin J. (1987): "Hypertext: An Introduction and Survey" - IEEE Computer, Vol.20, N.9, Sep.1987

Conklin J., Begeman M. (1988): "gIBIS: A Hypertext Tool for Explaratory Policy Discussion" - ACM ToOIS, Vol.6,N.4, Oct. 1988

Delisle N.: Schwartz M.: "Neptune: a Hypertext System for CAD Applications" - Tektronix Laboratories, Oregon

Delisle N.M., Schwartz M.D. (1987): "Neptune: A Hypertext System for Software Development Environment" - Database engineering, Vol.10,N.1,Mar. 1987

Foss C.L. (1988): "Efective Browsing in Hypertext Systems" - Proc. RIAO'88, MIT Press, Cambridge, Mar 1988

Frisse M. (1988): "From Text to Hypertext" - Byte, Oct. 1988

Garg P.K. (1988): "Abstraction Mechanisms in Hypertext" - Communications of the ACM, July 1988, Vol.31, N.7

Gibbs S.J. (1989): "LIZA: An Extensible Groupware Toolkit" - MCC, Software Technology Program

Hofmann M., Langendörfer H. (1990): "Browsing as Incremental Access information in the Hypertext System CONCORDE" - Proc. Conf. Interactive Communication

Hornung C., Santos A. (1991): "Proposal for a Reference Model for Cooperative Hypermedia Systems" - Eurographics Multimedia Workshop

Jones H. (1987): "Developing and Distributing Hypertext Tools: Legal Inputs and Parameters" - Hypertext'87, The University of North Carolina, Chapel Hill

Lamport L. (1978): "Time, Clocks, and the Ordering of Events in a Distributed System" - Communications of the ACM, July

Meiser D. (1990): "Die abstrakte Hypertextmaschine DAHM als Basis für große verteilte Hypertextsysteme" - Proc. of the workshop "Integrierte, intelligente, Informationssysteme", Sep. 1990

Phillips D. (1990): "Interactive SIGGRAPH Proceedings: A New Form of Publication" - Computer Graphics, Vol. 24, N. 1, Jan. 1990

Phillips R.L. (1990): "Multimedia Publications: Status, Opportunities and Problems" - Proc. of the Eurographics'90 Conference

Rada R. (1989): "Writing and Reading Hypertext" - Journal of the American Society of Information Scientists, Mar.

Rada R., Keith B. (1989): "Collaborative Writing of Text and Hypertext" - Hypermedia Vol.1,N.2, 1989

Raynal M. (1986): "Algorithms for Mutual Exclusion" - The MIT Press, Cambridge, Mass

Ricart G., Agrawala A. (1981): "An Optimal Algorithm for Mutual Exclusion in Computer Networks" - Communications of the ACM, Jan.

Santos A: (1990): "State of the Art Report on Multimedia" FAGD-90i034, Dez. 1990

Sculley J., Hutzel I. (1990): "Playing Author" - Computer Graphics world, Feb.

Streitz N.A., Hannemann J., Thüring M. (1989): "From Ideas and Arguments to Hyperdocuments: Travelling through Activity Spaces" - Proc. Hypertext'89, November 1989

Part VI

Information Systems

Chapter 17

An Open Hypermedia System for Multimedia Applications

Thomas Kirste and Wolfgang Hübner

Abstract

In this paper we present an architecture for an open hypermedia system that supports integrated multimedia applications. Besides support for the organisation and the manipulation of heterogeneous data types like text, raster pictures, vector graphics, video, animation and sound, open hypermedia systems include techniques to extend the system with new data types and tools as basic functionality.

Starting from a requirement analysis for an open hypermedia system, we identify the different task scopes of the system. We then map the task scopes onto a conceptual architecture and describe the different architectural and descriptive elements resulting from this mapping. The systems' architectural elements are the components *mass storage*, *object*, *session* and *presentation-interaction management*. On the descriptive side the HyperPicture concept provides *information objects*, *extents*, *functions bindings*, *events* and *actions* as atomic elements for the definition of the interaction between user, operating system and data objects.

Furthermore, we describe a prototype implementation of the HyperPicture concepts being developed at the Computer Graphics Center (ZGDV), the HyperPicture-Toolkit. Moreover, an application built on top of this toolkit – the satellite data retrieval system SpacePicture – illustrates the use and the potential of the HyperPicture-Toolkit and its underlying concepts. Finally, this paper contains a brief description of open issues and further development.

1 Introduction

The term *Hypermedia* today more and more stands for a trend towards *Integration*. Hypermedia comprises within the approach of a unified, integrated system the different aspects of hardware support, user interfaces, multimedia data, data manipulation and data organisation. A superficial analysis of these aspects yields three significant dimensions for the description of a system – *data types*, *application tools* and *system services & resources*. 'Full' Hypermedia is in essence identical to the complete volume defined by these dimensions. However, every currently available hypertext- and hypermedia-system[1] covers only a certain sub-volume of this space.

1 The differences between hypertext and hypermedia are summarised in [Streitz-90].

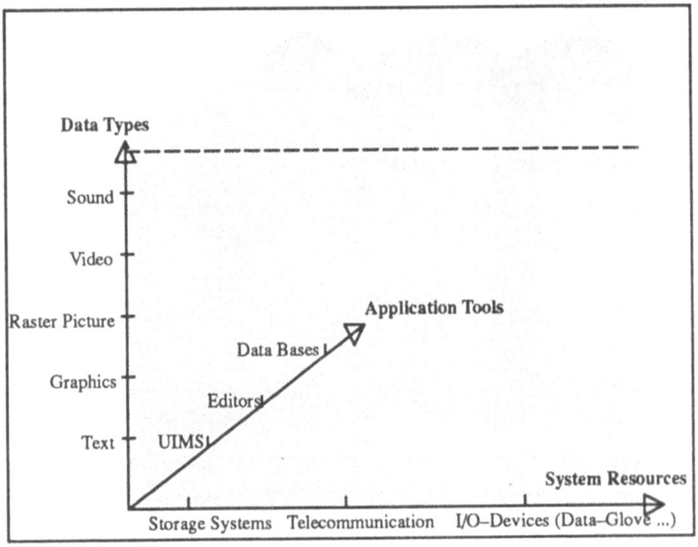

The goal of an *open* hypermedia system is to cover the complete space by providing generic tools for defining, accessing, organising and manipulating multimedia data objects.

1.1 Requirements

The concrete requirements that have to be met by an open hypermedia system directly result from the application environment they are intended for. However, these requirements may be grouped into abstract task scopes. This is shown for an example environment, where the system is used to perform the tasks of rendering systems, image archives, image processing systems, and multimedia information systems.

Organisation of heterogeneous data objects:

- Object types – e.g. scene definitions, geometries, textures, raster pictures, textual data.
- Object associations – e.g. complex objects like *scene* consisting of scene definitions, geometries, several textures and raster pictures; free associations like annotations.
- Object sets – e.g. user, application and project specific object sets ('John's objects', 'raster picture archive objects', 'project SpacePicture').

Presentation of data objects:

- Display of pictures, scene definitions, geometries etc.
- Interactive manipulation of the display, e.g., Rotation of a geometry, contrast enhancement for a raster picture.

Transformation and interactive Manipulation of data objects:

- Editing of scene definitions, geometries and annotations.
- Transformation of scene definitions into geometries, of geometries and textures into raster images.
- Creation of annotations and associations, following of associations.

Storage of voluminous data objects:

- E.g., high-resolution raster pictures and picture sequences for a scene definition.

Following from the tasks listed above, an open hypermedia system has to provide the user with all required mechanisms for the interactive organisation and manipulation of heterogeneous data objects *within a single integrated system.* An open hypermedia thus provides a high-level interface to the different 'classical' services of a computer system. From the user's point of view, it may therefore be regarded as a *replacement* of these services and their respective user interfaces (e.g. JCL for the operating system and SQL for the data base system) [McCracken-84].

In case of a system extension (e.g, towards animation in case of the example environment introduced above), new object types together with their specific manipulation, presentation and interaction methods have to be introduced. For this reason, an open hypermedia system has to provide the description tools for the definition of these new types and methods, in addition to the tasks already outlined above.

This means, that all mechanisms of the open hypermedia system have to be of an *inherently generic nature.* It must be possible to tailor the system's behaviour concerning specific object classes, applications etc. by *explicit description* the required reactions. Otherwise, an efficient and adequate support of a steady growing pool of heterogeneous data types cannot be maintained.

In case of the extension towards animation, additional requirements are introduced for the storage management, concerning large volume and isochronal data objects.

1.2 Current Concepts

In recent years, hypertext and hypermedia has received an increased attention, partially due to the flexible and individual data *organisation* obtainable through the use of these systems, and the easy interactive data access. This implies a certain appropriateness of the hypertext/hypermedia concepts for some of the requirements listed above.

However, currently available hypermedia systems, as well as the reference models for hypertext and hypermedia, do not cope very well with the manipulative elements required for a complete open hypermedia system. This is mainly due to the fact, that hypermedia defines itself by the concept of the 'hyperlink'. A link is an explicit connection between data objects, having an implicitly static nature. Therefore, a 'hypertext' is a structured document, where the aspects of data manipulation are only captured with respect to creating and accessing the document's structure. This is mirrored by the two modes offered by nearly every hypertext system: 'Authoring' – creation of the document structure, and "Browsing" – access of the document structure.

Hypermedia systems usually offer the possibilities to edit and structure documents, and to view these structured documents later on. The tools provided for document creation are partially very powerful. Some systems for example, KMS[Akscyn-88],[Feiner-82], Notecards[Halasz-88] and [Richartz-90] offer the 'active link' concept. An active link is a link, whose destination is a set of commands instead of a document. These commands are executed if the link is traversed. The result of the command execution is the actual destination document of the link, thereby offering certain dynamics for documents.

Nevertheless, these mechanisms are mainly intended for the production of information structures and the navigation (the access) within these structures. Active information processing like generating new information from existing data (e.g., through image analysis) or automatic creation of new structures is only supported for the specific application of document creation.

On the other side there are systems for dedicated complex information processing and data generation – however, without adequate means for organising and administering the data pools on which the systems work. These systems are, e.g, simulation packages, image processing and analysis tools and image generation (rendering) systems.

An open hypermedia system should be able to provide both aspects – the easy, individual information *access* and the powerful means for information *processing* – within an integrated, homogeneous environment.

2 The HyperPicture Concept

HyperPicture is a fundamental architecture for open hypermedia systems in graphics applications. The goal of this development is the construction of a hypermedia toolkit, that allows the realisation of information management systems based on multimedia data like raster images, motion picture and sound. The capabilities for data manipulation have been regarded as one of the key issues and are an integral part of the concept. With respect to the description of relations between data objects, the conceptually static 'Link'-model had to be extended. Furthermore, a finer grained approach to the underlying concepts of 'anchoring' and 'trigger' provides the descriptive tools to define complex interactions at the user interface.

2.1 The Architecture

Similar to the approach of current reference models for hypertext and hypermedia [Furuta-90] [Halasz-90] [Lange-90], the interpretation of heterogeneous object contents, like raster image, video and text is based on the separation of an object's abstract *identity* and its concrete *contents*[2].

Within an object-type independent system kernel, *abstract* object identities are used as synonyms for objects. Thereby the kernel mechanisms processing different objects and object structures can be realised independently of the contents interpretation. The kernel is surrounded by *content-specific* tools, that provide support for accessing and manipulating the contents of a given object.

One example is the definition of a part of an object. Since the object may possess arbitrary structure (a set or array of pixels, character sequences, a scene definition), a complete sub-part specification language is required, to render arbitrary parts of arbitrarily structured objects describable (e.g, "the texture of the round table in the second frame of the third scene"). It is by all means less expensive for the system kernel, to delegate the responsibility of the *interpretation* of a part definition to the respective content specific components. On the kernel level, only abstract *identities* are used (e.g., Object *XYZ* contains part *ABC*; with the mapping *XYZ*–>"Second frame of third scene", *ABC*–>"Texture of round table").

A second structural separation of HyperPicture is the differentiation between *dynamic* and *structural* behaviour. Dynamic behaviour describes and controls the user's interaction with the system, while structural behaviour captures the aspects of transformations between data objects and the mechanisms for creating and accessing information structures.

The structural layers of HyperPicture – abstract and contents layer, dynamic and structure layer – provide a framework onto which the system components can be mapped:

- Storage Management (STM)
- Object Management (OM)
- Session Management (SM)
- Presentation and Interaction (PIM)

	dynamic	structural
abstract	SM	OM
content–specific	PIM	STM

2 From this follows, that the identity of an object is independent from its contents. This property is, especially for integrity conditions, not without problem potential in the case of the modification of the contents. A solution as proposed for XANADU[Nelson-80], where *all* versions of an object are kept available so that the mapping between identity and contents remains unambiguous, seems not appropriate for voluminous multimedia data objects.

These components are responsible for the following tasks:

Storage Management – This component is responsible for mapping data objects to storage pools, accessing the contents of data objects, providing synchronous access to isochronal data objects and controlling the cache.

Object Management – The object management component is responsible for storing and accessing the abstract elements of HyperPicture; it is the abstract machine within the meaning of HAM [Campbell-88].

Session Management – Session management controls coordination and synchronisation of the different PIM-members of a session. It is responsible for the processing of abstract events and the execution of actions and functions.

Presentation and Interaction – These components manage the type-specific presentation of data objects, the interpretation of event- and extent-definitions and the generation of events. In addition, they provide object-type specific standard mechanisms for object manipulation.

In HyperPicture, object management, session management, and the respective PIMs may be realised as individual processes. Thereby the parallel processing of computation-intensive and i/o-intensive tasks in the case of object and session management is easily supported. This is especially valid in the case of several simultaneously active sessions. Implementing the PIMs as separate processes provides for a very easy system extension through the introduction of new type specific PIMs or the replacement of PIMs with improved or extended versions. The kernel system (below the PIM/session-manager interface) remains unaffected (in fact, fully operational) by the exchange procedure[3].

2.2 Storage Management

The specific properties of multimedia data with respect to such characteristics as storage requirements (e.g., for high-resolution raster pictures), storage type (e.g., motion picture, sound), heterogeneity and synchronisation mechanisms for presentation must be taken into account. Therefore, the storage management has to provide the following mechanisms:

- Support for the individual properties of the different storage pools (RAM, Winchester, WORM, IVD, LAN, WAN, etc.). Especially for WORM, new approaches are required [Kirste-90a]);
- Administration and retrieval of isochronal data objects (Sound, Video);
- Support for interactive retrieval of data objects in the context of the binding (link) concept;
- Support for large and/or variably sized data objects;
- Support for complex objects consisting of heterogeneous sub-objects;
- Support for data manipulation mechanisms.

The storage management component employs adaptive caching and migration algorithms that rely on the usage profile of the data pool and an analysis of the bindings (links) defined between data objects. In addition, mechanisms are required for the explicit (possibly temporary) assignment of data objects to specific storage pools. Further required properties for mass storage management are described in [Kirste-90a], [Kirste-90b] and [Woelk-87].

3 The easy exchangeability of PIMs allows, e.g., that a user chooses among different browser-PIMs the one best suited for his needs. This is similar to the situation in the window system X, where a user may choose a window manager based on completely personal preferences.

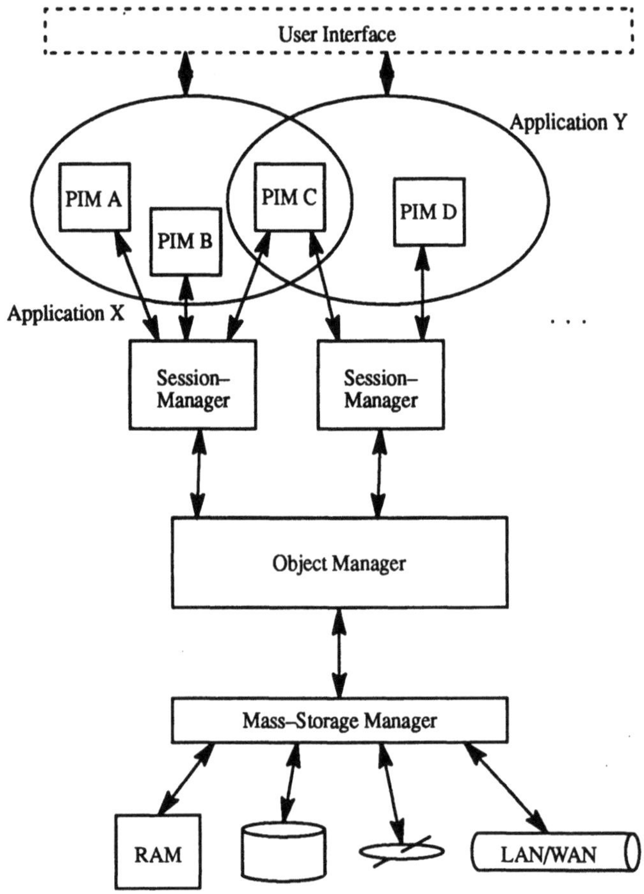

The system architecture of HyperPicture

2.3 Objects and Structural Behaviour

The system's structural behaviour is described using 'Information Objects' and 'Functions' operating on these objects. 'Bindings' and 'extents' are provided for the easy realisation of special-purpose structures.

2.3.1 Information Objects

Information objects are containers for application data. The structure and behaviour of an information object are defined by a class system. Every information object belongs to a specific class, giving it a unique type (e.g., 'Raster Picture,' 'Animation'). An object's class defines its structure and its instance variables and their respective types (e.g., Raster Picture = {width, height: integer; pixmap: array of byte}).

Each object class usually defines at least one content-specific tool; that is, the presentation and interaction method (PIM). The PIM is used to present an object[4], especially its contents, upon activation in an appropriate way to the user and provides a means for interacting with the object.

2.3.2 Extents

Besides references to complete objects, it is useful to be able to access specific parts (extents) of an object. E.g, for defining part of a raster picture object to use it as texture, or for defining a reference from one section of a text object to another section in the same object.

Because the method for specifying a part of an object depends on the part-notion appropriate to the type of the object's contents, the interpretation of an extent specification is the responsibility of the contents specific tools. Therefore, these tools are responsible also, for preserving the integrity of the extent specifications after an object's contents have been modified.

Example:

```
extents(ob#1) ->
  [xt#1: "pixelarea 10 10 100 100"]
```

For object ob#1 (maybe a raster picture object) a rectangular extent has been defined.

2.3.3 Functions

HyperPicture integrates functions for data manipulation, 'active links' and static links using one fundamental mechanism, the function.

$$\mathbf{f: X \to Y}$$

In HyperPicture, the function is the sole means for information access. It is used as well as for building structured data (like abstract data types), as for data manipulation. From the user's point of view it does not matter whether information belonging to an object is stored as a substructure of the object (e.g., `wheels(car) := car.wheels`) or computed from other data at the time of access (e.g, `edges(picture) = filter(picture,[[1,1,1],[1,-8,1],[1,1,1]])`). It is only relevant, that information has to be accessed that is a *function of* the respective object[5].

Using functional notation and a function 'jump', a binary hyperlink from X to Y may be written as:

$$\mathbf{jump: x \mapsto y.}$$

In HyperPicture therefore, hyperlinks are object-valued functions of objects.

Within this functional model, the 'computed link' and 'active link' concepts of hypertext may be interpreted as follows: Computed links are functions, that give a set of existing objects as result; they are to be understood as set-valued functions of sets. Active links are object-valued functions, that give *new* objects as results.

The means for defining functions and applying functions to argument is a central system component of HyperPicture. The user may anytime extend the system by introducing new functionalities through the definition of corresponding functions. Therefore, in contrast to hypertext, the canonical activity in HyperPicture is function application, and not link activation.

---

4 Subsequently, the term 'object' is used synonymously for 'information object.'

5 HyperPicture thus basically employs a functional data model ([Shipman-81],[Sibley-77]), like the IRIS data base management system [Fishman-89].

Besides the usual primitive data types, the set of possible types for function arguments and results contains the 'identifier' type. It is the type of the abstract representations of objects, extents and events[6].

2.3.4 Bindings

However, the approach presented above, oriented at the functional data model, evokes the following problems:

a) The evaluation of certain functions is much more expensive, than the storage of the evaluated result (e.g, rendering of a photorealistic image).
b) For some functions it is not possible to define a finite algorithm, that means, the cost of function evaluation is infinite (e.g., the function Counterposition: Proposal –> Rebuttal).

Therefore, it is useful (a) and necessary (b) to augment the functional model with a means for modelling these degenerate cases. A mechanism is required, that allows the *explicit declaration* of individual argument–result mappings for functions. In addition, it should store the result of a function evaluation.

In HyperPicture the Binding–concept fulfills this task. For any argument–tuple of a function, a result–tuple can be explicitly defined by 'binding' arguments and result. If the function is applied to a given argument tuple, it has to be checked by the system, whether a binding exists for this function/argument combination. If this is the case, the result value can be retrieved without executing a (possibly non-existent) result-yielding function body. Otherwise, the result is computed by explicit evaluation of the function body[7].

In order to provide a flexible and easy of the binding mechanism, the behaviour of HyperPicture functions may be attributed with respect to the binding. The following attribute values control the automatic instantiation of bindings by the system:

autobind
After evaluation of the function body, arguments and result are bound automatically;
demandbind
After evaluation of the function body, arguments and result are bound upon request;
nobind
Arguments and results are never bound;
bound
The function may only be applied to bound arguments.

Likewise, the evaluation of the function body can be made subject to the binding state of the function arguments. Parts of the function body can thus be declared to be evaluated only in the case of unbound arguments (e.g., for explicit computation of the result), while other parts are evaluated always (e.g., in order to implement a specific history management) or only if the arguments are bound.

Based on binding behaviour, a function 'annotate' may be implemented as an 'autobind' function. The Annotation is created in a part of the function body, that is only evaluated for unbound arguments.

---

6 The function/binding model does not contain explicitly definable attributes for 'links', as do some hypertext systems. However, link attributes may easily constructed. E.g., using constructs like `select (tag-jump (X,Y),2)` which accesses the tag-attribute of a link modelled with a function `tag-jump: A x B -> C x D x Tags`.

7 Functions and Bindings thus provide for the intensional and the extensional definition of predicates as defined by Woods [Woods-75].

2.3.5 Data Definition & Data Manipulation Language

For describing object classes and functions, it is necessary to provide a data definition (DDL) and a data manipulation language (DML). Besides constructs for creating, accessing and modifying HyperPicture-Elements and for controlling the system behaviour, the language has to offer the expressive power of a complete programming language in order to allow the definition of arbitrary functions on the object set.

2.4 The dynamic behaviour

Besides the description of data objects and functions, a means for defining the system behaviour in response to external events is required. This tool for the definition of dynamic behaviour is necessary as well as for describing the user interface (which interactions are possible, how does the system react to them ?), as for the definition of the object behaviour in the case of other events (what happens if the object is modified, what action is triggered by a timer interrupt ?).

The system's dynamic behaviour is described by events and actions. In the field of hypertext and hypermedia this differentiation between specifying an event and the activity possibly triggered by that event, is not usually made. Events and Activities (as well as Extents) are contained implicitly and in specific modality within the 'anchor' concept. An anchor is an extent whose manipulation (e.g. by a mouseclick) generates an event, that motivates the system to traverse a link. On the other hand, in User Interface development tools, especially for graphic applications, explicit definition mechanisms for trigger conditions are available [Hübner-90]. Moreover, object-oriented techniques exist to specify multimedia events and actions for prompt feedback and dynamic and semantic reactions [Hübner-89a] [Hübner-89b]. In HyperPicture, this finer grained view, consisting of extents, events, and actions, has been integrated in favour of the anchor-concept of classical Hypertext. Through this approach, the individual elements forming the dynamic system behaviour are readily available for the user. They provide him with the expressive power for a much more flexible definition of an object's behaviour, as well at the user interface level, as on the more abstract object evolution level ([Baumann-91]).

2.4.1 Events

Events are the fundamental mechanism that allow the communication between user or operating system and HyperPicture.

Events may be generated by a variety of different circumstances, e.g., the passing of a time interval, the deletion of a file, or a mouseclick in a specific screen area. In general, the set of event sources and the types of events generated cannot be determined beforehand. For this reason, the concrete specification of an event and its abstract identity are separated, as is the case for objects and extents.

For every object and class, the system maintains a set of events that can be generated by the object or an instance of the class. During object activation, the set event specifications associated with the individual object, as well as the event sets of its class and its superclasses are interpreted by the PIM[8] responsible for the object. If one of the specified events occur, its abstract identity is sent to the system kernel.

8 Arbitrary event sources ('event demons') can be realised based on specialised PIMs. These PIMs do not have to present a specific data object, instead they are used to manage and create events associated with a 'dummy' object. On the system level, this avoids the introduction of a separate concept for event sources.

Example:

```
events(ob#1) ->
  [ev#1: "mouseclick" xt#1,
   ev#2: "menuitem 'Tools' 'Filter'"]
```

The object ob#1 specifies two events, a mouseclick within an already defined extent, and the selection of the menu item 'Filter' of the Menu 'Tools'. The PIM responsible for ob#1 is obviously able to dynamically create new menus and menu items.

2.4.2 Actions

Events determine the atomic elements of a user or operating system interaction with HyperPicture; that is, the external incidents that are recognised as atomic input elements by the system. In order to translate events into activities, HyperPicture needs further information about the kind of activity, that has to be executed if a specific event or event-based condition occurs. In other words: events define only the lexical elements of an interaction, so that additional means for the syntax and the semantics of an interaction are required.

This information is defined by the 'action definitions.' An action definition is a set of productions consisting of condition and action clauses. A productions' condition clause defines an event-based condition. Its action clause defines the activity, that should be executed if the condition pattern of the condition clause is met by the actual state of the system[9]. One very important feature of this type of object-behaviour definition is the independence of the individual behavioural elements, so that the object behaviour can be modified easily by adding, removing, or changing individual action definitions.

Moreover, a kind of distributed system behaviour definition is supported. For each object (class) only the individual object (class) behaviour is specified[10]. New data types can thus be integrated easily into the system with respect to the user interface.

In the simplest case, an action definition consists of a single event as condition and a parametrised function call as action. However, the condition clause usually is more complex and contains a list of states and events, that have to hold for the action to be triggered. This allows to subject the interface behaviour of an object to the actual state of an application and its context.

Example:

```
  actions(ob#1) ->
[ev#1 .AND. (application.EQ."SpacePicture")->jump(ob#1,xt#1),
 ev#2 -> filter(ob#1)]
```

In this example, the first action is available only within a specific application context.

Through action definitions the behaviour of a PIM may be flexibly tailored, without internally affecting the PIM. Using this feature, a PIM can be implemented as a functionally empty shell, that provides only the user interface 'widgets'. The actual functionalities and the behaviour are then defined by the required action definitions.

Like events, actions may be defined locally, for individual objects, and globally, for complete object classes. Using actions and message events, the message/method concept of ob-

9 The fact that action definitions are basically production systems, provides two important elements. They allow an easy definition of *adaptive* behaviour, and provide a formal base, that can be used to verify certain properties of the specified behaviour (the latter characteristic has already been used on the base of Petri-nets [Stotts-89]).

10 This distributed interface definition should not be confused with 'inheritance' as provided by object-oriented programming systems. In HyperPicture, *individual objects* may independently specify their behaviour. The *cooperation* of active objects forms the actual user interface. 'Inheritance,' in contrast, allows an object to *inherit* the behaviour defined for its *superclasses*.

ject-oriented programming systems may easily be implemented. This feature is for example employed by the system during object activation (see next section)[11].

2.5 Processing sequences in HyperPicture

In contrast to classical hypertext systems, the processing sequences for certain activities in HyperPicture require more complex actions. The following three processes illustrate the internal action flow of HyperPicture.

1) Object Activation

In the case of the activation of an object, the actions defined for this object are loaded by the responsible session-manager. Then the 'activate'-message is sent to the object[12]. If the object defines an action for this message event, it is executed (this action usually transfers the object to the responsible PIM).

The object remains active until it receives the 'deactivate' message. Only during the active state of an object, it may receive messages and actively send messages and events itself.

2) Link Activation

The classical action of 'traversing a hyperlink' is performed in HyperPicture by the following sequence of actions:

	Preprocessing		Evaluation	Postprocessing	
Execution Agent	PIM	SM	SM/DM	SM	PIM
Activity	Event →	Action–Exec. →	Function–Appl. →	Activation →	Display
Definition	Event–Descr.	Action–Descr.	Function–definition + Binding	Action–Descr. (activate)	Contents (+ selected extent)

3) Link Creation

In order to create an interactively traversable point-to-point document connection of the popular 'hyperlink' variety, the extents, events and actions for activating the link have to be defined besides the function and the binding. The following definitions are required, e.g, for the creation of a binary hyperlink, that may be activated by a mouseclick in a certain area of the source object. The destination of the link is a – not further specified – extent of the destination object:

```
CreateExtent(ob#1): xt#1 = "pixelarea 10 10 100 100"
CreateEvent(ob#1): ev#1 = "mouseclick" xt#1
CreateAction(ob#1): ev#1 -> jump(ob#1,xt#1)
```

---

11 In fact, through actions and messages the complete *object behaviour* can be described, so that the effects of object manipulations with respect to the system [Baumann-91] becomes explicit. For example, automatic integrity checks after object modifications can be defined through this mechanism.

12 Interesting problems for architecture and synchronisation of various PIMs arise, if several objects have to be activated synchronously (e.g., Video and Audio). One possible solution is the definition of a three stage protocol: 'get-set->', '<-ready', 'go->', instead of 'activate->').

```
CreateExtent(ob#2): xt#357 = ...
CreateBinding(jump): ob#1 xt#1 -> ob#2 xt#357
```

2.6 Applications with HyperPicture

A central property of the HyperPicture-concept is the ability to create complete applications solely based on the description tools for data objects, functions and dynamic behaviour provided by HyperPicture. This means, that in the 'optimal' case, an application consists only of a set of object class definitions, function definitions and class specific event- and action specifications (roughly comparable to the 'stackware' of HyperCard [Apple-88]). In addition, some data objects for the creation of an initial user interface might be necessary.

All these definitions can be imported into the HyperPicture-system at any time, even without closing down the system. As result, an integrated, dynamically growing application environment is created. The gaps between individual applications vanish and the user sees a unified, dynamic world of objects and functions.

2.7 Relation to the Dexter Reference Model

The elements of the HyperPicture can be mapped to the concepts of the Dexter Reference model. Under this mapping, HyperPicture appears as a refinement and concretisation of the Dexter model, especially with respect to data manipulation and the definition of dynamic behaviour. A one-to-one mapping, however, does not exist. This fact is not really surprising, since HyperPicture comprises aspects, that are not of interest for pure hypertext and hypermedia system and vice versa.

Architectural elements:

(Dexter)	(HyperPicture)
Runtime layer	Session management and PIMs
Storage layer	Object management
Within-Component layer	PIMs and STM

Conceptual elements:

(Dexter)	(HyperPicture)
Components	Information objects, links
Links	Function bindings for objects and extents
Anchors	Extents
Resolver function	Function evaluation and function bodies

HyperPicture incorporates the additional concept elements *events* and *actions*, that are required for the definition of the object behaviour. Furthermore, the *resolver function* contained in the Dexter model is made explicit by the function/binding model of HyperPicture and extended to be used for data manipulation. However, the elements *presentation specification* and *accessor function* are not yet contained in the HyperPicture concept, and require further analysis (ref. sections "Storage Management" and "Conclusion").

3 The Realisation of HyperPicture

Based on the HyperPicture concept, an experimental toolkit system for organisation and manipulation of multimedia data objects has been developed at the ZGDV [Kirste-90b][Kirste-91]. In addition to analysing the various aspects of the realisation of the HyperPicture concept, this toolkit is used to demonstrate and evaluate the usability of the different elements of HyperPicture in the context of heterogeneous applications.

The HyperPicture toolkit[13] version described in this paper is currently used as the base system for realising various graphical applications for managing multimedia data. Examples of some application fields are:

- raster image archives [Kirste-90b];
- satellite picture retrieval systems;
- X-ray image analysis and documentation systems.

An application for satellite picture retrieval is described following the description of the toolkit itself.

3.1 The HyperPicture Toolkit

The toolkit incorporates the architectural concepts presented above. It is a system for interactive organisation and manipulation of heterogeneous multimedia data. The data objects are stored on optical discs; they are structured and manipulated using the function/binding concept of HyperPicture. The classical 'link'-concept is offered at the user-interface level as an independent metaphor. It provides functions for the automatic simultaneous creation of the events, actions and bindings that form a complete 'link' in HyperPicture. This allows the easy definition of static references and annotations, without introducing the requirement for a new conceptual element at the system level.

A graphical user interface based on X and the OSF/Motif toolkit provides easy interactive access to the stored objects and supports the interactive manipulation of the objects. The current HyperPicture toolkit version supports as fundamental data types:

- text,
- raster images,
- vector graphics,
- animation,
- video.

The HyperPicture toolkit consists of two layers:

- The object management system, containing the architectural components STM, OM and SM. It is an application independent Hyperlink-machine, responsible for processing access and modification requests of the data pool.
- For the various object classes, individual presentation and interaction modules exist. Included with these modules is a browser, that may be regarded as a special pourpose PIM for all object classes.

Similar to the CONCORDE system [Hofmann-90], HyperPicture supports several data spaces:

- a global space, accessible for every user;
- a private space for each user;
- a temporary work space for each user, that exists only during an active session.

For every active (displayed) object, the visible data spaces and the affected data space for link and object creation can be individually defined.

The toolkit provides as DDL/DML the HCL-dialect (HyperPicture Control Language) of LISP. Besides providing the usual mechanisms of LISP for defining functions, HCL includes additional features for defining HyperPicture data objects and object manipulation functions, as well as interface functions for accessing the internal HyperPicture functionality.

---

13 The development of the HyperPicture experimental toolkit at the ZGDV started in December 1989. Based on a HP9000/360 workstation running HP-UX, the first functional versions were presented at the CeBit '90 and during the GMD-Workshop Hypertext/Hypermedia '90.

3.1.1 The Browser

The HyperPicture toolkit contains a browser that supports the user to orient himself in the data network – similar to the browsing tool offered by several other hypertext and hypermedia systems. The browser is used for the visualisation of fragments of the hyperspace, by graphically displaying the objects and the links defined between them. The browsing tool of HyperPicture provides specific features for the support of data sets consisting of primarily visual data objects.

Objects are displayed by the HyperPicture browser as icons. These can be either symbolic, or a reduced version of the original image (bitmap or pixmap[14]). Through the use of appropriate icons, the content of an object is already recognisable in the browser display. Since the object does not have to be activated for display in the browser, this preview feature reduces especially for large objects, like raster images, the time required for searching an object with a specific contents.

The HyperPicture browser displays for a given object, the Point-Of-Interest (POI), all neighbouring objects; that is, all objects that are accessible from the POI through a single link traversal. A simple mouseclick on one of the displayed icons activates the corresponding object or changes the POI to this object. Furthermore, the browser allows the definition of the link types visible for the browser, so that simple structure queries are possible. Besides opening an object and changing the POI, the browser maintains browsing history information, so that the last visited POIs remain quickly accessible. The interactive definition of links is also supported.

3.1.2 The Presentation and Interaction Modules

The object type specific presentation and interaction modules available with the HyperPicture toolkit are simple examples of the PIM concept. All PIMs support the interactive activation, definition, and deletion of links. In addition, the PIMs contain several object type specific functionalities; e.g, the switching between private and global colourmap for raster picture objects, the sizing of raster pictures and vector graphics, or the editing of text objects[15].

A PIM presents its data objects in individual windows on the display[16]. The user may interact with the displayed objects by activating links, applying functions, and selecting specific functions of the PIM.

The interactive definition of a link is triggered by selecting the "Link To .." item accessible in the command menu of every PIM. The user may then define the object extent of the trigger and the destination object of the link. As trigger extents, the PIMs support character sequences (text), rectangular and polygonal areas (raster, vector), and time varying rectangular areas (animation and video). Link definition does not affect the navigation functions of the browser, so that the destination object may be searched actively with the browser. After defining the destination object, a link label and the link type (its associated function) may be defined optionally. The link is then available for activation.

3.2 SpacePicture – a HyperPicture Application

SpacePicture is a satellite picture retrieval system implemented using the HyperPicture toolkit system. It is an interactive retrieval system for accessing high-resolution satellite pictures (e.g.,

14 It is not necessarily trivial, to display several icons (or full-sized pictures) with large colour spaces simultaneously on an 8-bit CLUT display. Therefore, a special pourpose colourmap had to be developed for HyperPicture, that is used for icon generation and the display of pixmap icons and – if requested – raster pictures.

15 The PIM responsible for text objects is an example for a contents modifying content specific method, that has to update extent definitions according to the contents modifications.

16 HyperPicture supports imposes no limit on the number of objects, that may be active simultaneously.

6000 x 5000 pixel, 7 x 8 bits per pixel). It specifically supports geographical queries. As mass storage device for the images SpacePicture uses an EPOCH-I optical disk jukebox system. This device includes a winchester disk for caching.

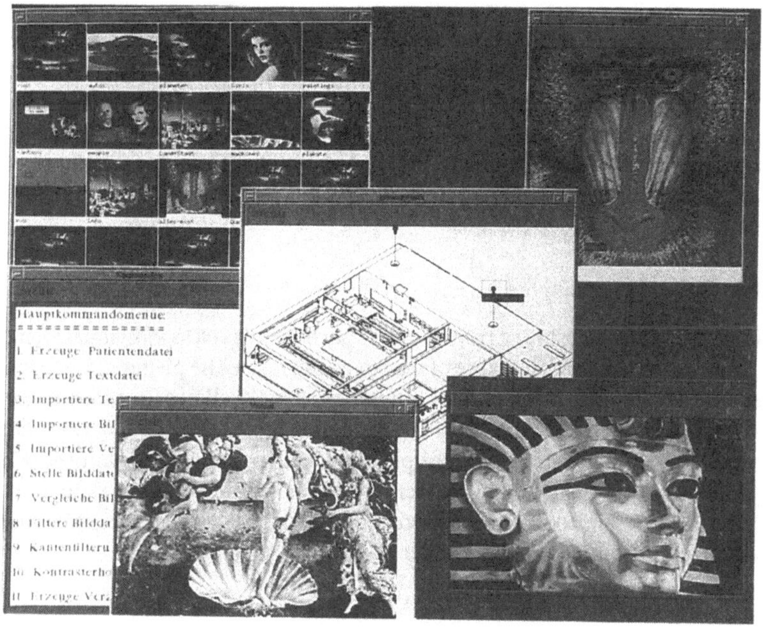

The HyperPicture raster image archival system
(Black and white reproduction of original colour picture)

A central feature of SpacePicture from the user's point of view is the possibility of using the geographic position of an image on the earth's surface as the key for image retrieval. The user can define an area on the earth's surface by graphical interaction. The system searches for all pictures contained in this area. A map browser for navigation on the earth's surface simplifies this task. It works on top of a map hierarchy that is created with digitized maps connected through hyperlinks of dedicated types. In addition to the geographic area-of-interest, secondary query specifications, e.g., creation date and sensor type, can be used to further restrict the result set of a query.

The object classes of SpacePicture are 'maps,' 'satellite pictures,' and 'sets' (query-results). The PIM 'Map Browser' is responsible for presentation and interaction with Maps and sets; satellite pictures are accessed by the PIM 'Quick Look Display'.

3.2.1 The Map Browser

The search for picture data is supported by the Map Browser, a visual retrieval tool. The Map browser provides the facilities for navigation on the earth's surface. They are used for an easy access to the best map of the geographic area of interest in question, on which a geographic query can then be started.

The hierarchy of maps is defined by links of specific types. Based on these links, the Map Browser supports the following navigation operations on maps:

- Selection of a more detailed map (down). By clicking on a point of the currently displayed map, the next more detailed map containing this point is selected, the user moves down one hierarchy level.
- Return to the previous (less detailed) hierarchy level (up).

- Return to the root of the map hierarchy (top).
- Navigation within a hierarchy level, based on a compass ("go west").

In order to start a geographic query on the current map, the user first defines the search area by interactively creating a search frame with the mouse. Through this search frame, the geo-coordinates of the area-of-interest are determined. Before starting the query processing, the user then may define the values of secondary query specifications (e.g., recording time and sensor type).

The query process then begins to scan the data pool for matching items. Hereby, the query function itself is implemented as a set-valued HyperPicture function of sets. Currently only one argument set, the set of all satellite pictures exist. The result of the query function evaluation is a temporary set, the set of all matching items. This set is then displayed as icons and labels in a dedicated window of the Map Browser.

3.2.2 The Quick Look Display

The set of satellite pictures resulting from a query may be displayed as individual elements using the PIM 'Quick Look Display'. Because of the large size of satellite pictures, a size reduced picture is used for the full screen display. This 'digital quick look' allows for a fast, yet sufficiently detailed display of a satellite picture on a high-resolution screen. The 'Quick Look Display' includes several tools for interacting with the picture. One block of functionality allows the user to improve the graphics display, e.g., by increasing contrast, lightness or saturation. Another function block provides the tools for transferring the picture or selected parts of it into the external file system, e.g., in order to apply further image analysis functions.

4. Conclusion

In its current version, the concept of HyperPicture provides an easy extendible platform for open hypermedia systems. It includes the mechanisms for describing, organising, manipulating, presenting and interacting with objects on an abstract level. Conceptually, there exist no limitations with respect to the specific types of objects, functions, and interaction methods that may be used within multimedia applications based on HyperPicture.

Some of the elements and components of the HyperPicture concept can be mapped to the framework provided by the Dexter reference model [Halasz-90]. With this mapping, the HyperPicture concept represents a refinement and concretisation of the Dexter model, especially with respect to the tools for data manipulation and the definition of the dynamic behaviour.

The fundamental appropriateness of the described concepts has been demonstrated in the implementation of the HyperPicture toolkit and the SpacePicture application.

The future development of the HyperPicture concept outlined above will lead towards a complete integrated information management system for multimedia data, if the individual components prove to be valid means for solving the assigned tasks. HyperPicture will then have to provide the combined features of operating systems, data base systems and user interface management systems used today for (mainly) textual and symbolic data.

Several aspects required for this goal are not provided by the current state of the HyperPicture system. These aspects need further analysis and work in order to acquire a satisfactory base system:

- The interfaces between PIM and session management, and between session management and object management lack formalisation and detail. Likewise, the complex problems of a distributed object management system need further thought. An important aspect here is the system's fault tolerance with respect to integrity violations. It has to be evaluated with respect to expense and usability, whether integrity conditions as used in data base management systems should be enforced, or whether other, more tolerant mechanisms are required for such a distributed, interactively used system.

- HyperPicture requires adequate mechanisms for controlling the evolution of a data object (version maintenance), as well as for describing and maintaining global and local integrity conditions for the different evolution stages. The separation of referential and contents-oriented identity of an object as in HyperPicture, needs special attention in the scope of this problem. One possibility would be the development of a concept of 'orthogonality' with respect to functions (in general: interpretations) modifying the contents, but maintaining the identity of an object. Based on this concept of orthogonal functions, the mutual influences of functions and content anchored references between objects may become describable.
- Although already in part contained in the SpacePicture system, set objects and operations on these objects (union, intersection, selection, ...) are not available in HyperPicture. However, they are required for powerful query operations. Here it is especially necessary, to evaluate the possibility to implement set objects with the help of standard data base systems ([Köhler-90]).
- The interactions between system kernel and a PIM during object activation needs to be analysed with respect to the influences of user identity, application context and activation source in order to provide the means for context specific modification of the display process employed. The current model uses presentation control variables stored in the session server to parametrise the presentation process (this is similar to the print control variables used in Common Lisp [Steele-84]).
- A 'Style-Guide' describing the required minimum functionality and the 'Look & Feel' of PIMs is necessary. This will facilitate the task to give the applications on top of HyperPicture a homogeneous behaviour.
- HyperPicture incorporates a standard mechanism for inter-session communication ('active atoms'), by which PIMs, even in different sessions, may exchange information. It remains to be proved, whether this mechanism is powerful enough to provide the synchronisation means required for cooperative work.
- The concept of 'virtual objects' is another possible extension of the existing concepts. Based on 'virtual objects,' it would be possible to describe complete complex processing sequences by connecting building the required processing tree based on functions, bindings and virtual objects. By instantiating the root of such a process tree with a real object, the process sequence is triggered and a copy of the process tree with real instead of virtual objects is generated.
- A graphical programming language for the easy development of complex functions and the building of process trees based on predefined 'function building blocks' might become part of an improved browser/net-editor.

Acknowledgements

The authors wish to express their thank to Prof. Encarnação and to the colleagues at ZGDV, FhG-AGD and GRIS for their helpful ideas and support.

The HyperPicture development has been supported by Hewlett-Packard, DisCom and DLR.

References

[Akscyn-88] Akscyn, R. McCracken, D.L., Yoder, E.A. KMS: A distributed hypertext for managing knowledge in organisations. *Communications of the ACM*, 31(7), 1988, 820–835.

[Apple-88] Apple Computer Inc. HyperCard Script Language Guide: The HyperTalk Language. *Addison-Wesley*, 1988.

[Baumann-91] Baumann, P. Die Spezifikation informationsverarbeitender Systeme mit Abstrakten Objekttypen, *Proceedings of the BTW-Fachtagung, Kaiserslautern*, Kaiserslautern, 6.–8. März, 1991.

[Batz-89] Batz, T., Baumann, P., Höft, K.-G., Köhler, D., Krömker, D., Subel, H.-P. PRODAT – Das PROSYT-Datenbaksystem. In Krömker, D., Steusloff, H., Subel, H.P. (Hrsg.): *PRODIA und PRODAT*, Springer, 1989.

[Campbell-88] Campbell, B., Goodman, J.M. HAM: A general purpose hypertext abstract machine. *Communications of the ACM*, 31(7), 1988, 856–861.

[Conklin-87] Conklin, J. Hypertext: A survey and introduction. *IEEE Computer*, 20(9), 1987, 17–41.

[Feiner-82] Feiner, S., Nagy, S., van Dam, A. An Experimental System for Creating and Presenting Interactive Graphical Documents, *ACM Transactions on Graphics*, 1(1), 1982, 59–77.

[Fishman-89] Fishman, D.H. et al. Overview of the Iris DBMS, *Technical report HPL-SAL-89-15*, Hewlett-Packard Company, 1989.

[Furuta-90] Furuta, R., Stotts, P.D. The Trellis Hypertext Reference Model. *Proceedings of the NIST Hypertext Standardisation Workshop*, Gaithersburg, Maryland, January 16–18, 1990.

[Halasz-88] Halasz, F.G. Reflections on NoteCards: Seven issues for the next generation of hypermedia systems. *Communications of the ACM*, 31(7), 1988, 836–855.

[Halasz-90] Halasz, F., Schwartz, M. The Dexter Hypertext Reference Model. *Proceedings of the NIST Hypertext Standardisation Workshop*, Gaithersburg, Maryland, January 16–18, 1990.

[Hofmann-90] Hofmann, M., Cordes, R., Langendörfer, H., Lübben, E., Peyn, H., Süllow, K., Töpperwien, T. Vom lokalen Hypertext zum verteilten Hypermediasystem. In Gloor, P., Streitz, N. (Hrsg.): *Hypertext und Hypermedia: Von theoretischen Konzepten zu praktischen Anwendungen*, Informatik Fachberichte Band 249, Springer, 1990, 28–42.

[Hübner-89a] Hübner, W., Lancastre, M. Towards an Object-Oriented Interaction Model for Graphics User Interfaces. *Computer Graphics Forum*, 3(8), 1989, 207–217

[Hübner-89b] Hübner, W., Gomes, M.R. Two Object-Oriented Models to Design Graphical User Interfaces. *Proceedings Eurographics '89*, North-Holland, 1989, 63–74.

[Hübner-90] Hübner, W. Entwurf Graphischer Benutzerschnittstellen. Springer, 1990.

[Kirste-90a] Kirste, T. Optical Disks, Technology and Application, *ZGDV-Report 43/90*, ZGDV, 1990.

[Kirste-90b] Kirste, T., Hübner, W. HyperPicture – ein Archivierungs- und Retrievalsystem auf optischen Speichermedien. In Gloor, P., Streitz, N. (Hrsg.): *Hypertext und Hypermedia: Von theoretischen Konzepten zu praktischen Anwendungen*, Informatik Fachberichte Band 249, Springer, 1990, 144–148.

[Kirste-91] Kirste, T. Ein offenes Hypermediasystem für graphische Applikationen. *Submitted to GI'91.*

[Köhler-90] Köhler, D., Baumann, P., Englert, G. Das Texturarchiv als Beispiel für den Einsatz nichtkonventioneller Datenbanktechniken. *Int. Workshop Integrierte, intelligente Informationssysteme*, Tuczno, Polen, September 1990, 156–175.

[Lange-90] Lange, D.B. A Formal Model of Hypertext. *Proceedings of the NIST Hypertext Standardisation Workshop*, Gaithersburg, Maryland, January 16–18, 1990.

[Nelson-80] Nelson, T. Replacing the Printed word: A complete literary system. In Lavington, S.H. (ed.): *Proceedings of the IFIP Congress 1980*, North-Holland, 1013–1023.

[McCracken-84] McCracken, D.L., Akscyn, R.M. Experience with the ZOG human-computer interface system. *Int. J. Man-Machine Studies*, 21, 1984, 293–310.

[Richartz-90] Richartz, M., Das Projekt NESTOR. In Gloor, P., Streitz, N. (Hrsg.): *Hypertext und Hypermedia: Von theoretischen Konzepten zu praktischen Anwendungen*, Reihe Informatik Fachberichte Band 249, Springer, 1990, 3–29.

[Shipman-81] Shipman, D. W. The Functional Data Model and the Data Langage DAPLEX, *ACM Transactions on Database Systems*, 6(1), 1981, 140–173.

[Sibley-77] Sibley, E.H., Kershberg, L. Data architecture and data model considerations. *Proceedings of the AFIPS National Computer Conference*, Dallas, Texas, 6/1977, 85–96.

[Steele-84] Steele Jr., G.L. Common Lisp: The Language. *Digital Press*, 1984.

[Stotts-89] Stotts, P.D., Furuta, R. Petri-Net-Based Hypertext: Document Structure with Browsing Semantics. *ACM Transactions on Information Systems*, 7(1), 1989, 3–29.

[Streitz-90] Streitz, N.A. Hypertext: Ein innovatives Medium zur Kommunikation von Wissen. In Gloor, P., Streitz, N. (Hrsg.): *Hypertext und Hypermedia: Von theoretischen Konzepten zu praktischen Anwendungen*, Informatik Fachberichte Band 249, Springer, 1990, 10–27.

[Woelk-87] Woelk, D., Kim, W. Multimedia Information Management in an Object-Oriented Database System. *Proceedings of the 13th VLDB Conference*, Brighton, 1987, 319–329.

[Woods-75] Woods, W.A. What's in a Link: Foundations for Semantic Networks, in Bobrow, D.G., Collins, A.M. (Eds.): *Representation and Understanding: Studies in Cognitive Science*, Academic Press, New York, 1975.

Chapter 18

The Manchester Multimedia Information System

Carole Goble, Michael O'Docherty, Peter Crowther, Mark Ireton, Costas Daskalakis, John Oakley, Stephen Kay and Costas Xydeas

1 Introduction

A Multimedia Information System (MMIS) is a repository for all types of electronically representable data (O'Docherty et al., 1990). Conventional databases provide a large set of operations for retrieval of simple data types. The simplest way of extending this to multimedia objects is to store and retrieve on the basis of a few manually entered associated attributes or links. The true potential of multimedia databases is realised when a rich set of operations is provided to allow transparent manipulation of data objects of all media. This can best be achieved through content retrieval, based on the automatic interpretation of medium objects. Automatic content retrieval avoids the problems of inconsistency, subjectivity and the labour-intensiveness of manual entry. MMISs with content retrieval will have wide application in industry, medicine, education and the military. The Multimedia Group at Manchester University have prototyped a MMIS for the content retrieval of images in a specific application domain and are developing a second system that includes content retrieval of text and documents. Hereafter, the term *instance* is used to refer to medium objects that are intended for interpretation in our system.

The project has four broad goals:

1. to prototype a general MMIS architecture and to demonstrate its applicability to images, text and documents.
2. to provide an object store for instances
3. to develop a representation of instances to support content retrieval
4. to investigate in depth the content retrieval of raster images

Raster images are a rich source of content at levels other than the representation; higher-level constructs range from related groups of picture elements (pixels) to much more abstract concepts such as 'bone', 'leaf' or 'road'. The abstract information in a raster image is hard to extract, but even simple extraction gives enormous help to queries. This potential, coupled with the group's signal processing expertise, has led us to focus on 2-D still raster images. Such work cannot be done in isolation from an application. An experimental prototype requires an application that has well defined images that are easy to obtain yet sufficiently complex and variable to pose an interesting problem. For demonstration purposes we have chosen as our application a database of images of deciduous tree leaves as this application satisfies the above criteria. We surmise that domain knowledge is needed to tailor the system, in particular the image interpretation, and we have access to local expertise.

The paper is divided into five further sections. Section 2 outlines the requirements of the ideal MMIS and of the Manchester MMIS in particular. Section 3 describes the proposed data model and the facilities required to use that model. In Section 4 the architecture of a general MMIS is proposed and mapped to the specific architectures for the Manchester prototypes. Finally in Section 5 we present our results and proposals for future work.

2 Requirements of a MMIS

2.1 The Ideal MMIS

This section comprises a general list of features for the ideal MMIS and is not intended to be specific to the Manchester MMIS. In this general description, the term *item* is used to denote an object that can be stored in and retrieved from a MMIS.

1. An MMIS should be able to store *everything* that can be represented digitally — principally facts, statistics, text, sound and images: raster, vector and moving.

2. Once everything has been stored, the user must be able to retrieve it. Retrieval falls into three categories:

   Presentation Retrieval by presentation relates to data type and data structure, without any sophisticated analysis. It is commonly applied to composite media, i.e. those containing other media. Examples of presentation queries[1] are "Find me all documents that have voice comments in them" or "Find me all images".

   Content Retrieval by content is the process of retrieving documents according to their semantic content. The simplest form of content retrieval is based on manually generated *labels* — i.e. descriptions entered from the keyboard by an operator. The other extreme is automatic semantic analysis — i.e. descriptions inferred by the system. In general, labelling makes things easy for the implementor, whereas automatic semantic extraction benefits the user. Although automatic semantic analysis will probably never be *better* than human analysis, human analysis followed by manual labelling is too time-consuming to be feasible in most cases.

   Association Retrieval by association is the process of retrieving items by associated links to other items. It can be used as a browsing mechanism and subsumes hypermedia (Meyrowitz, 1986).

3. There are a number of ways in which querying may be achieved from the user's point of view:

   By data model The user is familiar with the data model and can formulate queries such as "What text attributes are stored?" or when classification is provided: "What characterises this class?".

[1] For convenience, the term 'query' in this article refers to anything that specifies a subset of the items stored in the MMIS. Examples are natural language commands, relational algebra/calculus and first order logic.

Directly The user knows exactly what the system stores in relation to each item, e.g. the labels it uses, the primitives it extracts during semantic analysis, or the way it structures composite media. Direct queries are then expressed as logical expressions or set operators, as in conventional databases (Date, 1986).

By similarity Queries of the form "Retrieve images that are similar to this one" are desirable, but in general they are too vague to be soluble. However, examples do exist: for images, statistical *similarity measures* can be used (Gonzalez et al., 1978; Toriwaki et al., 1980); for text, an approximate measure of word content can be found using a hashing function to produce *signature files* (Faloutsos and Christodoulakis, 1984).

By prototype This technique is related to similarity retrieval. Queries take the form of a prototype presented to the database, where the prototype may be either of the following:

- A 'shorthand' version of an item is given on-line by the user and the system must try to match this *sketch* to stored items. The form that a sketch takes varies from one medium to another, and may be meaningless in some. An image sketch might comprise a rough outline of a particular style of house with salient features included such as rectangular Georgian windows with multiple panes. A voice sketch may be a sentence spoken by the user in a particular accent, dialogue or language. An image example that already exists is the Ledeen on-line symbol recogniser (Neumann and Sproull, 1981).
- The user presents an item as prototype. The system interprets the prototype to produce its semantic representation. The semantic representation is then matched against items in the database to retrieve those that are similar. The similarity measure in this case is most easily based on classification of the item or its sub-objects (see Section 4.2).

4. In a large system it is undesirable to present users with a large set of items as the result of a query; what is needed is a measure of the degree to which each item satisfies the query so that they can be ranked and the best matches examined first. For prototype retrieval, a ranking score can be obtained by measuring the distance of the retrieved item from the prototype. Another source of scores is to assign an importance to each clause of the query; items that satisfy the most important clauses receive the highest score and so on. Scores can be discrete (very good, good, reasonable, ...) or continuous (normalised to the range [0, 1] for item).

5. Another retrieval technique that should be provided is *browsing*, possibly using hypermedia as a mechanism. The user has a set of items (the entire contents of the system or a subset obtained by query) and is allowed to roam over them. Various browsing techniques are examined in (Christodoulakis and Graham, 1988; Irven et al., 1988). The user may wish to generate his own commented connections between items in a hypermedia fashion. The system should manage the connections for him as sets of 'webs'. Queries can then take the form "Get me web X".

6. In order to fit more items on the screen and to avoid getting the full versions from the system, retrieved items may be displayed as:

   Icons Small pictorial representations relating to the type of the original, but not the content.

Miniatures The original item reduced greatly in size.

Descriptions One-line comments about the item's content — for example, operator generated 'headers' or system generated type names.

7. Retrieval should be mixed-media, using the same language to express all forms of media, but possibly with sub-clauses specific to each medium to cope with their different semantics (Ceri and Tanca, 1990).

8. The system should have a reasonable response time in order to be interactive. Semantic analysis can sometimes take hours or days. Content retrieval can be based on analysis done *pre-query* — i.e. before the item is involved in a query — or *post-query*. Pre-query analysis increases storage requirements and post-query analysis increases response time. Lazy evaluation can be used as a compromise, so that analysis is performed on demand and the results retained in the database.

9. Editors should be provided so that users can modify or create new items. Although editors are medium specific, they should all have the same look and feel — e.g. all window based, with a similar menu hierarchy and similar high-level options. Editors for composite media (webs, documents) could call on the appropriate editors for the media they contain. Many media require modern workstations for display but in a multi-user, distributed system they will vary in resolution, number of bits per pixel and so on. Therefore a workstation will have to assess the incoming items and do one of:

   - Reject them as undisplayable.
   - Alter the items to fit its own screen by transforming resolution, converting colour to grey-level, reducing the number of bits per pixel and so on.
   - Display what it can and replace the rest with icons; this would allow a text-only screen to replace images in a page with a box containing the word IMAGE or a description, while retaining the text.

10. Storage requirements will be huge, running to hundreds of kilobytes for a single high-resolution colour image for example. Therefore, MMIS designers will have to consider each of the following:

    High volume storage technology Such as a 'juke-box' of read/write optical disks, or write-once optical tape.

    Multi-user access Since it will be expensive and sought-after, mass storage should be shared between users and ideally between machines.

    Distributed architecture More than one machine should be able to provide database resources. Ideally the location of a particular piece of data should not be apparent to the user, allowing controlled replication of data to speed access.

    Storage by reference An item appearing in more than one composite item is stored only once while the composite items each get a copy of a pointer to it.

    High bandwidth networks Local-area and wide-area networks to allow multi-user access and distributed architectures.

Version control A user may wish to modify an existing item and record the item from which it is derived. For storage efficiency, a new version could be stored as a description of the changes made to the parent.

Archiving Some technologies for mass storage are write-once. Therefore, items can remain in an editable state on magnetic disk until completed. Once complete they can be stored permanently or *archived*. If it is ever necessary to change an archived item, it must be retrieved into an editable state and re-archived. This is another reason to provide version control.

Data compression Data compression reduces storage requirements and speeds transmission through networks.

2.2 The Specific Requirements of the Manchester MMIS

The specific requirements of the Manchester MMIS, which are a subset of those in the previous section, are intended to provide a sound and extensible basis for a MMIS with automatic content retrieval. We contend that the core of such a system can be separated safely from the design of interface tools for the novice user; we have chosen not to provide such tools. Our requirements are:

1. An extensible architecture.
2. Storage of text, raster images, sub parts of images and hierarchical composite instances, specifically documents.
3. Creation and storage of automatically derived information about instances.
4. Storage of arbitrary, user-entered links between instances.
5. Retrieval based on presentation, content and association.
6. Direct retrieval.
7. Retrieval based on *browsing* using hypermedia links.
8. Mixed-media retrieval.
9. Reasonable but unoptimised query response time — although our system is biased towards pre-query analysis, the distinction is not apparent to the user and the analysis may be tailored to lazy evaluation.
10. User entered instances.
11. A client-server architecture that runs on a network of workstations and includes sharing, multiprocessor implementation and multiuser access (without protection) but that pays no attention to data distribution, storage technologies, version control or archiving.
12. Expressively complete retrieval mechanisms that range from the simple "What text instances are there in the system?" variety to the more detailed "Find me documents containing images of beech leaves".

3 Semantic Data and its Representation

This section describes briefly what semantic data is extracted from instances during interpretation as attributes and structural relationships and how that data is represented. The representation formalism used should ideally be application independent, medium independent, storage efficient and access efficient; it should be possible to express any information about an instance (*expressive adequacy*); it should be possible to deduce anything from the representation that could have been deduced from the original data (*logical adequacy*); finally, such formalisms should be easy to generate. No formalism will satisfy all these ideals; in particular, logical adequacy is probably impossible for complex instances such as images — consider the task of asking a human to describe a picture of a room exhaustively, concisely and without repetition — but expressive adequacy should still be sought. We propose semantic nets (Ringland and Duce, 1988) for the representation of still raster images and demonstrate their applicability to the representation of free text and hierarchical documents.

In the generation of semantic data, it is a general aim to progressively refine low-level data to provide data that is more helpful to users. It should be noted that low-level data is never discarded because it is impossible to predict at which levels users will wish to query and because low-level data may be used to infer other data in the light of future knowledge. There is always a trade off between the time taken to interpret instances in response to queries and the space required to store representations of the results of interpretation. Our systems cater for both approaches — currently, most interpretation is performed pre-query and the results held in an appropriate formalism but further processing can be performed post-query by the query engine.

3.1 The Data

3.1.1 Images

The basis of interpretation is that images such as the one illustrated in Figure 1 contain distinct regions of interest that in their processed form are referred to as **basic logical objects** or *blots*. This term was chosen to avoid confusion between the term 'blob' meaning an 8-connected[2] set of pixels in image analysis terminology, and BLOB meaning a Binary Large OBject in database terminology. In our application, blots may be leaves, scale markers or noise. Scale markers are used to standardise scalar measurements within the image, which are otherwise sensitive to camera sizing. The markers are designed to be easily distinguishable from other instances of interest and have a constant measurement between a pair of points — in this case, the marker is 5cm from end to end.

Image attributes include width, height, time of interpretation, number of leaves contained, number of pieces of noise contained and class. An image's class records whether it is binary, monochrome or colour; the class also indicates the number of bits per pixel for monochrome and colour images and thus indicates what sort of interpretation is required, whether it can be displayed on a particular workstation and so on. Finally, if a scale marker is identified, then images have a `length_scale` attribute for converting from pixels to metres.

An image has a structural relationship to its scale marker, each of its leaves and each of its pieces of noise.

[2]Two pixels are 8-connected if they are horizontally, vertically or diagonally adjacent.

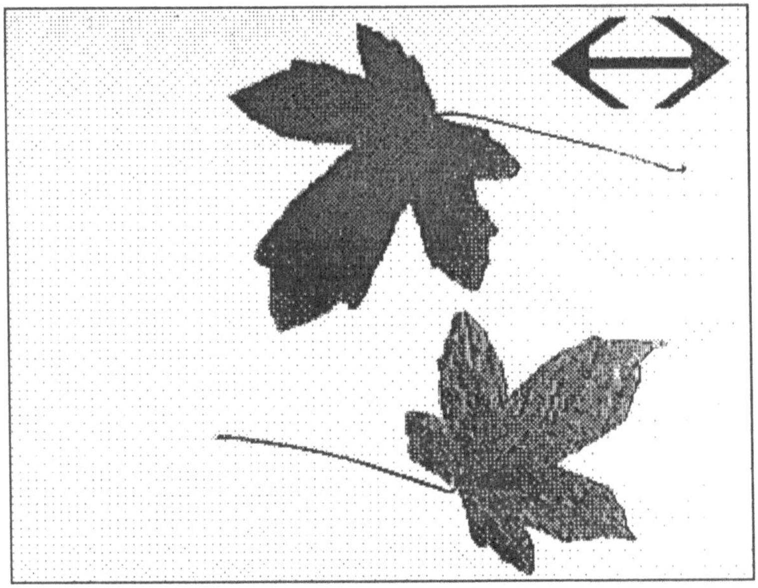

Fig. 1: A typical leaf image with scale marker

3.1.2 Blots

The main blot attributes are listed below and illustrated in Figure 2(a).

Area

Perimeter length

Circularity Circularity is the ratio $\frac{\text{Area}}{\text{Perimeter}^2}$ and is maximum for a circle $(1/4\pi)$ and minimum for a line (0). Here, it is normalised to give a value in the range 0% (line) to 100% (circle).

Upright bounding box The upright rectangle that exactly fits the outside of the blot.

Longest chord The longest line that can be drawn between any two points on the blot's perimeter.

True bounding box The rectangle that exactly fits the extremities of the longest chord and its two longest perpendiculars.

Length The length of the true bounding box.

Width The width of the true bounding box.

Aspect ratio The ratio $\frac{\text{Length}}{\text{Width}}$.

Hull area The area of the convex hull. A blot's convex hull is analogous to the shape of an elastic band stretched around its perimeter (see Figure 2(b)).

Transparency Transparency is the ratio $\frac{\text{Hull area}-\text{Area}}{\text{Hull area}}$. It is low for convex blots and high for incised blots. Here, it is normalised to give a value in the range 0% (completely convex) to 100% (completely transparent).

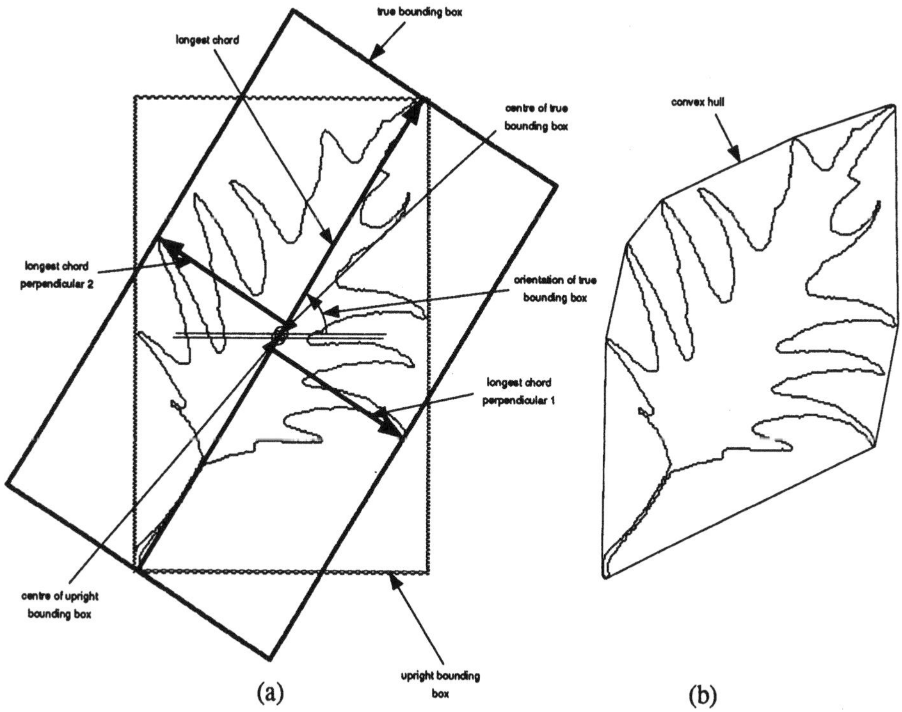

Fig. 2: Aspects of a blot that are expressed as attributes

Irregularity Irregularity is a measure of the unevenness of a blot's perimeter.

Shape class Each blot is given a classification (Section 4.2) based on the attributes that are considered to be good shape descriptors — in this case transparency, aspect ratio, circularity and irregularity.

If a scale marker is identified, then all attributes that have a length component are expressed using metres as well as pixels.

Blots have structural relationships to other blots in the image to describe relative positions in terms of bearing and bounding box overlap. The bearing of one blot from another is described by one of eight compass directions, (north, north east, east, etc), between the centres of their true bounding boxes; this is augmented by a test of whether or not their true bounding boxes overlap.

3.1.3 Text

Text instances in our prototypes are simple ASCII data with no formatting information other than newlines. Any formatting information is provided when text, images and blots are grouped as documents (see below). What is recorded is a structural relationship from each text node to each word, number, code and punctuation component. Each component has a set of position attributes to denote all its occurrences with respect to the start of the file. This enables all queries based on position and groupings such "Find me text instances that contain the words 'multimedia' and 'database' in the same sentence".

3.1.4 Documents

Documents are represented as components grouped hierarchically in a style similar to the Open Document Architecture, ODA (ISO, 1988)). This provides a representation formalism for multimedia paginated documents that describes a document's generic and specific logical (chapters, sections, etc.) and layout (pages, figures, etc.) structures, for transmission to any computer recognising the standard.

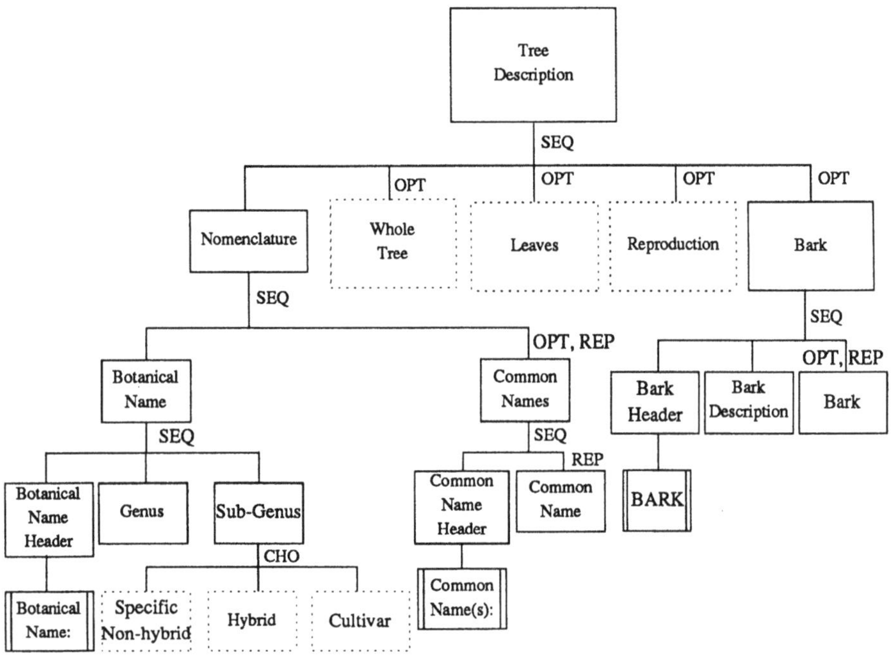

Fig. 3: Part of the generic logical description for a tree-description document

As an example, consider Figure 3 that shows part of the logical structure of a document that describes one particular tree. It corresponds to a regular grammar where each node in the tree is either *basic* (mapping to an instance that forms part of the document) or *composite* (composed of other nodes). Dashed boxes in the figure are composite nodes that have been omitted for clarity. The *subordinates* or children of composite nodes are generated according to one of the following:

- **SEQ**uence The subordinates occur in sequence.
- **CHO**ice Only one of the subordinates occurs.
- **AGG**regate The subordinates occur in any order.

Additionally, each subordinate may be further specified as:

- **OPT**ional The subordinate may occur 0 or 1 times.
- **REP**eated The subordinate may occur 1 or more times.
- **OPT**ional, **REP**eated The subordinate may occur 0, 1 or more times.

If a subordinate has no specifier then it must appear exactly once.

Basic nodes are mappings to actual, atomic parts of the document that appear on paper or screen. Each atomic part is called a *content portion*. A *generic content portion* is a piece of the document that always appears when the relevant branch of the tree is instantiated and is indicated by a box with double sides — eg. the string "BARK" is automatically included if the optional branch 'Bark' is filled in. Conversely, *specific content portions* are added below the generic basic nodes during the editing process when, for example, pictures of leaves are included.

The user is provided with extra, automatically extracted information such as the tree's family, the person who classified it, structural information about relative positions of component instances on the formatted page, and so on. The user can also access all the information known about each component instance (basic node).

3.2 The Representation

Each instance has an associated semantic description referred to as its *semantic representation*. The semantic representation is a set of facts about the attributes of instances and their structural relationships to other instances. For example, a text instance could have the attribute `author` with the value `fred` and a structural relationship `description_of` to some image in the system. Furthermore, a instance can have structural relationships to its own parts as in the case of a document with a structural relationship `has_title_page` to the output of a drawing package. The parts themselves can also refer to other instances to form hierarchical or graphical structures.

Here, the chosen representation is the semantic net. In its simplest form, a semantic net is a graph of unidirectional labelled arcs that can be used to describe structure as in:

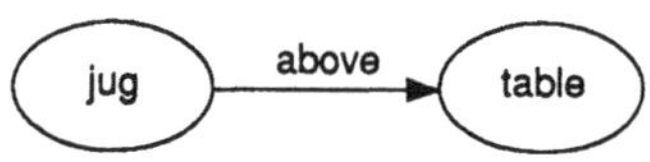

and attributes as in:

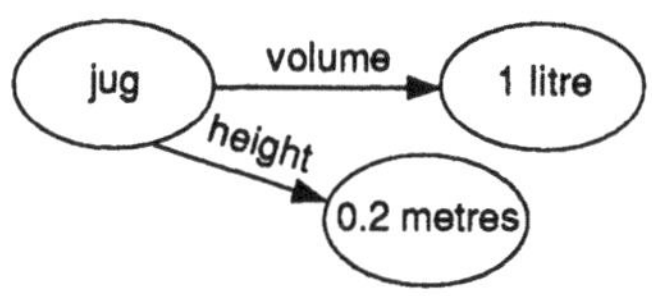

Each arc is a statement of fact; in the case of a structural relationship, both the source and destination of the arc are entities being described with the source having the stated relationship *to* the destination; for an attribute, the source is an entity and the destination is the value of the attribute, with the arc label being the name of the attribute. In practice, the user formulating queries is unaware of the fine distinction between attributes and structural relationships, especially if arc names are meaningful.

Semantic nets are generated by medium interpreters that know what attributes and structural relationships to expect and how to deduce them. All node and arc labels take the form

<*type*> / <*value*>

as explained in the following table:

Type	Value
int	integer
float	float
image	instance identifier
text	instance identifier
document	instance identifier
blot	instance identifier
dimension (SI units)	float
enumeration identifier	integer
atom	atom identifier
abstract node	abstract node identifier

Part of the semantic net generated for Figure 1 is shown in Figure 4; for clarity, the type (atom) has been omitted from all arcs in this figure. In the case of images, text, documents and blots, the value is a unique identifier referencing the actual instance in a separate repository (see Section 4). Units for floating point values that have dimension are the standard SI units with the addition of the sub-unit radian, a special unit for camera lengths called *pixel*, and without the dimension of quantity of substance (the mole). The pixel unit is abbreviated to p. The enumeration type is analogous to that used in C or Pascal and is allocated by individual applications. Abstract nodes are used to denote concepts that need more description than a single node allows, as in:

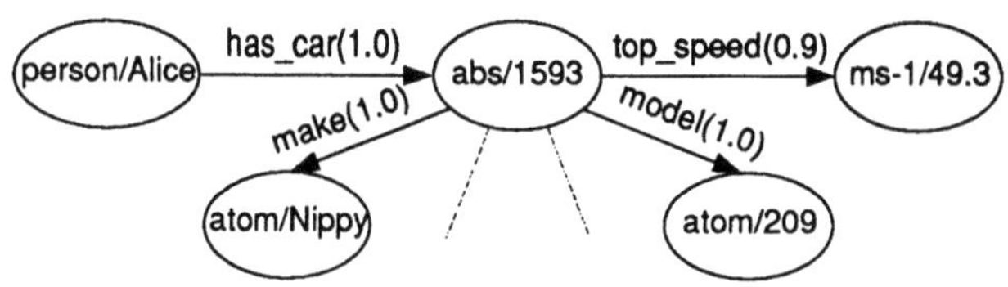

Here, the abstract node glues the reference from Alice to the description of her car.

All arcs have an extra floating point value called a *score*, that is used in the ranking of query results (see Section 4.3.1). In the examples in this section, all arcs have been given a certainty score between 0 (false) and 1 (true). Such values can be calculated in any way that is meaningful to the application (for examples, see Section 4.3.1).

Semantic nets can be conveniently described by a set of triples as in Figure 5. Each triple represents a fact (arc) as

<source><relationship><destination>

This approach leads to simple storage and optimised access. Triples require an unambiguous syntax if several are to appear in each query; for our systems they must also be compatible with Prolog which is used as the query language and query engine. One possibility is a quaternary predicate (from first order logic) called `triple` as in:

triple(source, relationship, destination, score)

This form is unambiguous but longwinded. A shorter form is to use the arc label as the name of a ternary predicate:

relationship(source, destination, score)

Thus the list of triples in Figure 5 becomes the list of ternary predicates in Figure 6. Note that representing arcs in this way allows navigation in *both* directions during querying.

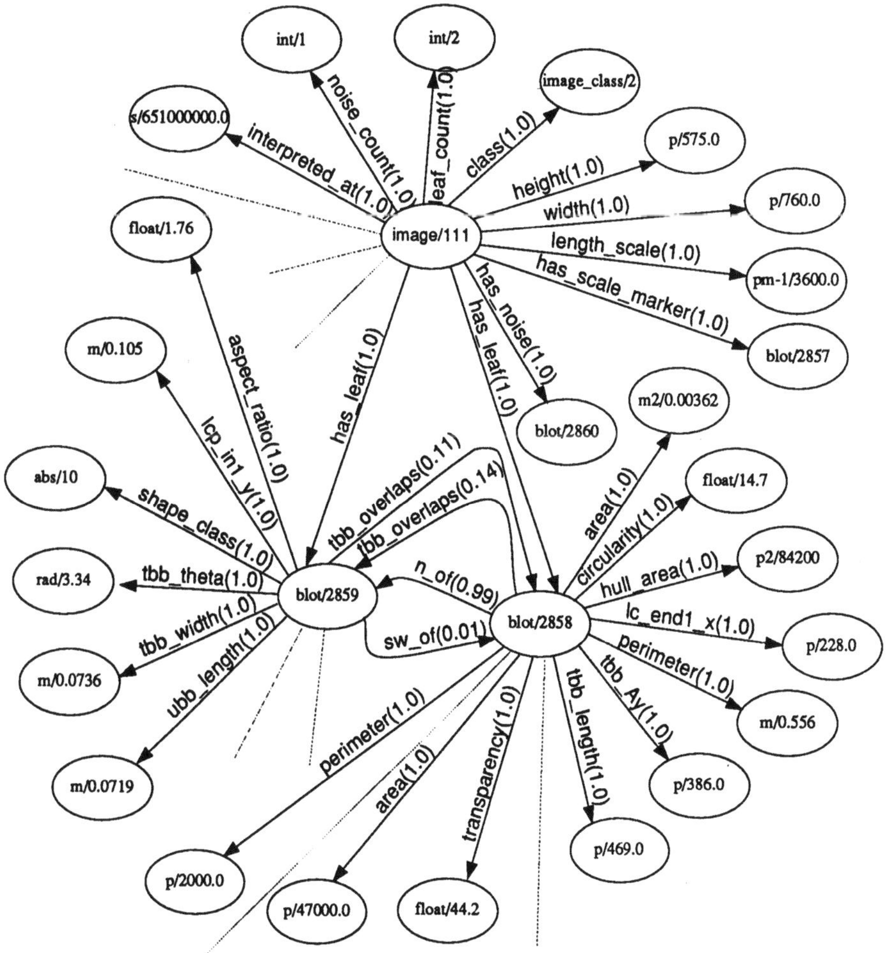

Fig. 4: Part of Figure 1's semantic net

image/111	class(1.0)	image_class/2
image/111	length_scale(1.0)	pm-1/3600.0
image/111	interpreted_at(1.0)	s/651000000.0
image/111	has_leaf(1.0)	blot/2858
image/111	leaf_count(1.0)	int/2
blot/2858	tbb_overlaps(0.14)	blot/2859
blot/2858	n_of(0.99)	blot/2859
blot/2858	area(1.0)	m2/0.00362
⋮		

Fig. 5: The triple representation of Figure 4

```
class(image/111,image_class/2,1.0).
length_scale(image/111,pm-1/3600.0,1.0).
interpreted_at(image/111,s/651000000.0,1.0).
has_leaf(image/111,blot/2858,1.0).
leaf_count(image/111,int/2,1.0).
⋮
```

Fig. 6: The predicate equivalent of Figure 5

Predicates can be represented readily as Prolog clauses with empty bodies and no variable arguments and can be used directly in Prolog queries (Section 4.2). For queries where the arc label is not known — eg. "What relationships are there between blot/20312 and blot/19978?" — the quaternary predicate `triple` is used as in:

```
triple(blot/20312, X, blot/19978, Y)
```

Henceforth, the terms fact, triple, attribute and structural relationship will be used as appropriate — facts are equivalent to triples; attributes and structural relationships are specific uses of triples; triples are expressed as ternary predicates in the query language.

4 Architectures and Capabilities of One Generic and Two Specific MMISs

4.1 The Generic Architecture

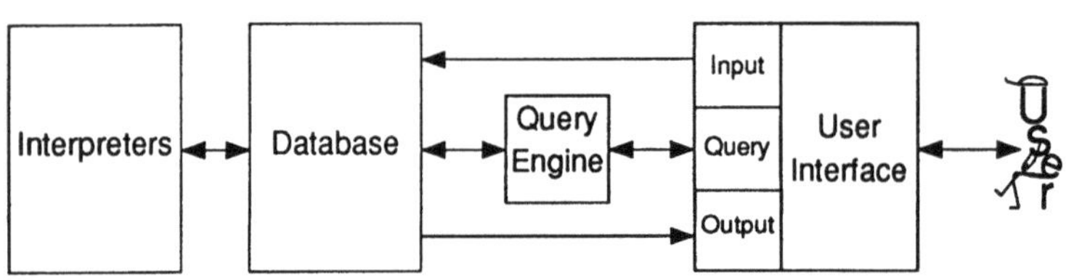

Fig. 7: An architecture for a generic MMIS

The generic architecture for a MMIS with automatic content retrieval is shown in Figure 7. The user interacts with a user interface that gives access to an input part for entering instances, a query part for formulating queries and an output part for presentation of query results and production of hard copy output.

Medium instances are stored in the database for access by the interpreters and retrieval by the user interface's output part.

An interpreter is provided for each medium and interpretation results are stored in the database.

The query engine resolves users' queries according to the interpretation results. The query may be translated into a form more suitable for optimal resolution.

4.2 MMIS-1

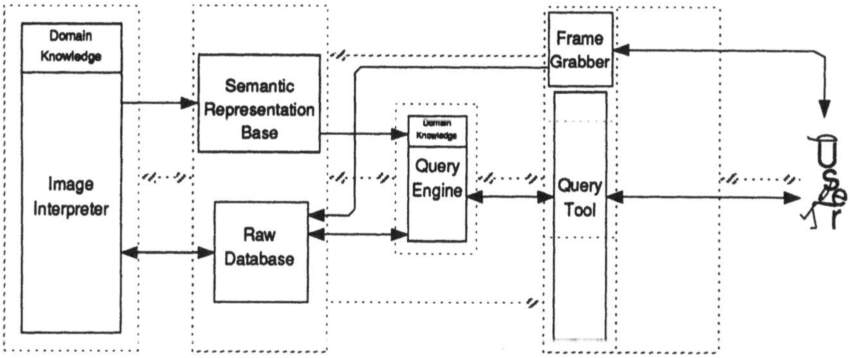

Fig. 8: The architecture of MMIS-1

The architecture of our first complete prototype, MMIS-1, is shown in Figure 8. The shaded boxes in the figure correspond to those of the generic architecture. MMIS-1 stores text and 8-bit grey-level images, but only the latter are interpreted. Both media may be retrieved in a hypermedia fashion. Image interpretation has two levels:

low-level blots are segmented from the image and their base attributes extracted using hard-coded but modular image analysis algorithms written in C++,

high-level a declarative style of program, written in Prolog, is used to derive more abstract attributes and structural relationships.

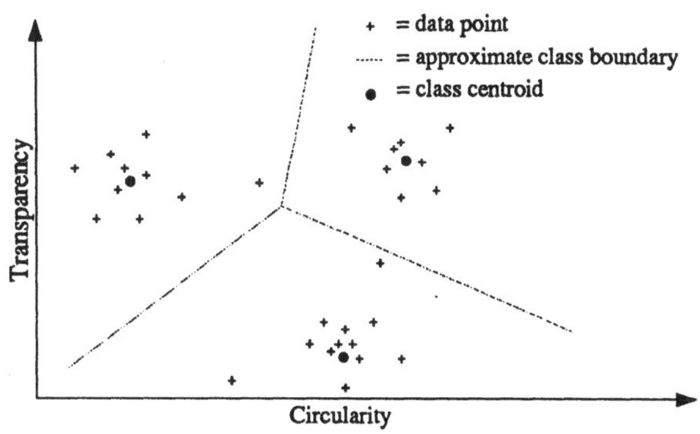

Fig. 9: A two-dimensional space for circularity and transparency

Each blot is given a shape classification based on clustering in a multi-dimensional attribute space (Ireton and Xydeas, 1991). As a simple example of clustering, consider the two-dimensional attribute space illustrated in Figure 9. To train the classifier, a large number of blots are plotted and the space is automatically partitioned into a number of disjoint classes. Each class represents a good cluster of data points and each is characterised by its centroid. Now, when a blot is presented to the system it is assigned to the class whose centroid is 'nearest' according to some distance criterion. This technique may be extended to an arbitrary number of dimensions, one per attribute. The set of attributes must be chosen so that each is relevant to a particular characteristic of the blot. In MMIS-1, the classifier has been tested for blots' shape characteristic, using circularity, transparency, aspect ratio and irregularity. A typical shape class is illustrated in Figure 10. Class membership is used as a key for prototype retrieval.

Fig. 10: A typical shape class

MMIS-1's interpretation is applicable to all images of 2D, non-overlapping objects except for the following domain-specific parts:

- Any blot that has an area of less than 500 pixels is regarded as noise.
- Transparency is only relevant to applications where blots are often incised.
- Irregularity is only relevant to applications where the micro-irregularity of edges is important.

Interpretation results are stored as semantic nets in the *Semantic Representation Base*, which is implemented as a set of triples in Prolog. The instances are referenced from the semantic net by their unique *instance identifier* and are stored in a separate object repository called the *Raw Database*. The raw database is implemented in C++.

The query engine is provided by Prolog's SL resolution theorem prover (Bratko, 1986). Approximately 10% of each semantic net is derived on demand by the query engine rather than being permanently stored in the semantic representation base. This is done where the cost of storing a particular arc is greater than the cost of slowing the query engine slightly.

A SunView based tool — *Query Tool* — has been implemented purely as a development environment for querying. A typical query session is shown in Figure 11. As can be seen from the figure, the semantic representation used in MMIS-1 is simpler than that described in Section 3. The main differences are:

- Instance identifiers are enclosed in single quotes so that Prolog can distinguish them from integers.

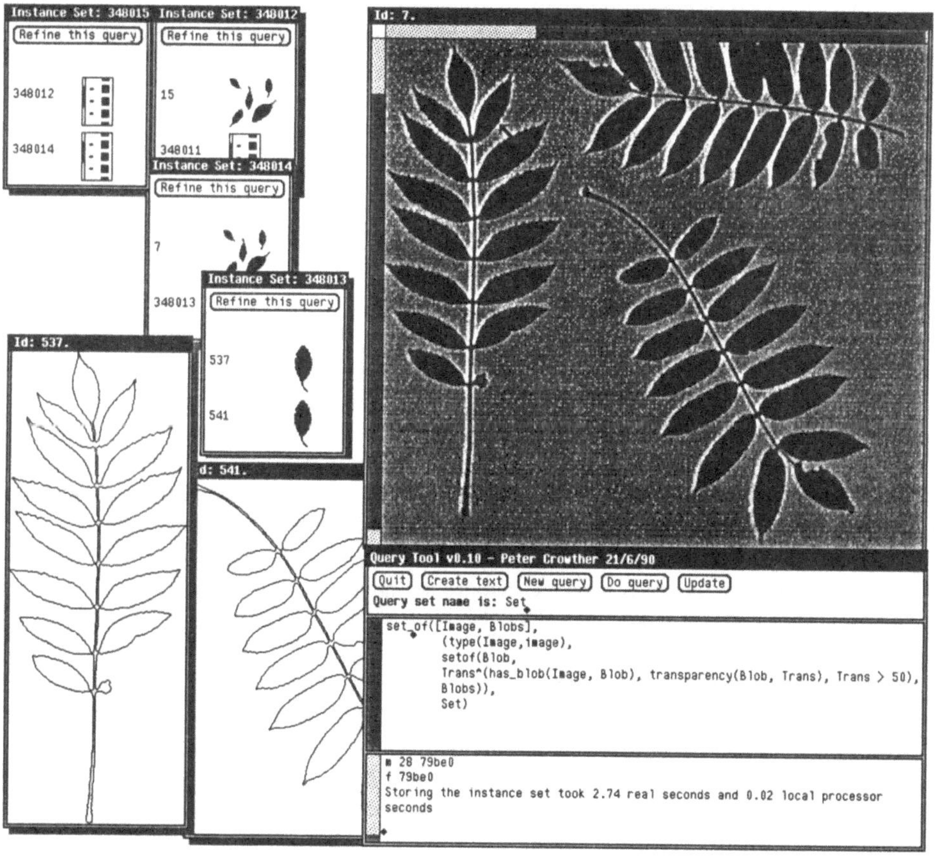

Fig. 11: The query interface of MMIS-1 showing the results of a hierarchical query

- Nodes have no type and therefore no dimension. The type of the instance referenced by each instance identifier is distinguishable by context, arc name, or by the attribute `type`.
- Arcs have no score — all facts are assumed to be certain.
- Regions within the image are referred to as 'blobs' rather than 'blots'.
- Pieces of noise are referred to as `bad_blobs`.
- Scale markers are not identified because the version used tended to be fragmented by the segmentation process. As a result, no distinction is made between leaves and scale markers: both are referred to as `blobs`.

Queries have mixed media semantics and return hierarchical sets of instance identifiers called *instance sets*. Instance sets are stored in the the raw database for progressive retrieval by the query tool. For example, the query in Figure 11 approximates to

> "Get me a set where each member contains an image followed by the set of blobs within that image that are more than 50% transparent"

The structure of the returned instance set is shown in Figure 12. The user can navigate down through this hierarchy by clicking on the iconic versions of the set members. In Figure 11, the user has followed the hierarchy down to the level of image 7 and its two highly transparent blobs. Hierarchical instance sets are a powerful conceptual grouping mechanism and can be used to retrieve hierarchical instances such as documents.

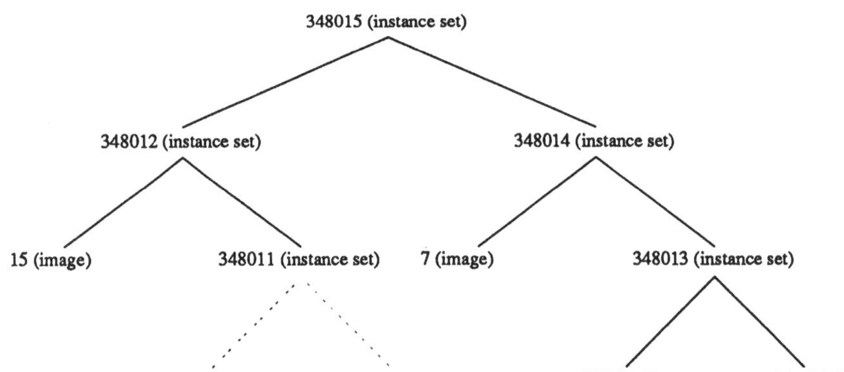

Fig. 12: The structure of an instance set

Users may create and destroy arbitrary hypermedia links between image, text and blob instances. The resulting 'web' can be browsed using the keyboard and mouse. Figure 13 shows some browsing in progress. Images are automatically connected to each of their good and bad blobs. All links may be navigated in either direction. A link from image 3 to its text description (23107) has been entered manually. Links are stored in the semantic representation base, but are kept separate from automatically derived arcs.

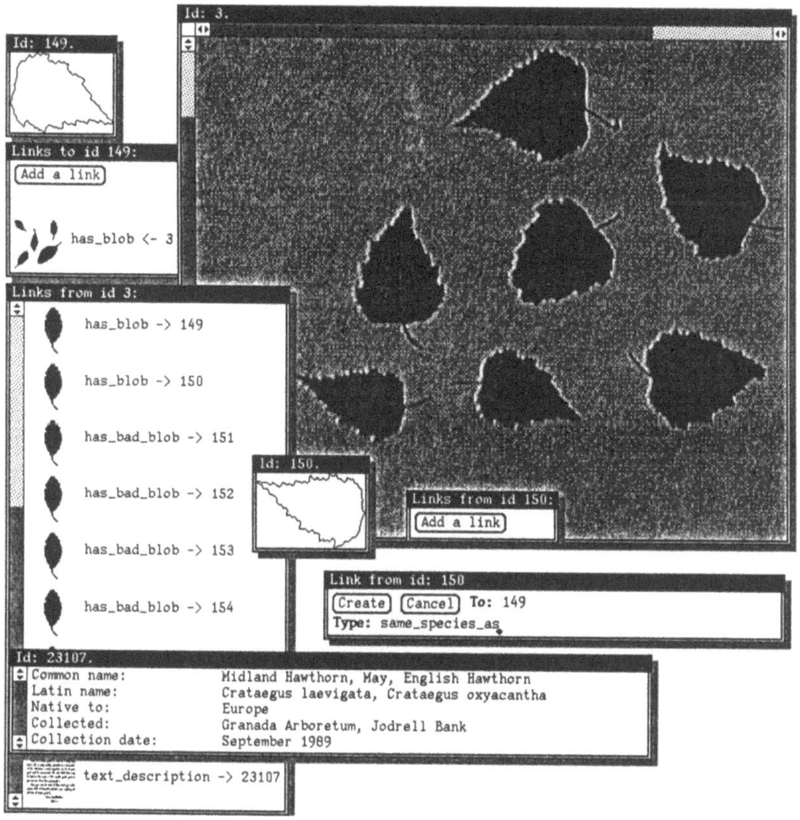

Fig. 13: MMIS-1's hypermedia facility

4.3 MMIS-2

4.3.1 Enhancements to MMIS-1

This section describes the shortcomings of MMIS-1 that will be removed in MMIS-2.

MMIS-1 stores images and text, but only interprets images. MMIS-2 will store and interpret images, text and documents.

The query tool only allows instance sets to contain complex types corresponding to instances and their sub-objects — namely images, blots and text. This is because it was envisaged that all queries put to such a system could take the form

> "Find me all instances that satisfy this query"

This is too restrictive — instance sets should be allowed to contain any type included in the data model, from integers to documents. This gives the user far more freedom of expression to formulate queries such as

> "How many times does the word **important** occur in document 15?"

Making the query tool capable of handling all types also allows the user, via hypermedia, to say anything that could be said by a medium interpreter.

Medium instances are entered into the raw database without first being compared with instances already present. This implies a many-to-one mapping between instance identifiers and instances, so the fact that two instance identifiers are different does not mean that the instances are different. MMIS-2 will provide a one-to-one mapping between instances and their identifiers.

For convenience in MMIS-1, the object representing a blot in the raw database contains more than just the chain code. This is so that the classification trainer, written in C++, does not have to interrogate Prolog. In MMIS-2, blot attributes will be stored in a triple format, accessible by both Prolog and C++. This means that the blot's chain code can be stored for display purposes only. The results of training the classifier will also be stored as triples, so that C++ need only derive the true base attributes and all other attributes and structural relationships can be derived more declaratively in Prolog.

Scale markers will be identified in MMIS-2, so that lengths can be expressed in metres as well as pixels.

The image interpreter will work more closely with the database to allow the system to accept less constrained input images. For instance, the image background will not need to be so uniform and foreground objects (leaves in our case) may overlap. The method will use the search speed of the database to match a large number of candidate leaf models against a representation of the image sub-part being analysed.

There are two ways of refining queries: the first is for the user to modify his initial query according to the system's answer; the second is to restrict the set of items that can be in the next query's answer to a proper subset of those that were in the initial query's answer. The first method would be expected in most systems. The second method can be used to reduce the proportion of the query that is re-evaluated or to reduce the number of objects over which the new query is evaluated. Due to the difficulty of inter-process communication between the user interface and the query engine, the second mode of refinement is not implemented in MMIS-1. It will be present in MMIS-2.

Attribute values in MMIS-1 may only be integer, float or atom (string). This means that the name of an arc is the only clue to the semantics of the fact that it represents. The only way to provide more information or to resolve ambiguities is to make arc names more verbose. For example, consider that image width is measured in pixels, and blot width is measured in metres. The only way of ensuring that users do not unwittingly combine these two semantically incompatible attributes in MMIS-1 is to use two long-winded arc names as in:

```
image_width_in_pixels('10', 760).
blot_width_in_metres('35', 0.05).
```

MMIS-2 will use the full data model of Section 3 that includes node type, so that the two attributes can be expressed as:

```
width(image/10, p/760, 1.0).
width(blot/35, m/0.05, 1.0).
```

This opens the way to a new class of expressive queries, such as:

"What instances have an area of more than $0.05m^2$?"

In MMIS-1, large instance sets are presented to the user with no conceptual ordering because all facts on which query resolution is based are assumed to be certain. What is needed is a method of ranking instances so that the user can first examine those that best match the query. Another motivation for ranking is that interpretation is never exact so query results are always uncertain. MMIS-2 provides scores for arcs so that uncertain statements can be represented. For example, each arc can be assigned a score from 0 to 1, where 0 represents false and 1 represents true. We have rejected the use of mathematical probabilities to produce scores because it is difficult to generate a distribution in order to give the probability any theoretical foundation. It is also unclear how to combine probabilities in complex queries when such probabilities may or may not be independent.

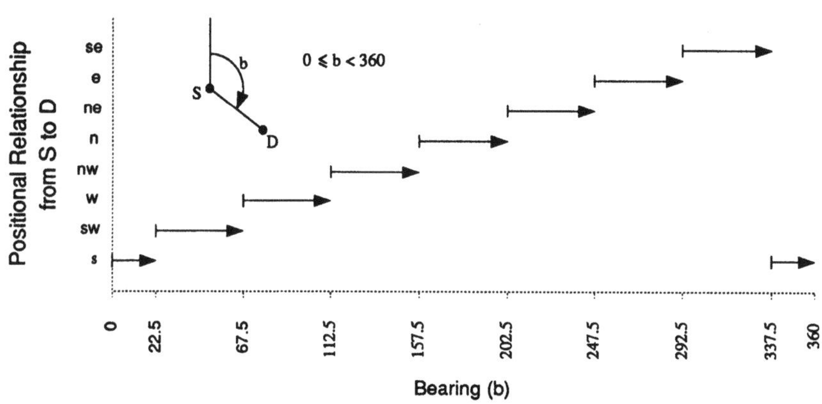

Fig. 14: Choice of positional relationships

There are situations, however, when a meaningful score can be generated. One example is the use of compass sectors to describe positional relationships. The relationship is currently decided on the basis of hard boundaries between compass sectors (see Figure 14). This scheme means that if b = 22.5° then S is considered to be south west of D, but if b = 22.499999° then S is south of D when there is clearly little difference. A better approach is to use inexact relationships similar to *fuzzy sets* as illustrated in Figure 15(a). Now if b = 65° then S is south west of D with score 0.56 and west of D with score 0.44. This makes the boundaries between classes of positional relationships blurred and more intuitive. This

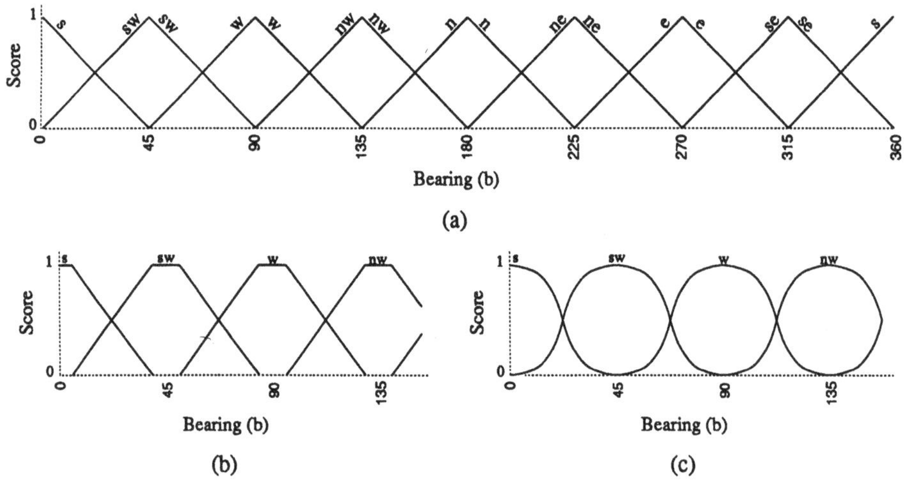

Fig. 15: Three inexact descriptions of relative position

technique can be adapted to give positional relationships a stronger influence close to the centre of their class either discontinuously (Figure 15(b)) or continuously (Figure 15(c)).

Another example is the assignment of a score to a blot's classification according to its distance from the centre of the class. This distance measure need not be Euclidean (Mahalanobis, 1936). Classes can be given non-sharp boundaries so that each blot has a degree of membership of several classes.

A final example is the degree of overlap of true bounding boxes, so that:

```
tbb_overlaps(blot/2859, blot/2858, 0.11).
```

means

"Blot 2859's true bounding box overlaps 11% of the true bounding box of blot 2858."

In order to speed development, MMIS-1's triples are stored in Prolog at run time, and in an ASCII file at other times. This is a disadvantage because:

- Data takes a long time to load and is held in a space-inefficient form in virtual memory.
- Since each Prolog process holds the entire semantic representation, updates have to be controlled carefully by the operator; therefore the system is not truly multi-process.

There are also problems associated with using Prolog as a query engine in MMIS-1:

- Prolog is not efficient at searching large data sets. Also, the indexing is optimised for predicates that can have variable arguments, non-empty bodies and arbitrary length argument lists.
- Prolog's resolution is optimised to provide individual solutions rather than sets of solutions, whereas our query tool retrieves sets.

MMIS-2's database will be a simulation of a hardware tuple store developed at the University of Essex (Lavington and Wang, 1990), capable of storing and efficiently accessing several million tuples.

4.3.2 General Description

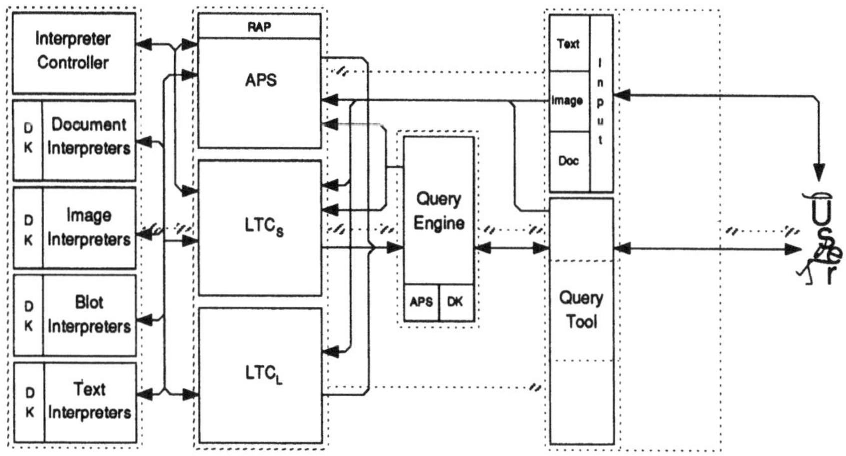

DK = Domain Knowledge
RAP = Relational Algebra Processor
APS = Associative Predicate Store
LTC$_{L/S}$ = Lexical Token Convertor for Large/Small objects

Fig. 16: The architecture of MMIS-2

The architecture of MMIS-2 is shown in Figure 16. Users may input text, images and documents to the database and all three media are interpreted. Interpretation tasks are allocated to individual interpreter processes by the *Interpreter Controller.* The interpretation is hierarchical: Document interpreters cause image and text interpreters to be spawned, image interpreters cause blot interpreters to be spawned.

The database has three components: the *Associative Predicate Store* (APS), the *Lexical Token Converter for Small objects* (LTC$_S$) and the *Lexical Token Converter for Large objects* (LTC$_L$). The APS holds the semantic nets as a set of triples where each third of a triple is a token. LTC$_S$ and LTC$_L$ translate tokens to and from small and large objects respectively. Small objects are numbers, atoms et al; large objects are images, text et al. Documents are unusual in that they have a hierarchical semantic net referencing other instances as their raw data representation, as well as a semantic net to represent the results of their interpretation.

The query engine is Prolog coupled to a special translator based on the ideas in (Draxler, 1990). The translator converts Prolog queries to triple store searches and relational operations. The relational operations are provided by the *Relational Algebra Processor* (RAP).

5 Conclusions

5.1 Results

We have shown that the notion of a MMIS with automatic content retrieval is feasible and conclude that our prototypes are a firm foundation for research and development. In order to exploit the full potential of MMISs, each must be tailored to the domain of a single application, trees in our case. This implies that the architecture should be easily configurable to new applications.

We have shown that a content retrieval database for heterogeneous objects can be implemented by separating storage structures from content querying structures. This database takes note of object-oriented database (OODB) research in that host language (C++) objects are stored in the large object store (Raw Database/LTC_L). However, a deliberate decision was taken to avoid storing any object schema in the large object store so we cannot claim to have built an OODB. Object inter-relationships are represented separately in semantic nets (in the Semantic Representation Base/APS).

Large amounts of data can be extracted using relatively simple analysis methods. Any system must be capable of storing and processing this data. Therefore a database capable of fast searching of many fixed-size, small objects is required.

Semantic nets have proved to be an expressive model for images and appear promising for other media. They can be stored in a simple fashion that allows searching to be highly optimised and even implemented in hardware. Other representations may be preferable in certain applications, but we have not attempted to use them in our system. We can conclude, however, that knowledge representation formalisms can be managed efficiently in a database if the emphasis is on a small set of high-level facts. If much reliance is made on the topological structure of nets to convey semantics then their database representation is far more difficult to achieve.

Deciding what facts to store in knowledge representations is a difficult task. It involves knowledge of the minimum requirements for describing a medium, what description is meaningful to users and what it is reasonable to try and deduce. This is exacerbated by the problem of whether deduction should be pre-query, post-query or lazy. There is also the question of whether knowledge is application-dependent — eg. a shape classifier for leaves — or application-independent — eg. extraction of chain codes and positional relationships. The end result has to be a compromise. In all cases, low-level information should be progressively refined to yield information that is more valuable to the user. This does not mean that low-level information can be discarded once high-level information is deduced; for instance, a system that reliably identifies leaves and stores only their species cannot easily answer the question "Which leaves have a transparency greater than 50%" except in general terms such as "Well, mature oak leaves are usually highly incised, therefore...". Unfortunately, progressive refinement plus retention of low-level data leads to redundancy. For example, all blot attributes can be derived from the chain code; this is unavoidable.

It is possible to build a system capable of retrieving images that are 'similar', provided that a definition of similarity is given in terms that the system can understand. The classification method used here, namely clustering in a multi-dimensional attribute space, provides an economical way of comparing image sub-objects for similarity on a number of criteria.

5.2 Future Work

We have not researched the types of query asked of a multimedia database. This makes it difficult to prove that all queries can be answered, although we have not found a query that cannot be answered by the system when extra domain knowledge is provided by the user. Future work should include the development of query languages that are safer than Prolog, that are more straightforward for novice users and that use graphical facilities.

One powerful consequence of using Prolog as query language and query engine is that rules can be added easily to perform post-query analysis or to implement user views of the data — eg. the renaming of attributes or the assignment of labels to ranges of values.

Verbalisation, or the mapping of a continuous value to one of a set of perceptual labels is an interesting area of research. For instance, an object's colour could be mapped to [very red, red, not red] to allow users to ask "What red objects are there in the system?". Another example would be the description of a shape class by the verbalisation of the attributes of its blots: "Shape class three is characterised by blots of very high circularity, low transparency, normal irregularity and very high aspect ratio".

The process of ranking query results needs further investigation; this involves the combination of arc scores and the importance scores assigned to query sub-clauses.

Hypermedia has proved easy to implement as a semantic net, but tools that allow browsing of the resultant webs as well as issuing queries have yet to be provided.

It may be possible in some circumstances for users to tell the system whether returned items match their query; positive and negative feedback could then be incorporated into the system to improve future analysis.

In MMIS-1, a simple meta-data description was used to indicate what attributes and structural relationships each instance should have and whether these were single or multiple, compulsory or optional. Meta-data languages could be developed for use with any application that can be described in terms of base and derived attributes and structural relationships; a description in this new language would then be used to generate an interpreter automatically — only the code to deliver base attributes would have to be written. The meta-data would be employed during interpretation to check that sensible data was being generated and during querying so that queries such as

```
set_of(image/I/S, shape_class(image/I, 2, S)), Set)
```

instead of producing no solutions would produce the system message "Instances of type image have no shape class".

Finally, the provision of MMISs with multi-user access and full management of user views, protection and updates needs to be investigated.

6 Acknowledgements

This work is funded by the Systems Integration Division of ICL and the Science and Engineering Research Council.

References

Bratko, I. (1986). *Prolog Programming for Artificial Intelligence.* Addison-Wesley, Wokingham.

Ceri, S. and Tanca, L. (1990). Retrieval of multimedia documents by imprecise query specification. In Bancilhon, F., Thanos, C., and Tsichritzis, D., editors, *Advances in Database Technology — EDBT '90*, pages 203–218, Venice. Springer-Verlag. Lecture Notes in Computer Science No. 416.

Christodoulakis, S. and Graham, S. (1988). Browsing within time-driven multimedia documents. *ACM SIGOIS Bulletin*, 9:219–227.

Date, C. (1986). *An Introduction to Database Systems*, volume 1. Addison-Wesley, fourth edition.

Draxler, C. (1990). Logic programming and databases. Technical Report 90.09, Institut fur Informatik der Universitat Zurich.

Faloutsos, C. and Christodoulakis, S. (1984). Signature files: An access method for documents and its analytic performance evaluation. *ACM Transactions on Office Information Systems*, 2(4):267–288.

Gonzalez, R. et al. (1978). A measure of scene content. *IEEE CH1318-5/78/0000-0385500.75*, pages 385–389.

Ireton, M. A. and Xydeas, C. S. (1991). Classification of shape for content retrieval of images in a multimedia information system. In *Submitted to the 6th IEE International Conference on Digital Processing of Speech in Communications*, Loughborough.

Irven, J., Nilson, M., Judd, T., Patterson, J., and Shibata, Y. (1988). Multi-media information services: A laboratory study. *IEEE Communications Magazine*, 26(6):27–44.

ISO (1988). IS 8613: Text and office systems — office document architecture (ODA) and interchange formats.

Lavington, S. and Wang, J. (1990). A formalism for the IFS/2 firmware — part 1. Technical Report CSM-159, University of Essex, Department of Computer Science.

Mahalanobis, P. C. (1936). On the generalised distance in statistics. *Proceedings of the Indian National Institute of Science*, 2:49–55.

Meyrowitz, N. (1986). Intermedia: The architecture and construction of an object-oriented hypermedia system and applications framework. In *OOPSLA '86: Conference on Object-Oriented Programming, Systems, Languages and Applications*, pages 186–201. ACM.

Neumann, W. and Sproull, R. (1981). *Principles of Interactive Computer Graphics*, pages 202–209. McGraw-Hill, 2 edition.

O'Docherty, M., Crowther, P., Daskalakis, C., Goble, C., Ireton, M., Kay, S., and Xydeas, C. (1990). Advances in the processing and management of multimedia information. *ICL Technical Journal.*

Ringland, G. and Duce, D., editors (1988). *Approaches to Knowledge Representation — An Introduction.* Research Studies Press.

Toriwaki, J., Hasegawa, J., Fukumura, T., and Tagaki, Y. (1980). Pictorial information retrieval of chest X-ray image database using pattern recognition techniques. In *Proceedings of MEDINFO '80*, pages 1154–1158.

Chapter 19

Database Requirements for Multimedia Applications

Matthias Rhiner and Peter Stucki

Abstract

The development of multimedia applications is an expensive process with regard to manpower, hardware, software, and multimedia resources that are spent on it. This fact asks for means that can help to protect and spread those investments, mainly the different types of multimedia and related description data. In computer science *database systems* are approved facilities to make data and conceptual knowledge, stored in a central pool, accessible to different users and applications. In the case of multimedia applications, there are many new implications, originating from the characteristic properties of multimedia, which must be considered in order to apply the traditional techniques of database systems to the much more complex domain of *multimedia database systems*.

Some of the most important properties, inherent to multimedia objects and applications, are treated in the first part of this paper. This examination results in explicit requirements towards database systems which have to support multimedia applications. These requirements and related consequences will be discussed and deepened in the second part of the this paper.

Keywords

Multimedia, hypermedia, database systems, physical objects, logical objects, object representation, object storage, object description, object retrieval, object rendering

1. Introduction

Multimedia applications are a representative example for the integration of modern *hardware technology* and *advanced software techniques*. New technical devices support the physical processing, storage, communication, and rendering of various types of media. Most of these hardware components have related counterparts on the side of software, such as device drivers or supporting software subsystems. Together they form an appropriate foundation for advanced applications in complex, heterogeneous environments (IEEE 1987).

Besides these more formally and physically oriented characteristics, sophisticated application types show a strong requirement for conceptual structures and logical relations. Contrary to basic multimedia representation systems, integrated, content-oriented multimedia applications require a much larger effort for the integration of logical and physical objects. This *dualism* of *form* and *content* can be made evident, for example, by the comparison of multimedia and hypermedia where multimedia is the formal foundation, conceptually augmented by the logical content of hypertext and hypermedia (Meyrowitz 1990).

The application development for a scenario, based on multimedia and hypermedia techniques, can be an expensive process with regard to various types of investments made in it. There is a strong need for *distribution* and *reusability* of physical and logical resources. These requirements can be satisfied in many respects by adopting the techniques offered by database systems and extending them to *Multimedia Databases* (Lockemann 1988). Multimedia databases provide a means to store and manage objects, to define and preserve consistent logical relations, and finally, to distribute this synthesis of objects and knowledge to an open number of applications and users.

In this paper fundamental concepts for the usage of databases within the domains of multi- and hypermedia will be discussed. First some thoughts are spent on the nature and characteristics of various *data types* in the domain of multimedia. Using an example of computer graphics, important *multimedia requirements* towards multimedia, non-standard database systems are expressed. These requirements are reinforced by the concepts, necessary for *multimedia object management*, such as object representation, object storage, object description, and object retrieval as major topics of interest within multimedia database applications. Based on these prerequisites of object management, various conclusions for the *integration* of a multimedia database system in heterogeneous application environments are deduced. Finally, the example of a hypermedia application resumes many of the previous aspects to a representative summary.

2. Multimedia Positioning

2.1 Multimedia Domains

There are several points of view from where to look at the field of multimedia. Primarily there are various *physical media* (graphics, images, sound etc.) which determine the principal characteristics of multimedia. But there are also different domains such as *computer graphics*, *image processing*, and *synthetic sound composition* which are involved in creating, processing, and transforming multimedia objects.

♦ **Computergraphics**
- Design, Modelling
- Scientific Visualization

♦ **Animations**
- Synthesis and animation of computer graphic elements
- Transformation to video, setting to music/sound

♦ **Image Processing**
- Transformations, Enhancement
- Analysis, Recognition, Understanding

♦ **Image Conversions and Archiving**
- Conversion between different image formats/standards
- Storing and archiving of images

♦ **Sound Processing**
- Composition, Synthesis
- Recording, Archiving

♦ **Multimedia / Hypermedia Applications**
- Integration and composition of various media
- Extending concepts of Hypertext to Hypermedia

Fig. 1: Multimedia: Domains of Interest

Finally, there are the environments of interactive *visual user interfaces* (VUI) or *multimedia user interfaces* (MUI) which are necessary for the presentation and rendering of multimedia objects with respect to end-user requirements.

2.2 Multimedia Data Types

Multimedia data can be separated into various types of data. But also within one specific data type there may exist different representation forms of objects. Multimedia objects can occur in a *readable textual, coded* form (tCod, see Fig. 2) or in a *binary, bit- or byte-mapped, coded* form (bCod). They can have internal structures (Struc.) such as part-objects, sub-objects, segments or they are mapped to flat, structureless representation forms (nStruc.) such as bytemaps of images). Objects in *formatted* form (Form.) are augmented by artificially imposed information. Special keywords (e.g. markup-tags) are included in the primary object representation. They allow the definition of additional information which concerns object-internal (e.g. object structure) or object-extraneous aspects (e.g. links to other objects). Contrarily there are unformatted objects (nForm).

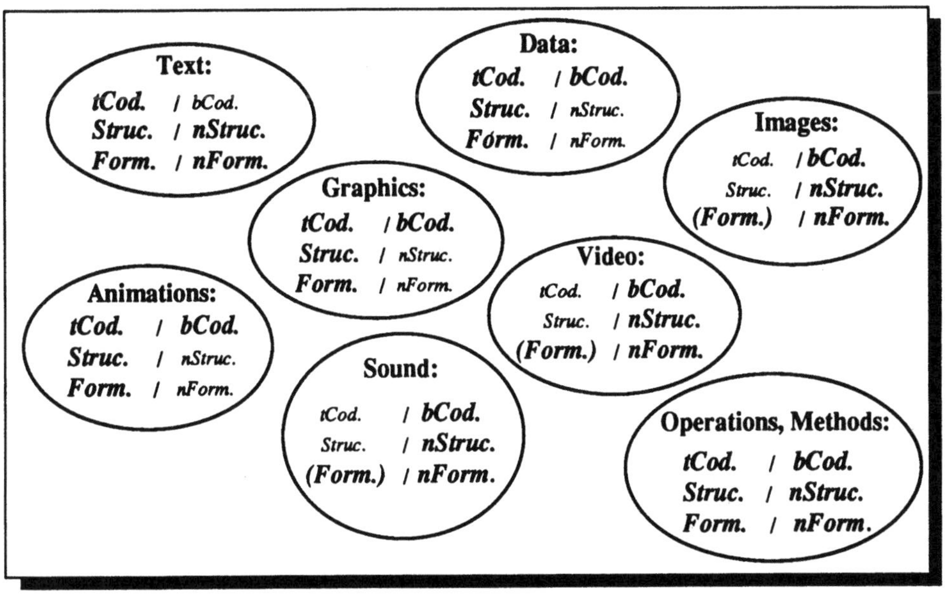

Fig. 2: Multimedia Data Types and Forms of Appearance

This classification essentially refers to basic, standard levels of object representation. Most object types can be combined to build coded, structured composites on conceptually higher levels or they can be transformed between different representation forms (see section 4.2).

3. General Multimedia Database Requirements

3.1 Data Processing Techniques and Databases

There is quite a difference in the way textual and numerical data is processed in conventional batch and transaction oriented environments, compared to the way, the access and the use of multimedia data is handled in a highly interactive environment (see Fig. 3).

In the first case, a data object is selected for a transaction based on certain explicit criteria. Then it undergoes a specific processing step. Finally, it is restored to a target database. Usually this is a quite linear and deterministic way of data processing.

In the case of non-trivial multimedia applications, (parallel) processing of various, heterogeneous objects takes place in a much more interactive way. For this reason operations are performed in a wider context than that of linear transactions, and there is a need for a more global view to the respective database.

Expressed in an exaggerated way: The database acts as an extension of an active workspace. There should be no distinction between objects currently existing in the workspace and those permanently stored in the database.

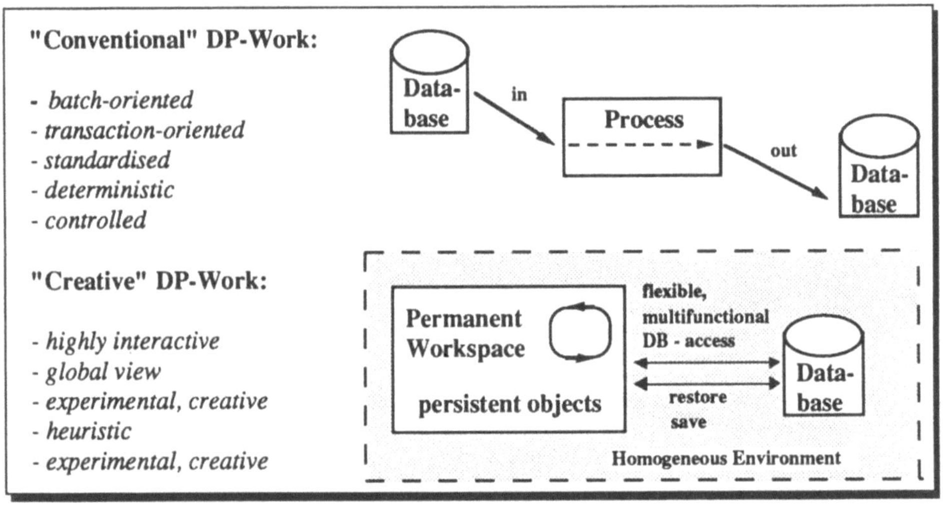

Fig. 3: Data Processing Techniques and Databases

3.2 Example: Computer Graphics Database

The preceding thoughts of extending an active workspace can be exemplified by defining requirements for a hypothetical database in the domain of computer graphics. An assumed database for this purpose must efficiently and transparently augment the workspace in which operations are performed on graphical objects. There are different requirements that must be fulfilled in order to provide this support.

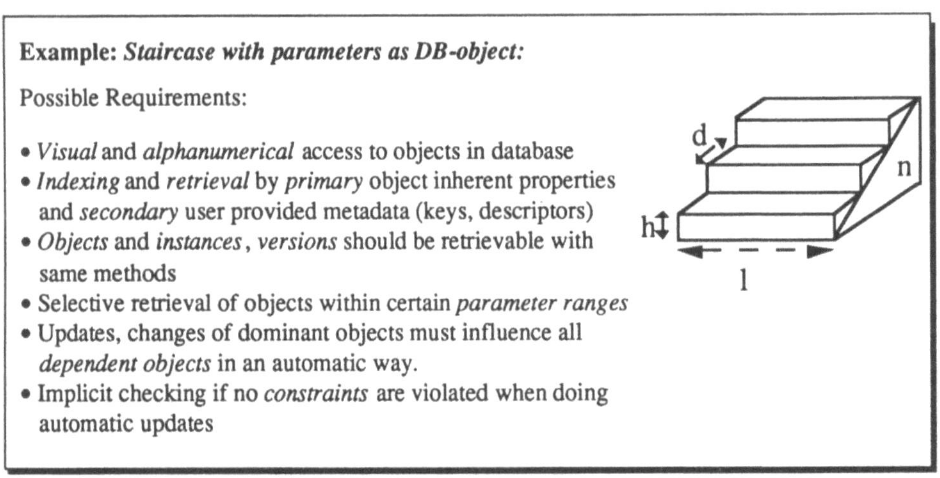

Fig. 4: Example: Computer Graphics Database

The requirements listed in Fig. 4 mainly refer to classical database features that have to be adopted and extended for highly interactive, visual applications which operate on complex, composite, graphical objects (staircase in this example), variants and versions of these objects.

4. Multimedia Object Management

4.1 Object Representation

The usage of databases, to support and extend multimedia applications, asks for appropriate representation schemes for the different types of media. The inherent characteristics of objects (coded, structured etc.) are decisive features with regard to potential mappings. There are several possibilities of mapping different data types to adequate representation forms (Fig. 5).

A textually coded, non-structured text can be mapped to the respective form of a plain text file. A binary coded, non-structured image can be mapped to a data structure containing the determining image parameters (which allow to interpret the data files) and three unstructured files which contain the proper image data (red, green, and blue pixel values). A graphical object, finally, may be mapped to a table containing all the primitives that define the respective object. Multimedia databases must be able to handle all these different forms of object representations.

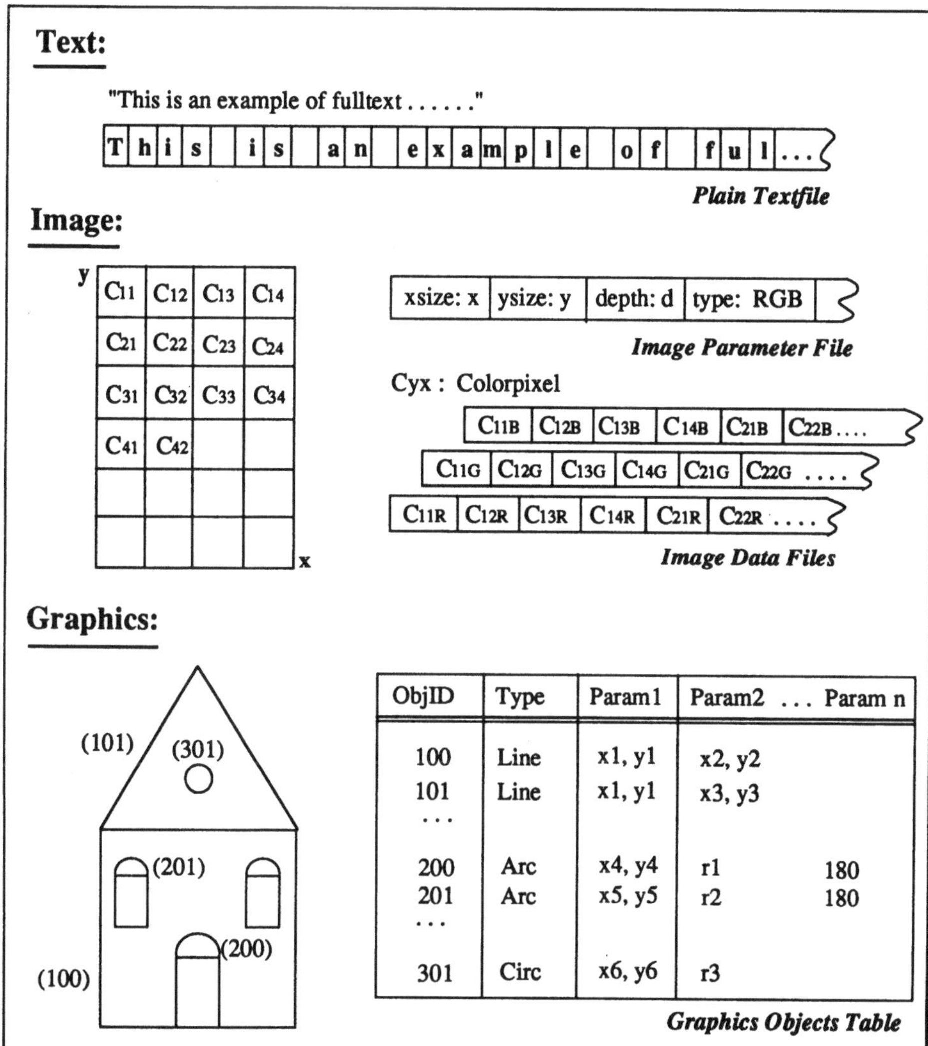

Fig. 5: Object Representation Techniques

4.2 Object Representation Example

In this subsection the principles of heterogeneous object representation forms, shown in Fig. 5, will be reinforced by explaining that the final visual appearance of an object in a multimedia environment can be independent from its internal representation model in a multimedia database.

The staircase, shown in Fig. 4., is the object of reference for the following example. Depending on contextual requirements, various methods of representing the concept of a staircase can be adopted. If the internal structure of the object is of interest, and if search facilities for specific components are a decisive criterion, a *tabular, structured* representation might be the ideal form. If structure is of importance, but if there is no reason to adjust all the information to a tabular raster, an *interpretable metafile*, containing all the information in a textually coded form, is a feasible solution. And finally, if the main focus is on a mere pictorial view, a flat, binary, *canonical bytemap* representation form may be appropriate.

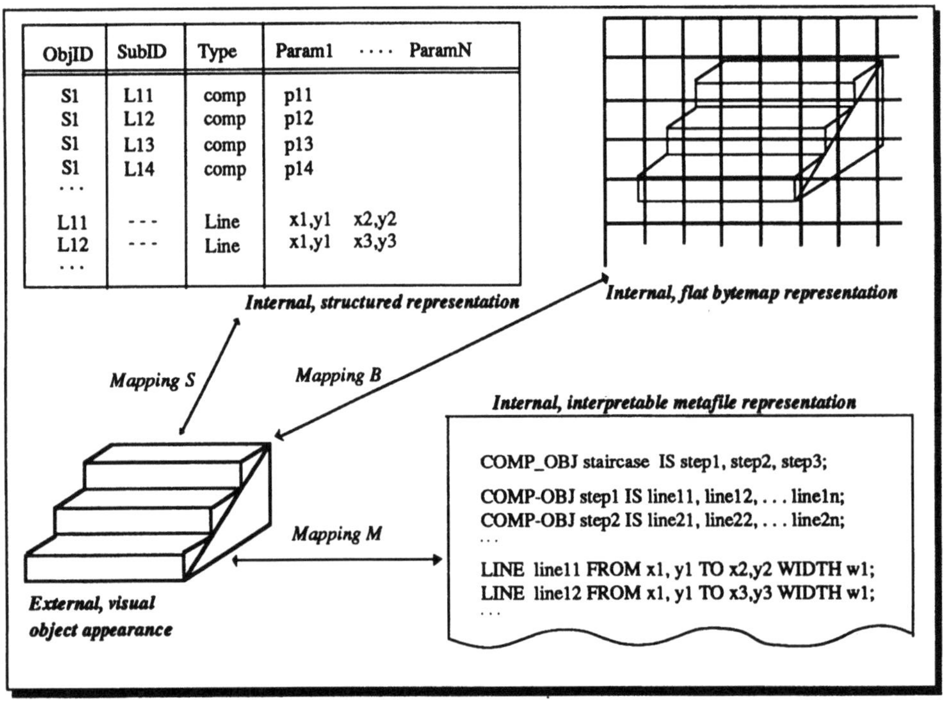

Fig. 6: Object Representation Example

Other forms of mapping are possible with regard to particular object representation requirements or specific database characteristics. Again, the multimedia database must provide techniques which allow the management of these heterogeneous representation schemes.

4.3 Object Storage

The example of heterogeneous object representation forms (Fig. 6) has given motivation for a closer look to the principles of object representation and respective object storage.

On one side, depending on specific requirements, different target instantiations of an object may be based on different internal representation forms of the respective object. On the other side, complex and composite objects may be a conglomerate consisting of heterogeneous sub-objects, for example, a basic image layer with complex graphical overlays (Rhiner 1991).

All the different ways of representing, accessing and finally rendering an object, mean that the manipulation of multimedia data has to be done by applying object- and target-specific methods.

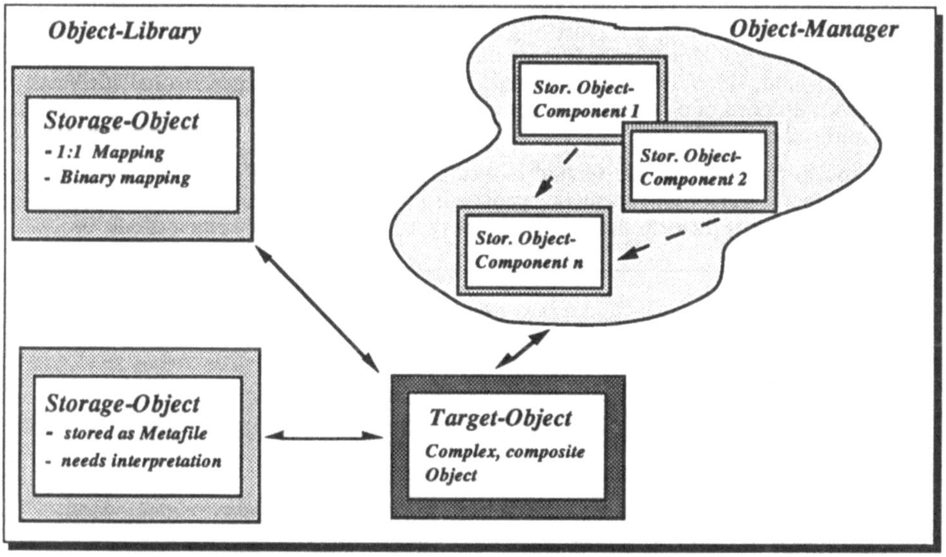

Fig. 7: Object Storage

4.4 Object and Method Storage

The different methods, required to handle objects, are in close relation with the objects they operate on. It is possible to define methods which are globally applicable for a whole class of objects, but there are other, dedicated methods that only operate on a single, unique object within a specific application context. Therefore, related forms of storing multimedia data and respective methods are required. A multimedia database must support and preserve this close relation of objects and methods.

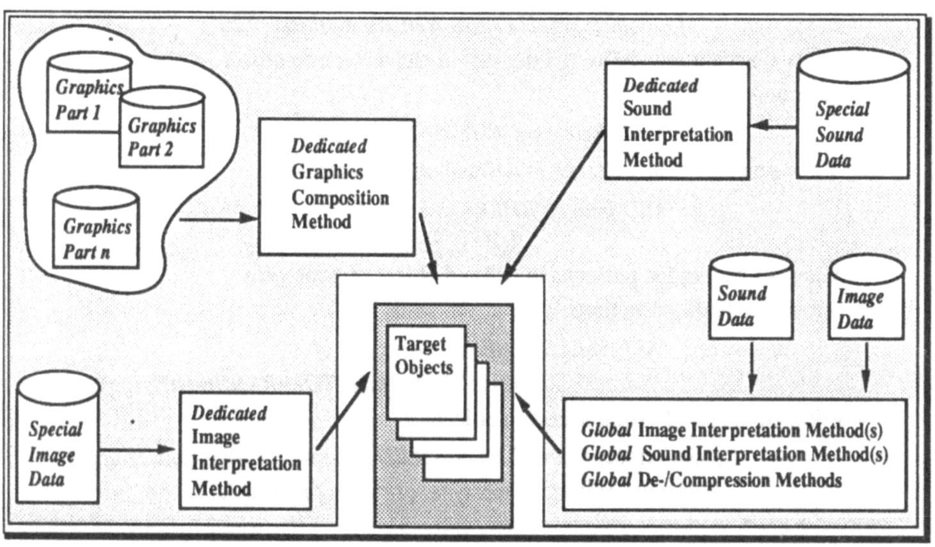

Fig. 8: Object and Method Storage

4.5 Indexing and Retrieval

Within multimedia environments a variety of objects that have totally different properties and forms of appearance has to be maintained. Textual descriptions are still the principal technique for the purpose of indexing and retrieving multimedia objects. Specific physical and logical properties of different object types (e.g. *spatial* properties for images and graphics; *temporal* aspects for sound, video) must be considered when assigning secondary, textual attributes or descriptors. All forms of object specific description modes must have corresponding opponents for the retrieval process.

In addition to the conventional textual indexing and retrieval methods, more multimedia-oriented methods, supporting automatic, media-adequate techniques, will become of increasing importance. Currently they are still restricted to very limited and specific applications.

Indexing Techniques:

- **Implicit:** Using directly obvious, immanent object information
  (e.g. Object parts or parameters in graphics, image regions)
- **Fully Automatic:** Extracting features, deriving key-data
  (e.g. Automatic image-feature extraction , automatic classification)
- **Semi-Automatic:** Extract features, 'manual' evaluation
  (e.g. Automatic feature extraction and 'manual' classification)
- **Fully 'manual':** 'Manual', explicit description of objects
  (e.g. provide descriptors, define areas of interest)

Retrieval Requirements:

- **Allow searching for components and composed objects**
  (e.g. "ALL circles WHERE diameter >20" ,
  "ALL objects WITH circles WHERE diameter > 20")
- **Allow searching by defining intervals of characteristic object parameters**
  (e.g. "ALL staircases WHERE 45 < slope < 60 ")
- **Allow searching for patterns in defined object regions**
  (e.g. "ALL images WHERE images[100-110,200-210]
  EQUAL pattern[0-10, 0-10])"
- **Allow searching for patterns in defined object regions with certain matching functions**
  (e.g. "ALL sounds WHERE sounds[x - y]
  MATCH pattern[z] TOLERANCE (t)")
- **Allow textual and visual access to objects**
  (e.g. Display (part of) an object library, retrieve all instances of a visually selected object type; use icons for images)

Fig. 9: Indexing and Retrieval

5. Multimedia Database System Integration

5.1 Multimedia Database Internals

Ways of structuring and storing objects have been described in the previous sections. Appropriate methods, stored together with the respective objects, are required for object composition, decomposition and transformation. Additionally there is a need for description data to define secondary attributes which are relevant for dedicated object management and selective object retrieval (Fig. 10). All these interrelated logical and physical object components must be stored in a multimedia database (Klas et al. 1989).

Considering these facts, there is a distinction between three major groups of elements within a multimedia database: 1. Proper *multimedia objects* such as images, sequences of sound or video. These objects may exist in various versions that are used for different application purposes or different target environments. 2. *Description data* covers a wide spectrum of information which describes primary and secondary object properties. 3. *Object-related methods* are the last group of relevant elements within the database.

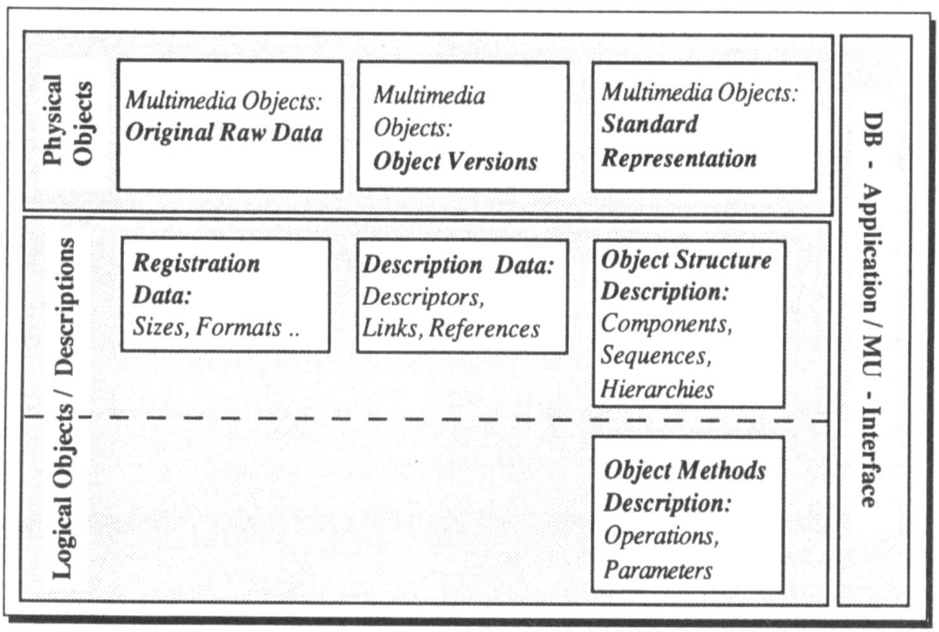

Fig. 10: Multimedia Database Internals

The elements of these three groups considerably differ with regard to object structure and object sizes. Therefore a multimedia database should support various logical concepts of *object management* and adequate, physical subsystems of *storage media*.

5.2 Heterogeneous Multimedia User Interfaces

A multimedia database is an important prerequisite for applications in different environments that are based on a common context. For the following example, a multimedia database is assumed, which contains a set of various objects representing the model of an engine. Several applications in different domains (e.g. configuration, diagnosis, education) access this common multimedia database and use the same logical object descriptions, but have to render different physical object instantiations to different multimedia user interfaces (MUIs, e.g. Windows®,

Presentation Manager®, X-Windows). In this way, various applications for different purposes within heterogeneous target environments can profit by a common multimedia database.

There are two principal ways of how to instantiate objects for a particular MUI:

(1) In a *specific mode*, environment-dependent and object-related methods are responsible for the physical transformations from database-internal object representation forms to specific environment-dependent object instantiations.

(2) In a more *general mode*, object-related methods produce an intermediate, environment-independent object instantiation that can be interpreted and consequently be rendered in the respective target environment (see also Fig. 12).

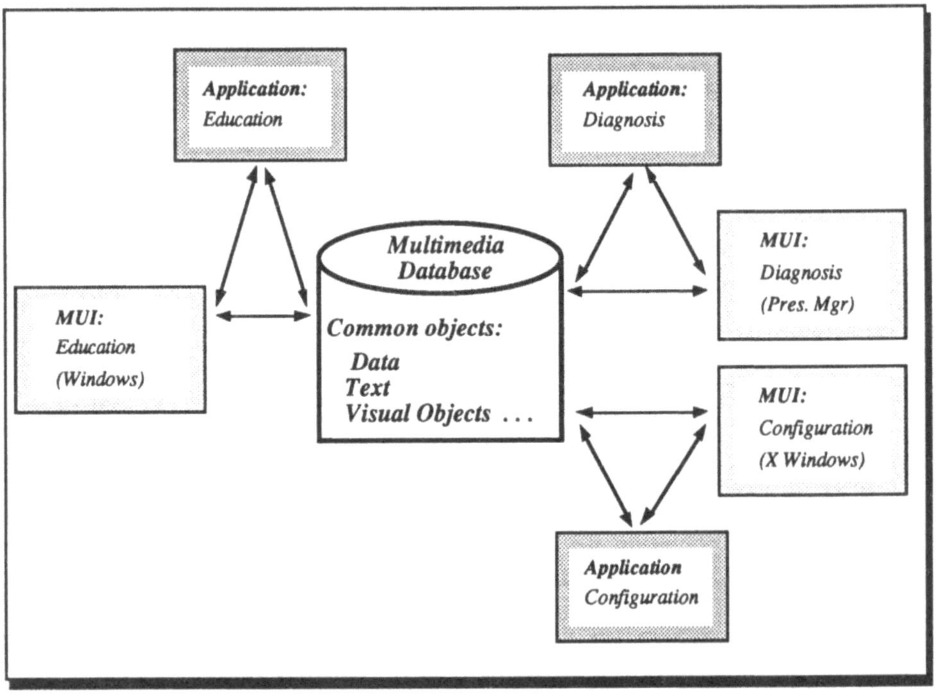

Fig. 11: Heterogeneous Multimedia User Interfaces

5.3 Object Rendering for a Specific Target MUI

Fig. 12 gives an rough impression of the complete process for rendering an object, stored in a multimedia database, within a specific multimedia user interface. Depending on the capabilities of the MUI internal object interpreter, the MUI requestor asks for different components of the respective object to be provided by the multimedia database:

In the case of a *functionally modest* MUI interpreter, the database object server and data server must return MUI specific object versions and appropriate instantiation methods that can be processed by the MUI interpreter and renderer. Object preparation mainly takes place on the side of the database.

In the case of a *functionally more sophisticated* MUI interpreter, the object server returns conceptual object descriptions that can be processed by the MUI interpreter in a more flexible way. As a consequence, specific and dedicated data requests can be sent to the data server. The data objects returned to the MUI can be manipulated locally, before being submitted to the MUI renderer, because the object structure is known to the MUI interpreter.

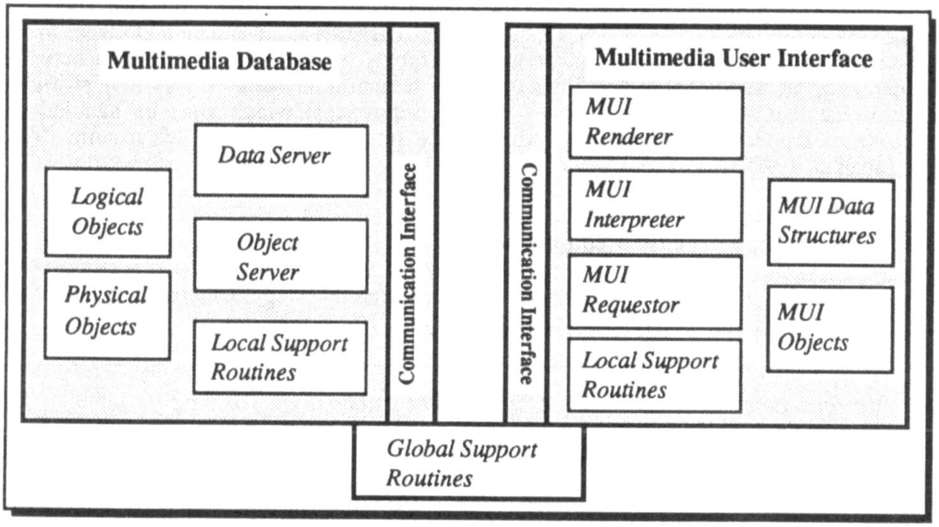

Fig. 12: Object Rendering for a Specific Target MUI

6. Summary and Conclusion

6.1 Hypermedia Example

As a summary, Fig. 13 represents some aspects of a composite hypermedia document. There are logical links between various types of heterogeneous physical objects. Again, objects and object-related knowledge, acquired and represented while preparing all the logical and physical components of such an interlinked hypermedia web, should be stored in a common hypermedia database which is widely available and accessible.

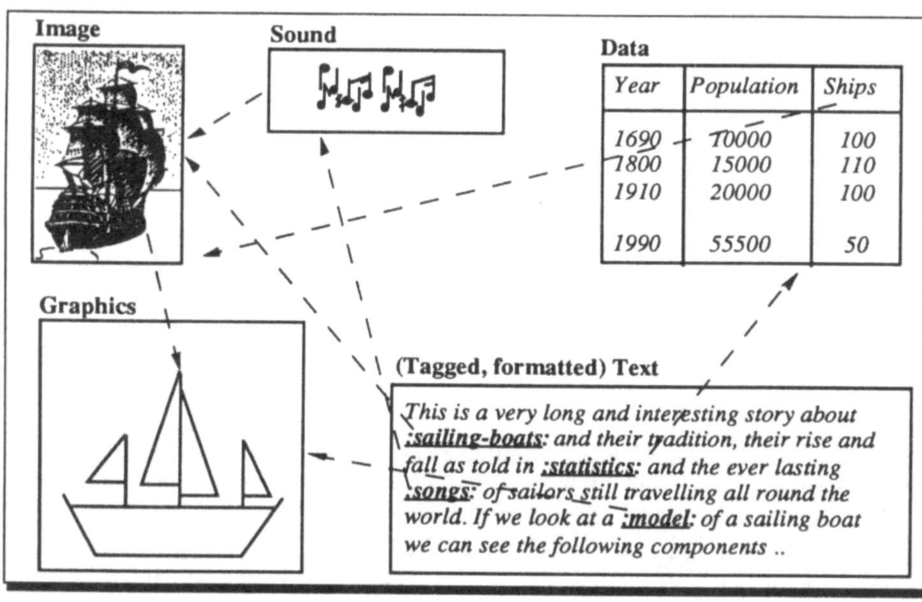

Fig. 13: Hypermedia Example

In addition to all the object and media specific characteristics, which have mainly been decisive in the case of pure multimedia databases, hypermedia databases attach special importance to the definition of associative relations between different objects. These relations may be implemented as traditional logical links (pointers, textual references) or they may profit by multimedia features (visual references, spoken references) which must be handled by appropriate database representation, indexing and retrieval techniques (Meyrowitz 1990, Paolino et al. 1990).

6.2 Hypermedia Database Requirements

The following requirements towards hypermedia databases are a representative summary of all the major keynotes emphasized in the previous sections.

- *Various, heterogeneous datatypes in the **same** database environment*
- *Complex and structured objects*
- *Non-textually coded, Binary Large OBjects (BLOBs)*
- *Formatted metafile information*
  (e.g. interpretable representation of graphical objects,
  fulltext with hypertext tags defining links, tagged hypermedia documents)
- *Objects related with operations and methods*
- *Support of various link-types between nodes*
  - ***implicit, logical, dynamic links (established, searched during run-time)***
    e.g. all text paragraphs containing word "sailor")
  - ***Explicit, physical, static, predefined links between related objects***
    (links between objects containing binary-coded, non-interpretable information)
- *Object and data type supporting, related query language*
- *Browsing and navigation tools for DB access*
- *Consistency and relation control when adding, deleting nodes*
  (e.g. detection of circularities, of dangling nodes)
- *Time-critical requirements*
  (e.g. synchronisation of sound with animations, image sequences)

Fig. 14: Hypermedia Database Requirements

6.3 Conclusion

All the database requirements, as stated in the preceding sections, are concepts which are required for the modelling of widely applicable and reusable multimedia and hypermedia databases. The concepts mentioned are not based on a specific database theory. Rather, they reflect foundations for a flexible model which defines general aspects of object representation for heterogeneous media within different, again heterogeneous application environments. The conceptual requirements expressed in this context can be satisfied and realized by appropriate mappings to existing relational (Meyer-Wegener et al.1988, Schütt and Streitz 1990) or object-oriented database systems.

Literature

IEEE COMPUTER SOCIETY (1987) *"Multimedia Systems"*. In: Proceedings of the IEEE Computer Society Office Automation Symposium, National Bureau of Standards, Gaitersburgh, MD, 27-29 April 1987. Computer Society Press of the IEEE, Washington, 1987. pp. 36-66, 180-204.

Klas, W., Neuhold, E.J., Schrefel, M., (1988) *"Visual Databases need Data Models for Multimedia Data"*. In: (Kunii 1989). pp. 433-462.

Kunii, T.L. ed. (1988) *"Visual Database Systems"*. Proceedings of the IFIP TC 2/WG 2.6 Working Conference on Visual Database Systems, Tokyo, Japan, 3-7 April 1989. North-Holland, 1989.

Lockemann, P.C. (1988) *"Multimedia Databases: Paradigm, Architecture, Survey and Issues"*. Interner Bericht Nr. 15/88, Fakultät für Informatik, Universität Karlsruhe, 1988.

Meyer-Wegener, K., Lum, V.Y., Wu, C.T. (1988) *"Image Management in a Multimedia Database System"*. In: (Kunii 1989); pp. 497-523.

Meyrowitz, N. (1990) *"Advanced Tutorial in Hypermedia Research"*. Documentation of the Tutorial at the first European Conference on Hypertext, ECHT'90, Versailles Nov 27-30, 1990.

Paolino, P., Caolini, A., Schwartz, R. (1990) *"Hypertexts and Databases"*. Documentation of the Tutorial at the first European Conference on Hypertext, ECHT'90, Versailles Nov 27-30, 1990.

Rhiner, M. (1991) *"Object Description and Representation for Visual and Multimedia Database Systems"*. (To appear) in: Proceedings of the 2nd IFIP WG 2.6 Working Conference on Visual Databases, Budapest, 1991. Elsevier Science Publishers B.V., Amsterdam, The Netherlands, 1991.

Schütt, H., Streitz, N. (1990) *"HyperBase: A hypermedia engine based on a relational data-base management system"*. In: Proceedings of the first European Conference on Hypertext, ed. A. Rizk et al., INRIA, France, November 1990. Cambridge University Press, Cambridge 1990. pp. 95-108.

Part VII

Systems

Chapter 20

A Transputer Based Multimedia System

Soo K. Chng and Mark J. Clark

Abstract

This paper presents the problems associated with multimedia interfaces for a network environment and proposes solutions to overcome them. The applications and characteristics of multimedia are discussed to provide a good understanding of the interface requirements for such systems. Transputers are applied as the parallel processing elements in a high performance multimedia system which provides an interface between the host system and the network to cater for the wide variety of traffic loads that the multimedia systems present.

1. Introduction to Multimedia Environment

As the processing power available for computation increases and the cost of the computer system decreases, it is becoming very attractive to incorporate multimedia within the computer environment. Many computer manufacturers are designing workstations to support multimedia with integral support for digital signal processing, audio capability, graphic accelerators, etc.

Multimedia will allow workstation users to communicate with each other using video and speech links. Workgroups will be able to share access to data comprising audio, graphics, video, hyper-media, etc. Workgroups may be located in the same building or separated by great distances. Multimedia stations will encourage home based working provided adequate communication infrastructures permit.

2. The Characteristics of Multimedia

To design a multimedia system, it is necessary to consider what makes multimedia different from conventional data communication. The answer is the varied requirements of the data which is to be transported and the factors associated with that transportation. Some of these factors are listed below:

- the delay that is acceptable to the media
- the bandwidth requirement for the media
- is the bandwidth requirement static or dynamic
- the error rate tolerable to each media
- the characteristics of the data, in particular the burstiness

Consider for example video which could require Mbs of bandwidth and would tolerate a few milliseconds of time delay, whilst in contrast, voice traffic would require less than 64kbs of bandwidth but is intolerant to delay.

It is not a trivial task for a system to determine the characteristics of the media it is handling, and provide services which can fully fulfil all the requirements. It is more practical to adopt a multimedia system which has processing elements to handle the multimedia. When communication come into consideration, it is not feasible to allow a separate network interface for each media, hence there is a need to investigate a sharing mechanism for the network interface in a multimedia system.

3. Network Services Requirements

The demands placed on the communications network for a multimedia system are much higher as compared to a conventional workstation of the 1980s. The multimedia system has to ensure that data is transmitted and received at the appropriate priority levels so as to minimise any delay. Conventional computer networks (such as Ethernet, Token Ring and etc.) were not designed to carry multimedia traffic. Fortunately, emerging networks such as DQDB[1], FDDI[2] or Orwell[3] tend to promise significant improvement of throughput and support for mixed traffic. In order to utilise the services offered by the network interface, the processing unit can no longer treat each media as a heterogeneous collection of data streams, but has to consider the different characteristics of each media.

A mixed traffic network that is required to support multimedia traffic should be able to support at least some of the following services:

- Isochronous traffic
  to handle data that require attention at fixed regular intervals.
- Priority services
  to handle media that require low delay and immediate attention.
- Asynchronous traffic
  to handle data that do not require synchronisation; this service class is suitable for data communication in a conventional workstation.
- Synchronous traffic
  to handle data that do not require services at fixed intervals, but need synchronisation mechanisms during the service.

The performance and capability of the interface between the media and the network plays an important role in a multimedia system. For example, voice data needs urgent attention as the frame interval approaches. A dynamic transportation approach is required since conventional protocols such as TCP/IP are inadequate due to the high processing overhead. A system that is designed to handle multimedia traffic has to be capable of guaranteeing the delivery of some of its data with a high priority level. This may seem trivial under the provisions of modern network interface which offers priority access, but unfortunately this is not true. Traffic at each priority level can queue on each of the priority services streams and the host processor would have to be responsible to dispatch the highest priority traffic to the network interface. For a network which does not offer sufficient buffering of data, such as DQDB, the buffering mechanism would have to be carried out by the system, which would result in a high overhead. Hence, an interface which could transparently handle the buffering and queuing of data on behalf of the host processor is needed.

As the performance of networks increases, there is an advantage of high bandwidth allocation to the user, but as the length of the network increases from a few km to a few hundred km, the latency (delay) of the network increases. Some of the modern networks tend to offer users a time slice for access which is very coarse, e.g. FDDI, only guarantees the waiting time for a user to access the network to fall within the interval of Token Rotation Time. The data produced by different media can have quite different frame intervals and hence it becomes necessary to buffer the data. See figure 1 & 2.

When a system is allocating network resources to a media, it cannot be based on a 'first come first serve' basis but has to base on the dynamic operating condition. For example, a system should prohibit a low priority media from continuously gaining access to the network service while a higher priority service is waiting to be serviced. Under such circumstances, when the system is servicing a particular media, it has to keep watching out for any new arriving request and always be prepared to give way when the later process has a higher priority. This introduces a high overhead and unnecessary multiplexing.

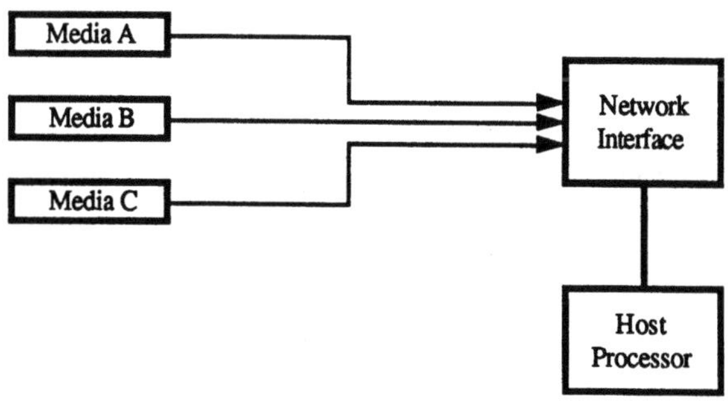

Fig. 1. Multimedia interface without queueing

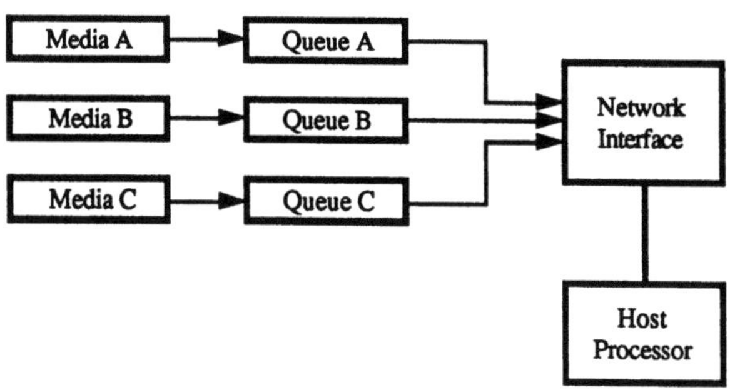

Fig. 2. Multimedia network interface with individual queue

The proposed interface to solve these problems allows each media to make its own requests to its own transputer control modules, and a master transputer would act as a scheduler on behalf of the host processor to schedule the transportation of the data. See figure 3. The scheduler can allocate the network resources according to the priority of each data. As a result, the schedule table is regularly updated such that it is possible to assume that the arrival of the most urgent services will comfortably wait until the next schedule interval. To ensure that urgent services are not being perturbed, the scheduler only allows a maximum number of resources to be allocated within each schedule table, thus in cases whereby lots of urgent services are active, services to low priority requests would not be guaranteed.

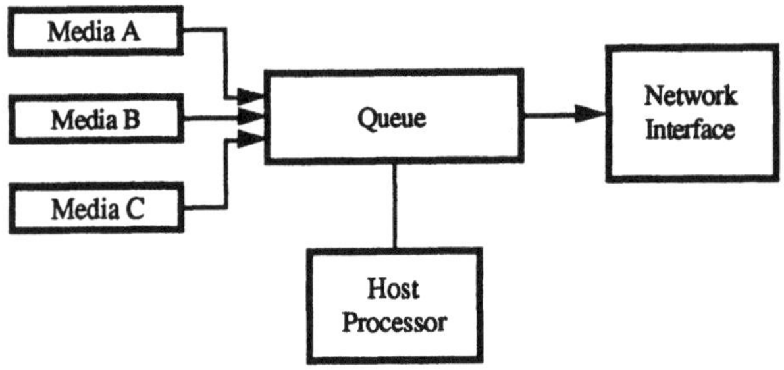

Fig. 3. Multimedia network interface with global queue

4. Problems in Dealing with Multimedia Network Interface

When building a multimedia system, it is possible that each media could be allocated a separate network interface[4], and allow the network interface to take care of the relative priorities of the multimedia. This would be a costly solution and it implies that there is little interaction between different media. A cost effective solution would be to allow multimedia to share a common network interface.

When integrating multimedia to a single network interface, data could either be buffered or unbuffered. If buffering is chosen, then a single global queue or multiple local queues could be used. However, regardless of the choice, there would be overheads in processing either in the host processor to maintain the single queue or on the network processor to decide which queue to service.

It is not difficult to realise that there are many potential problems in providing a network interface to a multimedia system. The main problems that we wish to address focus as follows:

- The handling of multimedia requests at the network interface.
- The allocation scheme of network resources to multimedia.
- The handling of transmission errors for different media.
- The buffering mechanism for different media
- The adaptation of the system to various existing network standards.

5. Parallel Multimedia Interface

The parallel multimedia interface proposed provides an architecture using transputers as an agent for data integration. See figure 4. The host workstation is only required to instruct the transputer unit to perform the necessary actions; hence the overhead on the host is minimal, enabling it to be free to provide computation necessary for a good user interface, or other processing functions. The transputers are responsible for dispatching data between the media processing system and the network interface and provide all the necessary adaptation (eg. sequencing error flow control) for the particular media.

The ideal implementation for the multimedia interface is to allow all the transputer modules to have common access to the data. But this requires the use of multi-port RAM and the number of transputer subsystems which could be connected will depend on the number of ports in the multi-port RAM.

The proposed implementation for the parallel multimedia interface, provides a direct shared communication path between the media processors and the network transputer. This allows first-in first-out memory (FIFO) to be used instead of multi-port RAM. The transputers are arranged to form a pipeline to handle controlling messages (see fig.1) by the use of transputer links. The proposed interface is more cost effective, and allows flexibility for expansion.

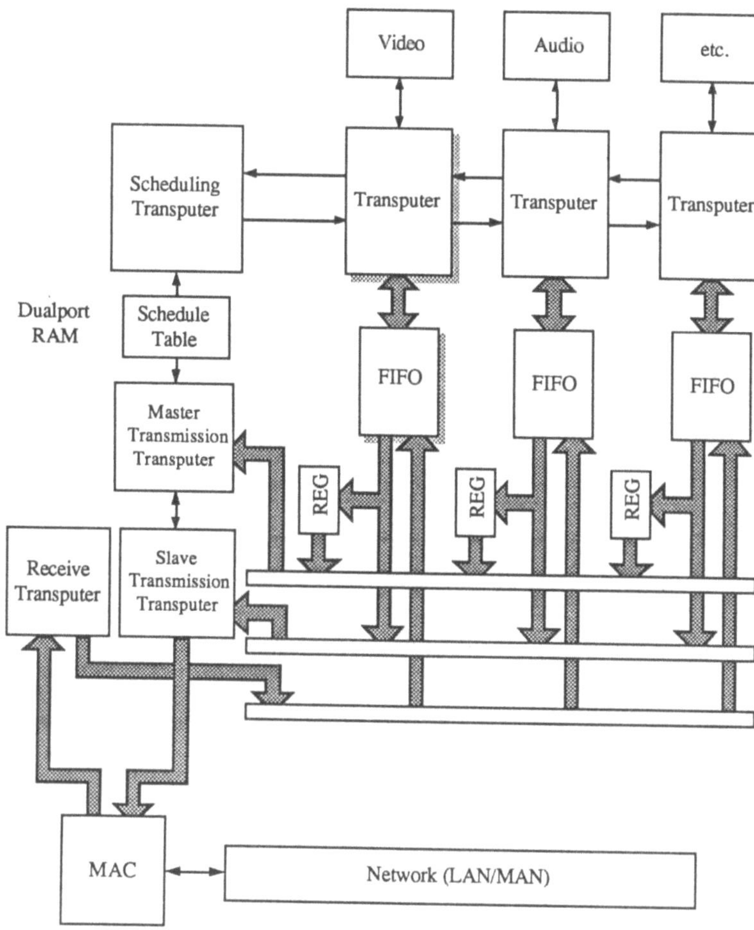

Fig.4. Parallel Multimedia System

In the control pipeline, each transputer signals to the scheduler to notify the state of FIFO and the types of traffic stored in it. Alternatively, this information could be registered in latches in order to allow the scheduling transputer to read them at any convenient time. The scheduler is responsible for generating a scheduling table which the network processor uses for the dispatching of the data. High priority services would be scheduled first, the remaining time slice would be allocated to less urgent services. With an efficient implementation of a scheduling algorithm, the system can perform a new schedule at every 1μs interval which would easily cope with a frame interval for voice (125μs) and other time critical applications. More importantly, the interface can provide multiple levels of services to a common network service without any buffer or queuing at the system or user levels.

The main advantage of using FIFO techniques is that while data is copied into one area of the memory, data in another area can be transmitted by the network processor. The use of FIFO memory in each transputer subsystem would allow data to be transported while the network interface is servicing a particular transputer subsystem. Hence at all times, the network processor would have data ready to be processed, and less time would be spent in waiting for data to be ready. The system can run at the maximum speed determined by the network interface, thus the speed of the transputer link does not limit the system performance because the control pipeline is dealing with relatively low amounts of communication as compared to that handled by a standard transputer switch implementation.

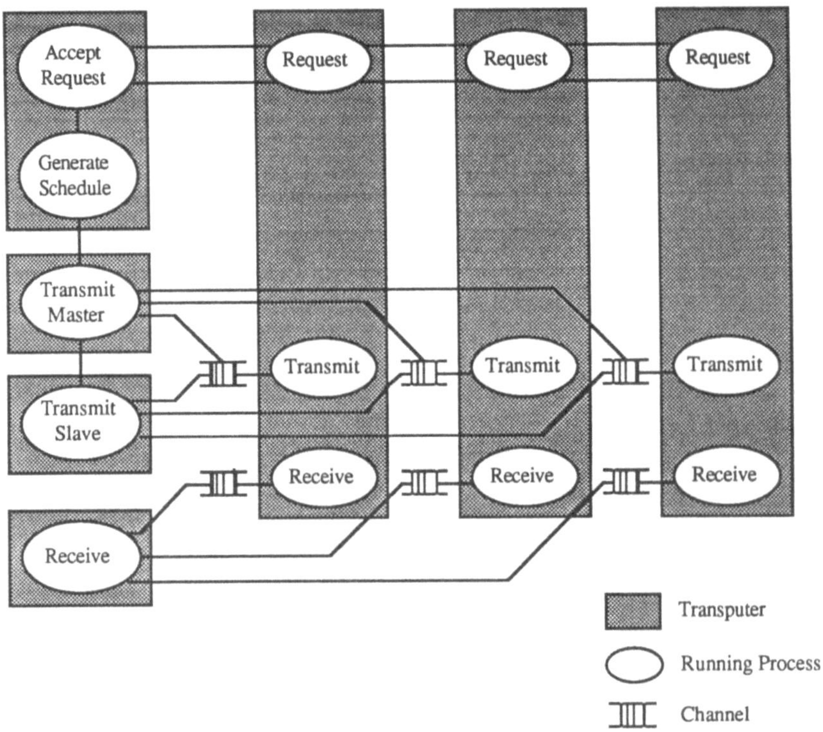

Fig 5. Processes on Parallel multimedia system

In the FIFOs, there is information indicating destination address or virtual communication port ID, user header and the actual data field. The data could be arranged to be packetised, so that it can conform to ATM[5] or FDDI format depending on the physical network being used. The flexibility of the data format in the data path improves the portability of the system. It is possible to chose a packet format which could adapt to various networks; protocols such as Multi Service Data Link (MSDL) [6] or ATM cell format are suitable because of its capability of supporting virtual communication channels.

Nevertheless, there is a disadvantage in the FIFO implementation, the sequential access nature of the FIFO makes the system difficult to handle error retransmission. The transputer channel has to request for a particular error packet from the sending process or processor, or the transputer node itself has to provide storage for the transmited data when an error occurs. This problem can be solved by the use of dual port RAM with additional logic gates to allow the dualport RAM to behave as an ordinary FIFO for normal access, but allow random access to the storage via a separate port.

The use of transputers allows multiple processes or threads to be executed in a single transputer node. See figure 5. Hence, it is possible to allocate one process for transmission, one for reception and an additional one for error handling if necessary. For media that requires a high bandwidth, it is also possible to combine multiple transputer modules to form a more powerful processing element.

Current transputers have a maximum data transfer rate in the region of 40 Mbyte/s, however, the new generation of transputers promises higher performance (5 to 10 times faster). Current transputers also offer a processor grain size of about 64μs which is very much faster than the frame interval of the network and the corresponding response required by most media. Therefore, transputers should be more than capable to handle most of the multimedia traffic.

6. Adaptation to Various Modern Multiservice Networks

There has been much discussion about modern multiservice networks. The parallel multimedia interface is intended to serve as a general interface block between the host and various networks. Let us consider some of them as the possible adaptable networks for our multimedia system:

- Orwell

  It is a packet network that is similar to Cambridge Fast Ring, a 100Mbs fast packet switch ring, but Orwell operates in destination release mode. The ring handles traffic in two stages, synchronous traffic (at 125ms) is being serviced before the asynchronous service. The parallel multimedia interface can be used to help to consolidate all the data of different kinds, and allows the scheduling of transmission of different traffic.
- DQDB

  It is a dual bus queueing network which provides 150Mbs per bus. It can support isochronous services based on pre-arbitrate access and asynchronous services at different priority levels under queue-arbitrate access. The parallel multimedia interface allows traffic of different types to select the appropriate priority services. Media that require isochronous services could make virtual connection to the isochronous service. It also allows each media to take full advantage of various services and allow the transparent sharing of network services. For example, a sub-band coded voice or video traffic could be routed via two different channels, where the channels could be separately handled by two transputers or two parallel processes running on a single transputer.
- CFR[7]

  based on slotted ring which provides fast packet switch at 100Mbs, does not provide provision in supporting prioritise service. The parallel multimedia interface can be used to manage the multimedia traffic by providing a priority queueing mechanism within the system.

For a network which does not provide error correction, the individual transputer can be used to perform error handling. Where errors do not matter, the particular transputer module may operate with the error handling mechanism disabled. This flexibility significantly improves the error handling mechanism for different media and minimises unnecessary retransmission.

Throughout the discussion, it had been assumed that the network interface always provides the required bandwidth for most urgent services. Nevertheless, under worst case considerations, it is possible for the network to be overloaded. Under such circumstances, the interface would ensure that higher priority data will be the first service irrespective of the backlog queue.

7. Conclusion

The parallel multimedia system has the capabilities of performing queuing, and providing prioritised services without the need for a global multiplexing scheme. The pipeline architecture in the system allows parallel processing to be performed which results in a very efficient implementation of the system. The use of transputers as individual multimedia processing elements allows the system to perform the appropriate error handling mechanism for each media. The application specific FIFOs can provide transparent sequential access and random access when required, with the additional advantage of providing a dynamically sizable buffer storage.

References

1. R.M.Newman, Z.L.Budrikis, J.L.Hullett, "The QPSX Man", IEEE Communication Magazine, Vol. 26, No. 4, Apr 1988, pp.20-29.
2. F.E.Ross, "An Overview of FDDI - The Fibre Distributed Data Interface", IEEE Journal on Selected Areas in Communications, Vol.7, No. 7, Sep 1989, pp.1043-1051.
3. R.M.Falconer, J.L.Adams,"Orwell: a Protocol for an Intergrated Services Local Network", British Telecom Technology Journal, Vol.7, No.7, Sep 1989, pp.1043-1051.
4. S.K.Chng & M.J.Clark "A Hyper Network For Multimedia System", Proceedings DECUS Europe Symposium, Cannes, France, 3-7 Sep 1990. pp.202-206.
5. M.J.Rider, "Protocols for ATM Access Networks", IEEE Network Magazine, Jan 1989, pp.17-22.
6. D.J.Greaves, I.D.Wilson, "Cambridge HSLAN Protocol Review", IFIP WG6.1/WG6.4 International Workshop on Protocols for High Speed Networks, Zurick, Switzerland, 9-11 May 1989. pp.257-268.
7. A.Hopper, R.M.Needham, "The Cambridge Fast Ring Networking System", IEEE Transaction on Computers, Vol.37, No.10, Oct 1988, pp.1214-1223.

Chapter 21

Managing Multimedia Resources in Process Control: Problems and Solutions

James L. Alty and Colin D.C. McCartney

Abstract: The case for using a multimedia approach when designing interfaces in process control rooms is put forward and some potential advantages outlined. In particular the distinction is drawn between conventional use of multimedia techniques in computer aided learning and the special problems of process control. The importance of the non-deterministic nature of process control operations is emphasised. This means that designers cannot be sure that devices will be available when needed so that alternative output mechanisms need to be provided. An immediate consequence of this is the necessity for a run-time media resource manager. The importance of synchronisation and concurrency are also stressed. The architecture of the PROMISE multimedia toolset is outlined.

1. Introduction

In recent years the role of the operator in process control has undergone an important change. There has been a major shift from the operator being a key element in the control loop to a new role as a plant supervisor and trouble shooter. In order to fulfil this role the operator must have a good high-level overview of the process and must be able to interact with higher level abstractions of the process. Furthermore, because of the inherent increased reliability of modern control systems resulting in far fewer incidents, operators are becoming less experienced in handling error conditions and therefore need access to a wider range of advisory facilities to assist them in their new role.

Process control advisory systems therefore need to provide more intelligent advice through the use of knowledge-based advisory systems using a higher bandwidth for communication. It is expected that the use of multiple media and parallel modes of interaction with the operator will offer an increased bandwidth for communication without a corresponding increase in operator information overload. Thus, the idea of providing a multimedia front-end to a knowledge based advisory system is an attractive one.

Single-media interfaces have already begun to show serious shortcomings in the new environment both in attention capture and in effective information display. It is likely that multimedia user interfaces will enable operators to reduce their cognitive overload by spreading information processing across different modal channels.

1.1 Terminology

In our terms a *Multimedia* interface involves multiple communication channels of the same or different modality, synchronised where appropriate. A *Multimedia Toolset* embraces an integrated collection of software modules using a knowledge based technology which will provides facilities for designing, creating, testing and delivering synchronised, concurrent and flexible multimedia user interfaces.

There seems to be no agreement over the terms medium, modality and channel, indeed, there is currently much controversy on this issue (Edwards, 1990). For example the differences between a multimedia interface and a multimodal interface are not clear. Breuker (1989) commented that multimedia and multimodality might be distinguished in the following manner

> "One can say that graphs and text are different media because their lexicon, syntax and pragmatics are completely different. It is not so easy to say that written and spoken language are different media however. Unless their lexicon, syntax and pragmatics are

all different they differ only with respect to channel i.e. mode of processing. Icons or graphs can only be presented in a visual mode but they are different media: these media can be combined easily. ...The distinction between medium and channel may look clean but there are many unresolved issues. "

Therefore, in the absence of any agreed standard definitions, this paper will arbitrarily adopt certain definitions for these terms. The following definitions may be assumed from now on:

Channel	The human sense used to perceive and communicate information, i.e. olfactory, taste, auditory, tactile and visual. Currently only auditory, tactile and visual channels are available to the user interface.
Media	The substance or agency by which information is conveyed to the user and vice-versa. Thus a medium implies a syntax for the interaction.
Mode	The style or nature of the interaction between the user and the computer which may be action-based (i.e. direct manipulation) or language-based (menu or command language).

It is important to note that the boundary between media and mode is very ill defined. For example, is natural language a mode of communication and text and speech different media for the transmission of natural language ? Are text and speech in themselves different modes of communication and the display and loudspeaker their underlying media ? Clearly no consensus on these issues exist other than the general hypothesis that a mode of interaction must be supported by one medium of communication. However, where *media* stops and *mode* begins will not be specified and, indeed, appears to be of little practical relevance.

1.2 What Advantages Could a Multimedia Interface Offer ?

Human beings communicate over a much wider bandwidth than that currently being offered by computer interfaces. We use voice, gesture, vision and tactile channels often in combination. Imagine the problem of explaining a complex diagram to someone. It would be much more powerful to have an explanation using highlighting (and possibly animation) on the diagram coupled with a voice explanation rather than text on the diagram. This allows the eye to see the important aspects of the diagram whilst simultaneously appreciating the auditory explanation. Communication using the same channel tends to result in degradation because different information sources are competing for the same channel. Different channels (such as the eye and the ear) can often operate simultaneously.

There is not a great deal of information in the literature on the benefits of a multimedia approach but it is generally agreed that an improvement in comprehension should result where multimedia are used appropriately. One important point however is that our approach should be user-centred rather than technology-centred. The important question is not "what can we do with multimedia technology ?" but rather "what might a user want to do with multimedia technology ?". Too much current exploitation of multimedia sytems tends to provide answers to the former question. This issue is discussed in more detail in (Alty, 1991).

1.3 Multimedia Support for Non-Deterministic Processes

Most multimedia ideas grew out of work in computer education. The educational multimedia approach involves the use of videocomputers, interactive television, and electronic books to provide a richer educational environment. It is envisaged that a user will be able "to browse through vast libraries of text, audio and visual information" (Ambron 1988). These libraries will be highly interlinked using a technique known as "Hypermedia" a concept developed from Hypertext which was first defined in the 1960's and led to the Xanadu system (Nelson 1981). Most of the current literature about multimedia approaches derives from the educational sector.

These educational applications tend to be activated by the learner alone where the user of the multimedia system is in complete control. For example, in Computer Aided Learning the information presented by the multimedia system is controlled via fixed courseware. The sequence in which the information is accessed may differ, but the information content of the interaction is known in advance by the system designer. Hence, the designer of the multimedia system can design the information presentation format in such a way that media channel conflicts (such as two voices simultaneously) will not arise.

In contrast the process control environment places extremely demanding requirements on the architecture of a multimedia presentation system.

- The operator may be engaged in many distinct tasks simultaneously, for example monitoring, tracking alarms etc..

- New tasks and hence interactions, may be instigated at any time by either system or operator.

- The process state may be extremely dynamic so information may need to be presented rapidly and in a form which is readily understood by the operator.

The designer of a user interface cannot know in advance what combinations of multimedia resources might be required. The problem may therefore be thought of as a resource management problem.

2. The PROMISE Project

The overall objective of the PROMISE project is the design, construction and evaluation of a multimedia toolset for:

> " improving user interfaces to advisory and diagnostic expert systems used by single operators in process control environments ".

The PROMISE System is multimedia, as it supports many ways of communicating information, and multimodal, as many styles of interaction are supported. The system will support of a number of multimedia options (Alty et al 1990) including:

- Text, Graphics and Sound output
- Full Colour
- Video Output
- Text and Mouse input
- Two and Three-dimensional Animation.
- Unmediated Video and Audio.
- Natural language Output.

The multimedia approach will be examined in two distinct types of environment which will help us in evaluation - a real-time application and a simulated one. The real environment puts serious constraints on the evaluation environment since the clock cannot be stopped, and unanticipated events can occur. Such an environment also poses other problems from an evaluation standpoint. Errors cannot be deliberately introduced or reproduced and controlled experiments are difficult. Therefore a simulated environment where we can control the nature of the upsets and monitor operator performance will also be used. The two application areas chosen are control of a chemical plant (DOW Netherlands) and the use of power station simulators (Scottish Power).

3. The Initial PROMISE M4I (Multimedia Man Machine Interface) Presentation Architecture

There were a number of key goals which the design of the PROMISE multimedia presentation system had to meet:

- Application Independence. The goal of the PROMISE project is a multimedia toolset for both knowledge based systems and process control systems. Therefore, the presentation system must be independent of the underlying application (although the problems of process control will obviously be taken into account).
- Exploitation of the potential of multiple media and modes of communication. The presentation system must be able to exploit the potential of multimedia and multimodal interaction with the user. This potential will take a number of forms including increasing the bandwidth of communication, reducing cognitive overload by presenting information in the most acceptable way, increasing redundancy by providing multiple views of data etc.
- Support of multiple interaction styles. As the presentation system is to be application independent it is not possible to identify a single style of interaction which will be universally suitable. Instead, the presentation system must be able to support multiple interaction styles with the most appropriate being used for a particular domain, i.e. direct manipulation, menu driven, conversational, hypercard etc.

Figure 1 illustrates the high level architecture of the PROMISE system as it currently stands in terms of its functional components and their relationships.

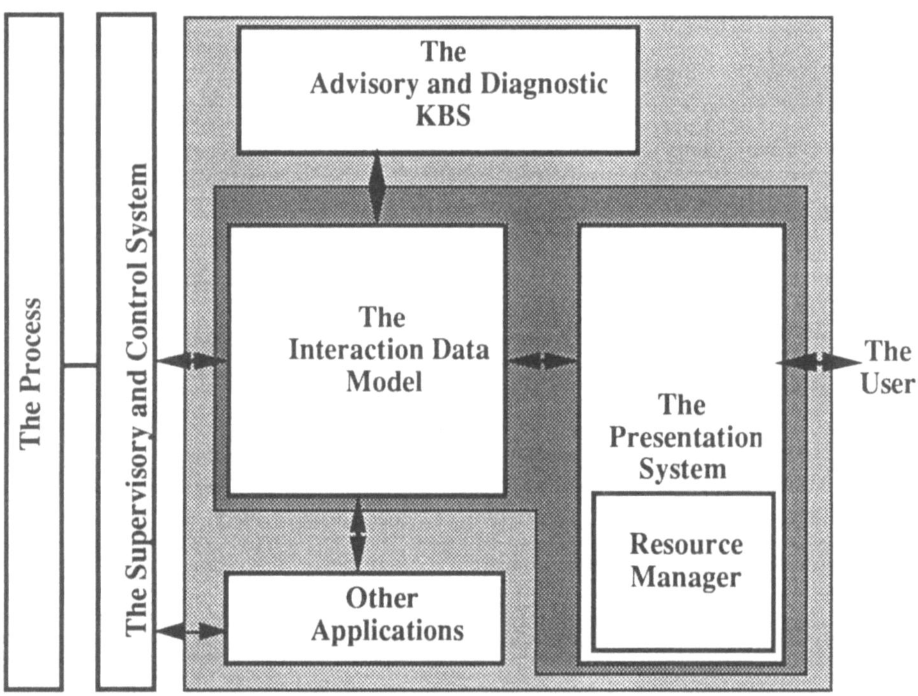

Fig. 1 High Level Architecture of the PROMISE System

This initial architecture involves the following major components - the Supervisory and Control System (SCS), the Interaction Data Model (IDM) and the Presentation System (incorporating the Resource Manager). These components interface with the Knowledge based Advisory System which provides assistance to the operator for certain tasks required to control the process.

3.1 The Supervisory and Control System (SCS)

The Supervisor and Control System (hereafter called SCS) component represents the existing process control software/hardware system. The data and events (e.g. alarms) produced by the SCS will be supplied to the Advisory/Diagnosis knowledge-based system (via the Interaction Data Model) which is in charge of the analysis of the process state. All operator process control input actions are handled by separate input controls (e.g. switches, toggles and other control equipment). This means that the M^4I Toolset can display meaningful system states but that overall control of the process is independent of the M^4I Toolset.

3.2 The Interaction Data Model

This system filters and accumulates raw data received from the SCS. It selectively cuts down the data flow from the process and updates client modules which have expressed an interest in certain process variables. It will contain a plant model of the relevant parts of the process. The main function of the IDM, however, is to describe, set up and maintain links between all components of the PROMISE system for general purpose communication and consistency maintenance. It also maintains consistency between application entities and their presentation on the user interface. This is particularly important in the multimedia situation because the same application data may be represented in many different ways and it is essential that all media views are consistent.

3.3 The Advisory / Diagnostic Knowledge Base

The Advisory/Diagnosis Knowledge Base system(s) is a key component of the system in giving the operator an overall view of the running process and in providing support during events analysis and fault diagnosis. When activated (either by the operator or by particular conditions of the process state) the system will try to relate events (e.g. alarms) to the current state of the process (e.g. the value of a subset of the process variables) with the goals of evaluating possible relations between alarms and predicting long term fault conditions.

The results of the reasoning activity of the expert system and their explanation will be provided to the operator via the M^4I toolset. We foresee a substantial use of interfacing techniques involving more than one interaction media, such as speech, animation, unmediated video and audio and graphics to convey the results produced by expert systems.

3.4 The Presentation System

The presentation system component is in charge of both the actual execution of the display requests coming from the other sub-systems, and the dispatching of operator requests. It is responsible for concurrent, synchronised multimedia input and output using abstract multimedia objects. It essentially consists of toolkit-based objects for different media, a media resource manager and a synchronisation mechanism.

Multimedia output scenarios are realised by the presentation server. Output scenarios are built using inputs from a library of template toolkit and scene classes (Toolkit and Scene Class Library). A scene is a collection of synchronised output sequences possibly involving more than one output media. The resource manager resolves conflicts in media resource utilisation by providing appropriate alternatives to presentation objects.

The resource manager consults a User Preferences Data Base (which contains a collection of default interaction preferences for both stereotypical users and defined groups of users) and a more general M4I Knowledge base to assist it in allocation decisions.

4. Media Resource Allocation and Management

4.1 The Resource Allocation Problem

The multimedia presentation system component must be concurrent in nature. Concurrency is essential for the following reasons,

- The presentation system must be able to cope with multiple, simultaneous interactions and asynchronous requests for new interactions from both user and system.

- Currently no true multimedia workstations exist. Instead, general purpose workstations have to be augmented with various external media devices residing on their own CPU's. Therefore, the presentation system has to be able to manage and synchronize the concurrent operation and output of these external devices.

- Concurrency is extremely useful in a multimedia presentation system. Many aspects of such a system are naturally concurrent in nature such as animation, rapid update of multiple displays, synchronized speech / sound and animation / video.

The presentation system must tackle the problem of resource allocation and management. It has a number of jobs (interactions), competing with one another for a limited set of resources (physical communication devices) to achieve some goal (effective communication between the system and the user). Viewed in this way the problem faced by the presentation system is very similar to that of the more general problem class of scheduling. However, one important difference exists, it appears very undesirable, in the majority of cases, for the presentation system to make use of temporal scheduling since interactions requested by the user or system are expected to take place immediately and not be rescheduled to some later point in time due to resource constraints.

The solution to this problem comes from a consideration of the properties of a multimedia. One of the powerful aspects of such a system is the ability to perform the same interaction in many different modes. This recognition of alternative media and modes of communication is the key to the solution of the resource management problem. If the resource manager cannot allocate a necessary resource for a particular interaction it may select an alternate media or mode for use by that interaction. However, certain modes are far more appropriate for a given interaction than others. If the resource manager simply selects resources on availability criteria then the results from the user perspective are almost certainly going to be very poor. Therefore, the resource manager must ensure that all required interactions take place by selecting available resources to satisfy each interaction's requests, in each case maximizing user comprehension.

To enable the resource manager to select resources on the basis of their appropriateness, it is obvious that certain constraints must be placed both on the external clients of the presentation system. The requirements are as follows,

- External clients of the presentation system must provide, in addition to the actual information to present and responses required, contextual information describing the nature and purpose of the interaction (Interaction Context).

- The designer of the presentation system must specify the characteristics of each available resource (device). For instance, which types of interaction a device is suitable for. (Device Characteristics)

- The presentation system itself must maintain, or have access to, a database of user preferences. For instance, which modes or media are prefered for which types of interaction. (User Preferences Data Base)

Furthermore, in order to be able to use the information detailed above to select resources, the presentation system must embody some form of knowledge of principles of the good use of multiple media and modes for performing interactions. This knowledge will be used to drive the resource allocation process and will be central to the resource manager.

4.2 The Importance of Designer Guidance

The necessity of a multimedia / multimodal presentation system having an intelligent, dynamic resource manager at its heart has been recognised before (for example in the Multimodal Response Planner (Gargan et al, 1988)). The goal of this Multimodal Response Planner was to provide a fully automatic and adaptive user interface system which derived from first principles the base modality of information from a semantic description of that information and a technique suitable for the presentation in that modality. In performing this task, the response planner made extensive use of knowledge of multimedia presentation and user models.

Such an architecture, where the presentation system takes all decisions on media and mode and automatically generates presentations based on user models is obviously attractive. However, a great many problems exist in implementing such a system. Even if such a system was feasible with current technology it is certain that, due to the extremely complex job of the underlying knowledge based system, the resulting system's performance would be completely unacceptable, particularly in real-time domains.

A different approach is thus proposed for PROMISE. In the PROMISE System the user interface designer must still design an interaction, give the media and modes to be used, the spatial and temporal organization of the interaction, the style of the interaction etc. However, in order that conflicts may be resolved between the media requirements of different interactions and that explicitly stated user preferences and device availability be considered the designer may specify alternative media or modes of communication for the interaction. The resource manager, therefore, becomes a designer support system whose function is to select between the alternatives specified by the designer. Because the resource manager is a support system for, rather than a replacement of, the designer, the success of the interface is the responsibility of the designer.

The priorities of the resource manager are thus as follows,

- To ensure each interaction is allocated sufficient resources in order that it may perform its function.
- To ensure that, where alternative resource allocations are possible, an allocation which maximizes user comprehension is selected.

It is inevitable that, in certain cases, the resource manager will be unable to satisfy the resource requirements of an interaction. No matter how many alternatives the designer specifies it cannot be guaranteed that one will be available. In such a case the interaction is said to be unrunnable, i.e. unable to perform its interaction. There are two possible courses of action for dealing with unrunnable interactions. The presentation system may simply discard the interaction or it may put the interaction to sleep until the necessary resources become available. However, both strategies are highly undesirable as the presentation of critical information may simply not take place or be postponed until it is no longer relevant. The solution to the unrunnable interaction problem proposed for the PROMISE presentation system is quite simple, the designer must specify an alternative resource which will always be available for allocation.

5. The Resource Management Process

The resource manager's goal is not simply to allocate resources to ensure that all interactions may run, but to allocate the various media and mode resources in order to maximise user comprehension of the interaction. Obviously, due to the nature of this task, a simple resource management strategy such as maximizing resource usage, is not sufficient. Instead, some more sophisticated, knowledge based, resource management strategy must be adopted by the resource manager.

Moreover, the problem faced by the Resource Manager may be thought of as a special case or sub-problem of the problem of intelligent, dynamic scheduling (Burke, 1988)(Burke et al, 1989) where the only temporal constraint that applies is that all jobs must run immediately. Several strategies current in scheduling appear to offer interesting approaches to the resource management problem. Two of the most important are Heuristic Rule Based Production and Constraint Satisfaction.

It is important that reallocation of currently used resources should occur only in rare circumstances. For the majority of the time a client should continue using the same resource throughout its lifetime. This has an important consequence for the Resource Manager. It is not acceptable to simply compute an entirely new set of resource allocations for each client every time a new request is made. Instead, the Resource Manager must consider the consistency of each client when considering resource allocation. Methods for integrating considerations of consistency into the heuristics or constraints of the Resource Manager will have to be found.

5.1 Heuristic Rule Based Production System

This approach employs the conventional A.I. approach of a state space search being guided by domain dependent and domain independent heuristics. In the resource management domain the state space is the set of all possible resource allocations, a set of rules would be used to determine legal resource allocations and the heuristics would embody information describing both general principles of good multimedia / multimodal presentation and information describing the specific characteristics of the problem domain. However, almost nothing is known about what constitutes the successful use of multiple media and modes of communication with the user. Hence, it is extremely difficult to specify any heuristics or constraints which may be successfully employed to drive a resource management system. Considerable further research and particularly prototyping is essential in order to derive further knowledge on this subject.

5.2 Constraint Satisfaction

In this approach a set of constraints is used to describe the legal allocations of resources to jobs and a general purpose constraint satisfaction system may be employed to satisfy these constraints. Constraints may be specified which describe many characteristics of multimedia resource allocation problems. For example, which devices conflict with one another, which devices are excluded by user preferences etc. In addition, due to the dynamic nature of the scheduling problem, a truth maintenance system may be employed to reduce the amount of work necessary when conditions are modified.

5.3 An Initial Approach

For the initial phase of the project at least, a heuristic rule-based approach will be adopted as the core of the resource management strategy. The mapping from the Resource manager to conventional AI terminology is as follows:

- A state is defined as a full or partial allocation of resources to the set of interactions. Hence the allocation of a resource to a particular interaction creates a new state.

- The intitial state is the state where all interactions in the system have no resources allocated and all resources on the system are unallocated.

- A goal state is a complete allocation of resources to interactions such that all interactions in the system have sufficient resources to run. Normally there will be many goal states, however some will be far more desirable than others.

- A rule defines a media resource which is a sensible selection for an interaction. By specifying many rules for the same interaction the choices of media for an interaction are defined. For example, the two extremely simple rules given below declare that an interaction using the high level resource Verbal can make use of the low level resource Speech or the low level resource Text.

  Resource(verbal) :- Resource (speech).
  Resource(verbal) :- Resource(text).

It is important to note that some rules are declared explicitly by the designers of media resources and some are implicit across all resources. For example, default rules exist to handle circumstances where none of the declared resources are available. Furthermore, rules may specify not only simple logical exclusive ORs of resources but also logical ANDs i.e. resource (A) AND resource(B) , and logical inclusive ORs i.e. resource(A) OR resource (B) OR resource(A) AND resource(B)

The resource management strategy consists of a simple forward reasoning, depth first search through the state space. However, as the state space may be very large and a better than-worst-case goal is being searched for, the Resource Manager must make use of heuristics supplied by the Multimedia Knowledge base to guide the search. In the initial system the heuristics take the form of rules to guide the selection of the most appropriate rule (Resource) to apply, and a heuristic evaluation function which returns a measure of how effective a given resource allocation is.

This heuristic function matches the Interaction Context attributes against the Resource Characteristics of a proposed resource, representing the closeness of a match by a numeric quantity. The various attribute matches are then multiplied by weights giving the relative importance of the various attributes. These weighted values are then summed and the resulting quantity rating describes the relative effectiveness of that resource allocation.

Figure 2 represents a simple example of a hierarchy of logical devices in the presentation system. The example represents a simple program which displays information to the user either textually in a text window or aurally via a speech synthesizer. In either case a window is also displayed to allow the user control over the application.

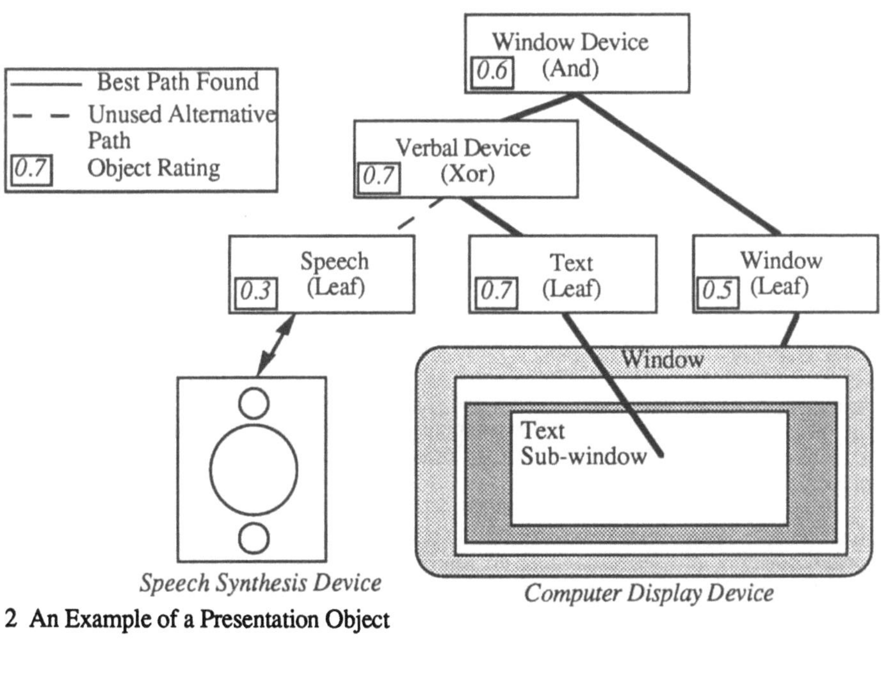

Fig. 2 An Example of a Presentation Object

It can be seen that at the lowest level of the hierarchy we have objects which communicate directly with physical devices, such objects are called *leaf* objects. In this example there are three leaf objects, a speech leaf connecting to the speech synthesizer, a text leaf connecting to a text sub-window and a window leaf connecting to a window. Above these leaf objects in the hierarchy are two media grouping objects, an XOR object, Verbal Device, which is used to specify an abstract device which uses either speech or text as a means of communicating with the user. As the verbal device can only select one of the speech leaf or text leaf it is an exclusive OR of these two leafs, hence, it is an XOR object. At the top of hierarchy is a logical device which combines the verbal device with a window. As this object needs both the verbal device and the window simultaneously this object is an AND object.

The diagram also shows the ratings attached to each object by the evaluation function. It is important to note that only the leaf objects have ratings generated by the evaluation function. Node objects such as XOR and AND derive their ratings from their child objects. The rules used to derive node values are simple, an XOR object takes the maximum value of all child objects, whereas, an AND object takes the average of all child objects (this is different than in other conventional approaches). In the example, it can be seen the the verbal device has a child with rating 0.3 and another with rating 0.7. As the Verbal Device is an XOR object it takes the maximum value of its children and hence has a value of 0.7. The Window Device, on the other hand, is an AND object and, therefore, takes the average of its child values, in this case 0.5 and 0.7, yielding a rating of the Window Device of 0.6. It is clear from this description how the best path through the hierarchy is selected, in this case the text sub-window and its parent window.

5.4 The M4I Knowledge Base

The Resource Manager must have certain knowledge describing which kind of media / mode logical devices (resources) are useful for the various types of interaction. This knowledge will be used by the Resource Manager to allocate media / mode resources to competing clients. No base of knowledge exists which we can use directly for this purpose so the initial contents of the knowledge base will be a set of heuristic rules derived pragmatically from any existing research work, *"common sense"* heuristics, system requirements, user consultation and existing project experience. It is also certain that the initial rules will have to be revised, replaced and added to by an extensive process of prototyping and further investigation throughout the life of the project and beyond. However, the current state of research in multimedia makes such an approach inevitable.

6. Presentation Synchronization

The synchronization problems associated with multimedia presentation systems are essentially concerned with the synchronization of the various multimedia input and output channels. From the users perspective, the output of these media devices may be related to each other in some way (i.e. generated speech describing the nature of a system being animated on a display) or unrelated (i.e. a voice channel being activated asynchronously to notify the operators of an alarm condition while an animation of some process is performed on a display).

The rate of output from the multimedia presentation system devices may also be hardware dependent. For example, the speed at which a three dimensional animation is carried out depends on the hardware that is being utilized and on any other load on the animation's host machine. Any change to the hardware or load will alter the duration of the animation. Furthermore, any modification to the interface generated by the presentation system may also highly affect the duration of output. For example, the duration of a passage of spoken text is dependent on the text itself, and if the text of a spoken description is altered, the duration of the speech output will inevitably change.

A time line based approach to synchronization (Christodoulakis et al., 1988) would not solve the synchronization problem since such an approach is both hardware and interface dependent. A better approach is to allow the output of each medium to be handled by a concurrent process.

The synchronization process is therefore the coordination of these concurrent processes. The main goal of such a synchronization mechanism is to allow the division of the output of the multimedia Presentation System into appropriate fragments and then to synchronize the output of these media fragments to their corresponding output channels (Sventek, 1987). In this way, multiple simultaneous media channels may be synchronized.

6.1 Multimedia Synchronization

The output of a multimedia system can be viewed as the sequential progression of several concurrent processes which are grouped in such a way that their output represents some specific information. We call such a group a *Scene*. The process whose sequential progression represents the output of a particular strand of information is called a *Sequence*. The smallest, identifiable step in each sequence is a typed entity called a *Segment*. Each segment is an atomic unit of information represented by some media.

In order to synchronize the progression of the sequences we introduce a metaphor called a *Gate*. Gates are abstract barriers controlling the progression of a scene's sequences. Each gate is known by a unique identifier. Sequences which wish to synchronize at some point utilize a gate by referring to that gate's unique identifier. On arrival at a gate, a sequence must wait until all other sequences synchronizing on that gate reach it. In this way sequences are synchronized in a time independent way.

There is a synchronization problem associated with termination of scenes. How does one terminate a scene while it is still in progress ? Immediate termination of a scene by simply killing the various sequences is not desirable. Consider the case where a particular display is playing a scene which has speech output (generated in a separate hardware unit). It may prove possible to terminate the other output channels of the scene but not the speech output as it is already being performed by an external CPU not under the direct control of the host machine. In which case certain portions of the scene continue to some indefinite point in the interaction while other portions terminate immediately producing confusion and a lack of synchronization. In order to achieve this a further entity is introduced, the *Mark*. Marks ensure that the termination of a scene is deferred until the progression of all sequences have reached a predefined point of sensible termination, i.e. a mark. These ideas are schematically represented in figure 3.

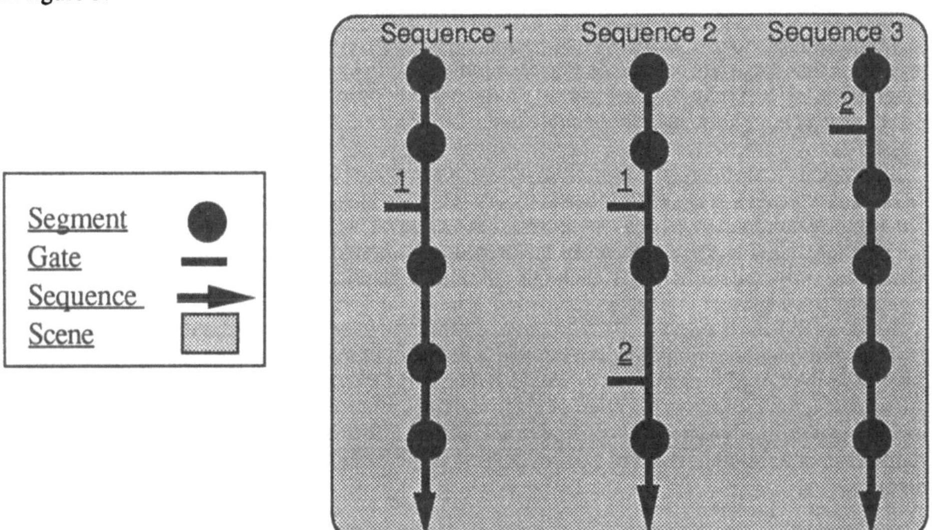

Fig. 3 Concurrency Objects

Another problem occurs when the resource manager reallocates resources to clients whose interactions contain scenes. It cannot simply reallocate a resource at any time as this will result in problems similar to those of scene termination. The solution to this problem is again found with the concept of a mark. Rather than simply reallocating a resource immediately, the resource manager will send a message to the scene which currently owns the resource to be reallocated. The resource manager then waits for an acknowledgement from the scene before performing the reallocation. The scene receiving the notification of resource reallocation from the resource manager may send the acknowledgment immediately, if the loss of the resource would not cause confusion or a loss of synchronization, or more probably it may defer the acknowledgement of reallocation until it reaches a predefined mark.

7. Object Handling in the Presentation System

At the heart of the Presentation System lies the presentation server. This sub-system is an Object Oriented Data Base containing all presentation objects currently used for communication with the user. Each object in the presentation server is an abstract presentation object. However, these abstract presentation objects can fall into a number of classes,

- Logical Device
  A logical device is a presentation object which provides some high level of abstraction of input and / or output to the user.

- Scene
  A scene is a presentation object which defines temporal organization of and synchronization of other presentation objects (these were already discussed in the previous section) .

- Geometry Manager
  A geometry manager is a presentation object which defines the spatial organization of other presentation objects on a display.

- Interaction
  An interaction is the highest level presentation object manipulated by an external client of the presentation system.

It is important to note, however, that the classes given above are not exclusive, i.e. a single presentation object may fall into one, more than one or all of the above categories. An important property of the abstract presentation objects, deriving from their nature as logical devices, is that they may be used as interface building blocks. One or more existing presentation objects may be combined to produce a new object. This new object will produce a further abstraction of the interaction and so on.

In object oriented design terminology the logical devices of the presentation system form a *class hierarchy*. At the top of this hierarchy lies a class which represents information and functionality common to all devices. Beneath this class come the sub-classes of the device class representing actual physical devices of the presentation system. The remainder of the hierarchy is made of a collection of classes, each one sub-classing and inheriting from one of the physical devices or from another logical device.

In addition to inheriting functionality and information for a device from that device's super-class, the sub-classed logical devices will also inherit the *characteristics* of the parent class. The device characteristics are a collection of class variables representing the capabilities of the device. As previously stated, this device characteristic information is used by the Resource Manager in determining which of a set of devices is the most suitable for performing a given interaction.

The sub-classed logical devices are not, however, limited to simple inheritance of their super-class's characteristics. They may also override the characteristics of the parent class or classes and include characteristics which may interfere with other devices. Hence, the Resource Manager will avoid allocating logical devices for simultaneous use which conflict. A logical device may also be allowed to override certain of the characteristics of its parent device.

7.1 The Presentation Object Hierarchy

The presentation object hierarchy describes the relationship between the various abstract presentation objects used for particular interactions. There are likely to be many hierarchies contained within the Presentation Server, one for each current interaction. For example, at the top of a hierarchy may be an abstract presentation object representing a window. Under the window object there may be a number of geometry management objects, each of which is used to group a number of button objects etc. This is a very simple example as it does not include objects for temporal or media / mode grouping. Nevertheless, it shows the basic structure of the presentation object hierarchies.

The principle use of the presentation object hierarchy, in addition to the obvious one of keeping track of which object belong to which other objects, will be for the dissemination of interaction context information. In a similar fashion to the Logical Device Class Hierarchy, each presentation object will inherit its context information from its parent object and be able to override portions of the context information if necessary. This has the notable advantage that a client of the presentation system need only specify context information for the top-level presentation object it opens. Any sub-objects created by that top-level object will simply inherit the context information supplied by the parent object.

It is important to note that presentation objects are, in fact, members of both hierarchies, i.e. each presentation object is an instance of a logical device class and also part of a hierarchy of presentation objects. Therefore, each object has the device characteristics of its device class and a presentation context at least partially derived from its parent objects.

8. Implementation

Initial prototyping on the Multimedia Resource Manager appears promising and a full system implementation is currently under way. The full system is being built on SUN Workstations using the HyperNeWS (Van Hoff ,1989) interactive user interface developent environment, C++ and Sun Common Lisp.

The resulting system will, when implementation is complete, undergo extensive testing and evaluation in both a Nuclear Power Station simulator and a live Chemical Plant.

9. Conclusions

The problems of supporting multimedia communication between an operator and a process information system in a non-deterministic process control application have been described. The outline of a mechanism for supporting knowledge based management of multimedia presentation systems in such applications has been presented. This system is under active development for use in actual process control applications.

It is hoped that the resulting system will offer tangible benefits both to operators (in terms of improved comprehension of process information) and designers (in terms of assistance in producing high quality multimedia process information systems).

10. Acknowledgements

There are many other people who have contributed to this design, in particular Massimo Zallocco provided many of the ideas for the IDM design and offered much valuable assistance towards the general design. The research described in this paper is funded as part of the European Community ESPRIT II programme. project 2397 (PROMISE), and we are grateful for this support.

11. References

Alty J.L., De Winter M., Dell'Olmo P., and Zallocco M., (1989), D2 - Interface Definition for First M4I Toolset (PRO/6), Deliverable No. 2, Esprit Project 2397.

Alty, J.L., (1991), "Multimedia: What is it and how do we exploit it ?", Keynote Address in Proc. HCI'91, (Edinburgh), published by Cambridge University Press, (to appear), or in LUTCHI Report No. 0110, available from the Author at the Dept. of Computer Studies, University of Loughborough, Leics. U.K.

Ambron, S., (1988), What is Multi-media ? In: Interactive Multi-media, S. Ambron, and K. Hooper, (eds.), Microsoft Press, Washington, USA, pp 5.

Baecker, R.M., and Buxton, W.A.S., (1987), "A Historical and Intellectual Perspective", Readings in Human-Computer Interaction; a Multidisciplinary Approach", Morgan Kaufmann, pp 41 - 54.

Breuker, J., (1989), Private Communication

Burke, P., (1988), Scheduling in a Dynamic Environment, IKBS in Production Control and Manufacturing, Research Report, University of Strathclyde, pp10, AISL - 38/35/37.

Burke, P., Prosser, P., (1989), A Distributed Asynchronous System for Predictive and Reactive Scheduling, Research Report, University of Strathclyde, pp1-9, AISL -42-89,.

Christodoulakis,S. and Graham,S., (1988), Browsing Within Time-Driven Multi-media Documents, Office Information Systems, Conference Proceedings, Palo Alto, California, 23-25 March, 1988. ACM, pp.219 - 227.

Edwards, A. D. N., (1990), Multi-what ?, Position Paper, CHI'90 Workshop on Multi-media and Multi-modal Interface Design.

Gargan, R.A., Sullivan, J.W. and Tyler, S.W., (1988), Multi-modal Response Planning : An Adaptive Rule Based Approach, CHI '88 Conference Proceedings : Human Factors in Computing Systems, ACM, pp 229 - 234.

Leffler, S. J., McKusick, M. K., Karels, M. J.and Quarterman, J. S., (1988), The Design and Implementation of the 4.3BSD UNIX Operating System", Addison-Wesley, pp 259 - 278, 282 - 307.

Nelson, T.N., (1981), Literary Machines, Edition 87.1, Swarthmore. P.A., available from the author.

Sventek, J., (1987), An Architecture Supporting Multi-media Integration, Proc. IEEE Office Automation Symposium, Gaithersburg, Maryland. pp.46 - 56.

Van Hoff, A., (1989), HyperNeWs User Manual, The Software is available from the Turing Institute, George House, 36 North Hanover St., Glasgow, Scotland, U.K.

Chapter 22

Support for the Authors of Multimedia Tutorials

David Bell and Peter Johnson

This chapter explores the communicative potential of multimedia with emphasis on the provision of support for authors of multimedia tutorials. The research reported here approaches the problems of describing and retrieving multimedia exhibits, and providing advice to compose them effectively.

Broad-based theories of communication, and theories of Natural Language are reviewed for application to multimedia, with the intention to provide structural support for tutorials. Hypotheses are derived from the current literature to enable the allocation of media to particular communicative acts in a given context.

These discourse theories and modality-allocation hypotheses are realised by the implementation of a prototype authoring tool, which segments tutorials using algorithms from the AI planning domain, and advises on the tutorial structure and media usage. An exploratory evaluation of the tool is described and the implications of the results are discussed.

1 Introduction

Multimedia provides a rich environment for exchanging information, binding the technologies from publishing, broadcasting and computing. Exploitation of graphics, text, sound, animation and video is crucial for effective communication. Instructors would be at a disadvantage if allowed only one medium from this selection, and Peeck (1987) has shown that multimedia presentation facilitates comprehension and retention.

Computer-based multimedia promises to provide greater excitement to hold the audience's attention and permit fast, accurate communication. This is emphasised by the rapid increase in demand for multimedia hardware and software.

Dedicated multimedia machines for the home are already on the market, integrating facilities to present high quality video and digital quality sound. Currently available systems include Commodore's CDTV, those using the Motorola/Philips CD-I[1] technology and those adhering to Intel's DVI[2] technology. In the research and development environment, all-purpose workstations such as Apple's Macintosh can be tuned into multimedia machines by the addition of plug-in audio-

---

1Compact Disc-Interactive

2Digital Video Interactive

video hardware, and software such as MacroMind Director™ or MediaMaker™. The aim of the work reported here was to provide some support to the many emerging creators capitalising upon the multimedia boom.

To make the task of analysing multimedia manageable in this paper, only text and picture combinations are considered, though the research and later implementation provide an extendible framework.

1.1 The need for authoring-support

Tutors compose tutorials to enable the audience to achieve some goal, but the tutorial is only effective if the audience both recognises and can act upon the author's intentions.

The combinations of multimedia, and communications performed by each channel are vast. Without some direction there is a great risk that authors will produce incoherent multimedia which smothers the intended communications. Multimedia software will be produced for a broad population, in the home or at work, so designers of authoring systems must consider the needs of the expected audience as well as the author, and provision of supportive authoring tools is one way forward.

We are concérned that the usage of Multimedia is integrated in such a way which reduces the audience's cognitive load, and efficiently uses the available communication channels to enable the audience to perform the desired task. ie.

(1) How can the author's construction task be supported so as to guarantee the communicative goal.

(2) How can support be given for the integration of multiple media in order to optimise the use of the available communication channels.

The goal of an instruction sequence is the audience's success in a specific task, or the acquisition of a particular skill or knowledge. The achievements of the audience depend solely upon the content and ordering of the instructions, thus a correct plan of instruction is crucial.

1.2 Elaborating the Communications problem

Those who ascribe to the Process School believe communication to be the transmission of messages, with both sender and receiver encoding and decoding the messages. Shannon & Weaver (see Fiske 1982) highlighted three problem areas of communication:

1. (technical) How accurately can the symbols of communication be conveyed via the chosen medium
2. (semantic) How precisely do the transmitted symbols convey the desired meaning
3. (effectiveness) How effectively does the received meaning affect conduct of the recipient in the desired way

Use of multimedia naturally encourages redundancy in communication, which can aid accuracy by adding predictability to an otherwise entropic message. The advantages are similar to teaching in front of a class with use of a number of presentation facilities such as speech, whiteboard and books; where misunderstandings of a communication in one medium, can be rectified by a similar communication via another medium.

Multimedia introduces a choice of communication channels for any given communication. Guidelines have been given for the allocation of these channels by Bieger & Glock (1986) and André & Rist (1990), but these guidelines need much development to consider the user-environment and preferences.

1.3 Can Discourse Theories help ?

André & Rist (1990) have investigated the application of a discourse analysis technique known as Rhetoric Structure Theory (RST) to the interaction between communications in a Multimedia environment. RST ordinarily is used to examine the relations between text spans within discourse, but André & Rist applied the same technique to textual and pictorial communicative acts. In this paper, the application of further multimedia analysis and construction techniques will be proposed, drawn from theories of natural language discourse. Plan-based approaches will be discussed in detail as will the use of a segmentation framework.

1.4 An experimental task-domain

The chosen domain for investigating multimedia support, and investigating the applicability of discourse analysis techniques, is an Authoring Tool for the production of multimedia tutorials for the usage and maintenance of a 35mm camera.

The chosen application domain has a target audience of a novice camera user who has just acquired a camera. Such a domain is viable, as the tutoring software would be distributed on a floppy or optical disk with the camera. It is assumed that the customer would have access to appropriate multimedia equipment. The author of such a tutorial will occupy a similar role to existing technical writers, having access to expert knowledge of the domain, but will use a multimedia authoring tool of the form defined in this project.

1.5 The outline of a software solution

Software providing advice on the structure of the tutorial and usage of media can help the author generate a Multimedia composition that will enable the audience to achieve the desired goal. A Multimedia Authoring tool could contain a knowledge-base for the domain of instruction, of the objects involved and the actions upon them, which could then be used to provide support for the generation and validation of plans of instruction, even plan recognition. A supportive tool could ease the author's task by recognising mistakes in the tutorial and suggesting corrections, as well as suggesting the pictorial and textual material to use. Finally, the tool can build the resulting tutorial in a form that is distributable to the audience.

2 Means of Providing Tutorial Support

A tutor requires high level support to ensure that the content and presentation of the tutorial meet the needs of the audience. Support can be given to ensure the coherence of the tutorial, and to advise on the use of the available communication media.

The coherence of the arguments in a tutorial can be tested using discourse-level techniques from the domain of natural language analysis. In order to perform such analyses, the low-level components of communication first have to be identified.

This section introduces sentential and discourse analysis techniques used within Natural Language, discussing their potential for integration and application to multimedia communications.

2.1 Using Discourse Analysis Techniques to Inform Tutorial Structure

The Chomskian approach to Natural Language analysis involves stages of parsing, semantic interpretation and contextual analysis. The parser applies grammar rules to the input sentence in order to match parts of the sentence with recognised components, such as noun phrase, verb phrase, etc. A parse tree, or deep structure, is the result. The semantic interpreter uses the parse-tree and the lexicon to investigate the meaning of the sentence, to estimate the actions on objects of the input and the relationships which exist. Contextual analysis enables a precise portrayal of the event described in the sentence; making reference to the semantics of surrounding sentences to identify exactly which actions and objects are referenced.

Discourse analysis considers language in context, examining the inter-relationships between sentences over time. Similar analyses can be applied to multimedia tutorials which involve sequential and parallel threads of communication in a number of media.

For the work reported here, it was not possible to parse pictures, or text and picture compositions. It was left to the developer to consider the syntactic and semantic information regarding the text and pictures used, and incorporate as much as possible of that information in the labelling scheme for pictures and text chunks.

The analysis techniques applied to multimedia tutorial construction utilised (1) dialogue segmentation and (2) plan-based (goal oriented) analyses. These techniques are described below.

2.1.1 Segmentation

Within text-based communication, certain sentences naturally cohere to form a segment; the same coherence is true of multimedia communications if the acts are sequential. Treating discourse as a number of successive segments provides a framework within which other discourse analyses can be carried out.

Allen (1987) defines a segment of discourse as having:

(1) a simple progression of time and location
(2) a common set of background assumptions
(3) a fixed set of speakers and listeners

A schematic diagram of a simple segment is shown below in figure 1, where all three of the above conditions are true.

Another segment (having a different topic for example) might occur between sentences three and four of the segment below, in which case we have a nested segment. During the period that the inner and outer segments are incomplete, we have to try and match each new sentence with both segments until the (inner) nested segment is closed.

figure 1

a simple segment, a sequence of five sentences

sentence1	sentence2	sentence3	sentence4	sentence5

When segmentation is used for discourse analysis, there are problems of allocating successive communications to existing segments. In an instructional domain, segments will be sequences of instructions which enable the audience to achieve one goal, thus there is little requirement to identify and clarify the relations between segments.

Filtering Rules

Plan filtering is used to ascertain whether a communication S continues the current segment, resumes another segment, or starts a new segment. S continues a segment if either the topic, an anaphoric reference, or causality (explained in section 2.1.2) match an existing segment; whilst S starts a segment if it introduces a new topic which does not match the reference or causality of an existing segment. We would expect an instruction sequence to exist as one coherent segment.

Segmentation relies greatly on the preservation of topic throughout a segment. A history list can be used to record topic changes and thus support the segment-matching algorithm. As each act is processed, associated details will be recorded in the history list, such as the potential foci, topic chosen, and candidates for a future topic. The segment-matching algorithm can then rely upon recency and look for the most recent topic match by searching backwards through the history list.

2.1.2 A Plan-based approach

A plan is a sequence of tasks which have been identified to achieve a goal (see the discussion of task knowledge by Johnson et al, 1988.) There are invariably plans behind action sequences and communication sequences. In the tutorial authoring tool, plan generation was utilised to provide basic instructional outlines for the author to build upon. Plan validation was utilised to check the integrity of the tutorials created by the author.

Plan generation and validation are founded on the assumption that a sequence of communicative acts (or actions) will be directed towards some goal. Plan generation is similar to natural language generation, which tackles the problem of identifying an action sequence which will bring about a goal-state given an initial state and a source act-set. Plan validation is performed to ensure that each act in a given act-sequence is executed in a state in which all of it's pre-conditions are satisfied, and that the plan will achieve the intended goal.

The function of an action which maps one world state to another can be termed it's causality, where the change is a result of the facts asserted or removed by the action. A causal connection between a communication and a segment (an instruction sequence) will exist if the causality of the communication has a place in the recognised causality of the segment.

Plans of actions, and likewise, plans of instruction, can be viewed hierarchically, by levels of abstraction. The example in figure 2 gives the hierarchic view of a plan to "attach the lens to the camera body". As it happens, the action consists of a sequence of subgoals, each having preconditions, action, and effect. This decomposition continues with each action until primitive actions are reached at the leaves (terminal nodes) of the tree, as shown schematically in figure 3.

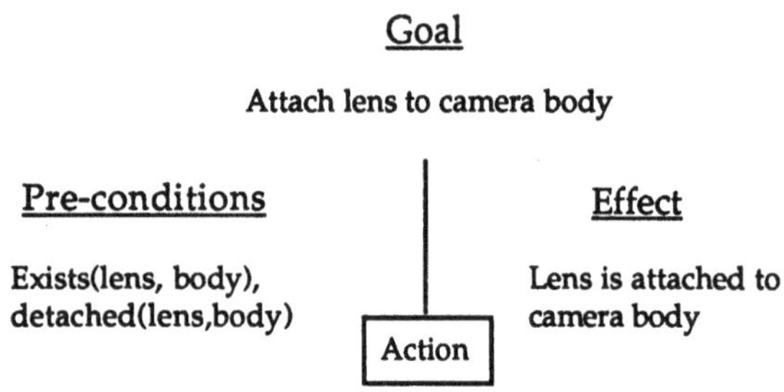

figure 2 The plan "attach the lens to the camera body"

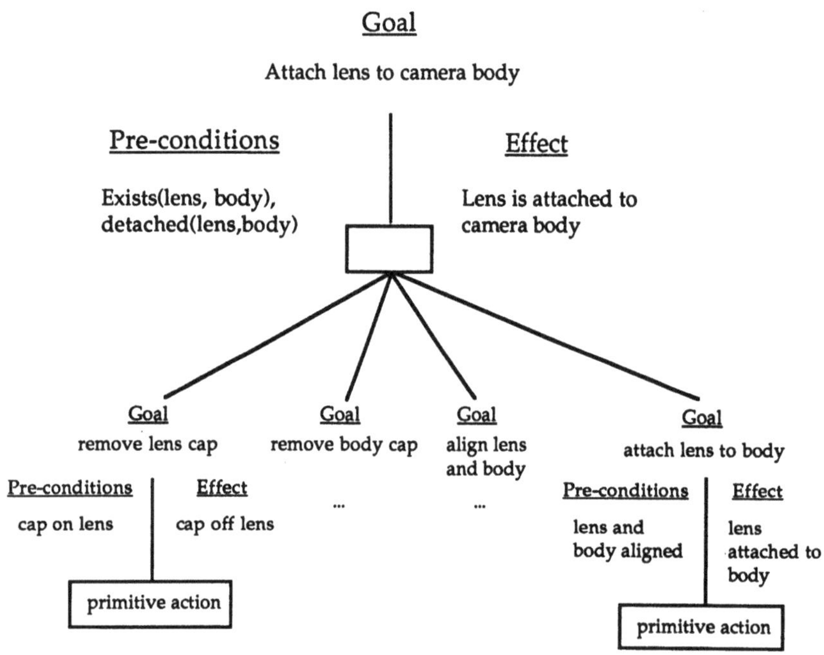

figure 3 A decomposition of the plan "attach the lens to the camera body"

Planning algorithms

The backward chaining algorithm was used for plan-generation, which, as it's name suggests, identifies the actions which achieve the goal state, and recursively identifies the action sequence from the initial state. The algorithm is:

(1) select a fact in the goal state that is not true in the initial state

(2) select an action, say action.1, from the knowledge base that has this fact as one of it's effects

(3) if the pre-conditions of action.1 are true in the initial state
then
good, action.1 can be appended to the plan and another fact in the goal state can be considered

else

(recursively) try to find an action (or actions) in the knowledge base which asserts the necessary preconditions of action.1

This recursive search is complete when the preconditions of the actions, which assert the required facts, have all been met.

A valid tutorial requires that:

(1) the preconditions for each instruction executed are true

(2) the plan transforms the initial state to the goal

Validity is checked by performing a *dummy execution*. To do this, if the initial world-state (or context) satisfies it's pre-conditions the first act in the sequence is executed, if execution takes place then the world-state is modified by asserting the effects of that action; then the next action in sequence is tested for executability, and so on. If the plan finishes and reaches the required goal the plan is valid. If any action fails, critical or not, then the whole sequence fails and the plan is invalid.

2.1.3 The choice of discourse techniques

A framework of segmentation was adopted, incorporating techniques of plan-generation and validation which operate *naturally* on the instructions (the communicative acts) of a tutorial.

The combination of these techniques is shown in figure 4.

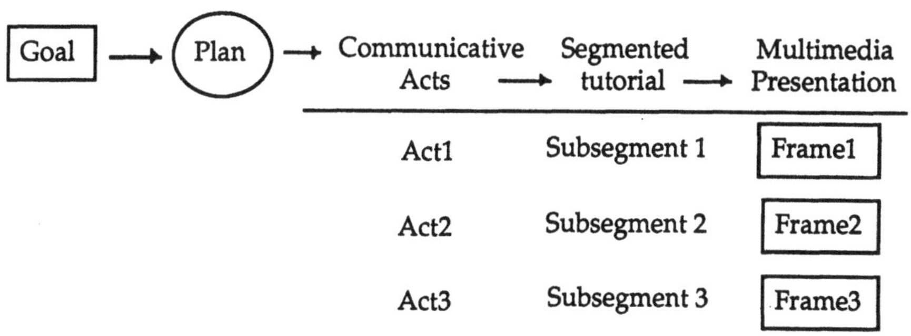

figure 4 The incorporation of Natural Language Analysis Techniques

Each frame in the presentation performs one communicative act of the plan (a multimedia instruction), with history-list update and analysis being performed after composition of each frame to ensure this. This frame-based model of construction is made explicit to the author.

2.2 Modality allocation - making the right choice

One aim of the project was to identify the optimal media for particular communicative acts in a given context. The type of a communication is given by it's content, which is either an *abstract* operation, a *spatial/structural operation*, or some *spatial/structural information*. Camera usage involves spatial actions such as *turn*, *press* and *open*, and tasks which contain abstract (non-spatial) tasks such as *focussing*. Focussing involves iterative and conditional actions, for example:

"Rotate the focus ring until the subject is in focus, continuing until the subject is blurred once more. Then rotate the focus ring to bring the subject into focus"

Bieger & Glock (1986) concluded that the presentation mode chosen for operational information had little effect on the accuracy or time for task performance. They also concluded that a textual rendition of spatial information reduced errors in the task, whilst a pictorial rendition of the same information reduced the time taken. Further authors have promoted pictorial presentation of spatial information such as André & Rist (1990) and Levin et al (1987).

2.2.1 Hypotheses for the project regarding modality allocation

The hypotheses made, based upon the research cited above, were:

(1) spatial information is better suited to a pictorial rendering.

(2) instructions which use iterative or conditional methods to reach a goal, are most effective if conveyed textually.

(3) *spatial* instructions, such as *open* or *turn,* can be portrayed equally well in pictures or text (in agreement with Bieger & Glock).

The hypotheses were tested by providing an advisory element in the tutorial authoring tool, which can suggest an optimal modality for the communicative acts performed by the author.

History-list support for multimedia advice

Traditionally, the history-list tracks the topic over successive sentences. In the multimedia authoring environment the history-list is used to ensure consistent modality usage for the presentation of given objects and activities, so as to minimise the cognitive load upon the audience.

3 The Tutorial Authoring Tool

Hypotheses regarding multimedia communication described above, and ideas drawn from the domain of discourse analysis were used to inform the design of a prototype authoring tool. The intention of the tool is to aid construction of tutorials for the operation & maintenance of a semi-automatic 35mm camera.

3.1 The intended function & capacity of the tool

The tool had to satisfy the following goals:

(1) to generate a tutorial which will enable the audience to perform the chosen activity.

(2) to provide the author with control over the content and sequence of frames of the tutorial

(3) to provide search, browse and select facilities for the textual and pictorial content of each frame

(4) to provide advisory support regarding tutorial structure and modality allocation

3.2 The development environment

SuperCard was chosen as a development platform because it provides a high level object-oriented toolkit of windows, menus, buttons, text-fields and graphical objects. Even with the speed handicap and inflexibility (there are no traditional programming tools such as arrays, pointers, or records) SuperCard provides those amenities required for a complete hypermedia application. An architectural view of the tool, with descriptions of the main functional components is given in figure 6.

3.3 The knowledge base

The knowledge base contains data of domain-based activities for plan generation and validation.

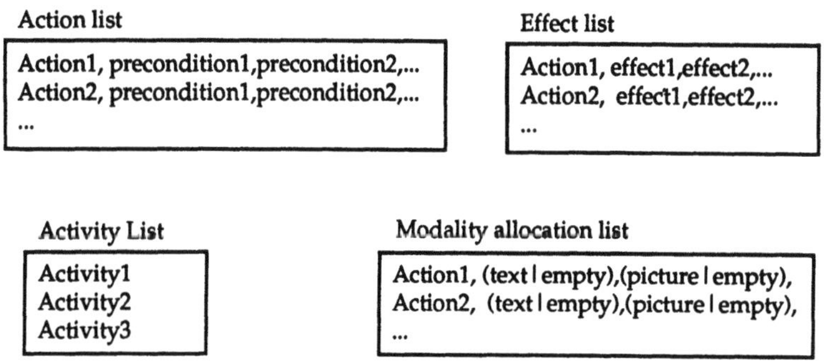

figure 5 The knowledge base

The activity list contains the activities supported by the tool, which is used when the author wishes to select a supported activity. The effect list gives all the actions supported and the facts they will render true on execution.

For each action, the *action-list* details the pre-conditions for execution. Actions are referred to by a description of the act they will enable the viewer to perform such as *attach(lens;body)* or *check(battery)*.

The *modality allocation list* gives a three-tuple for each action, consisting of the action name, the word "text" if it can be rendered in text, and the word "picture" if it can be presented pictorially. For example, by hypothesis(3) the instruction for the action *align(lens;body)* can be conveyed equally well in text or pictures (being a spatial action), so the entry in the modality allocation list is *....align(lens;body),text,picture,....* Whereas the instruction *giveCondition(battery replacement)* involves conditional statements, so by hypothesis(2) is recommended to be presented textually, and has the entry: *...giveCondition(battery replacement),text,,....*

3.4 Plan generation

Choosing an activity for the tutorial from the list of supported activities automatically invokes the backward-chaining planning algorithm to generate a suitable instruction sequence for the tutorial.

Starting with the *goal*, the algorithm takes an action and looks up it's preconditions in the action list. If there are any unsatisfied preconditions, each is taken in turn and a search takes place to identify an action in the effects list which achieves it. This precondition-action matching continues recursively until all preconditions are met and a valid action-sequence is found.

If the author decides to construct a plan manually or to edit the suggested tutorial plan, support is provided in the form of plan validation.

The Framework for a multimedia authoring tool

(1) The author has an intention towards the audience, to pass on some knowledge or give instructions in a tutorial.

(2) The plan of the tutorial can be entered manually by supplying actions, objects and a preliminary ordering

(3) The tutorial plan can also be built automatically by the planner, which uses backward-chaining to generate the required plan from the chosen goal

(4) The Goal ordering stage permits the author to edit or reorder the generated plan.

(5) Plan validation then ensures that each operation in the plan is executed at a stage when all of its preconditions are true

(6) Advice on modality usage for a communication is based upon recommendations in the knowledge base and the history of modalities used for the action & objects being portrayed

(7) A composition manager is required to build the resulting tutorial which can be passed on to a customer

u : indicates user interaction

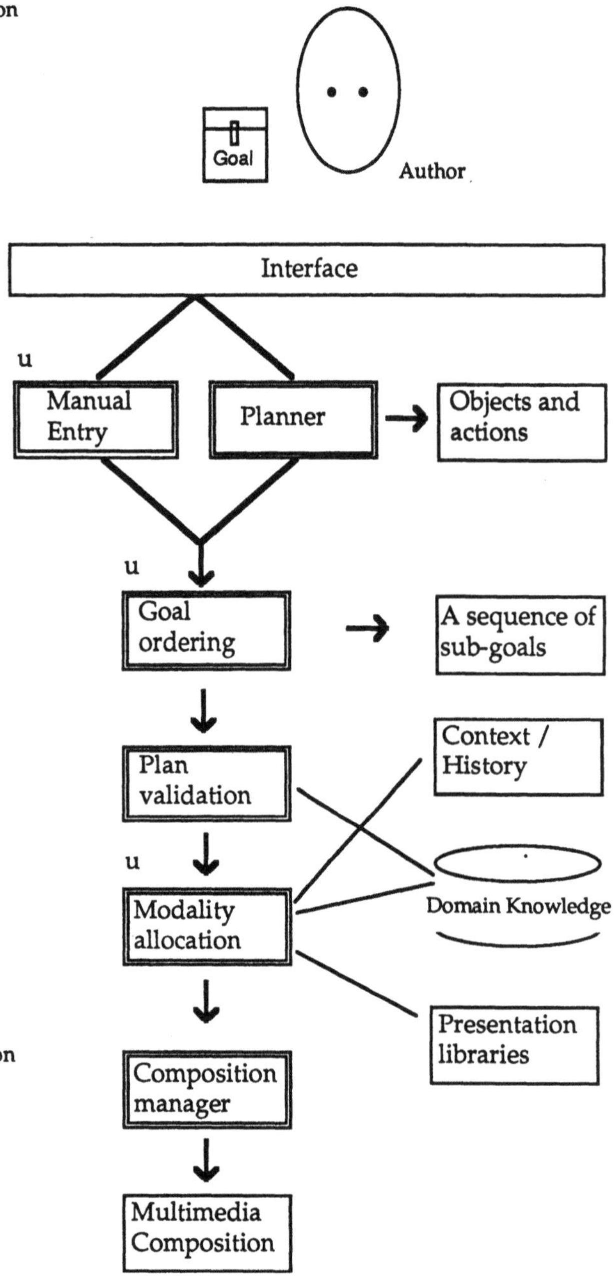

figure 6. An Architectural View of the Authoring Tool

3.5 Plan validation

Plan validation uses the *dummy execution* algorithm previously described in section 2.1.2. In addition, the results of the validation check are presented to the author in the form of a validation log, to aid any necessary debugging of the plan.
Validation of the author's instruction-plan consists of the following steps:

(1) take the first action, and the context of true facts
(2) if the preconditions of the action are met in this context
    then
        add it's effects to the list of true facts
        note the success on the log
    else
        set the failFlag
        note the preconditions missing on the log
(3) take the next action in the sequence and apply the same rules in the new environment of facts

If the failFlag is not set during validation then the plan sequence is valid and the author is notified, otherwise the author is notified that the plan sequence is invalid.

3.6 Mapping communications to frames

On completion of plan generation the author can move on to compose the tutorial. Due to the segmentation of the tutorial, reinforced by the application of the planning algorithm, each instruction in the plan equates to a frame of the final tutorial. The instruction numbers match those of the tutorial frames to reiterate the correspondence.
An overview of the developing tutorial is available to the author from which the author can:

- select, add, edit and delete frames
- build the final tutorial

Whilst editing a frame the author identifies appropriate text and/or pictures to achieve the desired communication.

3.7 Provision of pictorial material

Pictures for use by the author in the tutorial were scanned from camera manuals using an image scanner, edited using SuperPaint™ then imported to SuperCard. Due to copyrighting regulations, Canon (UK) Ltd were asked before pictures and text from one of their manuals was used.

Picture searching is performed for the author because of the large number of pictures that are available. The author will often be presented with a choice of appropriate pictures to perform the act required, with variations mainly in size or scope of the picture. The designer of the tool labels each picture with a description of the communicative act performed which enables this searching to take place.

3.8 Provision of canned text

The semantic content and communicative act of text used by the author in the tutorial has to be known for analysis and advisory purposes, but there is no parser or interpreter to analyse free text, so a choice of labelled sentential chunks are provided. For example, if presentation of a text chunk enables the audience to align the camera lens and body, then a descriptive label of the form *align(lens;camera)* is applied to the text chunk.

The text provided by the tool is based upon instructions in the Canon manual, but where it was desirable to remove dependency upon any associated picture (for evaluation purposes,) that dependency was removed. It is recognised that this chunking of text might bias the use of the system as it is an unnatural way to handle text.

Suitable text for an instruction is found in a similar manner to pictures. Clicking on a text chunk then copies it to the text field of the current frame. The act associated with the text in each frame is also recorded.

3.9 Building the History List

The history list records information necessary for a simple segmentation-like analysis of the tutorial. A comparison is made of the pictorial and textual acts of each frame, and information is recorded to enable analysis over the whole tutorial.
The information that is identified and recorded for each modality of each frame is:

- previous topics in the tutorial of that modality
- the chosen topic of that frame
- further potential topics
- the communicative act performed

The last item of the history list of each frame is the logical union of the communicative acts of the pictorial and textual analyses. The constraints of analysis performed mean that there should only be one act per frame, though evidence would indicate that concurrent, complementary communications are desirable rather than simple duplications.

The history-list is updated upon completion of each frame to ensure that successive history list entries contain correct details of the content of the tutorial.

3.10 Providing Advice

The author can request advice after the history list analysis is complete. The author is given an on-screen report which indicates:

1. If the communicative act of the frame is appropriate to that which is given for the frame in the tutorial plan.
2. If the desired communicative act of the frame has been achieved using the preferred media.
3. If the textual and pictorial communications conflict (if both were used)

It must be emphasised though that the author is free to disregard any or all of the advice that is given.

4 Evaluation of the Authoring Tool

A series of informal evaluations took place to investigate the general usability of the authoring tool, the plan generation and validation facilities, and modality allocation.

After a trial evaluation it was decided that the evaluation of modality allocation should take place away from the tool. This was because the facilities provided by the tool to utilise the available textual and pictorial media were found to bias the subjects' composition strategy.

The results of the study provided support for the hypotheses that conditional instructions were best conveyed textually, and that spatial information was better suited to pictorial presentation. However, the results gave less support to the hypothesis that spatial instructions could be rendered both pictorially and textually, supporting rather the conclusion that a pictorial representation is best.

4.1 Evaluation of Plan Generation & Validation

Two groups of two subjects (all MSc computer science students) were given the task of creating a tutorial to enable an audience to load a new battery into a camera.

The first two subjects had use of the plan generator, which provides a valid tutorial plan to achieve the instructional task. The second group of two subjects did not use the plan generator, but had to enter the instruction plan manually and validate it.

The first group did not need to perform any plan validation as the usefulness of a pre-generated instruction sequence was the concern. However, the second group was given an instruction plan with two actions intentionally out of place, in order to test the benefits of validation.

Comments made by the subjects were recorded, whether in distress or success during usage of the tool, as well as approximate timings for subtask completion.

4.2 Evaluation of Modality Allocation

As stated previously, modality selection experiments were carried out in isolation from the prototype, although the hypotheses implemented in the prototype were those being tested. Four subjects were asked to choose between a pictorial or textual communication for each act in a plan which enabled an audience to load a battery into a camera. The action sequence used was generated by the planner, and is shown below.

1 unscrew hand grip
2 remove accessory shoe cover
3 open battery chamber
4 orientate battery correctly
5 insert battery
6 give conditions for battery insertion

Users were not shown pictures or text, they were just asked to indicate which media they would use to convey the instruction. In this evaluation particularly, the subjects' comments were of importance, as well as the parity between the implemented hypotheses and the subjects choices.

4.3 Evaluation Results and Discussion

The results were qualitative rather than quantitative, consisting of subject's own descriptions of their difficulties as well as the experimenter's notes of error-points and timings for task completion. It was very much an exploratory study to test the novel components of the prototype.

In general, it appeared that defining a plan of instruction before constructing a tutorial hindered most subjects, possibly because communication planning in everyday communication is taken for granted. The benefit of planning is to make the communications required for instruction explicit, and hence make the tasks of the audience clearer to the author.

4.3.1 Plan generation

Subjects who had use of a suggested tutorial plan had to make the operation-to-frame inference and decide upon the content of the frames to build up the tutorial.

It was found that subjects in this group did not spend much time considering the instruction-plan. They tended not to consider the preconditions and effects of the instructions in as much depth as the second group, and therefore did not have as good an appreciation of the task they wanted the audience to achieve.

4.3.2 Plan validation

The subjects in this group were not given access to automatic plan generation and constructed a plan manually, spending considerably longer deliberating the meaning of the notation for actions than subjects who used a pre-generated plan. These subjects also spent a longer time thinking of the action sequence and precondition-effect constraints, thus gained a deeper understanding of the battery-loading task.

The plan validation log used by this group was confusing initially, especially the jargon terms that were used, such as *world state*. When confident in the task, subjects did not gain from using the validation log, which would likewise be the case if camera-experts were used as subjects. The delay while validation took place was found to be annoying, especially if only to report that the plan was valid.

4.3.3 Modality Allocation

Modality selection by subjects supported the hypotheses that spatial information is best presented pictorially and that conditional instructions were best conveyed textually.

The hypothesis that spatial instructions could be rendered in either text or pictures was not so obviously supported. This may be because it was not possible to separate the spatial actions from the spatial information that was conveyed pictorially, which resulted in the spatial instructions being rendered pictorially too. It must be reiterated that this evaluation was intended as an exploratory one, and it is expected that future, refined experimentation will yield clearer results.

Subjects chose to present the instruction sequence almost totally in pictures, just as the tool itself would have advised; though some subjects did consider the use of text support. This might indicate some bias introduced by the chosen task, or the bias of the domain as a whole.

One subject paid great emphasis and much gesticulation to the spatial nature of actions like *sliding off* or *snapping off* (for instructions 2 and 3), to justify their portrayal by picture.

One factor in choosing the textual modality was the difficulty of the communication. For example, one subject reported that the instruction indicating battery orientation was best conveyed textually because "it is difficult to convey the conditions for a camera to work using pictures alone".

A strong desire of three subjects was to combine the acts of informing the audience of the correct battery orientation and enabling the audience to insert the battery. A desire to combine complementary communications such as these had been recognised previously.

4.4 Conclusions from the experiment

From this initial study, support can be given for the conclusions of Bieger & Glock regarding the choice of media for *spatial* and *operational* communicative acts, but further investigation is required before any strict guidelines can be given. Certainly further investigation is required to determine if spatial instructions can be presented textually (or verbally) as well as they can be pictorially.

It has been shown that techniques from the AI planning domain have application to construction of multimedia tutorials, and can promote the author's awareness of the audience's tasks.

The aim of this study was to show that discourse analysis techniques can be applied to the analysis and construction of multimedia communication, and a number of issues were uncovered in that process. Certainly the range of permissible communication *types* needs to be considered in more detail, as well as further combinations of communications and richer multimedia environments.

4.5 Revised requirements of an authoring tool

From the evaluation it is possible to define more clearly the requirements of a tutorial authoring tool.

The tool needs to make a clear distinction between the audience's action sequence that will achieve a goal, and the communicative acts that the author must perform in order to enable the audience to perform that action sequence. Such a distinction could make considerable usability gains.

Some communicative acts are quite suitable for combination, such as *insert(battery)* and *illustrate(orientation)*, but the planning algorithm automatically allocates one act per frame. Greater flexibility is desirable where the ordering constraints are not breached, so that acts may be combined.

It is not clear at this point that the author should be made aware of the plans which exist for the activities of the camera-user and subsequent instruction sequences. Greater flexibility could be provided if the author's plan were recognised as the tutorial was built, and prompts could be given if the presentation sequence was incorrect or incomplete. This indicates that plan recognition in such a tool should be explored.

One drawback of the history-list analysis is the inability to record the changes at the instant they are made to the tutorial, ie it is not possible to update the history list when the author copies a new text-chunk or a new picture. A Multimedia interpreter is desirable, that will parse the content of each media, perform semantic interpretation within and across media, and identify the inter-relationships that exist between the acts within and across media. This desire is a long way from fulfilment.

The tool must not bias the author's choice of modality by providing media-slots in each tutorial frame. Once text and picture chunks have been copied to a frame, subjects are not inclined to remove either, a behaviour which tends to continue through the remainder of tutorial composition.

Coherent models of media-manipulation need to be explored, without resorting to the unnatural chunking which was used for text in the prototype. The chosen interaction model will also have to accommodate media which bring a temporal component such as animation, sound and video.

4.6 Requirements of future experiments

4.6.1 Plan Generation & Validation

There is a need to use author-subjects who are camera experts, in order to better assess the usefulness of plan generation and validation in this domain. The resulting tutorials should then be tested with a real audience of camera-novices, to test the resulting benefits of the authoring-tool. Such an evaluation would need the use of a camera as depicted in the tutorial.

An evaluation is needed which will measure the benefits of prolonged use of the authoring tool, so that the author gains familiarity with it. Over time the author may acquire an increased awareness of the audience's tasks, and improve the tutorials further.

Over successive experiments a wide range of tutorials could be constructed, to test the plan-generation and validation algorithms on longer tutorials which have greater constraints to instruction ordering.

4.6.2 Modality Allocation

Initial evaluations with the tool were biased because subjects saw that both text and pictorial *exhibits* were available to perform any particular communication, and tended to take the safe option of redundancy by using both media. An experimental method has to be found which will offset any influence of the tool, or the experiment, upon the user's choice of modality.

Similarly to the planning and validation components, it is necessary to test the success of the modality decisions by evaluating the performance of a real audience in a task using the resulting tutorials.

It was observed that redundant communication were often used, especially when the tool was not well understood. The advantages brought about by such redundancy need to be measured. Likewise, there is a need to measure the entropy of communications, and measure the degree of entropy that both the author and the audience can tolerate.

5 Conclusions

Implementation of the authoring tool has provided a platform for the production of multimedia tutorials, upon which further support can be added. The prototype has highlighted the restrictions that a framework of segmentation can impose by enforcing one communicative act per frame, as well as showing how an explicit plan of instruction can improve the author's comprehension of the audience's task.

Stress must be placed on the need for a set of guidelines to aid the usage of multimedia in a variety of circumstances. It is clear that the goal is to be able to interpret, or at least some make some headway in interpreting, the communicative acts that take place in each channel of a multimedia composition, without requiring the developer of such a system to label each available communication.

The concept of a multimedia interpreter is a giant leap from the current technology and techniques, but if experts can identify appropriate uses of media there is hope that similar skills of judgement can be embedded in a supportive tool.

Analysis of pictures using text-based tools, in a text-based planning environment, ignores much of the communicative power that a picture can provide. One of the future tasks is to define the communicative acts that are unique to pictures, rather than identifying the acts they perform in common with text or speech.

Acknowledgements

We would like to thank many people for their support in this work, including John Bell, Hilary Johnson and Steve Sommerville. Many thanks to Canon (UK) Ltd for allowing the use of material from the AE-1 camera manual. This work was funded by the Science and Engineering Research Council, UK.

References

Allen, J (1987) **Natural Language Understanding** Benjamin Cummings, California

André, Elisabeth & Rist, Thomas (1990) **Synthesizing Illustrated Documents: A Plan-Based Approach** paper presented at ECAI '90

Bieger, George R. & Glock, Marvin D. (1986) **Comprehending Spatial and Contextual Information in Picture-Text Instructions** Journal of Experimental Education Vol 56 (4)

Fiske, John (1982) **Introduction to Communication Studies** Methuen, NY.

Hovy, Eduard & Arens, Yigal (1990) **When is a Picture Worth a thousand Words? - Allocation of Modalities in Multimedia Communication** full paper presented at the AAAI Symposium on Interfaces, Stanford

Johnson, P. Johnson, H. Waddington, R. and Shouls, A. (1988) **Task Knowledge Structures.** In Jones, D. and Winder, R. (eds) People and Computers IV, CUP

Levin, J. Anglin, G & Carney, R (1987) **On Empirically Validating Functions of Pictures in Prose** in Willows & Houghton (1987), Vol 1, Chapter 2

McKeown, Kathleen R. (1985) **Discourse Strategies for Generating Natural-Language Text** Artificial Intelligence 27 (pp1-41)

Mann, William C. & Thompson, Sandra A. (1988) **Rhetorical Structure Theory: Toward a Functional Theory of Text Organisation** TEXT 8(3) pp243-281

Peeck, Joan (1987) **The role of Illustration in Processing and Remembering Illustrated Text** in Willows & Houghton (1987), Vol 1, Chapter 4

Treisman & Gelade (1980) in chapter 1, vol 1 of Willows & Houghton , 1987

Wilkins, David E. (1988) **Practical Planning: Extending the Classical AI Planning Paradigm** Morgan Kaufmann Publishers, San Mateo, Cal (Chapter 4, Hierarchical Planning at Differing Abstraction Levels)

Willows, D. & Houghton, H. (1987) **The Psychology of Illustration** (2 Vols) Springer-Verlag, NY

Chapter 23

An Object Oriented Architecture for Interactive Animation and Simulation

Rui Pedro Casteleiro, Fernando Vasconcelos and Mário Rui Gomes

1. Introduction

Direct Manipulation (Shneiderman 1993) at interface and application levels poses common requirements including sophisticated graphics, commands given at any time, different ways to give the same command, multiple input and output devices, complex dialogues, fast and continuous prompt/feedback and non static interfaces.

The OO-AGES Model (Gomes and Fernandes 1991) deals with these common requirements with the introduction of an integrated Model of Man Machine Interactive Graphic Systems based on Graphic Manipulation.

The Magoo Architecture (Gomes 1990) is an implementation of the OO-AGES Model, written in C++ and using the X Toolkit. Both Magoo interaction techniques and X Toolkit Interaction techniques ("widgets") are integrated.

In this paper we will first give a general overview of the MAGOO architecture showing how these concepts interact to form a consistent application. Then we will proceed to a more detailed description of the main classes that compose Magoo. Finally we will show how Magoo can be extended to support multimedia applications, such as animation and simulation.

A new Magoo implementation is under development and will be used in the HYPERFACE project (ESPRIT 5391). A set of CASE tools for industrial Simulators and Monitors will be developed.

2. Magoo Architecture

A MAGOO Application is composed of two main object family types: the Data objects and the Transformer objects.

Data objects are passive and are divided in two main classes. Some contain information about real world objects (2D and 3D objects), others represent the information used by the Man-Machine Interface (a screen content or a mouse position).

The transformers are active objects, usually organized in a pipeline. They are also divided in two main classes. Each object of an output pipeline is called a driver and is responsible for the creation of a data object view. The inverse transformation is performed by an input pipeline, where each object is called a dialogue.

So in the MAGOO architecture the application starts by creating a data object, transforming it through several output pipelines, displaying it in one or more displays, receiving information from the user to change the object, notifying the dialogue, changing the object if needed, and then restart all over again.

A Data Object can be anything from a simple integer to a hierarchical 2D graphical object, or a 3D object with texture and trajectory, or even an object representing a sequence of frames, that is, a movie. It can also be an object that contains a music staff, or even a book.

An output pipeline has the responsibility of transforming the data objects running through the several pipeline stages until the data objects needed for a particular display type are created. For example, if we have a 3D object, it can be transformed by a 3D -> 2D driver object and then by a 2D -> X driver resulting in an image on a X window. If we want a paper version produced by a PostScript printer, a 2D -> PostScript driver object should be used instead of the 2D -> X driver. If we have a 3D graphic engine the output pipeline will be composed only by a 3D -> PEX driver object.

A display is a low level data object, where output is shown and input is received. It can be an X window, a page from a PostScript printer, a NeWS window, a frame by frame recorder, a touch screen, a sound recorder, a data glove, or even a head mounted display.

An input pipeline is responsible for managing (creating, editing and destroying) a class of objects. In a factory, for example, it can be important to receive information, sent by sensors, about pressure or temperature. In those cases, special dialogues that know the received meaning information are needed.

The first input pipeline stage is a generic event handler that can subscribe several basic event types, like a button down in a X or a NeWS window, a data glove finger movement or even a pressure value.

Generic dialogues can implement a simple state machine, or in more complex cases, a Petri Net. The GKS input model or an event script language like Hill´s ERL (Event Response Language) (Hill 1987) can be used to define dialogue dynamics.

The application main dialogue subscribes a dynamic set of simple dialogues, forming a tree, managing all the Man-Machine Interactions using different types of feedback objects (still images, text, sound) and receiving information from different input devices (mouse, light pen, voice, data glove).

3. Magoo Classes

To create a Magoo application it is necessary to define both the Virtual World and lower level abstractions. The mapping between these two levels is a Driver´s (upper to lower level) and a Dialog´s (lower to upper level) Responsibility (Brock and Wilkerson 1989).

For example, an application that manages Splines must create Spline Graphic Objects, Magoo Displays and the same number of Drivers. Then all the Graphic Objects must be linked with the Drivers and each Driver to a Magoo Display. Any Spline modification will be updated in all Magoo Displays implementing multiple views of the Graphic Object (the Spline). Each Driver Object implements a Graphic Pipeline stage.

The transformation between operator actions and the Spline modification is a Dialog object responsibility. Each Dialog Object will define the dynamic of the Spline Direct Manipulation, implementing an interaction technique.

A Magoo application is a set of linked objects managing Virtual World entities. The programmer´s responsibility will be to create Dialog Classes that deal with an application's dynamics using the pre-defined Graphic, Driver, Dialog and Display Classes that we will describe in the next sections.

3.1 Magoo Display Objects

The first task of a Magoo Programmer is to define the initial application screen layout. All the Motif widgets are available and can be used. There is a 1:1 relation between a Magoo Display and a X Toolkit widget. The concepts are similar and so a Magoo application development will be a very easy task to a programmer with X Toolkit experience.

The XToolkit Arg list concept is supported. To parametrize a Magoo Display a **CArgList** should be created and initialized with the resource (name, value) tuples supported by the widget type the programmer wants to create.

In a Magoo application only a *MXtDisplayRoot* object, responsible for the communication with the Window Manager Application, is allowed. If the programmer wants to create a forest of widgets, where each root widget is managed by the Window Manager Application, another class *MXtDisplayApp* is available. A *MXtDisplayApp* object must be a MXtDisplayRoot object shell.

Often pop-up objects, connected with any widget, are needed. Magoo supports this requirements with the concept of Shells.

The last Magoo application instruction is normally to send a *mainLoop* message to the *MXtDisplayRoot* object, transfering the application control to the X Toolkit. Motif, Athena, Inesc, Hyperface (Marshall 1990) or any other XIntrinsics based Toolkit will be supported.

In Fig. 1 one MXtDisplayRoot has been created with 3 MXtDisplayApp shells, "A-App", "B-App" and "C-App". The Magoo Display "B-App" has 3 MXtDisplay children of different widget classes, "D-Window", "E-Button" and "F-Button".

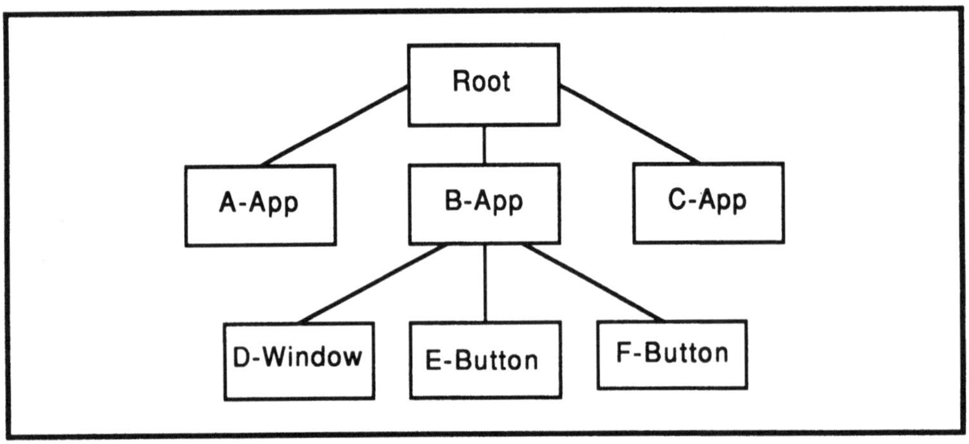

Figure 1: A simplified example of a Magoo Display Forest

3.2 Graphic Objects

After a Magoo Display tree or forest is created we can proceed to create Graphic Objects. A Graphic Object, as any other Data Object is composed by a set of components (other Data Objects) and a set of methods to define (*set*) or inquire (*get*) the value of each component. Any Data Object is editable. It is for instance possible to insert or delete a point in a polyline or change a circle´s radius.

Each Graphic Object is defined in its own coordinate space and is composed of a geometric and a graphic attribute part.

A list of points and a transformation matrix form the geometric part. The transformation matrix is implemented by the *MMatrix* class. There are several methods to change a Graphic Object matrix, including rotation, translation and scaling. Of course methods to set or inquire any other geometric attribute are also provided. A bounding box is automatically computed for each object. This is implemented through the *MBox* class. The Magoo set of data objects already include Polylines, Polygons, Splines, Circles, Arcs and Rectangles.

The GC class defines the graphical part of any data object. A GC is a shared attribute composed of references to a pre-defined set of graphic attributes needed to control the lowest level representation of any Graphic Object. Font, DrawMode, Pattern, LineWidth, LineStyle, Visibility, Detectability, Foreground (Colour), Background (Colour) are available. The sharing mechanism is inherited from the *MResource* base class.

An attribute object can also be used to create several GC. The attributes will then be shared by those GC objects. This mechanism is convenient for most application requirements and for the efficient use of X-Windows Server objects (X Window dependent Graphic Context).

3.2.1 Composed Graphic Objects

Most Virtual World entities are complex objects. Magoo deals with these requirements with the introduction of the Composed Graphic Object concept. Those objects will have an editable set of Graphic Object, a Transformation Matrix and a Graphic Context. Note that the Compose Graphic Object is also a Graphic Object.

A Graphic Object's coordinate space is defined in its father coordinate space. If a Graphic Object has no Graphic Context or doesn't have all the graphic attributes, the missing information will be inherited from its father.

Fig. 2 shows a Composed Graphic Object, the "Inesc Logo" composed by a set of Spline Graphic Objects. Two Attributes were created, "Colour Green" of class MForeground and "Width 2" of class MLineWidth. Both shared objects were used to create a Magoo Graphic Context, the "MGC". This Shared Data Object is referenced only by the Composed Graphic Object. None of the Splines has references to any Magoo Graphic Context. All of them are inheriting the "Inesc Logo" Graphic Context.

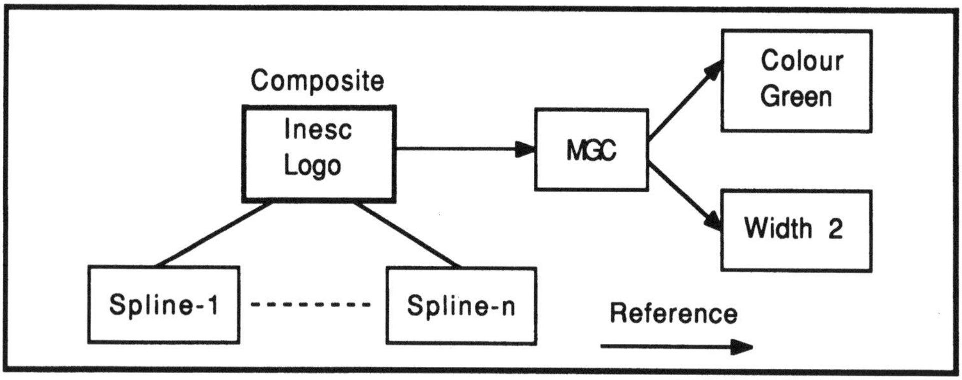

Figura 2: A Tree of Graphic Objects with references to Shared Data Objects

3.3 Driver Transformer Objects

To compute one or more lower level representation of a Graphic Object, *MDriver* objects must be created and linked with Magoo Displays. Finally the Graphic Object must be linked with the drivers. To create an image inside a X window a specialized driver, the *MXtDriver* must be used and linked with a *MXtDisplay* object.

Any *MDriver* manages a display list. The relative position of two Graphic Objects in a display list will define the sequence of the lower level Graphic Object creation. Methods to insert, insert before, insert after, update, remove or inquire a *MDriver* display list are also be available.

An update message will be sent to the driver object if an update of the lower level Graphic Object representation is explicitly needed.

Although data objects are mainly passive it is possible to send them a *setActive* message. From that point in time, after any object modification, update messages will be sent to all the Driver Objects to which the Graphic Object is linked. If a Graphic Object is often changed the automatic updating mechanism should be disabled and enabled only when needed.

A MXtDriver will use it's display list to automatically repair the contents of the Magoo Display window it is connected with. This functionality is not currently supported by XToolkit and is achieved with the X-Window dependent Graphic Object creation and management. Thus, the lowest level objects are not seen by the application programmer.

A contents window update due to an object modification is a two step process. Before repairing it is necessary to erase the previous object representation. However as the object as been changed it is usually impossible to identify the damaged area.

In Magoo a Graphic Object identification and it´s lower representation is stored in a tuple. The object has changed but its lower representation is still available and can be used to compute the damaged area. The low level primitive is then recalculated and redrawn by the MXtDriver. Thus the coherence between levels is reached.

Fig. 3 show the necessary links to obtain three different "views" of the Composed Graphic Object, the "Inesc Logo". The three images are computed by the three Drivers (MXtDriver) in the windows of three Magoo Displays. Any "Inesc Logo" modification will be visible inside the three windows.

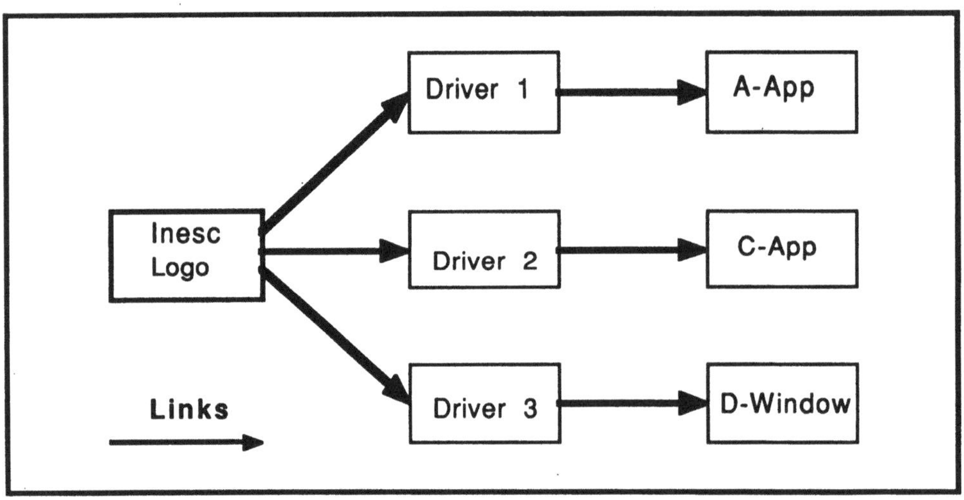

Figure 3: One Composed Graphic Object with 3 "Views"

3.4 Dialog Objects

Until now it was possible to create Graphic Objects and to display them in several Magoo Display windows. But most Magoo applications are interactive and, by definition, the human operator will be responsible for Graphic Object modifications. Magoo deals with this requirement by introducing Dialog Objects.

A *MDialog*, is an object responsible for implementing the application's dynamic. Most dialogs are responsible for the creation or management of a pre- defined class of Graphic Object.

To receive low level events a specialized Dialog is required, the *MEventHandler*. For the communication with a X dependent Display an *MXtEventHandler* will be used and will be responsible for managing X window dependent events.

After a MXtEventHandler and several DEvent creations we need to link them with a MXtDisplay.

The communication with a Dialog Object is also a two step process. First an object subscribes to the service. For example if a client wants to be informed of any button pressed he will send a subscribe message to the server. In this case as soon as a button pressed event is received the client will be informed through the call of a receive event message.

An event is a Data Object of *MEvent* class used both to define a subscription and to store a low level event message.

Figure 4 shows a Dialog Object responsible for the "Inesc Logo" editing. The editing operations will be based on "Move" and "Key Press / Release" event types. Although the Image of "Inesc Logo" is visible inside three different windows only "D-Window" is used for event input.

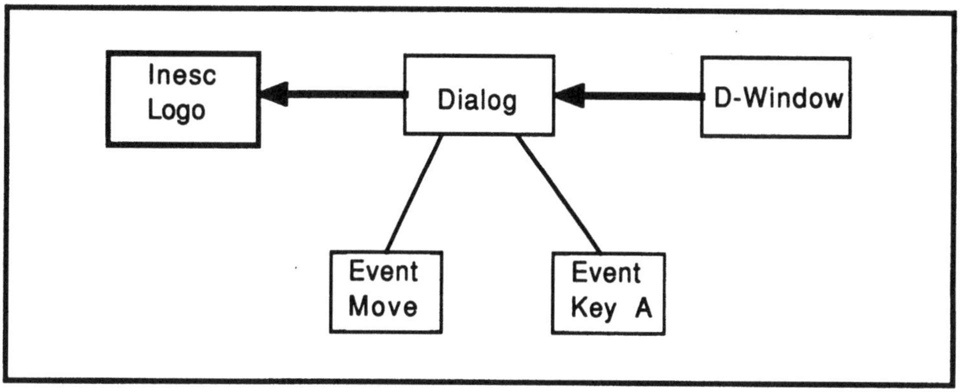

Figure 4: A Dialog Responsible enabling an operator to edit the "Inesc Logo"

4. Multimedia Applications

MAGOO has been used to create several applications, and will be used in the Esprit Hyperface Project (CASE for monitoring applications). New functionality towards Multimedia applications including Animation, Simulation and Monitoring is planned.

The Data object types needed to support those applications are very similar. They have a graphical representation, either 2D or 3D, and they can be composed objects forming a tree. The position, transformation, and graphic properties like colour and texture are propagated through that tree.

Trajectories will be modelled by a new movement data object type and they can also be composed. For example to obtain a complex trajectory it will be possible to compose several simple ones. For instance if we compose a linear acceleration with a circular trajectory we get a spiral trajectory. It will be possible to apply trajectories to any object type in any hierarchy level. The trajectories are also propagated through the tree defining the movement of any object.

As an example of a multimedia application we will consider monitoring. In this type of application beside the usual data objects that describe in some way the factory status, we will also consider special input devices, like cameras. These cameras will put on the workstation screen an image of some factory key points. In an Automatic Guided Vehicle (AGV) environment these could be for instance a trajectory crossing point, or an AGV loading target.

Another useful input device would be a voice recognition system to give orders in an environment where the use of a keyboard would be inadequate.

As output devices we will consider the use of special sound effects mainly to warn the operator of some pre-defined danger situations. Note that this information will be a very important complement to the visual representation of the factory status, where the high level of graphic complexity sometimes reduces operator reaction time.

In the Intelligent building field there is also a need for multimedia applications. In this case the tools previously described are almost sufficient (camera input and voice recognition) but we also would need some voice synthesizer objects.

We should emphasize that the integration of these special objects is fairly simple in the Magoo Architecture, and mainly reduces to the writing of a new layer of data, driver and dialog objects on top of the existing ones.

5. Animation

With the dialogues we can interact with the objects movement changing the trajectories. In an Animation application the dialogue can be a script containing all the steps describing the overall scene, similar to the orders given by an Actor´s Director. The script can specify the exact moment an actor (a hierarchical 3D object) enters in a scene, what movement he will perform, specifying a sub-actor movement or install a condition, defining for example, when an actor´s movement will change.

A very useful application in the Animation area is the preparation of a movie, where it is possible to try a lot of examples, interact with them, to change the scenes and to see all the editing implications before starting real production.

We have already developed a 3D Computer Animation System for CAD and Simulation, called GEAR (Domingos et al. 1988) which was originally written in C with a Data-Oriented internal architecture.

The main originality of GEAR is to support the application of movement (a hierarchy of trajectories) to an actor (a hierarchy of solids), as long as a mapping between the two topologies exist. If the topology of both trees is the same, the trajectories will be applied to all solids. In figure 1 the solid A will stay still because no trajectory is defined and the trajectory F will not be applied (Fig. 5).

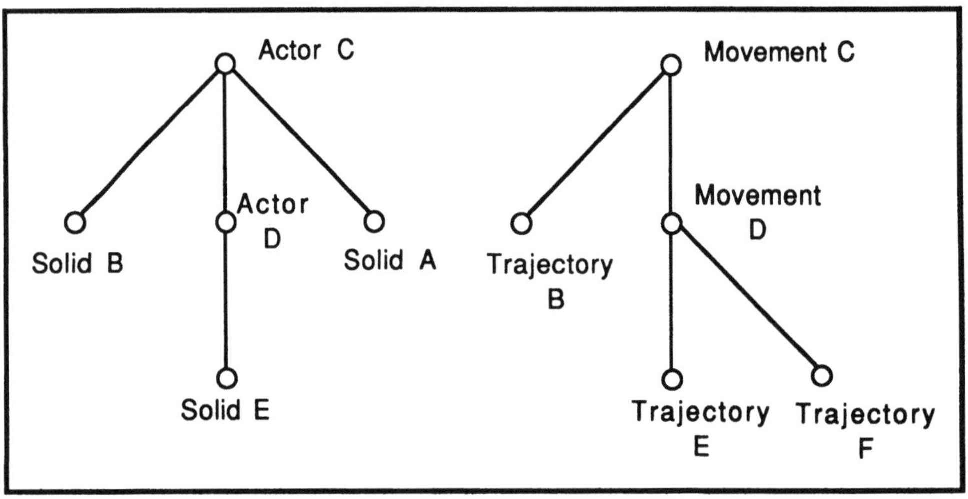

Figure 5: Mapping the Actor and Movement hierarchies

There are two ways to change the temporal behaviour of an actor which are to change the trajectories or to apply another pre-defined movement.

To advance from one frame to the next every actor, light and camera, position and orientation must be updated, all actors frozen and the resulting "scene" structure (composed of a camera specification, a list of lights and a list of solids) passed to the renderer for display.

To integrate Gear in the new environment it will be possible to use an important number of Transformer and Data Objects. This also will make available some new data types.

The GEAR system will use the new 3D Magoo Data Objects, including cubes, spheres and tors and the hierarchy of primitives, the actors. The new Magoo 4D Graphic Data Objects will also be used (figure 6).

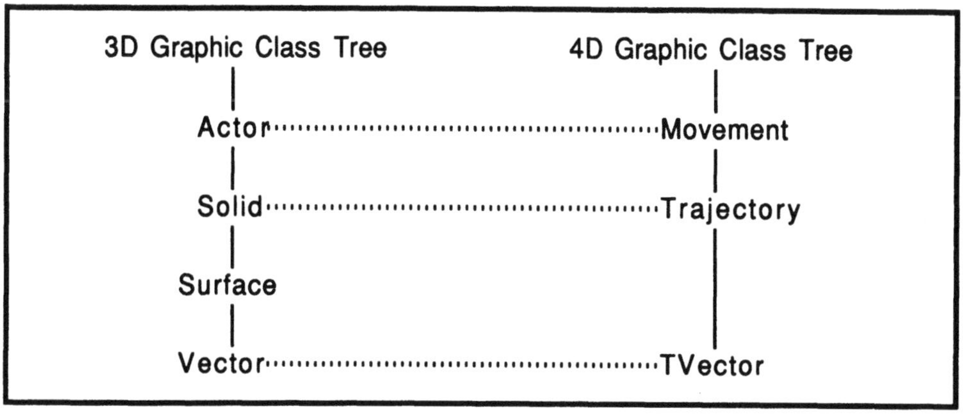

Figure 6: 3D and 4D Graphic Classes

New Gear application dependent Transformer Objects, like the animator, and new data objects, like the Light and the Camera will be created.

The new Data Objects will be derived from the Magoo 3D Data Objects. A Light will be modelled as a 3D point, a 3D line, a 3D cone, a 3D tor or a 3D sphere. A camera is also a 3D object with special application dependent attributes, like window dimension, orientation and perspective.

A new driver object, the Animator Engine will be created. A typical Gear Application will first create the Animator Engine, then the Render Driver Objects and all the other entities including Actors, Lights, Movements and cameras. Finally a trigger is sent to the Animator Dialog Object that will gain the execution control.

Animation is on our opinion one of the privileged medias to support multimedia applications.

6. Simulation and Monitoring

The Script concept can also be applied to simulation. However in this case the script is usually calculated by a simulation engine which reacts to special conditions called events. For each one of these events a certain behaviour of the simulated system is calculated and a graphical and animated representation of it can be provided.

To be more precise let us for instance consider the case of building a factory layout editor with simulation capabilities.

In this editor we will provide a library of commercially available AGV's each one of them represented by a different graphical appearance. In the editing mode we will also be able to create trajectories, set the different loading and unloading points and place Work Centres.

After the model creation we would then place the application in simulation mode. At this point the simulation engine will take in account the model built by the editor and using the graphical representation also available will provide suitable animation.

Consider for instance the arrival of an AGV at a loading point. Then the simulation engine could decide if that was the AGV target. In that case we would then see, for instance, the AGV being loaded with a set of boxes. That would be the graphical and animated representation of that event. Proceeding in a similar way for every event we then would have a complete animated representation of the simulation. Of course the animated sequence could also be described interactively using an animation editor.

What will we have to do to get such an Application? Well we will have to write some dialogs so that we could manage the details of this editor (note that these dialogs would inherit the existing set of lower level dialogs). We will also write some new data objects. Finally we will have a new driver which will also inherit from the existing ones so that he knows how to handle the new data objects. Please note the incremental (through inheritance) nature of writing a new Magoo application. This fact strongly suggests a high level of software reuse.

If we forget the editing part of the previous application and replace the simulation engine by position sensors we will have a monitoring application. Note that the editing portion of the previous application being restricted to the dialogs this is a really straight forward task. So with little work we can construct two different applications. We could even consider a third one that would compare the results of the simulation and the results of the monitoring and provide a graphical representation of such a comparison. This application could easily be built with the available Magoo objects.

7. Conclusions

Magoo is an Architecture suitable for Direct Manipulation requirements both at the Application and at the Interface level. The Object Oriented nature of the architecture allows an easy integration of any kind of output graphic pipeline, interaction techniques and new physical input devices.

The Magoo dialogue concept enables direct manipulation of any data object. So it is possible to change any object behaviour and observe the consequences. It is even possible to install a dialogue that checks physical restrictions, preventing if necessary, the changing of an object's trajectory or other attribute, like preventing a rope from stretching more than a physical defined value thus avoiding its rupture.

It must be highlighted that the same Model and main mechanisms, including composition, can be applied to different Medias, and different object's families from paper Images to 3D Animated objects or even Sound objects.

8. Acknowledgements

This work was partially financed by Esprit, under Project HYPERFACE 5391 contract.

References

Brock, R. W., Wilkerson, B. (1989) Object-Oriented Design: A Responsibility-Driven Approach. In: Norman Meyrowit (ed.) OOPSLA'89. SIGPLAN Notices 24 (10), pp. 71-75.

Domingos, P. et al. (1988) GEAR - a 3D Computer Animation System for CAD and Simulation. IEEE Student Papers Context.

Gomes, M. et al (1990) The MAGOO Architecture. European X-Conference Proceedings, pp. 14-20.

Gomes, M. R., Fernandes J. L. (1991) The OO-AGES Model - An Overview in User Interfaces Management and Design. In: D. A. Duce, M. R. Gomes, F. R. A. Hopgood, J. R. Lee (eds), Springer Verlag.

Hill, D. R., (1987) Event-Response Systems - A Technique for Specifying Multi-Threaded Dialogues. Proceedings of SIGCHI+GI 88, pp. 241-248.

Marshall R. (1990) The Hyperface widget set, Hyperface Technical Report TR 5.1.1.

Shneiderman, B. (1993) Direct Manipulation: A Step Beyond Programming Languages. IEEE Computer.

Part VIII

Conclusions

Chapter 24

Interactive Multimedia Information Systems for Education

Peter Ward and Farath Arshad

Abstract

As the computer based and audio–visual technologies have become integrated, hardware platforms are now available which allow the storage and integrated display of multimedia information. Access to multimedia information resources allows rich and high fidelity representations of the real world to be constructed. Education is an application area of great potential for computer based multimedia information systems (MIS). Interactivity at the interface, guidance within information spaces, strategic advice in the acquisition of knowledge and the negotiation of problem spaces are key issues to be dealt with in the design of effective educational applications. The engineering of such applications will require the combined efforts of computer scientists, psychologists and educators. A central issue in the design of relevant and effective systems is the involvement of target users – the course designers/tutors and learners.

This paper will focus on the place of multimedia technology in education, and the need to consider pedagogical concerns which must to be addressed for such technology to be successfully applied.

Introduction

A brief discussion of the evolution of multimedia technology, the nature of information systems and the application of computers to education will be followed by a consideration of the pedagogical requirements which such technology must address and the new possibilities and scope that interactive multimedia systems have to offer education. A clear understanding of these requirements is important if such systems are to provide useful tools and are to become a coherent part of the educational environment, both for the learner and the teacher.

Multimedia Technology

Computer based multimedia technology has evolved over the past ten years or so from the platforms handling information coded as numbers, formulae and text with alpha-numeric displays to platforms capable of processing and delivering all forms of information both analogue and digital. The audiovisual and computer technologies have become integrated and currently offer a variety of processing, storage and delivery platforms. An intermediate stage in this development path has been "interactive video" - a hybrid of audiovisual and computer technology with more or less interactive control of multimedia materials from the computer. Offering some flexibility in the organisation and access to materials, it employed the analogue optical laserdisc as the storage medium. While this analogue medium suffers from a lack of universal implementation standards, the digital optical laserdisc medium CD-ROM has been carefully introduced with a world standard in place at the outset.

Rather than just based on single stand-alone workstations, developments in Telematics are providing for networks and multiple platforms for the widespread distribution of information in all its forms. Thus, frameworks can become established for multimedia communication and collaborative interaction-essential ingredients in processes such as design and education. These will extend the possibilities for open/distance learning.

The cost of multimedia technology has initially been high but will become reduced as it is widely taken up. In many early systems involving often no more than the simple inclusion of token graphics and audio stimuli, its development has been technology (hardware) led rather than applications or user led. While there is now no shortage of sophisticated multimedia hardware, the development of software for the processing of multimedia objects and information systems which actually deliver the applications promised by the technology is in its infancy.

Computer based interactive multimedia technology offers the possibility of multisensorial stimulation. It becomes 'hypermedia' (cf. hypertext) when multimedia materials are organised into meaningful arrays (hypermedia nets/webs) in which logical and meaningful relationships between objects are explicit and accessible through a node-link arrangement e.g. information structures organised for optimised knowledge representation. To be truly "interactive" a computer based information system must provide ready and intuitive support for enquiry. It must provide all logical channels and modes of communication at an interface which is essentially transparent in the sense that it supports the intention of the user to search for, access, examine and make effective use of information. It must provide a range of simple tools for the manipulation of information which are easy to use. The interface should adapt to a variety of user types, from the 'power' user (experienced in the use of information technology) to the naive user coming to the system for the first time. It should positively stimulate interest and encourage further use. In an educational context, an interactive system should allow a self-paced access to learning materials.

Information Systems

A computer based information system model will include: a Database of information, an Interface (with access to application specific modules) and a means of translating the software to specific hardware platforms. While the technologist is concerned with the design of the formal data model, the low level machine interface and the overall efficiency of the system – the part of the system of interest to the applications builder and target user will be the interface. The interface will be configured with general tools to facilitate access and retrieval of information, allowing creative editing, formatting, and presentation. Application-specific tools will help target users access the information. Multimedia and the inclusion of hypermedia databases adds a new level of complexity to the design of information systems and to the material encountered by users. The general purpose of MIS is, presumably the encapsulation and the representation (communication) of information which is somehow closely related to the real world. As far as education applications are concerned, there is a need to focus on the design of the cognitive interface which must provide means of understanding the organisation of the information contained at a number of levels: both in terms of a rich but unstructured resource and in terms of a rich interlinked resource representing meaning. There is a need for high quality and variety of stimulating (interactive) communication channels. Both general and domain specific interface components must be provided ranging from symbols in menus that can be directly manipulated to high level schemata such as maps and representations of "hypermedia webs". This can only be achieved with the involvement of real users from a target domain.

At this point, basic questions which seem appropriate to address are how are MIS to be designed (can this be done in isolation from applications)? What added value can multimedia technology offer to enhance conventional computer based learning technology?

Currently, an object-oriented approach to the design of MIS is being adopted. This is consistent with the need to deal efficiently with very large amounts of data (e.g. including archives of still and moving pictures). The object-oriented approach provides a processing level within the system (virtual machine) so that complex multimedia objects are essentially portable and distributable and can be compiled and displayed on any machine.

Education and Computer Based Systems

There is a great deal of academic research being directed at the development of computer based systems (CBT, CAL, CAI* etc) for the delivery of education and training materials into various domains. The recent CEC DELTA 1989 initiative was established to focus on the development of general tools and systems with the potential to deliver flexible, adaptable, reusable and portable materials (including multimedia resources). However, the expectation of target users for readily accessible cost-effective deliverables has yet to be fulfilled and there has been considerable dissatisfaction expressed by those on the shop floor needing to develop and deliver education and training materials. They argue that they should have been consulted and that they have not been sufficiently involved in such developments so that real and immediate requirements are met (Ward 1990). The question remains: can Information Technology and MIS create alternative, effective, perhaps more naturalistic, ways of providing and stimulating learning opportunities?

Concerns of Education

Whilst technologies may be developed in isolation from applications, as far as education is concerned, it is important that the problems of education are carefully understood and that new technologies are engineered to address these specific problems. Bork (1989) has expressed concern about the tendency for the design of technologies for education to be technology led. He argues that a pragmatic approach should be based upon the major learning problems of knowledge/skill transfer and acquisition experienced by teachers and students alike, defined in current learning environments.

However, the other side of the coin is that, new technologies (such as computer based multimedia) can make education an exciting experience. As such, instead of just sticking to teaching for teaching's sake, learners and teachers can interact in an exploratory journey of discovery. Apart from the fact that they can push back the frontiers of what can be learnt, these technologies can define new ways of teaching and learning. Students can have a higher profile; through the medium of appropriately engineered systems, their state of knowledge and understanding and their approaches to learning can be made explicit to the instructor. This would lead to a focus and closer examination, on the part of the tutors, of the strategies for organising and expressing subject material in particular ways, and indeed how it can be assimilated by the student. Therefore, effort could be focused on integrating our current knowledge about learning and pedagogy with innovative teaching strategies supported by innovative technology.

The process of learning is an essentially dynamic and social process. An optimum environment for education is one in which dynamic and collaborative interactive communication processes between teachers and learners are supported within a context of a sound curriculum design and adequate material resources. Technologies for education must seek to provide support for these processes. There are a number of levels in formal education, each with its own characteristics:

– Primary, in which largely undeveloped minds and almost boundless energy are a challenge to educators who must establish key linguistic and numerate skills and begin to create a framework for thinking;

– Secondary, in which much subject matter must be dealt with and various techniques of learning are encouraged;

– Tertiary, in which there is focus on restricted domains and depth of study;

At the Primary and Secondary levels there is usually a formal role for the teacher and the instructional environment of the learner is generally quite closely controlled. Whereas, at the Tertiary level, the learner is confronted with responsibility for their studies which are not so closely directed. Support, in the form of sound guidance on learning-how-to-learn, negotiating the curriculum will be required.

Providing a learning environment which assists students to develop study skills (learning-how-to-learn) involves instructional planning. It is important that the students programme of work is coherently co-ordinated. This entails provision of mechanisms that assist not only in the selection and sequencing of appropriate study goals, but also suggests the use of suitable materials and guides how these materials can assist in the achievement of specific study goals (Arshad 1990). It is essential that such a support structure must adapt to the needs of different learner requirements. This can be designed and built into computer based systems which could provide an infrastructure for the delivery of effective educational support and adapt to the variety of learner types.

Learners differ from one another in many respects. Amongst other variants, there are differences in background knowledge and the need or preference for specific types of learning materials. It is the suitability of the learning materials which is the key issue here. The suitability (relevance), form (content & design) and level (complexity) of presentation determines the quality and type of processing or assimilation of the material achievable by the student (cf. Reigeluth 1983). These educational issues must clearly be addressed by significant multimedia teaching systems. At present these issues are unaddressed.

As well as information materials, an educational software resource must include authoring tools. Authoring tasks include formal information structuring (cf. classification and databasing; in the realms of library and information science), knowledge structuring (by domain experts, but not necessarily teachers), pedagogical design (of conceptual structures, by teachers who understand the cognitive and communication issues) and interface/presentation structuring (audiovisual/multimedia designers). These tasks should be considered and dealt with separately in the design of courseware. The designers of the pedagogical content require tools which provide a means for the decomposition of the domain and the specification of various structures. These include navigable knowledge frameworks with access organised to support specific learning goals, learning to particular levels of detail, and adaptation to various learning strategies indicated or preferred by individual students. Incorporating sound and pragmatic pedagogical principles, such tools could constrain the mode of delivery and interactivity and be instructional to the less experienced or less gifted teacher as well as to the student.

Education and Interactive Multimedia

In order to represent basic concepts and skills within a particular domain, information needs to be available in rich, high fidelity and organised chunks. A major component of a fertile learning environment is the provision of context. A system that provides multimedia materials organised into interactive hypermedia knowledge-based structures including realistic examples and simulations has the potential to enable the learner to learn within the context of real world representations and problems; to gather knowledge or to acquire a skill appropriate to a situation rather than just an exercise in the accumulation of information and rules.

Multimedia resources available within an interactive information system can provide ready access to a wealth of contextual material. Most importantly, they can enable a method of representation based on modelling and simulation as part of a process of experimental or situational learning. An example of this approach is given in ARK – the Alternative Reality Kit – in which all objects have a visual image, a position and velocity and are operated on by physical forces; the student can manipulate objects accordingly, with the possibility of experimental variation (Smith, 1987). Real world experience is highly complex – involving the interaction of multiple phenomena. Students can be provided with simpler microworlds and the opportunity to manipulate individual components experimentally (di Sessa, 1987). Computer based modelling tools are routinely used in the industrial sector and are an analogue for exploratory, simulation based discovery learning in the educational environment.

In the "electronic theatre project" (Clabaugh et al. 1989, Norman, 1990) a new environment for collaborative learning and research is being developed in which hypermedia is an essential feature. A key feature of this environment is instructional interaction among key agents: instructors, students, course materials and the products of instruction. Users have access to a wealth of multimedia materials, including hypermedia databases, simulations, exercises (which are continuously evolving) on a network. The system provides instructional models and tools for navigational support and guidance in the achievement of learning goals.

The current Apple (UK) Computers "Renaissance Project" (Apple, 1990) has been established to formulate some standards in the application of multimedia to education. It has as its stated premise that multimedia is ideally suited to the delivery of multi/inter disciplinary representations/views of rich and complex real world situations in context. One of its threads is the study of mathematics. The proposition is that mathematics in the curriculum has tended to become far too abstract, dry and lifeless and has lost touch with its historical and cultural roots, having little relevance to the practical world. The potential of interactive multimedia to alter attitudes to maths by allowing the learner to explore the way that maths relates to everyday life, thus enabling the appreciation of context as well as a detailed understanding, is being explored. A knowledge of maths is being developed to underpin a study of environmental phenomena. The implication here is that a knowledge of maths can be developed simultaneously with a knowledge of the environment in the process of environmental modelling and simulation.

Good design of content becomes very important when materials are extensive and complex. Methodologies for meaningful information structuring and chunking and the design of high level multimedia browsing mechanisms are the subject of considerable research interest (Shneiderman, 1989a) Environments provided by proprietary tools such as Hypercard (Goodman, 1987), Guide (OWL) and Hyperties (Schneiderman, 1989b) allow a beginning to made to the process of multimedia design. More extensive environments are provided in research tools such as Intermedia (Yankelovitch et. al., 1988), KMS (Aksycn et.al., 1988) and the Andrew System (Borenstein, 1990). Recently, a reference model for hypertext/hypermedia systems has been suggested as a basis for comparing various systems and for the development of interchange and interoperability standards (Halasz and Schwartz, 1990).

Conclusion

Computers have the potential to become an integrating medium for instruction. The potential contribution that computer based multimedia technology has to make to education is perhaps rather easier to conceptualise than to implement. More than merely a presentation technology, "hypermedia" as an extension of multimedia can provide a dynamic and interactive access to the world of objects, relationships and functional phenomena. Indeed, the object-oriented paradigm as a means of organising and linking formal data-structures is closely related to "hypermedia webs". Media objects can be constructed into meaningful information structures and knowledge representations which can constitute formal models in learning resources. Hypermedia certainly offers new possibilities for exploration and collaboration in learning processes and its introduction into the classroom presents a challenge to redesign the instructional environment.

Historically, the dynamic combination of language, image, sound and text for meaningful effect has been practised and developed into art forms in the theatre, education, and more recently in cinema and television. These predate the advent of computers as a means for organising and communicating information in which the storage and display technology required for multimedia information processing has only quite recently been developed. While the thrust of the technological developments has rather naturally been from the Sciences in these processes, there is much interest from the Arts and Humanities to become involved and make a contribution. High quality interfaces with good information modelling tools will put the technology at the service of those with creative imagination who are only latterly becoming aware of the possibilities that the technology offers. Good quality demonstrators of hypermedia are the surest way of communicating these possibilities. The makers of television programmes are taking an interest in computer based multimedia with a view to the exploitation of broad bandwidth cable-communications networks. Such networks could be used to deliver distance/open learning materials. There promises to be an interesting marriage of skills: the makers of programmes and the makers of software joining forces to develop interactive programmes to be delivered on intelligent home terminals. While there is currently no shortage of suitably sophisticated hardware, there is a shortage of high quality educational software. There is a need for a system/framework of design methods to guide the designers of educational and training materials.There are a number of priorities including, authoring tools embodying sound and pragmatic pedagogical strategies; presentation (formatting and media integration) formalism supporting optimum access to and communication of information; and the provision of navigational support so that the learner can understand the context of the current focus.

Education is an obvious application for computer based multimedia which will require the engineering of information systems whose design is modular, capable of encapsulating very large amounts of information with reusability (adaptation, versioning, repurposing) of information structures (resources and content) a priority. This is a truly interdisciplinary exercise.

Prototype MIS in which various strategies for media presentation, integration and synchronization are tried out must be evaluated with learners for their effect in the communication of meaning and knowledge.

There are a number of priorities for the design of MIS in the education and training domain. Re-usability of materials,maintenance of materials/system, and upgrading are all essential practical features required by developers of courseware.

As well as the need to verify the actual effectiveness of an interactive computer based multimedia learning environment, there remains the requirement to provide tests of understanding: interactive procedures producing diagnostic data indicative of the level, extent or deficiency of knowledge acquisition. Given that there may be different types of knowledge that can be represented and acquired (eg conceptual, procedural, operational), then different tests for these must be devised and made available. The results would be accumulated in the individual student record and would influence their subsequent interaction with the computer assisted learning system (or other means of knowledge acquisition). Perhaps imaginative variations or even alternatives to the standard text based MCQ (multi choice questionnaire) test format could be designed and implemented. For example, operational simulations in which there would be various opportunities for intervention and problem solving. Computer based Multimedia offers a rich environment for the construction of such test-simulations. There is little doubt that considerable value can be added to computer based learning by enhancement with well designed multimedia materials and hypermedia structures. The notion of edutainment is useful: learning can be an exciting and enjoyable experience. If a learner smiles with pleasure when confronted with educational computer based multimedia materials, then is this not a major achievement (supporting multimedia interactive learning environments, (Ward 1987)?

What is good multimedia design? The developers of traditional education and training courseware, who have been encouraged to have great expectations of the multimedia technologies, have expressed a need for the development of guidelines and formal strategies for the organisation and presentation of information. Good design of content becomes very important when materials are extensive and complex. A number of different design skills are required: including pedagogical design, media design and communication. These must be integrated in order to manufacture elegant designs. Work on these issues has really only just begun.

References

Apple Computer (UK) (1990) The Renaissance Project: An overview, aims, developments and products (version 3). Apple Computer(UK) Limited, Higher Education Division, 6 Roundwood Avenue, Stockley Park, Uxbridge, Middlesex UB11 1BB, UK.

Arshad, F.N. (1990) The Design of Knowledge based Advisors for Learning. PhD Thesis, University of Leeds, UK.

Arshad, F.N. & Kelleher, G. (1991) SOLA*: Students' On-Line Advisor. Accepted for publication in Int J. Man-Machine Studies.

Aksycn, R., McCracken, D.L., and Yoder, E.A. (1988) KMS: A distributed hypertext for managing knowledge in organisations. Communications of the ACM, 31 (7) pp820-835.

Borenstein, N.S. (1990) Multimedia Applications Development with theAndrew Toolkit. Prentice Hall.

Bork, A. (1989) Suggestions for developing technology based learningmaterials. Interactive Learning International 5 (1) pp25-38

Clabaugh, S., Destler, W.W., Falk, D.S., Gilbert, W., McDaniel, C.K.,Power, D.J., Ricart, G., & Schneiderman, B. (1988) The AT&T teaching theater: An environment for collaborative learning and research. College Park, MD, University of Maryland.

di Sessa, A. (1987) Towards an Epistemology of Intuitive Knowledge in Physics. University of California, Berkley.

Goodman, D. (1987) The Complete HyperCard Handbook. Bantam Books, New York.

Halasz, F., and Schwartz, M. (1990) The Dexter Reference Model. The NIST Hypertext Standardisation Workshop, Gaithersburg, MD.

McLeese, R. (Ed.). (1989) Hypertext: theory into practise. Osney Mead, Oxford: Blackwell Scientific Publications.

Norman, K.L. (1990) The Electronic Teaching Theater: Interactive Hypermedia and Mental Models of the Classroom. In P.S.Ward (Ed.) Hypermedia and Artificial Intelligence, Special Edition: Current Psychology Research and Reviews, 9 (2) pp 141-161

OWL Guide Hypermedia information System. Office Workstations Limited, Edinburgh UK.

Reigeluth, C.M. (1983) Meaningfullness and instruction: relating what is being learned to what a student knows. Instructional Science, 12 pp 197-218.

Schneiderman, B. (1983) Direct manipulation: a step beyond programming languages. IEEE Computer, 16 (8) 57-69.

Schneiderman, B. (1989a) Reflections on Authoring, Editing and Managing Hypertext. In: Barrett, E. (ed) The Society of Text: Hypertext and Hypermedia, the Social Construction of Information. MA: Cambridge, The MIT Press.

Schneiderman, B. (1989b) Hypertext on Hypertext. Addison-Wesley: New York.

Smith, R.B. (1987) Experiences with the Alternative Reality Kit: An exam of the Tension Between Literalism and Magic. IEEE Computer Graphics and Applications Vol. 7 No.9 pp40-50.

Ward, P.S. (1987) SMILE: Supporting Multimedia Interactive Learning Environments - an approach to information modelling in education. Report HM/87 IBM Academic Systems Cambridge UK.

Ward, P.S. (1990) Delta HeltaSkelter, In Interactive Media International 3 (10) pp 3-6

Yankelovitch, N., Haan, B., Meyrowitz, N., and Drucker, S. (1988) Intermedia: The concept and the construction of a seamless information environment. IEEE Compter, 21 (1) pp81-96

Chapter 25

Collected Conclusions

edited by Lars Kjelldahl with contributions from David Bell, Carole Goble, Richard Guedj, Nils-Erik Gustafsson, Hans Marmolin, Yngve Sundblad, Roger Took and Peter Ward

During the workshop there were many interesting presentations and discussions. The conclusions in this chapter are not the direct result of a general discussion at the workshop. Rather they are conclusions and opinions inspired by the workshop and put together after the workshop through contributions sent to the editor. The chapter is organised as a number of questions with discussion, opinions and/or conclusions.

What is multimedia?

The terminology associated with multimedia causes confusion. Multi-sensory, multi-channel, multi-tasking, multi-user: frequently these terms are used interchangably and mean different things to different workers. One might think that multimedia is something were new, which in some respects is true. It may however be interesting to study an old paper and to note that the spelling in (Kolodin Irving, "The new world of sight and sound, live and recorded", in Saturday Review, MultiMedia, January 30, 1971.) is "MultiMedia", showing a parsing of the word. From this article on MultiMedia we extract the following aspects:

1 "MultiMedia is the name of a supplement devoted to new dimensions in sight and sound made possible by fast-moving developments in the world of electronic technology".

2 "MultiMedia will explore new opportunities for education as well as entertainment"

3 "MultiMedia will take as its stage everything that has meaning to the eye and ear"

4 "...the eye long restricted by its structure and perception to immobile or reproduced things has never enjoyed the ear's priviledge of servicing and educating itself instantly..."

5 "...the moving and the evanescent it was dependent upon means it could not enjoy when and as wanted"

In quoting this 20 years old article, the intention is to stress the "accidental" insight of the author, bringing together essential aspects, namely:

- we can notice that emphasis is on perception through the ear and the eye.
- emphasis on perception
- meaning for ear and eye
- education and entertainment
- self-educating, therefore allowing autonomy

In terms of the representation and communication of information, 'multimedia' can be defined as : text/natural language; pictures (including symbolic graphics, cartoons, animations and both still and moving real world images) and sound (speech and ambient). Computer based interactive multimedia technology offers the possibility of multisensorial stimulation.

As well as visual and auditory channels, haptic (touch), kinaesthetic (force and movement), vestibular (positional sense) and olfaction (taste and smell) may be included in a consideration of potential interface components and channels of communication. Indeed, for the unsighted the development of the sense of discriminative touch is an important perceptual modality and means of communication (e.g. Braille). The sense of smell is a potent cue in long-term memory and is a medium for the communication of behavioural (e.g. fear) and physiological (e.g. reproductive) states. The 'virtual reality' systems of the future may be expected to include these modalities of communication.

Why use the term multimedia systems, when media systems will suffice?

Graphics systems and CAD systems are well described by the names used, so why can the term media systems not be used when the major characteristic of the systems are described.

There are at least two reasons: The term Media is too often used to refer to the agencies who disseminate information, such as the newspapers, television and radio. The use of the term Media is too closely related to the use of one media at a time. The term Multimedia ensures that the concept of multiple, integrated, concurrent communications is understood.

What is hypermedia?

The term "hypermedia" was most likely coined by Theodor Holm Nelson in his paper "A File Structure for the Complex, the Changing and the Indeterminate" (Proc. ACM, 1965). It refers to the possibility of the "reader" of the thus packaged information content to traverse the information nodes in a non-sequential fashion.

It is doubtful whether information with a number of different possible traversal routes predetermined by the information author/designer is truly "hyper" enough to earn the description hypermedia (or hypertext, if limited to textual presentation). Rather like an encyclopedia, a truly hyper information system should allow the reader to traverse the information nodes completely at will (irregardless of the authors/ designers intentions!).

In the context of hypermedia, the author constructs hypermedia graphs by relating nodes of information of differing media. The author of a hypermedia graph makes the connections so as to convey a particular meaning. Subsequent browsers, or readers, of this graph are then an audience to a presentation – a presentation which they are able to direct the progress of by their choice of link traversals – they therefore experience hypermedia. Multimedia presentations which the audience cannot direct the progress of (by following links) are not hypermedia.

What is the relation between CSCW and multimedia?

When discussing CSCW one should separate out the components: work (tasks), computers (computer related tasks), multimedia representation(s) etc.

CSCW (Computer Supported Cooperative Work) often needs multimedia although it can do well with just text. CSCW can be seen as one application of multimedia and it can be used within different areas e.g. CAD/CAM Design

Given a situation where a number of people at remote sites have to work together, multimedia provides many benefits.

The collaborators need shared access to information, possibly the same focus within that information and maybe exactly the same view (using the same medium) onto that shared focus.

There may be occasions when having extra media available means that an information item can be conveyed in a number of ways – to ensure it is expressed accurately to those who do not understand one particular representation.

Flexibility to present information in multiple media means that information can be disseminated regardless of the hardware and software at collaborator sites; if collaborators cannot access the information in the optimal media, they can access it using the best media they have available.

Communication

To support group work, meta level discussion is required in addition to discussion directly related to the artifact (the content or result) of the group task. Such meta-level discussion is required to organise stages of brainstorming, ordering of ideas and elaboration of content. Meta-level discussions may take place about the discussions that the group will have and how the work that the group must undertake is divided to complete the task.

A basic means of discussion is via shared text windows, but much greater perception of group membership and participation will be achieved if audio and video channels are available. Richer channels for communication increase the degree to which group members know what others in the group are doing, increasing the shared context.

There are arguments for and against the use of video communication; its benefits are much harder to gauge than those achieved by audio communication channels. Video communication is much harder to perfect due to logistic difficulties of lighting and positioning (keeping the subject in shot). There are also psychological difficulties to overcome, such as the need to provide eye-contact between collaborators, and the need to preserve privacy.

How shall we design multimedia systems?

Should users provide requirements for multimedia system development, or should designers push forward the available technology for users to try out. The debate is whether the development of the domain should be requirement driven or technology driven.

Up to now multimedia has been very much technology driven. Only now are we beginning to step back from this technology to ask some more fundamental questions. How should we go about designing a multimedia document or database? Do the old design strategies still hold? Who uses multimedia – does anyone? And if so how and why? We have mainly taken the system point of view rather than the user's point of view. There are few experiences (of failures OR successes) to guide new developments, neither are there techniques to generate user requirements and specifications for multimedia systems based upon existing work environments or systems. Requirement gathering and early evaluation techniques have to evolve in order to provide specifications for multimedia environments that allow concurrent (possibly interacting) communications.

On the other hand there has been some activity from companies producing multimedia material. Particularly in the USA it is those companies which have developed multimedia authoring tools, but these have often been ad-hoc, one-offs and the engineering principles have often been poor.

Developers of multimedia hardware and software have to be able to rapidly prototype, evaluate, and revise the systems that are being produced, until optimal uses of the available media and standard multimedia interfaces become apparent.

The time has come to acknowledge that multimedia is a genuine area of work and a truly cross-disciplinary activity. The system designers need to understand how and why multimedia is used; the users need systems that are generic and extensible; and both need people who have traditional skills in multichannelled communications, namely those film-makers and cinematographers who understand how to communicate complex ideas in a multisensory way. Some work has already been done in this area (e.g. NUNTIUS, Macromind Director 2 the work of MIT Media Lab). Cross-disciplinary work necessitates the close collaboration/interaction/understanding/agreement with common focus between key personnel with key skills and target users (as opposed to two techies producing things on the basis of their intuition – which is characteristically misguided – and a few conversations with their friends, some of whom may know something about an application).

One solution to the problem is to optimize for user-tailorable interfaces, where an administrator for an installation, or the individual, can decide the configuration of the multimedia system. – Maybe optimal configurations will become apparent quicker, or perhaps a greater variety of incoherent systems will result. However other experiences say that it is better with a limited facility to reconfigure (within standard design constraints ensuring design elegance and continuity of e.g. presentation standards within an application). Most people only want and in fact only use a small part of the functionality available. People want to do simple things, in various combinations, quickly and easily. This is probably true also for MM Systems.

What kind of experiences can be gained from the development of other areas in the computer field?

We can draw an analogy with Desktop Publishing – its introduction enabled publishing to come within the control of anyone. There was a proliferation of inspired but often very badly designed documents. The use of multimedia will not compensate for a badly designed database or tutoring system. Multimedia needs to stop being a decorative gimmick and become serious with properly developed support methods and tools if it is not soon to be perceived the emperor's new clothes.

The design of multimedia support systems is at the same stage of development as window systems when raster technology first became available. We can see now that window systems have not been "cleanly" designed: implementations of the windowing interface (icons, menus, scroll bars etc.) and its metaphor (desktop, rooms etc) are often limited by the implementation of the underlying screen and input handling facilities. In addition, these basic facilities often lack generality (there are many geometric limitations in window systems, for example). Yet because window systems form the basic presentation medium for many applications, they possess a great deal of inertia and are difficult to change.

It is important, with this experience of designing window systems behind us, that systems to support multimedia interaction do not fall into the same trap of implementing a narrow metaphor in such a way that it cannot be extended or modified. It is important that the fundamental functionality of multiple media and their interactions be studied carefully and thoroughly (ideally formally) before large scale implementations are started. In particular, it is important that multimedia management systems (to coin a phrase) be cleanly modularised into a subsystem to support, as generally as possible, the display and input handling of multiple media, and, separately, a subsystem to generate particular user interfaces or user interface metaphors or styles.

Are there any successful applications of multimedia systems and how can multimedia be used?

Up to now there have been very few really successful applications of multimedia, except perhaps of education systems (including museum applications). Experiences from real applications and evaluation of those systems are needed. Is multimedia suitable for all kinds of application domains, or should its use be restricted? As with many new trends, there are attempts to apply multimedia to all kinds of application domains. In spite of all the good things with multimedia, there are also some disadvantages to be considered. There are as always cost-benefit trade offs concerning costs, interface complexity, installation problems etc. Therefore it could be worthwhile to attempt to formulate recommendations about when to use and when not to use multimedia.

Could the multimedia and the AI approach be integrated or are they fundamentally different ways of solving problems. In order to answer that question one has to specify the kind of problems that multimedia tries to solve. Is multimedia a solution to interface problems or is it a solution to the problem of user or systems control or is it a solution to the problem of representation of information etc

What is the relation between multimedia and the old techniques of graphical presentation and the new area of virtual reality? Is multimedia just a step on the way from graphics to virtual reality, or does multimedia mean something more? Is it a fundamental new approach to systems design and a new paradigm in computer science?

What kind of programming tools are needed to build multimedia systems?

Programming tools should be simple and intuitive to use, which enable other (sophisticated) tools to be used to generate data eg wordprocessors and graphics editing so that such data can be imported as standard data format eg ASCII text and TIFF 24 bit graphics and then subsequently manipulated into various screens.

Object-oriented methods seem axiomatic to the design and realisation of multimedia systems, e.g. OODBMS, the separation of rendering from object type, the synchronisation of objects for multichanneling. Multimedia will promote the use of OOPS.

Direct manipulative and object oriented techniques are also important when building programming tools for devopment and when experimenting with prototypes of multimedia systems. Prototyping with user participation is crucial for good systems design especially in an area as new, immature and fast developing as multimedia. An interesting possibility is to extend the now so popular direct manipulative interface building techniques for graphic interfaces to mutlimedial interfaces.

Have data bases been used in a good way in multimedia?

Little seems to have been done to address the issues of retrieval of multimedia objects by the setting of criteria and the use of query languages. In order not to throw away all the benefits of databases encrued over the past few decades, we must continue to look at how we might express the semantic content of multimedia objects such that those objects can be retrieved by query expressions. Databases must take on the challenge of multimedia.

List of Participants

J. L. Alty, Multi-media Research Group, Department of Computer Studies, Loughborough University, Loughborough, Leics, LE 11 3TU, England

J. Andersson, Infologics, Box 91, S–191 22 Sollentuna, Sweden

F.N. Arshad, Worsley Building, University of Leeds, Sch of Medicine, Leeds LS2 9JT, England

D. Bell, Department of Computer Science, Queen Mary andWestfield College, London University, Mile End Road, London E1 4NS, England

R. Casteleiro, INESC, Rua Alves Redol 9-2 D, Apartado 10105, 1017 Lisboa Codex, Portugal

S.K. Chng, Electronic Systems Engineering, University of Essex, Wivenhoe Park, Colchester CO4 3SQ, England

B. Eiderbäck, Numerical Analysis and Computing Science (NADA), Royal Institute of Technology (KTH), S–100 44 Stockholm, Sweden

D. Frohlich, Advanced Information Management Department, Hewlett-Packard Laboratories, Filton Road, Stoke Gifford, Bristol, BS12 6QZ, England

S. Gibbs, Centre Universitaire d'Informatique, Université de Genève, 12 rue du Lac, CH–1207, Genève, Switzerland

C. Goble, Department of Computer Science, Oxford Road, University of Manchester, Manchester, M13 9PL, England

R. A. Guedj, Institut National des Telecom, Charles Fourier, 91011 EVRY, France

N.-E. Gustafsson, Infologics, Box 91, S–191 22 Sollentuna, Sweden

W. Herzner, Austrian Research Centre Seibersdorf, Department IT , A–2444 Seibersdorf, Austria

P. Hoepner, Gesellschaft für Mathematik und Datenverarbeitung (GMD), Forschungszentrum für Offene Kommunikationssysteme (FOKUS), Hardenbergplatz 2, W–1000 Berlin 12, Germany

C. Hornung, Fraunhofer–Gesellschaft, Arbeitsgruppe für Graphische Datenv, Wilhelminenstr 7, D–6100 Darmstadt, Germany

W. Hübner, Computer Graphics Center (ZGDV), Wilhelminenstr 7, D–6100 Darmstadt, Germany

H. Hämmäinen, Helsinki University of Techn, Laboratory of Information Proc Science, Otakaari 1 A, SF–02150 Espoo, Finland

P. Johnson, Department of Computer Science, Queen Mary and Westfield College, London University, Mile End Road, London E1 4NS, England

T. Kirste, Computer Graphics Center (ZGDV), Wilhelminenstr 7, D–6100 Darmstadt, Germany

M. Kummer, Austrian Research Centre Seibersdorf, Department IT , A–2444 Seibersdorf, Austria

L. Kjelldahl, Numerical Analysis and Computing Science (NADA), Royal Institute of Technology (KTH), S–100 44 Stockholm, Sweden

A. Lundeberg, Sony Corporation, Telecommunication and Information Systems Laboratory, Information Systems Research Department, 6–7–35 Kitashinagawa, Shinagawa–ku, Tokyo, 141, Japan

H. Marmolin, Numerical Analysis and Computing Science (NADA), Royal Institute of Technology (KTH), S–100 44 Stockholm, Sweden

R. Mäntylä, Helsinki University of Techn, Laboratory of Inform Proc Science, Otakaari 1 A, SF–02150 Espoo, Finland

C. McCartney, Multi-media Research Group, Department of Computer Studies, Loughborough University of Techn, Leics, LE 11 3TU, England

M. O'Docherty, Department of Computer Science, Oxford Road, University of Manchester, Manchester, M13 9PL, England

D. Penna, Philips Research Laboratory, Cross Oak Lane, Redhill, Surrey RH1 5HA, England

P. Rajka, Department of Speech Communication and Music Acoustics, Royal Institute of Technology (KTH), S–100 44 Stockholm, Sweden

M. Rhiner, Multimedia Laboratory, Department of Computer Science, University of Zürich, Winterthurerstr 190, CH–8057 Zürich, Switzerland

A. Santos, Fraunhofer–Gesellschaft, Arbeitsgruppe für Graphische Datenv, Wilhelminenstr 7, D–6100 Darmstadt, Germany

Y. Sundblad, Numerical Analysis and Computing Science (NADA), Royal Institute of Technology (KTH), S–100 44 Stockholm, Sweden

K. Tollmar, Numerical Analysis and Computing Science (NADA), Royal Institute of Technology (KTH), S–100 44 Stockholm, Sweden

R.K. Took, Computer Science Department, University of York, Heslington, York YO1 5DD, England

T. Ungvary, Department of Speech Comm and Music Acoustics, Royal Institute of Technology (KTH), S–100 44 Stockholm, Sweden

T. Usuki, Sony Corporation, Telecommunication and Information Systems Laboratory, Information Systems Research Department, 6–7–35 Kitashinagawa, Shinagawa–ku, Tokyo, 141, Japan

H. Vin, Department of Computer Science and Engineering, University of California, San Diego, La Jolla, CA 92093–0114, USA

K. Väänänen, Telecom Finland, Business Systems R&D, P.O.BOX 140, SF–00511 Helsinki, Finland

P. S. Ward, Worsley Building, University of Leeds, Sch of Medicine, Leeds LS2 9JT, England

T. Yamamoto, Sony Corporation, Telecommunication and Information Systems Laboratory, Information Systems Research Department, 6–7–35 Kitashinagawa, Shinagawa–ku, Tokyo, 141, Japan

EurographicSeminars

Tutorials and Perspectives in Computer Graphics

Eurographics Tutorials '83. Edited by P. J. W. ten Hagen.
XI, 425 pages, 164 figs., 1984

User Interface Management Systems. Edited by G. E. Pfaff.
XII, 224 pages, 65 figs., 1985

Methodology of Window Management. Edited by F. R. A. Hopgood, D. A. Duce, E. V. C. Fielding, K. Robinson, A. S. Williams.
XV, 250 pages, 41 figs., 1985

Data Structures for Raster Graphics. Edited by L. R. A. Kessener, F. J. Peters, M. L.P. van Lierop. VII, 201 pages, 80 figs., 1986

Advances in Computer Graphics I. Edited by G. Enderle, M. Grave, F. Lillehagen.
XII, 512 pages, 168 figs., 1986

Advances in Computer Graphics II. Edited by F. R. A. Hopgood, R. J. Hubbold, D. A. Duce. X, 186 pages, 96 figs., 1986

Advances in Computer Graphics Hardware I. Edited by W. Straßer.
X, 147 pages, 76 figs., 1987

GKS Theory and Practice. Edited by P. R. Bono, I. Herman.
X, 316 pages, 92 figs., 1987

Intelligent CAD Systems I. Theoretical and Methodological Aspects.
Edited by P. J. W. ten Hagen, T. Tomiyama. XIV, 360 pages, 119 figs., 1987

Advances in Computer Graphics III. Edited by M. M. de Ruiter.
IX, 323 pages, 247 figs., 1988

Advances in Computer Graphics Hardware II. Edited by A. A. M. Kuijk, W. Straßer.
VIII, 258 pages, 99 figs., 1988

CGM in the Real World. Edited by A. M. Mumford, M. W. Skall.
VIII, 288 pages, 23 figs., 1988

Intelligent CAD Systems II. Implementational Issues. Edited by V. Akman, P. J. W. ten Hagen, P. J. Veerkamp. X, 324 pages, 114 figs., 1989

Advances in Computer Graphics IV. Edited by W. T. Hewitt, M. Grave, M. Roch.
XVI, 248 pages, 138 figs., 1991

Advances in Computer Graphics V. Edited by W. Purgathofer, J. Schönhut. VIII, 223 pages, 101 figs., 1989

User Interface Management and Design. Edited by D. A. Duce, M. R. Gomes, F. R. A. Hopgood, J. R. Lee. VIII, 324 pages, 117 figs., 1991

Advances in Computer Graphics Hardware III. Edited by A. A. M. Kuijk. VIII, 214 pages, 88 figs., 1991

Advances in Object-Oriented Graphics I. Edited by E. H. Blake, P. Wisskirchen. X, 218 pages, 74 figs., 1991

Advances in Computer Graphics Hardware IV. Edited by R. L. Grimsdale, W. Straßer. VIII, 276 pages, 124 figs., 1991

Advances in Computer Graphics VI. Synthesis, Analysis and Interaction. Edited by G. Garcia, I. Herman. IX, 449 pages, 186 figs., 1991

Intelligent CAD Systems III. Practical Experience and Evaluation. Edited by P. J. W. ten Hagen, P. J. Veerkamp. X, 270 pages, 116 figs., 1991

Graphics and Communications. Edited by D. B. Arnold et al. VIII, 274 pages, 84 figs., 1991

Photorealism in Computer Graphics. Edited by K. Bouatouch, C. Bouville. XVI, 230 pages, 118 figs., 1992

Advances in Computer Graphics Hardware V. Rendering, Ray Tracing and Visualization Systems. Edited by R. L. Grimsdale, A. Kaufman. VIII, 174 pages, 97 figs., 1992

Multimedia. Systems, Interaction and Applications. Edited by L. Kjelldahl. VIII, 355 pages, 129 figs., 1992

In preparation:

Advances in Scientific Visualisation. Edited by F. H. Post, A. J. S. Hin. Approx. 260 pages, 1992